Second Edition

Knowledge Management
An Integrated Approach

Ashok Jashapara

University of London (Royal Holloway)

Financial Times
Prentice Hall
is an imprint of

PEARSON

Harlow, England • London • New York • Boston • San Francisco • Toronto
Sydney • Tokyo • Singapore • Hong Kong • Seoul • Taipei • New Delhi
Cape Town • Madrid • Mexico City • Amsterdam • Munich • Paris • Milan

Pearson Education Limited
Edinburgh Gate
Harlow
Essex CM20 2JE
England

and Associated Companies throughout the world

Visit us on the World Wide Web at:
www.pearsoned.co.uk

First published 2004
Second edition published 2011

ISBN: 978-0-273-72685-2

British Library Cataloguing-in-Publication Data
A catalogue record for this book is available from the British Library

Library of Congress Cataloging-in-Publication Data
Jashapara, Ashok.
  Knowledge management : an integrated approach / Ashok Jashapara. -- 2nd ed.
    p. cm.
  ISBN 978-0-273-72685-2 (pbk.)
 1. Knowledge management. I. Title.
  HD30.2.J38 2011
  658.4'038--dc22

10 9 8 7 6 5 4 3 2
14 13 12 11

Typeset in 9/13 Stone Serif by 30
Printed by Ashford Colour Press Ltd, Gosport

Knowledge Management

This book is dedicated to the inspiring life of

SPUD BAKHLE
(1929–2003)

for our numerous conversations over a glass of wine.

Custom publishing

Custom publishing allows academics to pick and choose content from one or more texts for their course and combine it into a definitive course text. Content choices include:

- chapters from one or more of our textbooks in the subject areas of your choice;
- your own authored content;
- case studies from any of our partners including Harvard Business School Publishing, Darden, Ivey and many more;
- third party content from other publishers;
- language glossaries to help students studying in a second language;
- online material tailored to your course needs.

The Pearson Education custom text published for your course is professionally produced and bound – just as you would expect from a normal Pearson Education text. You can even choose your own cover design and add your university logo.

To find out more visit **www.pearsoncustom.co.uk** or contact your local representative at: **www.pearsoned.co.uk/replocator**.

Brief contents

Contents

Part 2 LEVERAGING KNOWLEDGE

Part 3 CREATING KNOWLEDGE

Part 4 KNOWLEDGE ARTEFACTS

7 Knowledge management tools: component technologies   185

Epilogue KNOWLEDGE MANAGEMENT

The stimulus for this book came from the fact that I wanted a single knowledge management text for my postgraduate and doctoral students. During my deliberations, I was surprised that I could not find a single book that covered the breadth and range of material in knowledge management. Some of the scholarly offerings came from a human resource perspective, some from practitioner orientations, while others came from strong information systems directions. A cursory look at these texts showed that there was little crossover between these three dominant dimensions. Scholars from one perspective were rarely cited in the other and vice versa. The situation was as if each perspective of knowledge management was engrossed in its little world without having the language or foresight to engage in the other perspective.

Such a situation is not totally surprising given that knowledge management as a discipline is little over ten years old. There is currently a tremendous drive and popularity in knowledge management as practitioners and academics have accepted that we are collectively moving into a knowledge economy. To survive as individuals or companies in this knowledge economy, we need tools and shared understanding of potential challenges and ways of dealing with them in knowledge-based organisations.

This book is intended for students and practitioners of knowledge management and recognises the relevance of the book for students from a multitude of different industrial sectors. The problems of managing knowledge and the everyday needs of knowledge workers are common across many sectors. This book should appeal to students and practitioners looking for a comprehensive coverage of theoretical debates and best practice in knowledge management. The book is likely to be challenging as it demands some philosophical introspection on the nature of knowledge given the argument that we cannot begin to manage knowledge until we know what knowledge is. Certain management or information systems aspects may also appear daunting to the uninitiated, particularly if this is not your background.

I suggest that you work through the uncomfortable feelings as I believe that the strength of this emerging discipline lies in an integrated approach to knowledge management. There are rich rewards as we move into a new paradigm of work. The material in this book is intended to provide you with some pertinent and practical frameworks as well as offer a source of stimuli to think and find out more in depth where needed. Even though there are questions within the text related directly to material found in each chapter, the 'Questions for further thought' were designed to help you think 'outside the box' using material from your experience and wider reading.

Facebook, Twitter and Second Life didn't exist five years ago when this book was first published. There have been major advances in Web 2.0 technologies that facilitate interactive knowledge sharing, interoperability and collaboration. In this second edition, I have brought these latest technologies up to date. I was never happy with the structure of the first edition. This is inevitable when you're trying to break new ground in an emerging disciple. For this reason, I have revised the structure of the second edition, which provides much greater coherence.

One of the shortcomings of the first edition was the lack of real-life case studies for class discussion. I found myself using different sources with limited success. I have rectified this situation by writing ten new case studies for class discussion. For my source material, I have only used companies that have won the MAKE (Most Admired Knowledge Enterprises) award. I felt that these international organisations would provide exemplars and important sources of learning. I have stitched together the case studies from a variety of publicly available sources and followed the traditional case study format of starting with a problem that needs to be resolved and set within the context of limited real-life information. I have taken some poetic licence in order to reinforce the intended learning.

Ashok Jashapara
November 2010

 **Dr Ashok Jashapara** is an internationally recognised expert in the field of knowledge management. He has published widely in leading books and journals and has won a number of awards for his writing. He has secured a number of research awards from notable national and international funding bodies such as the ESRC, NIHR, EU and the United Nations. He has acted as External Examiner at the University of Sheffield and led the information studies discipline in teaching and learning as Associate Director for the Higher Education Academy. He is a Founder Member of the Knowledge Management Research Group at Loughborough University and the iCOM Research Group at Royal Holloway (University of London).

Author's acknowledgements

My special thanks go to my partner Karin. I would like to thank her for her tolerance of my many absences from family life, as well as practical and moral encouragement throughout the writing period. She was terrific! My two daughters, Nicole and Anna-Tina, have been an inspiration to me and I have valued their hugs and mischief when I have become overly involved with writing this book. My parents, Ramnik and Nilu, have also provided much-needed warmth and reassurance over the past year.

A large number of people have helped me with the preparation of this book, not least Gabrielle James and Emma Violet at Pearson Education, whose assistance and advice guided my perceptions of a good textbook. I would like to thank colleagues in the School of Management at Royal Holloway (University of London) for their kind words and feedback on chapters and early drafts of the book, in particular Professor Duska Rosenberg, Dr Bill Ryan, Dr Leonardo Rinaldi and Dr Gloria Agyemang. A special acknowledgement goes to members of the Knowledge Management Research Group at Loughborough University who read draft chapters and gave me their valuable comments that helped improve the final version. I would like to thank Professor Ron Summers, Dr Mark Hepworth, Dr Tom Jackson and Dr Ann O'Brien in this regard.

I owe a debt of gratitude to my friends at the 'Swan, Hope and Windsor' for their great forbear-ance at my ramblings when I have needed to talk to someone outside the confines of knowl-edge management. John Mack and Tony Zajciw at the 'Swan' have provided perfect diversions into conversations around the arts. Similarly, Glen Thumwood, Graham Farenden, Roberto Sarah Sanchez, Terry Prudham, Tony Vaghela, Celis and Tommy have provided much-needed humour, wit and hilarity to balance the serious-ness of writing a book. I am similarly grateful to my biking friends Al and Blossom at the 'Coffin Scratchers' for the long bike rides and music fes-tival diversions during the writing of this book. I cannot forget Roger Faulks and Manu Frosch at Swithland Woods for their friendship and tacit encouragement in this process.

Finally, I would like to thank the reviewers of this second edition and draft chapters. They steered the book into new and uncharted waters and, while I do not claim to have incorporated all of their comments, they certainly caused some heart-searching reflection.

During the course of writing the first edition of this book, my close friend, Spud Bakhle, died. I would like to dedicate this book to a celebration of his life and acknowledge our numerous conver-sations and ideas that have found their way into this book. Spud Bakhle was a Hegelian and Kantian scholar among other things and ideas around a dialectic are directly attributable to him.

Publisher's acknowledgements

We are grateful to the following for permission to reproduce copyright material:

Figures

Figure 2.3, 2.4, 11.1 adapted from *Sociological Paradigms and Organizational Analysis: Elements of the Sociology of Corporate Life*, Ashgate (Burrell, G. and Morgan, M. 1985) copyright © Ashgate Publishing; Figure 2.5 adapted from 'The paradigm is dead, the paradigm is dead... long live the paradigm: the legacy of Burrell and Morgan', *Omega – The International Journal of Management Science*, Vol 28 (1), pp.249–268 (Goles, T. and Hirschheim, R. 2000), Copyright © 2000 Elsevier Science Ltd. All rights reserved; Figure 2.6 adapted from *Method in Social Science: A Realist Approach*, Routledge (Sayer, A. 1992) copyright © Cengage Learning EMEA Ltd; Figure 2.8 from 'Moving beyond tacit and explicit distinctions: a realist theory of organizational knowledge', *Journal of Information Science*, Vol 33 (6), pp.752–766 (Jashapara, A.), Sage Publications. Copyright © 2007, Chartered Institute of Library and Information Professionals; Figure 3.1 adapted from *Intellectual Capital: Navigating in the New Business Landscape*, Macmillan (Roos, J., Roos, G., Edvinsson, L. and Dragonetti, N.C. 1997) p.15, figure 1.2, Reproduced by permission of Palgrave Macmillan; Figure 3.3 from 'The Balanced Scorecard – Measures that Drive Performance', *Harvard Business Review* (R.S. Kaplan and D.P. Norton, Jan–Feb 1992), copyright © Harvard Business School Publishing; Figure 3.4a from 'Dow's journey to a knowledge value management culture', *European Management Journal*, Vol 14 (4), pp.365–373 (Petrash, G. 1996), Copyright © 1996 Published by Elsevier Science Ltd; Figure 3.4b from *Intellectual Capital: Realizing Your Company's True Value by Finding Its Hidden Brainpower*, Judy Piatkus (Publishers) Ltd (Edvinsson, L. and Malone, M.S. 1997) copyright © 1997 by Leif Edvinsson and Michael S. Malone. Reprinted by permission of HarperCollins Publishers and Little, Brown Publishers Ltd; Figure 3.4c from *Strategic Management of Professional Service Firms*, Handelshojskolens Forlag (Lowendahl, B. 1997) reproduced with permission; Figure 3.4d from The Danish Confederation of Trade Unions, 1999, reproduced with permission of LO, Landsorganisationen Islands; Figure 3.4e from *Profiting from Intellectual Capital: Extracting Value from Innovation*, Wiley (Sullivan, P.H. 1998) Reproduced with permission of John Wiley & Sons, Inc.; Figure 3.4f from *Intellectual Capital*, Thomson Publishers (Brooking, A. 1996) copyright © Cengage Learning EMEA Ltd; Figure 3.6 adapted from 'Developing and managing knowledge through intellectual capital statements', *Journal of Intellectual Capital*, Vol 3 (1), pp.10–29 (Mouritsen, J., Bukh, P.N., Larsen, H.T. and Johansen, M.R. 2002), Copyright © 2002, MCB UP Ltd; Figure 3.7 adapted from 'Knowledge management: auditing and reporting intellectual capital', *Journal of General Management*, Vol 26 (3), pp.26–40 (Truch, E. 2001), copyright © The Braybrooke Press Ltd; Figure 4.1 adapted from 'Of strategies, deliberate and emergent', *Strategic Management Journal*, Vol 6 (3), pp.257–272 (Mintzberg, H. and Waters, J.A. 1985), Copyright © 2010 John Wiley & Sons, Ltd; Figure 4.3 adapted from 'The effective organisation: forces and forms', *Sloan Management Review*, Winter, pp.54–67 (Mintzberg, H. 1991), © 1991 from MIT Sloan Management Review/Massachusetts Institute of Technology. All rights reserved. Distributed by Tribune Media Services; Figure 5.2 adapted from *The Fifth Discipline: The Art and Practice of the Learning Organisation*, Doubleday Currency (Senge, P.M. 1990) copyright (c) 1990, 2006 by Peter M. Senge. Used by permission of Doubleday, a division of Random House, Inc.; Figures 5.5, 5.6, 5.7 adapted from "Organisational learning: the contributing processes and the literatures", Organization Science, Vol 2, pp.88–115 (Huber, G.P. 1991), reproduced with permission. Copyright © 1991, the Institute for Operations Research and the Management Sciences (INFORMS), 7240 Parkway Drive, Suite 300, Hanover, Maryland 21076, USA; Figure 6.2 from *The Learning Organization*, Gower (Garratt, B. 1987) copyright © Professor Bob Garratt; Figure 6.3 from *The Learning Company: A Strategy for Sustainable Development*, McGraw-Hill (Pedler, M., Burgoyne, J. and Boydell, T. 1991) Reproduced with the kind permission of The McGraw-Hill Companies. All rights reserved; Figure 6.4 from The Knowledge Creating Company, *Harvard Business Review*, 69 (Nov–Dec), pp. 96–104 (Nonaka, I. 1991), copyright © Harvard Business School Publishing; Figure 6.5 from 'Cognition, culture and competition: an empirical test of the learning organization', *The Learning Organization: An International Journal*, Vol 10 (1), pp.31–50 (Jashapara, A. 2003), Copyright © 2003, MCB UP Ltd; Figure 6.6 from 'A Typology of the Idea of Learning Organization', *Management Learning*, 33 (2), pp.213–230 (Ortenblad, A. 2002), Copyright © 2002, SAGE Publications; Figure 7.13 adapted from John Risch at the Pacific Northwest National Laboratory, www.cybergeography.org/atlas/info_spaces.html, reproduced courtesy of Pacific Northwest National Laboratory; Figure 9.3 from 'Handy's typology of culture' *from Understanding Organisations*, Fourth edition 1993, Penguin Books 1976 (Handy, C.B.) copyright (c) Charles Handy, 1976, 1981, 1985, 1993, 1999. Reproduced by permission of Penguin Books Ltd; Figure 9.4 from

THE NATURE OF KNOWLEDGE

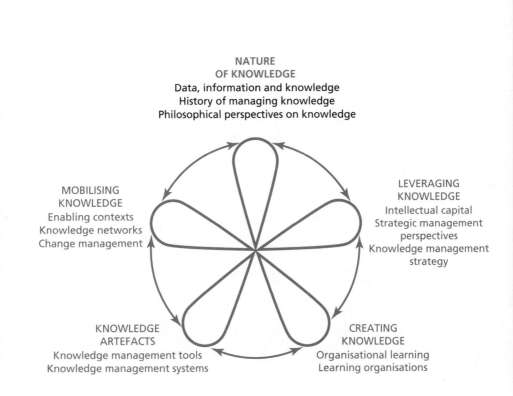

NATURE
OF KNOWLEDGE
Data, information and knowledge
History of managing knowledge
Philosophical perspectives on knowledge

MOBILISING
KNOWLEDGE
Enabling contexts
Knowledge networks
Change management

LEVERAGING
KNOWLEDGE
Intellectual capital
Strategic management
perspectives
Knowledge management
strategy

KNOWLEDGE
ARTEFACTS
Knowledge management tools
Knowledge management systems

CREATING
KNOWLEDGE
Organisational learning
Learning organisations

Chapter 1

Introduction to knowledge management

Learning outcomes

After completing this chapter, the reader should be able to:

- distinguish between different perspectives in the knowledge management (KM) literature;
- explain the diversity of disciplines and content that make up the field of knowledge management;
- describe the differences between the terms data, information and knowledge;
- assess the differences in the management of knowledge from ancient to modern times.

Management issues

An introduction to the discipline of knowledge management implies these questions for managers:

- What is knowledge management?
- How can knowledge improve actions in an organisation?
- What is the difference between information management and knowledge management?

Links to other chapters

Chapter 2   examines the history of philosophical thought on the notion of knowledge which links directly to the history of managing knowledge from the oral traditions to the storage of knowledge in libraries.

Life in an interconnected world

FT

'Tech companies are hoping that the latest innovations in the sphere of "collaboration software" will revolutionise the way in which we work,' writes Richard Waters.

The Digital Age has bred a new class of information slaves. They process endless streams of e-mail or waste time hunting for information on their hard disks and corporate intranets. Edited and re-edited versions of the same document bounce back and forth on long e-mail threads among co-workers, challenging them to keep up.

For the tortuous and time-consuming nature of this work, you can blame some of the world's biggest technology companies. Much of the 'collaboration software' that most workers use to communicate and work together – in particular the e-mail systems that dominate white-collar working life – has barely changed in a decade, even as the tide of messages and documents has risen.

'It's almost been criminal, the lack of innovation on the e-mail client,' says Matt Cain, an analyst at Gartner, the technology research firm.

Even in areas where technology has advanced, many workers are still in the Dark Ages – either because their companies have yet to give them the latest tools, or because they don't have the time or inclination to try them out.

'It's a constant challenge for us to make people engage with new technologies,' says Stephen Elop, president of Microsoft's business division, which makes the widely used Office applications.

The sheer number of applications that the average worker has to juggle hasn't helped. These now range from corporate document-sharing sites and web conferencing to Facebook and Twitter, which are starting to encroach from the consumer world.

'If you count up all the applications people are being asked to use, it's probably a dozen,' says Ted Schadler, an analyst at Forrester Research. The result, he says, is overload and frustration. In a survey last month of how 2,000 office workers use their PCs, Forrester concluded that the take-up of collaboration tools has 'stalled out', leaving e-mail as the all-purpose default option. Change, however, is finally in the air. The market for collaboration software, dominated for years by Microsoft and IBM, is now under attack from all sides as other technology companies hunt for ways to make so-called 'knowledge workers' more productive.

Cisco Systems showed its hand last month with the announcement of a $3bn (€2bn, £1.8bn) agreement to buy Tandberg, a Norwegian video-conferencing company, to add to widening portfolio tools. Google launched a limited test version of its own all-purpose online tool, known as Wave, in September.

Undaunted by the coming clash of giants such as these, several start-ups have also set their sights on the market. Typical of the breed is Xobni, whose technology rides on top of the widely used Microsoft Outlook e-mail software and aims to help users find and make use of information in their e-mail inboxes more effectively than Microsoft's own tools can.

Most of these companies have their sights set on the same things: simplification and convergence.

One manifestation of this is the growing use of 'dashboards' – screens that bring a number of applications together in one view. They are usually centred on the e-mail inbox, with parts of the screen given over to other applications.

Designs such as this are meant to help workers complete a task without having to close and open multiple windows on their PCs. They aggregate multiple sources of information and provide a limited amount of information integration.

'For instance, when opening an e-mail from a customer, a user of Xobni's dashboard might see information alongside it drawn automatically from the company's internal customer relationship management system,' says Jeff Bonforte, the company's chief executive. 'The bigger operators are also moving quickly in this direction, with most likely to announce similar products in the coming months,' says Mr Schadler at Forrester.

Aggregating and integrating e-mail with other sources of information and applications is only part of the answer. Eventually, to solve e-mail overload, the inbox itself needs to become smarter. 'It should be able to aggregate all the sources and recommend priorities,' says Doug Heintzman, head of strategy for IBM's collaboration software.

Research labs at companies such as IBM and Microsoft have been working for some time on the algorithms to do this, but according to Mr Heintzman, a working system is still three to five years away.

A second approach to simplification and convergence focuses on ways for workers to collaborate on tasks without having to resort to endless group e-mails with multiple 'cc's' and attachments.

Most new approaches revolve around software that keeps information in a central place and lets staff jointly access and work on it. Microsoft, for instance, has devised a way for people in different locations to 'co-author' a document simultaneously, though their employers will need to buy the latest versions of its Office and server-based Sharepoint software for this to work.

Google is now trying to go one better. If people can communicate in the same place that they create and edit information, it calculates, then many of the complexities caused by current software would fall away.

The result is Google Wave, an online application built for both consumer and work use that merges multiple ways of working and communicating. That makes it the Swiss Army Knife of software, and its early reception has been mixed, reflecting the difficulty of such an ambitious undertaking.

'It's the opposite of simple,' says Mr Cain at Gartner, though he adds that it is 'really innovative'. 'There's no doubt it will have an impact on the evolution of this market,' he says. For the average information slave, meanwhile, none of this guarantees a quick or sure route to higher productivity and lower blood pressure. Though many of these new ways of interacting have already been tried out in the consumer world – 'social' software such as wikis, or co-authored documents were a staple of the Web 2.0 movement – it will be some time before they find their way into office life.

It takes time for experimental consumer services to evolve into the stable, secure applications that corporate IT departments feel comfortable with. Also, the slow upgrade cycle of corporate software feels glacial compared to the red-hot pace of innovation currently seen on the internet. The biggest challenge of all, though, comes from workers themselves.

'Any collaboration tool that is not adopted widely will, by definition, fail, yet devising software that appeals to a broad group of users is hard,' says Mr Heintzman at IBM. 'There are so many different work styles, people have so many different roles and come from different cultures,' he explains.

They also come from different technological eras: a generation of workers wedded to e-mail is starting to encounter a generation that grew up on social networks and instant messaging. Keeping them all on the same page will not be easy.

Surf the Wave
It was classic Google ambition. Earlier this year, Lars Rasmussen, one of the company's star developers, stood in front of thousands at a company-sponsored conference and said that Google was about to reinvent e-mail.

Google Wave, now in a limited test, has been hailed as a radical departure in internet-based communication, though it has also been faulted for its complexity and poor design – criticisms that Mr Rasmussen and his fellow developers accept, though they say they will correct these glitches.

Like an expanded instant messaging system, Wave lets groups of users hold a text conversation while also creating, commenting on and jointly editing documents in the same window. In a head-turning gimmick, words can be seen by anyone connected to a 'wave' as they are being typed.

'Making one tool with such broad utility is the way to go,' Mr Rasmussen says. 'You don't have to learn a new way of sharing something for every different collaboration task. Everything is just a wave.' In spite of the simplicity which that implies, getting the most out of Wave will demand a lot from its users. 'We weren't trying to hit something that you could learn in an afternoon,' he says. 'We were trying to build a tool that will be with you for many hours each day. You can even imagine, in time, people will be teaching courses in Wave.'

Source: from Life in an interconnected world, *The Financial Times*, 03/11/2009 (Waters, R.), copyright © The Financial Times Ltd.

Questions

1 How can 'information slaves' overcome problems of 'information overload'?

2 What are the problems of collaborative technologies for 'knowledge workers'?

3 How can Google Wave improve collaboration and communication among 'knowledge workers'?

Knowledge management: an integrated approach

The aim of this book is to provide a comprehensive and integrated discourse on the various facets, emerging issues and perspectives on knowledge management. There are numerous accounts of knowledge management as a process and a continuous cycle and this representation has been used as a structure for this book, as shown in Figure 1.1. The generic activities in the knowledge management cycle are subdivided into the five parts of this book: the nature of knowledge, leveraging knowledge, creating knowledge, knowledge artefacts and mobilising knowledge.

◗ Part 1: The nature of knowledge

Part 1 explores all the different aspects related to the notion of knowledge and knowledge management. An historical perspective on how knowledge was managed across the centuries from the bardic oral tradition to the current digital revolution is provided. Philosophy is not often taught in our universities and its central role in understanding knowledge is examined. This will allow future students to move beyond the current structural, process and practice perspectives in the literature.

● *Chapter 1: Introduction to knowledge management.* This chapter provides an exploration of the emerging discipline and forwards an integrated model. The differences between data, information and knowledge are examined. An historical perspective on knowledge management illustrates the central function of libraries in knowledge creation, sharing and transfer.

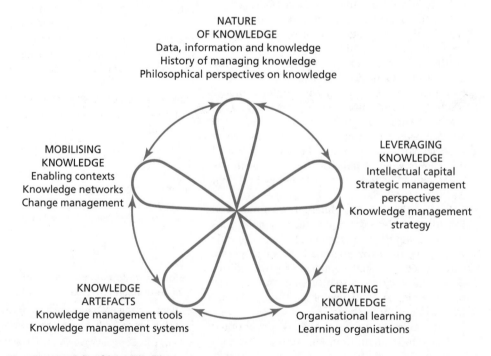

Figure 1.1 **Web of knowledge management**

- *Chapter 2: The nature of knowing.* This is a thought-provoking chapter exploring issues of ontology and epistemology. What is the nature of knowledge and reality? What are the aspects of knowledge that we can know? The contributions of major philosophers in the knowledge debate are examined and the current notions of knowledge in the knowledge management literature are assessed.

▶ Part 2: Leveraging knowledge

Part 2 explores the fruits of knowledge management in the formation of intellectual capital within an organisation. Knowledge is considered as the critical factor for competitiveness and economic growth. The knowledge management strategies underlying innovation and growth are assessed.

- *Chapter 3: Intellectual capital.* This chapter examines some of the limitations of traditional financial measures in performance measurement and the search for non-financial measures such as intellectual capital to supplement these conventional sources. Several models of intellectual capital are compared and generic notions of human capital, social capital, organisational capital and customer capital are presented.
- *Chapter 4: Strategic management perspectives.* This chapter contrasts the difference between three dominant strategy schools of thought: industrial organisation, excellence and turnaround, and the institutionalist perspective.

▶ Part 3: Creating knowledge

Part 3 examines the different organisational processes involved with knowledge creation. At its heart are the various learning processes intrinsic to organisational survival and growth. The organisational learning literature has led to the conception of a 'learning organisation'. The nature and debates surrounding a learning organisation are explored.

- *Chapter 5: Organisational learning.* This chapter outlines the nature of individual, team and organisational learning. An information processing perspective is adopted to examine the processes of knowledge acquisition, information distribution, information interpretation and organisational memory. The development of organisational routines and dynamic capabilities are discussed.
- *Chapter 6: The learning organisation.* This chapter contrasts the terms 'organisational learning' and the 'learning organisation' and articulates the diversity of US and UK models associated with the learning organisation. Empirical research in this field is assessed.

▶ Part 4: Knowledge artefacts

Part 4 examines knowledge artefacts, which occur as different forms of information and communication technologies to enable effective utilisation of knowledge. This part provides an understanding of the different technologies used to mobilise knowledge, especially the new Web 2.0 platform with applications such as Twitter, Facebook and Second Life. A number of these technologies have been integrated as knowledge management systems to allow organisations to manage the high load and complexity of knowledge.

- *Chapter 7: Knowledge management tools: component technologies*. This chapter provides a grounding in the variety of knowledge management tools that can be used at different stages in the knowledge management cycle. These include ontology and taxonomy tools, information retrieval tools, personalisation tools, data mining tools, case-based reasoning tools, groupware tools, video-conferencing tools, e-learning tools and visualisation tools.

- *Chapter 8: Knowledge management systems*. This chapter elaborates on a variety of knowledge management systems including document management systems, decision support systems, group support systems, executive information systems, workflow management systems and customer relationship management systems.

◗ Part 5: Mobilising knowledge

Part 5 examines the softer aspects of mobilising knowledge through people and technology. Apart from conducive social environments, organisations are increasingly providing a mixture of physical and virtual spaces for their knowledge workers. The intention is to enable them to engage actively in discussion and dialogue in formal and informal settings. Innovation and new initiatives can often face hostility and difficulties. The various human resource interventions for the successful implementation of such initiatives are explored.

- *Chapter 9: Enabling knowledge contexts and networks*. This chapters contrasts the literature on organisational climate and culture and explores the debates around knowledge-sharing cultures. Informal networks called 'communities of practice' are explained along with the role of storytelling and narratives within them.

- *Chapter 10: Implementing knowledge management*. This chapter provides the latest thinking on the effective implementation of knowledge management initiatives. It examines how high levels of commitment can be developed through leadership and a variety of human resource interventions. The role of politics in change management programmes is highlighted.

Introduction

Knowledge management has similar parallels with the rise of English as an academic discipline in the early twentieth century. In the 1920s it was unclear why anyone should study English and, by the 1930s, it was a question of whether students should study anything else at all. English was initially a poor man's Classics and was taught in working men's colleges and mechanic institutes. The subject was considered an upstart and rather amateurish affair compared with the traditional subjects such as Classics and Philology. Similarly, knowledge management in the twenty-first century has risen from practitioner and consultancy knowledge and has only recently become a subject for academic study. Today English is often associated with creative or imaginative writing. However, in the eighteenth century, English covered all the valued writings in society including history, philosophy, essays, letters and poems (Eagleton 1999; Palmer 1965). Similarly, today knowledge management can be confused with information systems by some commentators and human resource management by others. In reality, it has roots in a wide variety of disciplines such as philosophy, business management, anthropology, information science, psychology and computer science.

In fashioning knowledge management into a serious discipline, this chapter will explore the nature of knowledge management and propose a definition of this field from an interdisciplinary perspective. To provide a balanced appraisal of the literature, a critical understanding of reservations in this field will be forwarded. The terms 'data', 'information' and 'knowledge' can often be used synonymously in the literature and the distinction between these terms is explored.

Knowledge, and the way it is managed, has been with humankind since the beginning of time. This chapter shall proceed to explore the history of knowledge management, taking a broad perspective and including the vital role of libraries in the ancient and modern worlds. The development of oral knowledge from the oral traditions to the first writing of cuneiform among Sumerians is discussed. A journey is conducted through the flourishing libraries in ancient Greek and Roman periods such as the Alexandria library and the Ulpian library. The influence of Christianity in the rise of monastic and cathedral libraries is explained together with the emergence of early universities. The paradigm leap in knowledge creation and dissemination that has occurred through the development of print, computers and telecommunications is fully explored.

The knowledge economy

Peter Drucker (1992, 1993) argued that the workplace was changing and there was an increasing distinction between the manual worker and the 'knowledge worker'. To him, a manual worker used his hands to produce goods and services, whereas a knowledge worker used his head to create ideas, information and knowledge that could add value to the firm.

Subsequently, knowledge workers have been defined as professionals, associate professionals or managers with graduate level skills in critical thinking, communications and technology. In 2006 knowledge workers accounted for 42 per cent of all employment in the UK (Brinkley, 2006). The concept of a knowledge economy has emerged to represent a 'soft discontinuity' from the past. It is not a new economy with new laws. Instead it is an economy driven by knowledge intangibles rather than physical capital, natural resources or low-skilled labour. The OECD (1996) has recognised that knowledge and technology have become drivers of productivity and economic growth in modern economies. The new focus for economic performance is on knowledge, technology and learning. The role of governments and policy makers is shifting towards the greater development and maintenance of this knowledge base. It is not purely an increased commitment to R&D but rather the mobilisation of knowledge to add value to goods and services. A number of definitions of the knowledge economy are provided below:

'....one in which the generation and exploitation of knowledge has come to play the predominant part in the creation of wealth. It is not simply about pushing back the frontiers of knowledge; it is also about the most effective use and exploitation of all types of knowledge in all manner of economic activity.' (DTI 1998)

'. . . economic success is increasingly based upon the effective utilisation of intangible assets such as knowledge, skills and innovative potential as the key resource for competitive advantage. The term 'knowledge economy' is used to describe this emerging economic structure.' (ESRC 2005 quoted in Brinkley 2006)

Unlike the use of scarce resources in previous economies, knowledge is not a resource that is depleted after its use. Instead, knowledge grows through transfer and exchange and an abundance of knowledge can be seen to exist on the internet. Firms are no longer restrained by the physical location of partners in a supply chain. Instead they can exist as virtual organisations and engage in economic activity within virtual marketplaces across the world. This can make it difficult for governments to regulate and control this economic activity through laws and taxes on a national basis.

Globalisation is closely related to the knowledge economy. Firms have added value through knowledge to new products in the West and have had them built and assembled in lower-wage economies such as China and India. However, the same low-waged economies are now investing heavily in knowledge through greater investment in R&D as a proportion of their GDP and increased numbers of home-grown graduates. They are developing their knowledge economies through greater share of highly educated labour and greater production and utilisation of information and communication technologies. In 2007 a Booz Allan Hamilton (a consulting firm) report on global innovation showed that the top global innovating firms had established 80–90 per cent of their new corporate R&D sites and personnel in India and China (Teagarden *et al.*, 2008). Is this an example of the use of 'cheap smarts' rather than use of more expensive home-grown talent?

What is knowledge management?

In the post-industrial or knowledge economy (Bell 1973; Drucker 1992), knowledge management has become an emerging discipline that has gained enormous popularity among academics, consultants and practitioners. It has been argued that it is no longer the traditional industrial technologies or craft skills that drive competitive performance but, instead, knowledge that has become the key asset to drive organisational survival and success.

To the uninitiated reader, the multitude of offerings on knowledge management in books, journals and magazines can appear rather daunting and confusing at first. The fact is that it is a relatively young discipline trying to find its way, while recognising that it has roots in a number of other, very different disciplines. Some literature on knowledge management is heavily information systems oriented, giving the impression that it is little more than information management. Other literature looks more at the people's dimension of knowledge creation and sharing, making the subject more akin to human-resource management. These are the two most common dimensions and there is often little crossover between them. Each world fails to comprehend the other, as the language and assumptions of each discipline vary significantly. However, it is precisely these interdisciplinary linkages that provide the most rewarding advances in this field.

Given the interdisciplinary nature of this emerging field, conventional academic demarcations in traditional subject areas do not help. For example, it is relatively rare for computer or information science graduates to gain sufficient grounding in human resource management and vice versa with traditional business management students. This impasse is often based on fear on both sides about the nature and relative merits of their respective skills and expertise. Beyond these two dominant dimensions, there are some additional perspectives within the KM literature, ranging from strategy to cultural change management. It is not surprising that there is little coherence between these offerings, as many authors orientate the subject area to their singular discipline perspective.

Critical thinking and reflection

What does knowledge mean to you? If you were asked to detail your specialist knowledge, how would you describe your knowledge? Have you ever thought of the market value of your knowledge and what this may be? Given that there is a competitive market for knowledge and skills, how do you ensure that your knowledge is state-of-the-art and kept up to date?

The strength and challenge of knowledge management as an emerging discipline comes from its interdisciplinary approach, as shown in Figure 1.2. For example, if knowledge management was purely information systems, current tools and business processes would suffice. However, the reality is that different information systems approaches such as data processing, management information systems and strategic information systems have been found wanting. There are numerous examples of major investments made in this area, particularly in the financial services sector, that have yielded little or no benefit to host organisations. Instead, the real synergies in knowledge management are more likely to occur from boundary-spanning individuals who can see beyond the narrow margins of their own disciplines and recognise the value of dialogue and debate with other disciplines.

Given the multidisciplinary nature of knowledge management, it is not surprising that the variety of current definitions comes from a number of different perspectives, as shown in Table 1.1. Some come from an information systems perspective (Mertins *et al.* 2000), while others suggest a human-resource perspective (Skyrme 1999; Swan *et al.* 1999a). A few definitions have begun to adopt a more strategic management perspective, recognising the importance of knowledge management practices for gaining competitive advantage (Newell *et al.* 2009; uit Beijerse 2000). However, none of these definitions expands on the alliances with particular strategic schools of thought, and the basic assumptions of the nature of competitive environments (such as highly turbulent) or strategic positioning (such as continuous innovation) need to be questioned

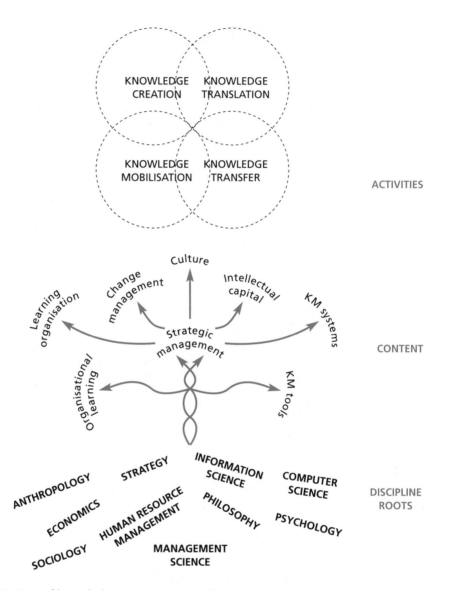

Figure 1.2 Tree of knowledge management – disciplines, content and activity

(Newell *et al*. 2009). External environments may shift from turbulent to more stable environments over time and competitive environments may favour efficiency rather than innovation in a given period. The basic fact is that we live in uncertain times and any assumptions about competitive environments and approaches to organisational alignment and adaptability need to be considered carefully.

Table 1.1 **Representative sample of knowledge management definitions**

Author/s	Definition	Perspective
Davenport and Prusak (1998)	'Knowledge management draws from existing resources that your organisation may already have in place – good information systems management, organisational change management, and human resources management practices.'	Integration (information systems and human resources)
Swan *et al.* (1999b)	'… any process or practice of creating, acquiring, capturing, sharing and using knowledge, wherever it resides, to enhance learning and performance in organisations.'	Human resource process
Skyrme (1999)	'The *explicit* and *systematic* management of *vital* knowledge and its associated *processes* of creating, gathering, organising, diffusion, use and exploitation, in pursuit of organisational objectives.'	Human resource process
Mertins *et al.* (2000)	'… all methods, instruments and tools that in a holistic approach contribute to the promotion of core knowledge processes.'	Information systems
uit Beijerse (2000)	'The achievement of the organisation's goals by making the factor knowledge productive.'	Strategy
Newell *et al.* (2009)	'… improving the ways in which firms facing highly turbulent environments can mobilise their knowledge base (or leverage their knowledge 'assets') in order to ensure continuous innovation.'	Strategy

From the definitions of knowledge management given in Table 1.1, it is clear that any advancements in this field need to adopt an integrated (Davenport and Prusak 1998), interdisciplinary and strategic perspective, as shown in Figure 1.3. The strategic purpose of knowledge management activities is to increase intellectual capital and enhance organisational performance (see Chapters 3 and 4). There is a human dimension of developing knowledge in individuals, teams and organisations and this fundamentally occurs through different learning processes (see Chapter 5). Once knowledge is created, the sharing of knowledge remains one of the fundamental challenges in this field. As human beings, we need support to help us explore and exploit knowledge (tacit – 'know-how' – and explicit – 'know what', see Chapters 2 and 5) more fully. There is a wide variety of tools, technologies and systems that can fulfil these functions, such as the continuous cycle of knowledge creation, capture, organisation, evaluation, storage and sharing (see Chapters 7 and 8). However, KM tools and organisational processes are insufficient in themselves to achieve success. Many well-planned initiatives have proved futile, as they have failed to acknowledge the cultural and change-management dimensions (see Chapters 9 and 10) of successful implementation.

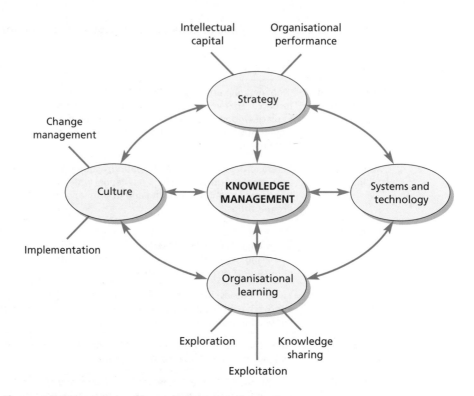

Figure 1.3 Dimensions of knowledge management

These different dimensions of knowledge management have been brought together into an integrated definition. From an interdisciplinary perspective, knowledge management can be defined as:

> *'the effective learning processes associated with exploration, exploitation and sharing of human knowledge (tacit and explicit) that use appropriate technology and cultural environments to enhance an organisation's intellectual capital and performance.'*

Is knowledge management a fad?

As is common with any new field of discourse, knowledge management has its critics and its antithesis. The most vociferous so far has come from information scientists who appear to feel threatened by the prospect that it may marginalise their own discipline (Ponzi and Koenig 2002; Wilson 2002). This is clearly unjustified, as information science is an essential component of knowledge management, although not the only one. A number of arguments have been put forward to show that knowledge management is no more than 'old wine in new bottles' where, as with Alice through the looking glass, terms can mean what anyone chooses them to mean. Let us explore some of the arguments.

The first argument posed is that knowledge management is no more than a fad or a fashion. The difference between a fad and a fashion is the duration of time over which the phenomenon lasts. Fads develop a high level of interest in a short time, then die away. However, fashions have a much longer maturity of interest. Bibliometric techniques have been adopted to examine the volume of bibliographic records as an indicator of discourse popularity over time. The assumption is that knowledge management is similar to other management fads such as quality circles, total quality management and business process re-engineering. However, the empirical evidence goes counter to these arguments. Bibliometric studies (1991–2001) show that knowledge management has had almost exponential growth in the past six years and shows no signs of abating (Ponzi and Koenig 2002).

The second argument posed by such critics is that knowledge management does not stand up to rigorous analysis, as it has emerged from consultancy practice (Wilson 2002). This is clearly not the case, since knowledge has roots within organisational learning and strategy literatures with a much older lineage of rigour. The organisation of knowledge was being considered by some scholars as early as the 1960s (Etzioni 1964). More recently, scholars have been debating the knowledge-based view of the firm (Grant 1996; Spender 1996) descending from a resource-based view of the firm (Barney 1991; Barney 2001) and institutional theory (Penrose 1959; Selznick 1957). At practitioner levels, there have been studies exploring knowledge management strategies and approaches in eminent journals such as the *Harvard Business Review* (Hansen *et al.* 1999; Nonaka 1991). The corpus of rigorous knowledge is emerging in this field, including critical analysis of the literature as well as alternative insights such as postmodernist orientations (Kalling and Styhre 2003; Styhre 2003).

The third argument against knowledge management is that many top business schools have failed to respond to these advances in knowledge management in their curricula (Wilson 2002). Some business schools may incorporate the material associated with knowledge management on a variety of modules such as strategic management, human resource management and information management strategy. It would be remarkable if any business school ignored the learning base associated with knowledge management. At some schools in the UK, such as the Open University Business School, there is a specialised module on knowledge management attracting a significant number of students. The knowledge management discipline is around seven years old, and it is not surprising that some business schools have been pioneering in this new field whereas others have been assessing its likely impact.

The final argument is that knowledge management is no more than 'search and replace marketing' (Wilson 2002). This means that many software houses simply relabel their products with 'knowledge' or 'knowledge management' somewhere within their brand. There is certainly an element of this. Such organisations may be forgiven for cashing in on the popularity of knowledge management in the corporate marketplace. An example of this is Lotus Notes software relabelling itself as 'Knowledgeware' rather than groupware. However, knowledge management is more than software and systems, even though they are important aspects of it. Some confusion may arise when critics wrongly assume that knowledge management has developed an entirely new toolkit in the past five years rather than building and adapting existing information systems to serve its own ends. Future KM technologies are likely to explore ways of tapping into the vast reservoir of tacit knowledge in organisations.

Table 1.2 **Some typical examples of knowledge management job titles**

• Chief knowledge officer	• Director of knowledge management
• Director of intellectual capital	• Knowledge department manager
• Knowledge manager	• Knowledge economist
• Knowledge consultant	• Knowledge resources librarian
• Knowledge management analyst	• Knowledge administrator
• Knowledge coordinator	• Knowledge management project manager

A convincing counter-argument against many critics is the clear empirical evidence demonstrating that knowledge management has become an accepted part of the corporate agenda, particularly among large firms. Specialist roles have emerged such as chief knowledge officers, knowledge managers and directors of intellectual capital (see Table 1.2 for a list of typical KM job titles). For instance, a survey conducted by KPMG Consulting in 1999 (KPMG Consulting 2000) of 423 organisations in the UK, mainland Europe and the US showed that 81 per cent were considering a KM programme, and 38 per cent of these already had one in place. This survey was conducted predominantly among executives and chief executives of large organisations with a turnover exceeding £200 million a year. The survey confirmed that 64 per cent of these firms had a knowledge management strategy and the main drivers of KM strategy were senior management or board level engagement. The most common KM problems encountered were information overload, lack of time for sharing knowledge and the inability to use knowledge effectively. The main causes of failure in KM initiatives revolved predominantly around human resource issues. These included the lack of user uptake due to insufficient communication, inability to integrate KM practices with normal working practice, the lack of time to learn and the lack of adequate training. In addition to this survey, there are numerous well-documented examples of firms engaged in KM strategies and practices, such as Buckman Laboratories and BP in the private sectors and World Bank and the United Nations in the public sectors.

What are the differences between data, information, knowledge and wisdom?

▶ Data

The dictionary definition of data is 'known facts or things used as a basis of inference or reckoning'. Let's try to unravel this multifaceted term and show that a definition of data depends on context. We acquire data from the external world through our senses and try to make sense of these signals through our experience. This external data becomes internal fact. The assumption about facts is that they are true. But our senses can play games with us. An example is the optical illusions contained in Escher's drawings, which can be seen in two different ways. Escher made an art of creating impossible figures, such as people ascending and descending stairs at the same time, that were clearly contradictory. We can also exclude data in a number of ways that can affect our inference or reckoning of it. The first is by not focusing on the data, such as with the 'cocktail party' effect where we are bombarded with lots of data but are able to ignore most of it (background noise) and concentrate on the data of the person speaking to us. We also exclude data when our senses are not able to respond to signals such as ultraviolet light or ultrasound, and we may exclude data voluntarily by putting on a blindfold or inserting ear plugs (Meadows 2001) or involuntarily through data overload.

So far we have explored data from the perspective of the receiver of the signal. In this context, a signal is a set of data transmitted to our senses. What about the source of the signal and the channel or medium through which it is transmitted? Each one of these can contain a distortion and this can affect the nature of data coming to us. The traditional game of 'Chinese whispers' at the dinner table shows how an initial message can become totally distorted by the time it has gone around the table.

There are differences between quantitative and qualitative data. For example, the numbers 72 and 83 per cent are pieces of data that can have multiple meanings and are highly context dependent. They may refer to mean examination scores or the performance of a new carburettor undergoing trials, so the data is meaningless when taken out of context and requires an association with something else. Qualitative data is much more troublesome as it depends on the perceptions of the transmitter and receiver of the data. Ten participants in a meeting are likely to provide ten totally different accounts depending on their perspective and their selective inclusion or exclusion of data. In this sense data is also value laden. An example of this is two artists, one European and the other Chinese, who painted 'faithful representations' of the same landscape in the English Lake district (Gombrich 1960). To European eyes, the painting by the Chinese artist was typical of a Chinese painting. This example shows the 'conceptually saturated' character of observation and data where it is difficult to distinguish between what is observable (empirical) and what is unobservable (theoretical or conceptual). We may have 'sensations' in our eyes without concepts, but we have no perception of data without concepts (O'Connor and Carr 1982).

▶ Information

The dictionary definition of information is 'something told' or 'the act of informing or telling'. However, this doesn't help us distinguish between data and information. Information could be considered as 'systematically organised data' (Meadows 2001). The notion of 'systematic' implies the ability to predict or make inferences from the data assuming it is based on some system. If we are given a sequence of odd numbers such as 7, 9, 11, 13, we can predict from the information that the next number in the sequence will be 15. To inform, the data needs to be organised. This may be done through some form of classification scheme set up to provide a framework for our thinking. For example, libraries classify their books using a bibliographic classification scheme. A common one is the Dewey Decimal Classification which is based on dividing all of knowledge into ten fields ranging from 0–999. Dewey has essentially followed a Darwinian model in which different aspects and parts of knowledge are related to each other either by direct descent or by collateral kinship. All knowledge is divided into *genera* and *species* using a similar approach to Darwin's. The ten encompassing classes (000, 100 … 900) are subdivided, first into 401, 402 …, then 410, 411, and then by adding further numbers after the decimal point that are related to numbers which can also appear before the point (an example is that the number after the decimal point is the same for certain periods covered in related subject domains such as English history and English literature).

Another conception of information is data that are endowed with meaning, relevance and purpose. This does not have to have a scientific meaning such as the Dewey classification system but may have a subjective meaning given by the receiver of the data or message. Information gives shape to the data and makes a difference to the outlook or insight of the receiver of the data. In this sense, it is the receiver of the data that determines whether a message is data or information. A consultancy report may be written to inform senior managers of critical issues but may be judged as ramblings and noise by the recipients (Davenport and Prusak 1998). Meaning in data often occurs through some form of association with experience or relationships with other data.

Critical thinking and reflection

From your experiences, can you describe situations where you have made decisions with wrong data or information? How do you guard against this? What strategies do you adopt to evaluate a situation with conflicting information or data? How do you manage 'noise' or irrelevant data or information related to a particular problem? How do you manage too much data or the problem of 'information overload'?

▶ Knowledge

In a practical sense, knowledge could be considered as 'actionable information', as shown in the hierarchy of data, information and knowledge in Figure 1.4. Actionable information allows us to make better decisions and provide an effective input to dialogue and creativity in organisations. This occurs by providing information at the right place, at the right time and in the appropriate format (Tiwana 2000). Knowledge allows us to act more effectively than information or data and equips us with a greater ability to predict future outcomes.

However, knowledge is much more complex than this simplistic notion. We have devoted the whole of the next chapter to exploring how over the past two millennia western philosophers have grappled with the question of what knowledge is. There is still no consensus on the nature of knowledge except that it is based on perceptions that can provide rational justifications for it. Such perceptions are based on our ontological and epistemological assumptions of reality. Put simply, we all wear 'different coloured glasses' whether we are aware of it or not. These 'glasses' contain assumptions about reality, such as whether it is subjective or objective (ontology) and assumptions about what we can know (epistemology). Continuing this analogy, the knowledge of a certain phenomenon is likely to be different if one individual wears 'pink' glasses and

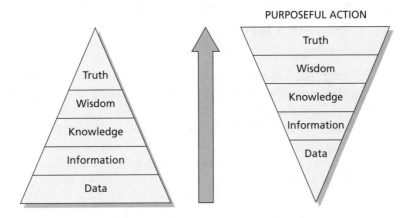

Figure 1.4 **Data, information, knowledge and purposeful action**

another wears 'blue' ones. Hence, for example, it is no surprise that the knowledge of costs and benefits of organisational restructuring is often viewed very differently by the workforce and by senior management. The interpretation of the same data and information will vary significantly depending on these perceptions and the original knowledge base of the individual.

The most common notion of knowledge in the current KM literature has its roots in the ideas of logical behaviourism based on the writings of Gilbert Ryle and Michael Polanyi. From this perspective, knowledge exists along a continuum between tacit knowledge (know-how) and explicit knowledge (know what) (Polanyi 1967; Ryle 1949). (See Chapter 2 for more in-depth coverage of knowledge frameworks and typologies.) One of the major challenges in knowledge management is exploring creative ways to convert the tacit knowledge base in organisations into explicit knowledge (Nonaka 1994). Organisational routines, practices and norms can also act as part of this tacit knowledge base. Despite the logical behaviourist perspective of tacit and explicit knowledge being dominant at present, there are numerous alternative perspectives on the nature of knowledge. As the literature gains in maturity, it is likely that other perspectives such as postmodernism, critical theory and realism may provide new insights and advances in this field.

❱ Wisdom

Wisdom and truth have been shown to have higher qualities than knowledge in the hierarchy of Figure 1.4. These terms are even more elusive than knowledge. Wisdom is the ability to act critically or practically in a given situation. It is based on ethical judgement related to an individual's belief system. Wisdom is often captured in famous quotes, proverbs and sayings. Some examples of proverbs from around the world include the following:

● Children have more need of models than of critics (French).

● You can't see the whole sky through a bamboo tube (Japanese).

- There is plenty of sound in an empty barrel (Russian).
- Trust in Allah, but tie your camel (Muslim).
- Wonder is the beginning of wisdom (Greek).

Truth is even more problematic, since there is a growing realisation that social phenomena are theory laden, as illustrated in the above example of the Chinese and European artists. Theory-neutral observations do not exist, as our tacit theories or conceptions of the world affect our observations. The notions of 'truth' and 'objectivity' can appear meaningless if the social world can be understood only through particular ways of seeing. This implies that there are multiple truths rather than one absolute truth of social phenomena. A pessimistic outlook on information, knowledge and wisdom has been captured in the well-known lines from T.S. Eliot in the 'Choruses' from *The Rock*:

> *Where is the life we have lost in living?*
> *Where is the wisdom we have lost in knowledge?*
> *Where is the knowledge we have lost in information?*

Early history of knowledge management: oral tradition to cuneiform

One of the oldest forms of managing knowledge is the oral tradition and the use of human memory to store knowledge. This oral transfer of knowledge occurs through a process of transmitting messages by word of mouth over time, as can be found in many bardic traditions around the world. The process of transmission begins when messages are repeated over time and ends when they disappear, for a variety of reasons. The message may represent news such as eyewitness accounts, hearsay or visions, dreams and hallucinations in some societies. The other group of messages are interpretations such as reminiscences of childhood, explanatory commentaries and historical tales, poetry, songs and sayings. Epic poems may be memorised to achieve a consistency over each recitation, but the fact is that actual wordings are likely to change over time. Songs provide more faithful transmission of messages as their melodies act as mnemonic devices.

Critical thinking and reflection

Think about your work or social life. What are your difficulties in people giving you knowledge or information verbally? Despite these difficulties, what do you prefer about the spoken word over other forms of communication? Have you ever played Chinese whispers at dinner parties? What are the likely problems with passing down knowledge second, third or fourth hand? Are there similar problems with spoken knowledge being passed down over many years?

The unique characteristics of the oral tradition are that messages are not written down and they accumulate interpretations as they are transmitted. Successive accumulation and selection of interpretations can mean that messages from the oral tradition become constrained by previous interpretations. Consequently, although the reliability of messages from oral traditions may be questionable, nevertheless they do provide 'inside' knowledge about how news is interpreted by a community of people.

The limitation of the oral tradition is the fallibility of our memories and the divergence from or direct contradiction of written sources. This can occur when certain groups or individuals selectively discard certain knowledge and retain only that which they consider important at the time. People may also add new meanings to the old knowledge, giving a degree of bias to the former knowledge. Oral traditions that are older than two or three generations can also suffer from the unreliability of the knowledge that is preserved (Vansina 1985).

Given the limitations of the oral tradition, the first evidence of attempts to preserve knowledge through writing dates back to around 3000 BC. The Sumerians settled in southern Mesopotamia and found that their rivers had a plentiful supply of good clay and reeds. They fashioned the clay into tablets, the reeds into three-cornered writing instruments or styluses and perfected a style of writing called 'cuneiform' based on simple lines and wedges (see Figure 1.5). The combination of these simple wedges (Latin *cunei*) and lines represented many hundred words and sounds. Scribes or '*dubsar*' underwent many years of training as apprentices to a headmaster or '*ummia*'. The scribes were highly venerated in this society, ranking just below high priests in social status. The knowledge recorded on these clay tablets ranged from administrative records, Hammurabi's laws and marriage contracts to legends and mythology.

Before long, collections of these clay tablets developed and the challenge became one of organising knowledge in tablets into some form of cataloguing system. In 1980 archaeologists discovered a room full of clay tablets at the ancient royal palace of Ebla in Syria dating back to around 2300 BC. The Eblaites gave us our primitive form of catalogues in the shape of long lists of words, objects, place names and species. The palace library provided a training ground for scribes and promoted the creation and preservation of knowledge similar in nature to our modern universities (Lerner 1998).

Figure 1.5 **Example of cuneiform writing (this records the allocation of beer)** (© The Trustees of the British Museum)

One of the greatest stores of knowledge in the ancient world covered over 10,000 works contained in 30,000 clay tablets found at Assurbanipal's palace library (around 650 BC) in Nineveh. These Assyrian collections were essentially archives created as a public memory for the state. Scribes and scholars were employed to compile, revise and edit different varieties of knowledge. The tablets were kept in earthenware jars, properly arranged on shelves in different rooms. Each tablet had an identification tag showing its precise location in a jar, shelf and room. There were also 'catalogue' tablets in each room providing a brief description of the tablets and their location in the room (Harris 1995). Even though the library contained literary materials such as the *Epic of Gilgamesh*, omen texts tended to predominate, reflecting some of the preoccupations of that society. These included astrological omens, dream omens and practices for conducting exorcisms.

In ancient Egypt the chosen medium for transmission and storage of knowledge was papyrus. This was made from the stem of the common reed found growing abundantly on the Nile delta. Papyrus had the advantage over clay tablets of being much lighter, easily transportable and much less brittle. Papyrus was essentially used for less formal records. More formal records were inscribed on stone, as can still be seen on many Egyptian monuments today. The most famous library of Pharaonic Egypt was the complex built by Rameses II called the 'sacred library' and inscribed with the phrase 'Healing place of the Soul' (Lerner 1998). The library contained texts on poetry, astronomy, history, engineering, agriculture and fiction that awaited the king in his afterlife.

Knowledge management in ancient Greece and Rome

While literacy was the sole domain of scribes and scholars in ancient Mesopotamia and Egypt, it was much more widespread in ancient Greece. Books were written on papyrus even though parchment was also available. One of the central events of ancient Greek history was the Trojan Wars, captured and shaped by Homer in the epic poems, the *Iliad* and the *Odyssey*. These verses were recited and transmitted orally by generations of bards. One of the early concerns was to establish a complete text of Homer's epics. This was attempted in the sixth century BC by the tyrant Peisistratus who also founded the first public library in Athens (Lerner 1998).

The selling of knowledge through books was flourishing by the time of the famous philosopher Socrates towards 400 BC A few decades later, book collecting became more common and it is most probable that Plato's Academy and Aristotle's Lyceum possessed their own private libraries. Alexander the Great, a Macedonian, recognised the contributions that books and libraries made in the classical Hellenic culture he had conquered. However, it wasn't until after his death in 323 BC that Ptolemy I, one of his generals, became king of Egypt and commissioned the greatest library of antiquity in Alexandria. This library was housed in the Museum, which flourished for hundreds of years, attracting many noted writers, poets, scientists and scholars and over 600,000 rolls of text. The Museum or 'the place of the Muses', included works of history, philosophy, music and the visual arts. In addition, it provided studies in language and literature and a multitude of commentaries, glossaries and grammar on such notable texts as the *Iliad* and the *Odyssey*. Rare and archaic words found in Homer were given meaning in a compilation by Philitas called *Miscellaneous Works*. This glossary of difficult or metaphorical words was a tremendous success among the many avid readers of Homer. The great library of Alexandria came to an end in 48 BC when 400,000 rolls were accidentally destroyed in Caesar's brief Alexandrian war.

The main rival to the Alexandria library was the library of Pergamon, built in the time of Attalus I (247–197 BC). This possessed around 200,000 rolls and focused more on Homeric studies, geometry and art criticism. There was tremendous rivalry between Pergamon and Alexandria for scholarship and their collections. However, this came to an end in 41 BC when Pergamon came under Mark Anthony's rule and he gave the entire collection of 200,000 rolls to Cleopatra, presumably in compensation for the losses by Julius Caesar in the library at Alexandria.

Critical thinking and reflection

Imagine that you were tasked to collect all the knowledge and received wisdom in your organisation. How would you go about carrying out this assignment? Where would you start? For example, what do you think would be the most appropriate medium for storing your found knowledge? Do you think paper records could play a role? If so, how? How would you go about organising all the knowledge you had collected? What are the main difficulties with such an assignment?

Even though the Romans conquered Macedonia in 168 BC, the invading forces were astonished by the richness of Greek culture and their collections of books. Many of these books found themselves back in Rome as spoils of war. The learning captured in these books was revered by many generals such as Paulus Aemilius who developed one of the first notable Roman libraries (Harris 1995). Julius Caesar commissioned a public library in Rome to surpass the library in Alexandria, but the plan was never realised due to his untimely death.

The first public library in Rome was founded in 39 BC by a politician and general named Gaius Asinius Pollio. He had made a personal fortune from the conquest of Dalmatia and used part of this to amass a number of private collections and form a library in the Temple of Liberty (Atrium Libertatis) on the Aventine Hill, containing both Greek and Latin books. The tradition of founding public libraries continued throughout the Roman era, although private libraries were also common in this period and their size was often related to the wealth of the owner. One of the greatest of Roman libraries was the Ulpian library found in the Forum of Trajan and built by Emperor Trajan in 114 BC. This was a public library on a grand scale, with two large chambers, one for the Greek collection and the other for the Latin one. Their sole purpose was to serve the readers of their collections in large and sumptuous surroundings. The chambers were decorated with huge sculptures, with lavish use of stone and marble throughout. Books were easily accessible to the reader and not stacked in vast rows, as was common in Greek libraries. The organisation of the library required the services of a specialist for cataloguing, reshelving and repairing damaged rolls. Some remains of the Forum of Trajan still exist in Rome near the Via dei Fori Imperiali (Casson 2001).

The knowledge contained in rolls among Roman libraries was susceptible to a number of hazards. These included frequent fires, insect attack on the rolls and dampness in the libraries. Various scholars and poets might also fall out of favour with an emperor and have their entire collection banished from library shelves. This occurred with Ovid under the rule of Augustus and the works of Livy and Virgil under the rule of Caligula (Wiegand and Davis 1994). Hence, the selectivity of knowledge from the oral tradition can apply equally to knowledge arising from written sources.

Management of knowledge in monastic and cathedral libraries

The rise of Christianity in the fourth century had a dramatic influence on the nature of the knowledge that was collected and stored in libraries. Religion was elevated above other knowledge domains and libraries became associated more with churches and monasteries. The most common western library for the next millennia was found in a monastery where monks were involved with reading scripts, copying theological texts (scriptorium) and writing commentaries on key texts. This was the main form of learning in this period. The Bible was of course the core text and numerous volumes and print sizes would be kept. Other texts in these collections might include works by early church fathers, lives of martyrs and saints, church service books, Latin textbooks and classics, and local literature and history (Harris 1995). Many of these collections were kept in book chests or small closets and were closely guarded under lock and key. Monks were often allowed to gain access to only one book at a time.

Flavius Aurelius Cassiodorus, a politician and intellectual in Rome, abandoned public life around AD 550 to set up a model monastery called Vivarium. The name derived from a common daily activity conducted by monks of raising fish (*vivaria*). Cassiodorus's private collection became the core of the monastery's library which contained Christian writings and all the major 'pagan' Latin and Greek authors. His major contribution to monastic life was the publication of *Institutiones Divinarum et Saecularum Litterarum*. This provided the template for monastic practice and a curriculum of theological study which influenced many future monasteries and cathedral schools. Cassiodorus elevated the role of monks as scribes in the scriptorium (see Figure 1.6) as one of the highest duties to God. Apart from reading and understanding the Bible, theological study included history, science and mathematics as part of understanding God's creation (Casson 2001; Lerner 1998). Similarly, a key figure in western monasticism was St Benedict. When he established Monte Casino and established his rule, a key element was the requirement on all monks to read and copy manuscripts. The scriptorium and the library became a central part of the Benedictine discipline. Like Cassiodorus, Benedict had been educated in the classical and Christian traditions and did not ban the reading or copying of pagan classical texts – a critical factor in their survival.

In the twelfth century intellectual life was moving from the rural monasteries back to urban centres, as there was a need to educate and train people in the growing and increasingly complex economies and governments of Europe. Cathedrals had traditionally acted as training grounds for monks in theology, music and canon law. They took on the new role and enlarged their book collections to include more secular interests such as arithmetic, rhetoric and astronomy. Some cathedral libraries such as Canterbury

Figure 1.6 **Scribe comparing two texts in a monastery** (© The British Library Board (Lansdowne 1179 f34v))

contained around 5,000 books by 1300. This led to the demise of many monastic libraries. The rule of Henry VIII in England led to a further fall in scholarly collections with the dissolution of the monasteries in the 1530s when numerous collections were scattered or destroyed (Harris 1995). Yet, despite the loss of thousands of manuscripts, relatively little knowledge was lost compared with that lost in the fifth and sixth centuries when various Germanic tribes destroyed the western Roman empire.

At the same time as the emergence of cathedral schools, certain cities became renowned for groups of teachers with specialities in particular subjects such as law or theology. This started to attract many students, and before long teachers and students were organising and regulating themselves. The resulting bodies were called universities or organised guilds. For example, the University of Paris evolved around 1200 and was renowned for theology. It gained recognition to certain rights and privileges through a charter from King Philip II. In 1167 some English students withdrew from the University of Paris and went back to England to help in the foundation of Oxford University. The undergraduate student was more likely to be a twelve-year-old schoolboy and the six-year curriculum contained the seven liberal arts (Lerner 1998). Surprisingly, classical literature from Greek and Rome was absent from this curriculum, being treated with great suspicion. The *trivium* helped to train the student in reasoning and argument:

- grammar;
- rhetoric;
- logic.

The *quadrivium* helped to train the student in the natural laws of the universe:

- arithmetic;
- geometry;
- music;
- astronomy.

The early university libraries resembled monastic libraries. They were normally formed through the bequests of ecclesiastical or lay patrons, such as the collection of Robert de Sorbonne which led to the founding of the Sorbonne in 1257. The predominant part of the collection was religious works, followed by classics and, lastly, the natural laws of the universe (mathematics, medicine, astronomy and law). There were strict rules and regulations for library membership and conduct in the library. For instance, students at Oxford could use the library only if they had studied philosophy for eight years, and there was a fine at the Sorbonne for leaving books lying open (Harris 1995). Books were expensive and knowledge was for the privileged few.

Paradigm shift from print to a digital age

The dramatic change in the storage and dissemination of knowledge came with the advent of print in 1455. Johann Gutenburg of Mainz is normally credited with the invention of printing in the West even though it is most likely to have been a Chinese invention in the eighth century. The first printed book in Europe was Gutenburg's 42-line Bible which resembled a fine manuscript. Manuscripts were expensive to produce, whereas printed texts cut the cost of books and allowed much wider dissemination. An example of Gutenburg's fine print is shown in Figure 1.7. Soon thousands of volumes were rolling off presses, with particular demand for Greek and Latin classics. These books found their way to private collections as well as to communal use in monasteries, cathedrals and the emerging universities.

The consequence of print was the striking rise in the size of libraries and their complexity. This gave way to modern librarianship so that basic functions of collection, organisation, preservation and access to this ubiquitous knowledge could be conducted. In 1545 Conrad Gesner, father of modern bibliography, published his

Figure 1.7 Paradigm shift to print: an example of Gutenburg's print (© The British Library Board (C.9.d.3))

Bibliotheca Universalis to help keep track of the ever-increasing volumes of books. An early attempt to index and find an appropriate classification scheme in libraries was made with the *Index Librorum Prohibitorum* in 1559.

The impact of this growth in libraries was to attract new readers and increase the levels of literacy among ordinary people. The introduction of printed texts also allowed lay people to enjoy a private reading of the Bible which had been the select domain of monastic and cathedral libraries in the past. Around the seventeenth century, there was an explosion of learning and knowledge concerning science and this saw the formation of many learned societies which started to disseminate the latest thinking and specialist knowledge in their fields through journals (Eisenstein 1979; Wiegand and Davis 1994).

The next major quantum leap was the introduction of computers in the late twentieth century which resulted in an explosion in the ways in which knowledge could be captured, organised, stored, shared and evaluated. Digital computers operate by converting symbols, pictures and words into a binary digit called a *bit* (represented by 0 or 1). A string of eight bits is called a *byte*. The advancement of computer technology has meant that greater quantities of knowledge can be stored on computers at lower costs each year. A *megabyte* (million bytes) of computer storage capacity is fairly common for individual users and large organisations can have knowledge repositories measured in *terabytes* (1 trillion bytes). The increase in microprocessor power has meant that some powerful computers can process a single machine instruction in a *nanosecond* (a billionth of a second).

Critical thinking and reflection

How important are computers in your everyday life? For example, do you feel you could live without them? As the power of computers and telecommunications has increased, what real differences have they made to your daily life? For example, how do computers assist you in making better-quality decisions or storing your personal knowledge for later retrieval? Are there aspects of your personal knowledge that would be impossible to store in a computer?

The major impact of computers has come through telecommunications, allowing computers to link up and knowledge to be shared through networks across the world. This can be local area networks (LANs) in an organisation or more global networks such as the information superhighway (internet). Technology has also developed wireless communication where knowledge can be transferred over a mobile phone or through personal digital assistants (PDAs). The most common form of knowledge transfer is electronic mail. The physical separation of people over long distances has become less of a barrier. Groups of people can meet electronically over the phone through teleconferencing or can modify data files simultaneously through data conferencing or meet each other visually on video screens through video-conferencing. The World Wide Web is at the heart of this knowledge explosion, with a subsequent rise in the publishing of knowledge over the internet. The new Web 2.0 applications means that there is greater ability of diverse organisations and systems to work together, users to interact with one another and change website content at an instant. Control has shifted from governments and organisations more towards the user. This will have new and exciting challenges for the future management of knowledge.

Ernst & Young (US)

Mala Garg, Ernst & Young's Chief Communications and Knowledge Officer, had just returned from the MAKE (Most Admired Knowledge Enterprises) awards having won the top award in the 'learning organisation' category. This was their eleventh consecutive MAKE award. But this morning there were more pressing issues ahead. Paul Smith, Managing Partner of Ernst & Young Ireland was making a special trip to meet her on Friday to discuss the ongoing knowledge crisis involving an ageing workforce that was having an adverse effect on their activities in Ireland. The 'brain drain' from the retirement of senior colleagues had become of strategic importance. Many retired colleagues had critical knowledge and expertise of certain aspects of the consultancy business that could not be found elsewhere.[1] Was this purely the fault of careless succession planning or were there creative solutions to this problem?

Mala joined Ernst & Young as it was one of the 'Big 5' consulting firms with a presence in over 130 countries. However, consulting was a highly competitive market with the advent of globalisation and the main tool of consultancy was adding value to client products and services in the form of knowledge and information. Knowledge management was critical to organisational survival in this industry where consultants primarily sold their knowledge and expertise. With a total workforce of over 80,000, there was the additional problem of dispersed knowledge and getting the knowledge or expertise to the right person at the right time; namely 'just-in-time' knowledge.[2] In this regard, consultants worked in teams to enable sharing of their disparate knowledge. But this could be a 'hit and miss' affair as teams were put together for the needs of any project rather than the needs of the individual in the form of interpersonal knowledge sharing.

In order to facilitate organisational-wide knowledge sharing, four centres were set up in the 1990s: the Centre for Business Innovation, the Centre for Business Transformation, the Centre for Business Knowledge (CBK) and the Centre for Technology Enablement.

The Centre for Business Innovation was the ideas and thinking arm of Ernst & Young. It scanned for new ideas, theories and conceptual frameworks that could be applied to businesses. The centre collaborated with universities and research centres and was on the look out for innovative solutions to business problems.

The Centre for Business Transformation was about transforming knowledge into tools and methodologies that consultants could apply efficiently and effectively to business problems.

The Centre for Technology Enablement was concerned with research and development of tools, information systems and technologies to improve and leverage business processes.

The Centre for Business Knowledge (CBK) was the backbone of Ernst & Young's knowledge management activities. The centre created, revised and maintained a repository of knowledge used by consultants in their everyday work. A consultant could make any enquiry to the call centre. If a query was not answered within thirty minutes, it was referred to the Business Research division. CBK held the latest client and industry specific information including all consultancy reports. One essential component of CBK was the development of 'Powerpacks'; vital filtered information database used by consultants in their everyday work – the consultant toolkit.

Despite these important structures, there was crucial knowledge lost each day from the retirement of the first baby boomers. These skilled workers possessed crucial technical and managerial knowledge of specific industries such as aerospace, nuclear and the defence industries that was difficult to replicate. Clear and major voids of knowledge were looming in different parts of the business.

Mala decided to ring Helen Walsh, Director of Ernst & Young's alumni, to ask about the recruitment of 'boomerangs'; employees previously employed by the firm who returned after a period of absence. Helen's words were encouraging and she suggested that boomerangs represented over 25 per cent of current recruits. As a former boomerang herself, Helen Walsh indicated that boomerangs were also a good vehicle for encouraging women back into the workplace.[3] However, it was much harder recruiting retired ex-employees as the tax system could work against people in some countries. For example, a British employee cannot receive a pension and a salary from the same employer. However, there are ways around this difficulty and firms have sought to sub-contract this work through other legal entities.

Mala takes a break and logs onto Ernst & Young's Facebook website. At Ernst & Young, at least 16,000 workers have a Facebook account.[4] She smiles as she remembers social networking was about meeting at the water cooler or a drink after work. Times have changed. She decides to put her deliberations about older workers into the forum. Within five minutes, she has over twenty replies from around the world and to her surprise most of the responses are from older employees. This certainly defies any notion of Facebook as a tool for the younger generations.

Mala picks up the phone to Geoff Trotter, Chief Knowledge Officer at CBK and a partner at Ernst & Young, to ask him about how knowledge management activities would be affected by the ageing workforce. Geoff Trotter is rather frank on the business aspects. 'If a business is agile it can deliver a competitive advantage, and KM builds on the theme of agility to deliver a sustainable competitive advantage. A business can then leverage people and information and is generally better organised to manage a fast pace of change and uncertainty. We have the necessary processes in place to capture, store and share know-how, know-what and know-who, and we are optimally organised across our organisation to make great use of newer technologies'.[5] His reservations are more about the agility and openness of older people towards new technologies. For him, it is the ability of CBK to embed older people's knowledge into services that is the key to competitive advantage. It is how one codifies this knowledge into the 'Powerpacks' for use by all employees at Ernst & Young.

Finally, Mala Garg decides to watch an archived video of James Harrington, past president of the International Academy for Quality and currently serving as international quality advisor to Ernst & Young. James Harrington sees five key pillars to performance improvement in any organisation: process management, project management, change management, knowledge management and resource management. He believes in a balanced approach between these five elements and stresses. 'Top management's job is to keep all of them moving ahead at the same time. To concentrate on one or two of them and let the others slide is a surefire formula for failure.'[6] He sees it as the leveraging of the interdependencies between the pillars that leads to business transformation rather than considering each element in isolation. And it is the knowledge rather than the information in organisations that leads to competitive advantage. He contends that there is too much information in organisations and not enough knowledge.

Mala removes two pieces of paper from her desk. One piece is to help her understand the nature of the problem she is tackling and the other is to explore potential solutions. She starts doodling on each paper and a mind map slowly emerges on each.

References

1 Schweywer, A. (2006) 'Knowledge crisis ahead?' *Human Resources Magazine*.
2 Lara, E. (2002) 'A case study of knowledge management at Cap Gemini Ernst & Young', Cranfield, UK, The European Case Clearing House.
3 Special Report (2006) 'Turning boomers into boomerangs – The ageing workforce', *The Economist*.
4 Green, H. (2007) 'The water cooler is now on the web; With a nod to Facebook, large companies are starting in-house social networks', *Business Week*.
5 Gyopos, S. (2008) 'It's what you know; Pooling stores of information in an organisation is a key way for business to stay ahead in today's globalised economy', *South China Morning Post*.
6 NZ Management Magazine (2006) 'In touch: Five pillars of wisdom', *NZ Management Magazine*.

Questions

1 What are potential ways forward to overcome the problem of an ageing workforce at Ernst & Young?
2 How would you codify critical knowledge of clients and industries currently being lost when employees retire?
3 What are the strengths and pitfalls of using social networking sites such as Facebook for Ernst & Young?

Summary

This chapter has elaborated on five key areas of knowledge management:

1 The different current definitions of knowledge management predominantly from information systems or human resource management perspectives. The diverse dimensions of knowledge management are brought together in an integrated definition from an interdisciplinary perspective.

2 The arguments providing an antithesis to the emerging field debating that it is no more than 'old wine in new bottles'.

3 The distinction between data, information and knowledge, particularly acknowledging the role of the sender, receiver and medium of the messages and signals.

4 The bardic oral traditions presented as the earliest form of managing knowledge in civilisation and their strengths and limitations. The movement of knowledge from word of mouth to writing cuneiform on clay tablets is explained.

5 The central role of libraries in knowledge creation and dissemination from ancient Greece to the formation of university libraries. The quantum leap in knowledge transfer occurring from the invention of print and the development of computers and internet technologies are discussed.

Questions for further thought

1 Given the highly specialised nature of traditional academic research, how can interdisciplinary research in fields such as knowledge management succeed and provide fresh insights?

2 What is the difference between information and knowledge management?

3 What are the strengths and shortcomings of academic knowledge and practitioner knowledge?

4 What does knowledge management mean to a small organisation?

5 How do you overcome the 'theory laden' nature of observations among managers in organisations?

6 What are the difficulties in the notion of knowledge as 'actionable information'?

7 How can lessons from the old bardic traditions assist modern-day knowledge management?

8 What are the advantages and disadvantages of different writing media such as clay, papyrus and parchment for storing knowledge?

9 How fallible is modern-day storage of knowledge on computers when many software programs become obsolete in less than ten years? How easy will it be to decipher the bytes on DVDs and CD-ROMs in 100 years?

10 What lessons can we draw from ancient libraries and librarianship for the creation, storage and preservation of knowledge?

Further reading

1 Newell *et al.* (2009) is a good all-round book on knowledge management predominantly from a human resource perspective and contains some good case study material.

2 Davenport and Prusak (1998) helped popularise the field of knowledge management and comes from a consultancy and practitioner background.

3 Harris (1995) provides an excellent historic background on the development of libraries and the management of knowledge through the ages.

References

Barney, J. B. (1991) 'Firm resources and sustained competitive advantage', *Journal of Management*, 17(1), 99–120.

Barney, J. B. (2001) 'Resource-based theories of competitive advantage: A ten-year retrospective of the resource-based view', *Journal of Management*, 27, 643–650.

Bell, D. (1973) *The Coming Post-industrial Society*, Basic Books, New York.

Brinkley, I. (2006) *Defining the Knowledge Economy*, London, The Work Foundation.

Casson, L. (2001) *Libraries in the Ancient World*, Yale University Press, New Haven.

Davenport, T. H. and Prusak, L. (1998) *Working Knowledge: How Organizations Manage What They Know*, Harvard Business School Press, Boston, MA.

Drucker, P. (1992) 'The new society of organizations', *Harvard Business Review*, September/October, 95–105.

Drucker, P. (1993) *The Post-Capitalist Society*, New York, Harper Collins.

DTI (1998) *Building the Knowledge Driven Economy: Competitiveness White Paper*, London, Department of Trade and Industry.

Eagleton, T. (1999) *Literary Theory: An Introduction*, Blackwell Publishers, Oxford.

Eisenstein, E. L. (1979) *The Printing Press as an Agent of Change*, Cambridge University Press, Cambridge.

Etzioni, A. (1964) *Modern Organizations*, Prentice-Hall, Englewood Cliffs, NJ.

Gombrich, E. G. (1960) *Art and Illusion*, Phaidon, London.

Grant, R. M. (1996) 'Toward a knowledge-based theory of the firm', *Strategic Management Journal*, 17, 109–22.

Green, H. (2007) 'The water cooler is now on the web; With a nod to Facebook, large companies are starting in-house social networks', *Business Week*.

Gyopos, S. (2008) 'It's not what you know; Pooling stores of information in an organisation is a key way for businesses to stay ahead in today's globalised economy', *South China Morning Post*.

Hansen, M., Nohria, N., and Tierney, T. (1999) 'What's your strategy for managing knowledge?', *Harvard Business Review*, March–April, 106–16.

Harris, M. H. (1995) *History of Libraries in the Western World*, The Scarecrow Press, London.

Kalling, T. and Styhre, A. (2003) *Knowledge Sharing in Organizations*, Copenhagen Business School Press, Copenhagen.

KPMG Consulting (2000) 'Knowledge Management Research Report 1999', Atos KPMG Consulting, London.

Lara, E. (2002) 'A case study of knowledge management at Cap Gemini Ernst & Young', Cranfield, UK, The European Case Clearing House.

Lerner, F. A. (1998) *The Story of Libraries: From the Invention of Writing to the Computer Age*, Continuum, New York.

Meadows, J. (2001) *Understanding Information*, K.G. Saur, München.

Mertins, K., Heisig, P. and Vorbeck, J. (2000) *Knowledge Management: Best Practices in Europe*, Springer-Verlag, New York.

Newell, S., Robertson, M., Scarbrough, H. and Swan, J. (2009) *Managing Knowledge Work and Innovation*, Palgrave Macmillan, Basingstoke, Hampshire.

Nonaka, I. (1991) 'The knowledge-creating company', *Harvard Business Review*, 69 (November–December), 96–104.

Nonaka, I. (1994) 'A dynamic theory of organizational knowledge creation', *Organization Science*, 5(1), 14–37.

NZ Management Magazine (2006) 'In touch: Five pillars of wisdom', *NZ Management Magazine*.

O'Connor, D. J. and Carr, B. (1982) *Introduction to the Theory of Knowledge*, Harvester, Brighton.

OECD (1996) *The Knowledge-based Economy*, Paris, OECD.

Palmer, D. J. (1965) *The Rise of English Studies*, Oxford University Press, London.

Penrose, E. T. (1959) *The Theory of Growth of the Firm*, Blackwell, Oxford.

Polanyi, M. (1967) *The Tacit Dimension*, Doubleday, New York.

Ponzi, L. J. and Koenig, M. E. (2002) 'Knowledge management: Another management fad?', *Information Research*, 8(1), 145.

Ryle, G. (1949) *The Concept of Mind*, Hutcheson, London.

Schweywer, A. (2006) 'Knowledge crisis ahead?' *Human Resources Magazine*.

Selznick, P. (1957) *Leadership in Administration: A Sociological Interpretation*, Row, Peterson and Co., Evanston, IL.

Skyrme, D. J. (1999) *Knowledge Networking: Creating the Collaborative Enterprise*, Butterworth-Heinemann, Oxford.

Special Report (2006) 'Turning boomers into boomerangs – The ageing workforce', *The Economist*.

Spender, J. C. (1996) 'Making knowledge the basis of a dynamic theory of the firm', *Strategic Management Journal*, 17, 45–62.

Styhre, A. (2003) *Understanding Knowledge Management – Critical and Postmodern Perspectives*, Copenhagen Business School Press, Copenhagen.

Swan, J., Newell, S., Scarborough, H. and Hislop, D. (1999a) 'Knowledge management and innovation: Networks and networking', *Journal of Knowledge Management*, 3(4), 262–275.

Swan, J., Scarborough, H. and Preston, J. (1999b) 'Knowledge management – The next fad to forget people?', *Proceedings of the 7th European Conference on Information Systems*, Copenhagen.

Teagarden, M. B., Meyer, J. and Jones, D. (2008) 'Knowledge sharing among high-tech MNCs in China and India: Invisible barriers, best practices and next steps', *Organizational Dynamics*, 37, 190–202.

Tiwana, A. (2000) *The Knowledge Management Toolkit*, Prentice Hall, Upper Saddle River, NJ.

uit Beijerse, R. P. (2000) 'Knowledge management in small and medium-sized companies: Knowledge management for entrepreneurs', *Journal of Knowledge Management*, 4(2), 162–179.

Vansina, J. (1985) *Oral Tradition as History*, James Currey Ltd, London.

Wiegand, W. A. and Davis, D. G. (1994) *Encyclopedia of Library History*, Garland, New York.

Wilson, T. D. (2002) 'The nonsense of "knowledge management"', *Information Research*, 8(1), 144.

Chapter 2

The nature of knowing

Learning outcomes

After completing this chapter the reader should be able to:

- describe the underlying philosophical traditions and their quest for knowledge;
- evaluate the competing paradigms in knowledge management;
- identify and understand the current typologies of knowledge within the knowledge management literature.

Management issues

The philosophical perspectives on knowledge imply these questions for managers:

- What are the problems of an action-oriented organisation?
- How can reflection be incorporated into organisational routines?
- How can tacit and explicit knowledge be managed effectively?
- How can 'past experience' be stored in a manner that is useful and meaningful to staff on a daily basis?
- Can a philosophical understanding promote double-loop learning in organisations?

Links to other chapters

Chapter 5   to understand some of the philosophical underpinnings of theory linked to individual, group and organisational learning.

Chapter 7   to recognise the different approaches to cultural management and their philosophical bases.

Business must learn from the new tribe

FT

So-called 'digital natives' are bringing down the barriers to collaborative working, finds Jessica Twentyman.

'To read the criticisms about the Net Generation,' writes author Don Tapscott in his latest book, *Grown Up Digital*, 'you might conclude that they are a bunch of dull, celebrity-obsessed, net-addicted, shopaholic exhibitionists.'[1]

Such a bleak view, he goes on to say, belies the fact that the children of the baby boomers – now aged between 12 and 30 and reared in an era of digital technologies – are poised to transform society in profound and largely positive ways.

In the workplace, he adds, their aptitude with technology and willingness to collaborate could provide their employers with a real source of competitive advantage.

But whether they are referred to as the Net Generation, digital natives, Millennials or Generation Y, this new tribe of employees can only make its mark if the businesses they work for are able to accommodate and capitalise on a host of new attitudes, beliefs and ways of working. 'Listen to young people,' Mr Tapscott urges business leaders. 'Put them in the driver's seat alongside you when designing work spaces, processes, management systems and collaborative working models.' In other words, be prepared to make big changes in order to unleash the power of these new employees.

Are businesses ready to heed that advice? 'In truth, many are not,' says James Callander, managing director of recruitment consultancy FreshMinds. 'This new generation is well known for its unrestrained ambition, but its largely unparalleled handle on technology presents a significant management challenge,' he says. 'I think one of the biggest problems is that older members of the workforce feel scared of looking foolish in the face of new technology and are threatened by these younger peers who seem to hold all the cards.'

He observes two common approaches to tackling this challenge. 'The first is almost a "divide and conquer" approach, consigning technology to different divisions or units in the business. But the internet and mobile technology is now so all-encompassing ... that separation is all but impossible. The second and better approach is to encourage younger workers to train and enfranchise their older colleagues.'

'In principle, that makes good sense, because while they may be reluctant to admit it, older business leaders have much to learn from their younger co-workers,' says Urs Gasser, executive director at the Berkman Center for Internet and Society at Harvard University and co-author of *Born Digital: Understanding the First Generation of Digital Natives*.[2]

As principal investigator on the Digital Natives project, an academic collaboration between the Berkman Center and the Research Center for Information Law at the University of St Gallen in Switzerland, he has devoted the past few years to studying how people who grew up immersed in digital technologies interact with the world.

'Three characteristics distinguish a digital native in today's workplace', he says. The first is their relaxed attitude to information disclosure; the second, their aptitude at social networking; and the third, the very different way they process information, as compared with previous generations. It is this first trait that causes business leaders most concern, according to Prof Gasser. 'Digital natives are generally more open about themselves and have fewer reservations about sharing their thoughts and opinions with the world. The fear is that this will lead them to share information about their jobs and the organisations they work for, without reflecting on how appropriate it might be to divulge information that might be considered confidential or commercially sensitive.'

Tackling the issue is a matter of education, he argues. Where corporate policies are thoughtfully applied (and observed), that propensity for self-disclosure can be a positive force, building trust between colleagues and opening the door to deeper collaborations. It also offers organisations a chance to get to know young employees better, to understand what motivates them and the best ways to channel their energies to reap better business results.

But it's the second and third traits that offer companies the greatest chance to get ahead. 'For years, organisations have been investing heavily in knowledge management initiatives to tap into the collective expertise of their workforce, but the results have been mixed. Suddenly, the cultural barriers to information sharing are crumbling with the emergence of social networking and the rise of a new workforce that is more than comfortable with working online with their peers to solve a problem.'

'This', he says, 'has huge implications in many aspects of business, such as developing products, identifying market opportunities and generating sales leads.'

'But the issue of working hours can be contentious', says Claire Schooley, an analyst with IT market analyst firm Forrester Research. 'Work–life balance is paramount to Millennials. These young people do not work by the clock – rather, they work by the task. Let them know what they need to do and when assignments need to be done. With mobile technology, they'll be online at night completing projects.'

As the connected world evolves, it is therefore vital that organisations adapt policies and tools to suit the style of new workers. In economies where the working population is ageing, this may not just be desirable but essential to survival.

References

1 Tapscott, Don (2008) *Grown Up Digital*, McGraw-Hill.
2 Palfrey, J. and Gasser, U. (2008) *Born Digital: Understanding the First Generation of Digital Natives*, Basic Books.

Source: from Business must learn from the new tribe, *The Financial Times*, 29/05/2009 (Twentyman, J.), copyright © The Financial Times Ltd.

Questions

1 How can organisations effectively manage the 'Net Generation'?

2 How can organisations harness the power of technology through the 'Net Generation'?

3 What are the best working hours for the 'Net Generation'?

Introduction

Much of the current literature in knowledge management is based on the writings of two philosophers, Gilbert Ryle and Michael Polanyi. These names and their ideas of logical behaviourism come out predictably within the literature and there seems to be relatively little questioning of their underpinnings. This chapter intends to explore the nature of knowledge more fully to enable the reader to gain a firm grounding of the different perspectives and to engage in some level of philosophical introspection. For example, the reader may find the competing postmodernist notion of production and consumption of knowledge much more attractive than the traditional viewpoint of logical behaviourism.

As a starting point, this chapter begins by looking at how western philosophers have grappled with the 'knowledge' question over the centuries. This forms the rich tapestry against which one can develop new perspectives and understandings of knowledge. As a way of aiding the uninitiated reader, western philosophers have been grouped into idealist and empiricist perspectives, as shown in Figure 2.1. This simplistic notion can act as a useful basis for the reader's future inquiry into the debates surrounding knowledge.

A closer examination is made of Gilbert Ryle's notion of 'knowing how' and 'knowing that' and Michael Polanyi's understanding that these concepts exist along a continuum rather than occurring as distinct and separate entities. The myriad epistemological positions are developed using Burrell and Morgan's framework and four

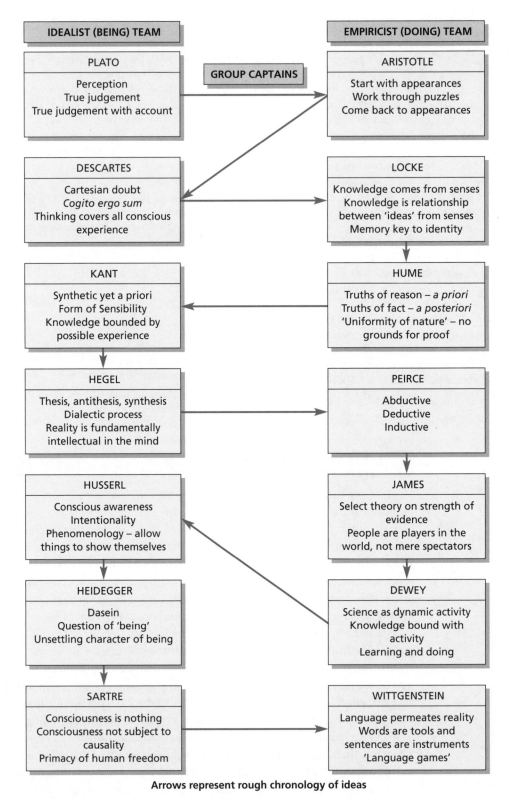

Arrows represent rough chronology of ideas

Figure 2.1 Idealist and empiricist perspectives on knowledge

common philosophical positions are explored in greater detail: positivism, constructivism, postmodernism and critical realism. The aim is to enable the reader to have a
greater understanding of the assumptions behind the writings of different scholars in
the area of knowledge management.

The different typologies of knowledge within the current knowledge management literature are forwarded to avoid confusion between different terminology used to describe
the same concepts of 'knowing how' and 'knowing that'. A realist theory outlining the
structure of knowledge based on 'past experience' is presented that builds on Ryle's concepts and suggests that the occurrence of a reflection phase may determine the difference
between single-loop and double-loop learning within the structure of knowledge.

What is knowledge? Philosophers from Plato to Wittgenstein

▶ Plato

Plato (427–347 BC), as a pupil of Socrates, wrestled with a wide variety of moral and
philosophical questions in the form of dialogues. He expressed his 'idealist' doctrine
mainly through the mouth of Socrates in the form of 'Socratic questioning'. Socrates
would start with a concept and get his pupils to understand the problems with the
concept until they formed an answer to the problem. In subsequent dialogue, Socrates
would then show the inadequacy of their answers by revealing contradictions within
them. The end result was not to provide a firm answer but to gain a better grasp of
the problem. Plato believed that 'conclusions' did not have any special status as our
assumptions and beliefs are open to perpetual questioning.

In a later dialogue, *Theaetetus* (360 BC), Plato explores the nature of knowledge. Is
knowledge purely subjective and why is it better than opinion? Plato provides three
answers to the question of 'What is knowledge?':

● Knowledge is perception.

● Knowledge is true judgement.

● Knowledge is true judgement together with an account.

Each answer is knocked down in true Socratic style. There is no consensus to this day
about knowledge except that it is derived from perception that can provide a rational
justification for it.

▶ Aristotle

Aristotle (384–322 BC), Plato's star pupil, saw philosophy as an ongoing attempt
to explore the complexities of human experience. After a sharp reaction against
Platonism, he achieved a synthesis of the natural and rational aspects of the world in
The Metaphysics (350 BC). In every area, his approach was to start with 'appearances'
(ordinary beliefs and language), work through puzzles (work through contradictions
and find beliefs that were most basic and central) and come back to 'appearances' with
increased structure and understanding.

Critical thinking and reflection

Reflect on your way of looking at the world. Have you ever done any philosophical introspection to understand your own position in amongst the diverse ways of looking at the world? Are you more of a thinker or a doer? Do you think that this has any impact on how you see the world? Have you ever thought about the effect that diverse ways of thinking about a problem may have on the functioning of a team? What do you think could be the implications of this?

▶ Descartes

René Descartes (1596–1650), a rationalist philosopher, struggled with the question 'Can we know anything for certain and, if so, how?' He saw 'certainty' as a state of mind and 'truth' as a property of statements about the external world. He developed scepticism to an art form and promoted doubt as a method which later became known as 'Cartesian doubt'. In *Meditations* (1641), Descartes provides three stages of doubt in order to know something:

1 Lay aside things on commonsense grounds that are doubtful.

2 Doubt that at any given moment you are awake or perceiving anything at all, i.e. you may be dreaming.

3 Imagine that a malign spirit or a malicious demon has the sole intent to deceive you.

This led Descartes to his first certainty:

'Cogito ergo sum' or 'I think, therefore I am'.

In *Meditations*, Descartes sees 'thinking' to mean all forms of conscious experience including pain, perceptions and feelings. The true value of Descartes comes from his questioning different aspects of knowledge:

● What do I know?

● What can I doubt?

● How can I know whether any of my beliefs are true?

● What is the difference between my beliefs and prejudices?

● Is there room for scepticism?

▶ Locke

John Locke (1632–1704), an empiricist, believed that everything we conceive or construct has come from experience. His dictum was:

'Don't blindly follow convention or authority. Look at the facts and think for yourself.'

In *An Essay Concerning Human Understanding* (1690), he develops the concept of 'idea' as something sensory that has the properties of a sensory image before the mind. An 'idea' can also cover thoughts, pains and emotions. He views reasoning as a mental operation of these 'ideas' which leads to knowledge or belief. In this sense, knowledge is a perception of relationships between ideas. He accepts that our senses provide us with knowledge of the existence of things but not knowledge of their nature or essence. Locke saw Newton's laws as a kind of crude fact. They were a good description of how things behave but not an explanation. He was keen to point out Newton's most quoted words: '*Hypotheses non fingo*' ('I'm not offering explanations'). Locke saw memory as key to personal identity as each person's awareness of history makes them the individual they are.

▶ Hume

David Hume (1711–76) knocked the bottom out of science with his insights into causal links. He acknowledged that one could make 'inductive inferences' about 'matters of fact' such as A causes B from observation of A followed by B, such as day follows night and night follows day. But he argued that past experience could not justify a conclusion about future behaviour. Even though defenders of induction invoked the principle of 'uniformity of nature', there were clearly no grounds to prove that this principle was correct. This insight showed that scientific laws gained through observation were no longer universal statements as previously held (Hume 2000). Subsequently, the doctrines of 'logical positivism' have been derived from Hume. He divided propositions into 'truths of reason' (analytic or *a priori* – from theory) and 'truths of fact' (synthetic or *a posteriori* – from practice).

▶ Kant

In *Critique of Pure Reason* (1781), Immanuel Kant (1724–1804) suggested a third proposition to Hume's truths of reason and truths of fact. This proposition was synthetic yet *a priori*, namely the Form of Sensibility, and concerned space and time. He argued that space and time were inescapable modes of experience and could be specified in an *a priori* manner (space with geometry and time with arithmetic). He saw knowledge as bounded by 'possible experience'.

▶ Hegel

Georg Wilhelm Friedrich Hegel (1770–1831) viewed the primary goal of knowledge as the greater development of the mind towards freedom. In *The Philosophy of History* (1837), he considered all concepts historically as part of a 'dialectic process'. Using the example of Greek society, the dialectic process starts with a 'thesis', where there is harmony between reason and desire in society. However, he argues that this stable condition cannot persist indefinitely and gives rise to its 'antithesis' through 'Socratic questioning' and the subsequent breakdown of Greek society. In turn, the dialectic process moves forward to create 'synthesis' of these opposing views to give way to a new thesis. Hegel's view of reality is '*Geist*' (mind or spirit) which is fundamentally mental or intellectual in nature.

❱ Pragmatists

The primary contribution of the American Pragmatists (Peirce, James and Dewey) towards knowledge was to create a link between belief, meaning, action and inquiry. Charles S. Peirce (1839–1914), often seen as the father of pragmatism, was principally focused on the question of how we are able to investigate the world rationally. In his *Theory of Inquiry* (1867), he suggests that we inquire by testing hypotheses and holding certain beliefs constant that may be revisable or fallible. In scientific inquiry, he proposes the following phases in the development of knowledge:

- 'abductive' inquiry – presenting theories for consideration;
- 'deductive' inquiry – preparing theories for test;
- 'inductive' inquiry – assessing results of the test.

William James (1842–1910) presents a pragmatic theory of truth where our beliefs need to be in accord with the underlying evidence (1909). For instance, he suggests that our preferences for one theory over another need be based purely on the strength of the competing evidence. In circumstances where evidence is equal, James suggests that we can use other criteria such as bias. He views people as players in the world rather than mere spectators.

John Dewey (1859–1952) applied Peirce's theory of inquiry to social and political philosophy. In *The Quest for Certainty* (1929), he sees science as an activity and process of 'inquiry' that is essentially dynamic in nature. He is against a 'spectator' view of knowledge. Instead, he views human activity as a concern for survival in a dynamic environment where knowledge is the most important survival mechanism. For Dewey, knowledge was closely bound with activity, and notions of truth and meaning also needed to have some connection with it. Dewey made a significant contribution to the philosophy of education (Dewey 1990, 1991) by highlighting the interconnectedness of learning and doing and the need to encourage children to learn by doing, by activity and by adopting a problem-solving approach.

❱ Phenomenology and existentialism

Edmund Husserl (1859–1938) influenced a number of philosophers such as Heidegger, Sartre and Merleau-Ponty and established a movement known as phenomenology. In addition, he made a crucial impact on the development of continental and analytic philosophy.

Critical thinking and reflection

On many levels, the pragmatist perspective may be considered to be the most appropriate one for managers. What do you think are the strengths and limitations of this perspective? Can you think of any circumstances when a pragmatist perspective could be detrimental to an organisation? Why do you think problem solving could be enhanced by this perspective?

In his masterpiece *Logical Investigations* (1901) Husserl starts his general theory of knowledge on the basis of our conscious awareness being undeniably certain. He continues that our consciousness is always an awareness of something and, in practice, it is difficult to distinguish between states of consciousness and objects of consciousness. He calls the directedness of mental content 'intentionality' and the aspect of the mind that accounts for this directedness 'intentional content'. He argued, for example, in his account of intentionality that it didn't matter whether there was a chair out there or not. He could bracket it and perform a 'phenomenological reduction'. This meant that all that was needed was that he took there to be a chair in the world of objects. He further argued that no one could experience anything without this directed mental content (intentionality). This became his unquestionable foundation for all understanding. For Husserl, phenomenology was allowing things to show themselves as they are in themselves.

Martin Heidegger's (1889–1976) predominant philosophical preoccupation was to answer the 'question of being'. In *Being and Time* (1927), he views human beings as '*Dasein*', meaning existence, and sees activity characterised by humans coping in certain situations. Heidegger suggests that we become '*Dasein*' when we conform to public norms and become socialised in shared coping skills. Any *Dasein* is aware that the way of the world is ungrounded. He uses the word '*Unheimlich*' (not being at home) to describe the anxiety in the form of guilt caused by the unsettling character of just being. This notion is taken up by existentialists in their liberation philosophy to accept no meaning in *Dasein* and the unsettling groundlessness of experience.

Jean-Paul Sartre (1905–80) was a student of Husserl and Heidegger and was also greatly influenced by Descartes' notion of human consciousness as free and distinct from the physical universe. In *Being and Nothingness* (1943), Sartre describes consciousness as 'nothing' ('not-a-thing') but an activity ('a wind blowing from nowhere towards the world'). As consciousness is nothingness, it is not subject to the rules of causality. This is fundamental to Sartre's thesis as it forwards the primacy of human freedom. He argues that consciousness is always self-determining and follows a playful paradox:

> *'It is always what it is not, and is not what it is.'*

▶ Wittgenstein

Ludwig Wittgenstein (1889–1951) was primarily concerned with the role of language in human thought and life. In *Tractatus Logico-philosophicus* (1922), Wittgenstein argues that if language represents reality and sentences represent states of affairs, there must be something in common between sentences and states of affairs. As part of his 'picture theory of meaning', he regards sentences as a picture of possible fact and the fundamental unit of meaning. Furthermore, he views the arrangement of words ('names') in sentences corresponding to possible arrangements of objects in the world. This leads to his premise that the structure of the real world determines the structure of language.

In his later work, *Philosophical Investigations* (1953), Wittgenstein employs a 'tool' conception of meaning whereby words are tools and sentences are instruments. The meaning of a word is its use in language and the structure of language determines how we perceive the real world. Language is not strictly held together by a logical structure, as argued earlier in the *Tractatus*, but consists of a multiplicity of simpler substructures or 'language games'. In this analysis, as language permeates all thinking and human experience, the notion of thinking can exist only with expressions. This resulted in some controversy over the 'private language' argument where critics argued that individuals could use words to name private sensations that no one else understood.

Contemporary philosophers: Ryle, Polanyi and Macmurray

The most dominant concepts within the current knowledge management literature are the notions of 'tacit' and 'explicit' knowledge (Nonaka 1994). The underlying philosophy of these constructs can be traced back to Gilbert Ryle (1900–1976) and Michael Polanyi (1891–1976). In the same period that Wittgenstein held the Chair of Philosophy at Cambridge, Ryle held a similar Chair of Philosophy at Oxford. In *The Concept of Mind* (1949), Ryle's major work, his philosophy of mind is focused on a destruction of Cartesianism. He argues that the world of experience is composed of two entities: physical things and mental things.

Ryle's most important contribution is demonstrating the difference between 'knowing how' and 'knowing that'. He makes a distinction between intelligence ('knowing how') and possessing knowledge ('knowing that'). For him, intelligence can have meaning only in activity and is associated with the ability of a person to perform tasks. It is the action that exhibits intelligence. In contrast, 'knowing that' is holding certain bits of knowledge in one's mind such as the names of Snow White's seven dwarfs. He defends his type of logical behaviourism by arguing against the Cartesian idealism that sees knowledge and intelligence as part of the same mental process. He contends that when a person does something intelligently, they are doing only one thing, not two. Knowing how cannot be defined in terms of knowing that. For instance, a chef doesn't recite his recipes to himself (knowing that) before he can cook according to them (knowing how).

Michael Polanyi comes from a similar behaviourist background as Ryle in his book *The Tacit Dimension* (1967) and develops the notion of tacit knowledge from a number of experiments involving hypothetical shock treatments reminiscent of the stimulus–response model of behaviour (Skinner 1938). His starting point of human knowledge is 'the fact that we can know more than we can tell'. He uses Ryle's distinction between 'knowing that' and 'knowing how' and suggests that each aspect of knowing is ever present with the other. They are not distinct entities and his assumption is that they exist together along a continuum, as shown in Figure 2.2. He uses the example of riding a bicycle and the need to have tacit knowledge to stay upright. Staying upright and engaged in the activity of riding is part of 'knowing how' to ride a bicycle. However, many people may find it difficult to articulate clearly (knowing that) what keeps them upright.

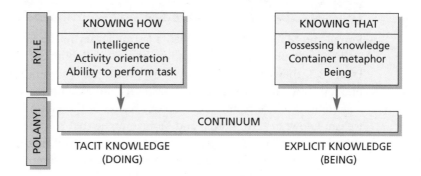

Figure 2.2 **Philosophy of Gilbert Ryle and Michael Polanyi**

Critical thinking and reflection

How appropriate do you believe it is to define and classify roles in organisations under 'know that' and 'know how'? When employers ask for skills and experience in person specifications, are they purely looking for 'know how'? Passing a football around an organisation provides a useful metaphor for knowledge sharing in organisations. What is wrong with this metaphor? Can you think of a better metaphor for describing knowledge in organisations?

A recent revival in the writings of John Macmurray, a realist philosopher who held the Grote Chair of Philosophy of Mind and Logic at London University from 1928 to 1944, saw realism as the unity of theory and practice. The realist position represented a radical departure from the dominant European idealist tradition which divorced theory from action. Macmurray (1933) believed the primary function of thought was to enable action to become 'effective' and 'right'. He insisted that action was more primary than thought with the assertion that:

'Thought begins only where action fails.'

Macmurray (1961) claimed that western philosophy had become ensnared by adopting a position that was theoretical and egocentric. The self was treated as pure, withdrawn and a detached subject. He recognised that to isolate mental activity as the distinctive feature of the self was to exclude the possibility that action, the material world and other persons were of definitive importance in understanding what it is to be human. He suggested (1957) that we substitute the Cartesian dictum:

'Cogito ergo sum' (I think, therefore I am)

with

'Ago ergo sum' (I do, therefore I am).

Burrell and Morgan's framework on philosophical paradigms

Burrell and Morgan (1979) have left a lasting legacy in the field of organisational studies by developing our understanding of the production of knowledge. As shown in Figure 2.3, they begin their analysis by examining the ontological assumptions which may underlie any epistemological positions and assumptions. Ontology relates to our assumptions of reality and epistemology relates to our grounds of knowledge and what we can know. In turn, Burrell and Morgan argue that it is the epistemological assumptions together with assumptions about human nature that determine the nature of methodology chosen by a particular perspective. The assumptions of human nature are principally focused across the polarities of free will and determinism.

From these assumptions, they produce a map of four 'sociological paradigms' by mapping the major belief systems of academics along a subjective–objective dimension and a free will (sociology of radical change) – determinism (sociology of regulation) dimension (see Figure 2.4). Paradigm is used to mean a 'commonality of perspective which binds together the work of a group of theorists'. The functionalist paradigm is concerned with a positivist, realist and social engineering perspective where organisational life is about creation and control and not letting matters fall apart. The interpretivist paradigm seeks to understand reality through the realm of individual consciousness and subjectivity. The radical structuralist paradigm emphasises the need to overthrow or transcend limitations placed on social and organisational arrangements by analysing economic power relationships. The radical humanist paradigm seeks radical change and emancipation by overcoming distorted ideologies, power and psychological compulsions and social constraints.

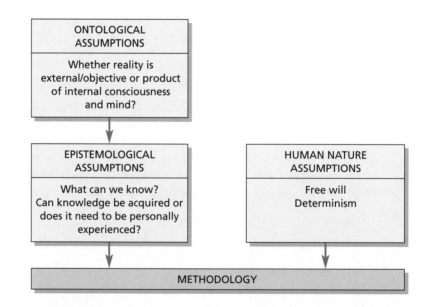

Figure 2.3 **Assumptions about social science research** (adapted from Burrell and Morgan 1979)

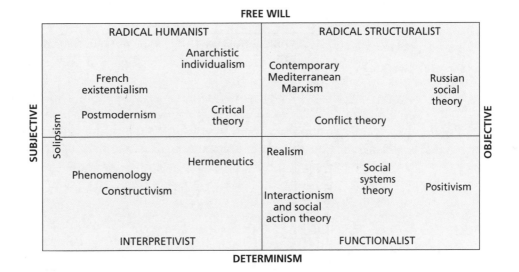

Figure 2.4 Burrell and Morgan's four paradigms and different epistemologies (adapted from Burrell and Morgan 1979)

The dominance of the functionalist paradigm and the paucity of radical structuralist or humanist perspectives in knowledge management research makes the current reality of research resemble much more closely the representation forwarded by Goles and Hirschheim (2000), as shown in Figure 2.5. This position has arisen from similar searches for respectability on the part of young and emerging fields to align themselves to the more respectable 'hard' sciences and the failure of young researchers exploring different paradigms to get published or obtain tenure owing to the well-meaning constraints presented by academic departments and journal editors. In addition, radical humanist and structuralist perspectives can be seen as a threat to traditional organisations as they advocate some form of rebellion against the current orthodoxy. In some quarters this may be seen as an unwelcome insurgence, in others as a transformation of the organisation.

Fortunately, there has been a positive development of Burrell and Morgan's contention that the four paradigms are mutually exclusive, and a greater move towards multiparadigm research. Gioia and Pitre (1990) argue that the four paradigms can be bridged by transition zones and provide examples of structuration theory, critical theory, Marxism, Weberian theory and solipsism that can exist in more than one paradigm.

Critical thinking and reflection

Look closely at Burrell and Morgan's (1979) four paradigms. Why do you think that there has been almost negligible management research from a 'radical humanist' or 'radical structuralist' perspective? What are the problems of 'free will' assumptions in management research? Do you believe that the objective scientific approach is the best perspective for management research and organisational problem solving? What may be some of the limitations of this approach?

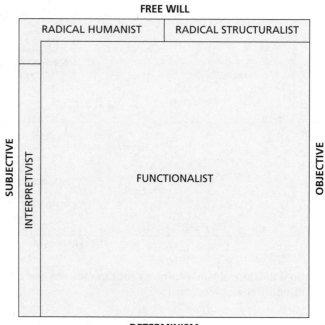

Figure 2.5 Proportional representation of Burrell and Morgan's four paradigms in knowledge management research (adapted from Goles and Hirschheim 2000)

Competing philosophical positions in knowledge management: positivism, constructivism, postmodernism and critical realism

Given the large array of philosophical positions, it is not astounding that there are often 'paradigm wars' between adherents of different epistemologies. It is also not uncommon to find open warfare within the same camp where further distinctions of epistemology are made by adding prefixes such as radical, post, critical and neo to the philosophical positions. As positivist science tends to dominate research, there is an uneasy tension between positivists and anti-positivists. The positivists view social phenomena as essentially not different from the natural sciences with a distinct and independent subject–object relationship as shown in Figure 2.6. In the 'naturalism debate', the argument against this position is that the social world is radically differ-ent from the natural world. The independent subject–object framework excludes social relations where subjects (let's say academics) may have their own language community as well as being engaged as objects of the social phenomena (see Figure 2.6).

Another argument against the positivist stance is that social realities are often not directly observable. This implies that knowledge of social phenomena is not as certain as in the natural sciences as there are no ways of justifying or falsifying general state-ments. Similarly, such knowledge does not tend to produce universal laws and logically coherent theories.

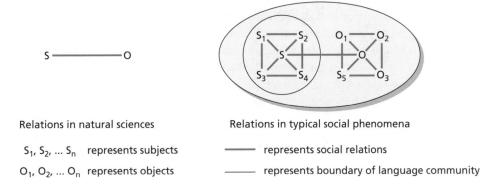

Relations in natural sciences

$S_1, S_2, \ldots S_n$ represents subjects

$O_1, O_2, \ldots O_n$ represents objects

Relations in typical social phenomena

——— represents social relations

——— represents boundary of language community

Figure 2.6 **The naturalism debate** (adapted from Sayer 1992)

Criticism of the positivist stance is also levelled at its underlying premise that the social world is characterised by a closed system. The absence of constant conjunctions in the social world is echoed in the physical world. A closed system is one where such conjunctions are invariant while open systems are those in which events do not follow a regular, fixed and repeated pattern. In reality, it is almost impossible to create a closed system in the social world similar to those obtained from laboratory practices. Some commentators have argued that the variability of events in the social world may not be due to the inherent uncertainty and chaos as suggested by the 'turbulent environment' thesis, but rather the conjunction of real causal mechanisms at work in open systems.

In their classic *The Social Construction of Reality* (1966), Peter Berger and Thomas Luckmann examine commonsense knowledge of what individuals take for granted as real. They recognise that the 'obvious' facts of social reality may differ among people of differing cultures and even within the same culture. The objective becomes the analysis of the processes by which people come to perceive what is 'real' to them. The constructivist perspective argues that our social and organisational surroundings possess no ultimate truth or reality but are determined by the way in which we experience and understand the world we construct in our interaction with others. Critics of this position have argued that social constructivists selectively view certain features of social reality as objective and others as socially constructed. In addition, this perspective fails to accept that there may be broader social forces such as capitalism or materialism that act as powerful influences on observable social outcomes.

One of the main exponents of a 'postmodern' perspective is Jean-François Lyotard in his book *The Postmodern Condition* (1984). He argues that the notion of history shaping phenomena and leading to progress has collapsed. He contests that there are no longer any 'grand narratives' or meta-narratives of history or society that make sense. As individuals are engaged with countless videos, films, TV programmes and websites, they come into contact with a multitude of ideas and values that no longer have a basis in their personal or external history. He rejects two influential meta-narratives on the goals of knowledge and asserts that there is no ultimate basis for settling disputes over these goals that:

● knowledge is produced for its own sake;

● knowledge is produced for people in a quest for emancipation.

Another important theorist of postmodernity is Jean Baudrillard (1988). He contends that electronic media have destroyed our relationship to the past and reversed the Marxist theory that history and economic forces shape society. Instead, he argues it is signs and images from electronic communication and mass media that shape people's lives.

Michel Foucault is another key contributor to postmodern thought, even though he refuses to call himself a postmodernist. He forwards important ideas about the relationships between power, ideology and discourse. The role of discourse is central to understanding power and control in society. Power works through discourse to shape popular attitudes towards social phenomena. For example, expert discourses can become powerful tools to restrict alternative ways of thinking. In this way, Foucault (1980) argues that knowledge becomes a force for control and is linked to technologies of surveillance, enforcement and discipline.

Critics of the postmodernist viewpoint argue that attempts to understand social phenomena or change the world for the better are doomed by this perspective. Also, it impedes any development of general theories of the social world that can help us to intervene and shape matters in a positive manner. One of the central planks of post-modern theory was the discovery of the complexity of the social world, language and meaning. For some critics there was no possibility of encapsulating the complexity, so that postmodern theory became the complexity itself. This is reflected in the wildly conflicting theories, practices and knowledge gained under the umbrella of postmod-ernism. Some critics of postmodernism have argued that its influence is going out of fashion at the start of the twenty-first century and that its most radical propositions are no longer outrageous and have a clichéd ring about them. In opposition to the ambigu-ity and complexity of this perspective, it is suggested that the clarity and simplicity of a critical realist perspective may provide the explanatory power and utility to follow the potential demise of this school of thought.

From a realist perspective, there are four misconceptions about knowledge (Sayer 1992), as shown in Table 2.1. First, knowledge can come from participation and inter-action with others as well as from observation. Second, spoken and written forms of language are not the only ways to communicate, appreciate and apply knowledge. Everyday skills such as experiencing sight, sound and smell can provide knowledge about, say, being in a large crowd or a threatening environment. Third, knowledge is not a finished product but rather an 'ever present' and 'continually reproduced' outcome of individuals. Last, science cannot be assumed to be the highest level of knowledge derived from the first three misconceptions.

Table 2.1 **Four misconceptions of knowledge** (Sayer 1992)

1	That knowledge is gained purely through contemplation or observation of the world
2	That what we know can be reduced to what we say
3	That knowledge can be safely regarded as a thing or product that can be evaluated independently of any consideration of its production and use in social activity
4	That science can simply be assumed to be the highest form of knowledge and that other types as dispensable and displaceable by science

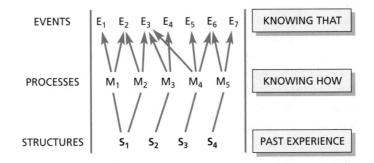

Figure 2.7 **Realist theory of explanation**

To ask for the cause of something is to ask what 'makes it happen', what 'produces', 'generates', 'creates' or 'determines' it. These are all metaphors by which change can occur (Bhaskar 1975). Realism does not view causality as a relationship between discrete events. Instead, realism is concerned with the 'causal powers' or processes and structures that operate in the social world, as shown in Figure 2.7. The causal powers can exist whether or not they are exercised. For instance, unemployed workers have the power to work even though they are not doing so now. Knowing an event 'A' has been followed by an event 'B' is not enough – we need to understand the continuous process by which 'A' produced 'B'. The process of change usually involves several causal mechanisms. Depending on the conditions, operation of the same process can produce different results or, conversely, operation of different processes may produce the same results. The underlying structures can be identified through abstraction and looking for what might produce the effects at issue. Examples with underlying structures are bureaucracies, religious organisations and industries.

Critical thinking and reflection

How would you describe your own knowledge? Do you use words such as 'know how' and 'know that'? Spend some time thinking about your own knowledge and make a list of words that describe your knowledge base. Can you recognise any similarities or differences in the words that you have used? Do your descriptions compare with any words found in this chapter? If you have some atypical words and descriptions, could they be used to formulate a new theory of knowledge?

The taxonomic perspective of knowledge

The taxonomic perspective of knowledge (Tsoukas 1996) treats knowledge as a commodity or substance rather like a football that can be traded according to its supply and demand characteristics (Abrahamson and Eisenman 2001 p. 67). Similarly, Hansen and Haas (2001, p. 2) adopt a metaphor of the possession of knowledge when they describe the internal market for the dissemination of electronic documents within an organisation. The popular conception of this taxonomic perspective makes a distinction between explicit and tacit knowledge. Such a logical behaviourist perspective derives from the philosopher Gilbert Ryle (1949), who made a distinction between 'knowing what' (explicit) and 'knowing how' (tacit). Michael Polanyi (1967) helped clarify our understanding that these two forms of knowledge were not distinct entities but existed along a continuum. A theoretical development of this structural notion of knowledge has been the articulation of processes that convert one form of knowledge into another. Nonaka (1994) proposed four separate processes in this knowledge conversion process: socialisation, combination, externalisation and internalisation. Chapter 6 explores these processes in more detail.

The philosopher Descartes saw a clear distinction between the mind and body which is now referred to as 'Cartesian dualism'. The philosopher Gilbert Ryle criticised Cartesian dualism and couldn't see the need to involve the mind in any way. Instead, he argued that descriptions of human behaviour need never refer to anything but the operations of human bodies. Behaviour was everything for him. This logical behaviourist perspective is easily undermined by a simple example – that of someone in pain. If one only observes the person's behaviour, how can one know whether the person is actually in pain or only pretending? Also, this perspective assumes that individuals can only have access to their experience and belief in pain through observing their own behaviour. Clearly this is not the case as some of us may be less expressive of our painful feelings than others.

Spender (1996, 1998) has adopted this taxonomic perspective of knowledge (tacit and explicit) but has made a distinction between where the knowledge resides: in the individual or in the social domain. He argues that social knowledge exists beyond the individual – in the culture of the organisation in terms of norms, values and underlying assumptions. This tacit 'collective' knowledge is considered the most valuable for any organisation.

Blackler (1995) reviewed a number of studies of organisational knowledge and suggested five different types of knowledge. Four of them were similar to Spender's (1998) framework linking tacit and explicit forms of knowledge to individual levels (embodied and embrained knowledge) and collective levels (embedded and encultured knowledge). He proposed a fifth form of knowledge which he called 'encoded' knowledge. This was conveyed by signs and symbols within organisations. He argued that different types of organisations had a propensity towards one of these forms of knowledge. For example, 'adhocracies' such as management consultancies had a propensity towards 'encultured knowledge' formed through a collective focus on novel problems where tacit knowledge was more valuable.

This functionalist view of knowledge, knowledge as possession, has been challenged on the grounds that it fails to take into account the subjective, dynamic and uncertain nature of knowledge. Gourlay (2006) argues that tacit and explicit forms of knowledge are 'mutually constituted' and their level depends on what is communicated in any dialogue or discussion. He points out that Polanyi originally argued that all knowledge has a personal component and our awareness of it may change over time.

The process-based perspective of knowing

The diametrically opposite 'subjective' perspective to the functionalist paradigm is linked to idealism. The process perspective of knowing draws on the traditions of 'social constructivism'. This perspective places greater emphasis on 'knowing' as a social and organisational activity rather than 'knowledge' as a possession. Constructivism holds that the only reality we can know is one represented by human thought. Reality is independent of the mind but knowledge is always a human construction arising from an individual's thought processes. Knowing, in this context, is a form of 'sensemaking' (see Chapter 5) where individuals interact in social contexts and negotiate their meanings and understandings of the world. It is the individual's mental models that are important. From this perspective knowing has a number of characteristics (Weick 1995, Berger and Luckmann 1966):

- knowing is dynamic and subject to change as individuals and contexts change;
- knowing is equivocal or uncertain as intersubjectivity and interpretations may change through different interactions, roles and structures;
- knowing is context-dependent and inseparable from its social and political environment.

This process perspective asserts that the only reality is one of ideas and is constituted by our perceptions. Hence, instead of making knowledge claims answerable to an independent reality, we make external reality answerable to our representations (Searle 1999, p.16). The problem with this perspective is that it isolates mental activity as the distinctive feature of the self and excludes the possibility that action and the material world have definitive importance in terms of our knowledge (Jashapara 2007). Social constructivism can reduce to a form of relativism where there are no absolute truths and each individual has a different, socially constructed truth in their minds.

One extension of the process perspective is postmodernism. Postmodernist perspectives emphasise the diversity of the world, the plurality of perspectives and the difficulty of obtaining reliable knowledge (Stone 1996, p. 2). Such relativist perspectives where knowledge is divided into discrete systems of thought can nullify the key role of criticism and evade critical evaluation. The problem of 'incommensurability' is that we cannot understand radically different discourses while we retain our own beliefs. However, in practice, some form of translation is always possible and incommensurability can be seen as a way of protecting favoured discourses from criticism (Collier 2003).

Feminist critique of 'malestream' science has contributed the notion of 'situated knowledge' concerning questions of power in what constitutes knowledge (Grimshaw 1996; Haraway 1991; Harding 1991). Situated knowledge is knowledge specific to a particular situation, such as experiential learning arising from trial and error. This knowledge bears the social markings of its context including the sex, race and gender of its authors as well as the media through which it is transferred. From this perspective, the dominant position of the western, white, heterosexual male in research provides one situated view of knowledge, even though it may be often passed off as having universal applicability within an academic community (Sole and Edmondson 2002). Such a feminist perspective would also support a drift towards a relativist position. However, this stance would deny the role of critical enquiry, particularly where feminist standpoints argue that certain positions are more advantageous than others (Jashapara 2007). In essence, all knowledge can be considered social, situated and contextual. However, the feminist perspective becomes problematic when it is assumed that certain forms of knowledge are only applicable to the groups from which they arise. If this was the case, we would only have acupuncture for the Chinese and French social theory for the French! Also, while there is clearly a need for reflexivity to guard against myopia and bias, it would be wrong to dismiss research *a priori* from certain groups such as white males as distorted but not that conducted by black females on the same grounds (Sayer 2000, p. 55).

The practice-based perspective of knowledge and knowing

Action rather than thought is the primary focus in a practice-based perspective. Knowledge and knowing are seen as inseparable from human activity and practice (Orlikowski 2002). Knowing is argued to be 'embedded' in human activity. The realist philosopher, John Macmurray, suggested that we substitute the Cartesian (idealist) dictum *'Cogito ergo sum'* (I think therefore I am) to *'Ago ergo sum'* (I do therefore I am). He insisted that action was more primary than thought, with the assertion that thought begins only where action fails (MacMurray 1933). From this perspective, knowing is seen as something we do rather than an entity we possess.

Orlikowski (2002) argues that knowing and practice are mutually constituted and knowing is enacted through people's everyday activities. Knowing does not exist externally in objects or systems or internally in human brains or communities. Instead, knowing exists in the whole human body and is 'an ongoing social accomplishment, constituted and reconstituted in everyday practice'. However, she contends that material objects and artefacts such as information and communication technologies play an important role in knowing. She uses the metaphor of a 'scaffold' to describe how material artefacts such as mobile phones and laptops structure/'scaffold' particular social activities at any given time. She argues that the social and material are 'constitutively entangled' in everyday life (Orlikowski 2007). The design of material artefacts such as computer systems influences human activity and knowing but is also changed by the same activity.

Language is used in social activity to convey meaning. From a practice-based perspective, the meaning arising from language can be 'ambiguous' as knowledge depends on context and the changing nature of social activity in different environments. A positivist perspective would assert that language has a fixed and objective meaning.

The practice-based perspective is rooted in realist philosophy. Realists explain social phenomena in terms of three aspects: the underlying structures in a social context, the social processes and the external behaviours we observe at any given time (Bhaskar 1978). The premise is that any social activity has underlying structures that lead to the enactment of certain social processes which, in turn, lead to certain social behaviours and actions. Jashapara (2007) has adopted this realist theory of explanation to describe the nature of organisational knowledge as the capacity for action, as shown in Figure 2.8. He argues that the organisational knowledge structures are composed of

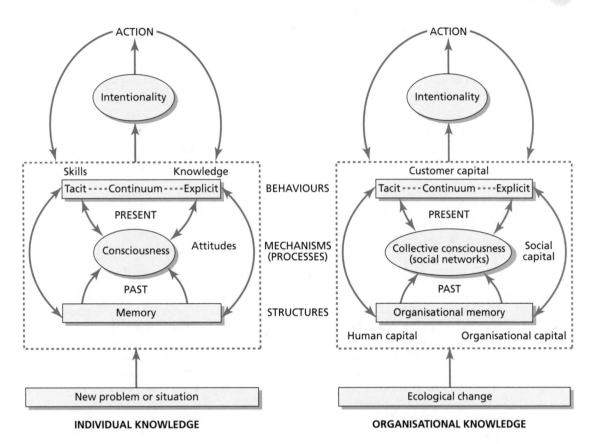

Figure 2.8 **Realist conception of organisational knowledge** (Jashapara 2007)

the collective memory. This memory develops its coherence by connecting and inter-weaving along social and temporal dimensions. The social space of meaning allows the continuous flow of actions, narratives and images to pass from one generation to the next. This enables practical and theoretical knowledge to be preserved and transmitted, as well as formative past experiences (Cohen and Levinthal 1990).

In this conception Jashapara (2007) proposes that the main knowledge processes are associated with collective consciousness. From a realist perspective, consciousness is at the same time a mental state and an internal biological phenomenon arising from brain activity (Searle 1999). At the organisational level, collective consciousness is still experienced at the individual level as a mental state which is constituted and reconsti-tuted in everyday experience. It is not some form of Hegelian spirit floating above an individual's head. Instead, collective consciousness is produced in a process through interactions in work teams and communities of practice. Such consciousness is situated in the historical, socio-materialistic and cultural context in which it occurs (Gherardi and Nicolini 2000). These shared mental models are influenced by the strength of per-sonal relationships, the stories that provide cognitive and social embedding of ideas and people as well as the dynamic construction of meaning through language.

Jashapara (2007) argues that the drivers or sparks for organisational knowl-edge creation and transformation are routines and sense-making processes.

Organisational routines provide the coordination mechanisms for integrating spatially and temporally dispersed knowledge. They allow different perspectives to be explored and common understandings to be developed within an organisational context of power relations, performance expectations and organisational identity. From this theoretical perspective, sense-making processes are not about the accuracy of organisational interpretations but rather the search for plausible stories that incorporate observations and past experiences (Weick 1995; Weick *et al.* 2005). This overall conception of organisational knowledge acknowledges the key role of memory and consciousness which has been missing in recent debates.

CASE STUDY

World Bank (US)

The gauntlet had been thrown down. James Wolfensohn, president of the World Bank, wanted a shift in paradigm from knowledge repositories and communities of practice. He was looking for a deepening in maturity of KM activities more towards engaging with external partners and utilising the combined knowledge towards effective local solutions. This was a tall order and Bruno Laporte, Manager of Knowledge and Learning Services at the World Bank, was tasked with putting forward workable proposals for their next meeting in two weeks. Bruno decided to have a cup of coffee and reflect on how he might go about this assignment.

In 1996 James Wolfensohn put forward a bold vision of the World Bank as a 'knowledge bank'. His vision was clear.

'We have been in the business of researching and disseminating the lessons of development for a long time. But the revolution in information technology increases the potential value of these efforts by vastly extending their reach. To capture this potential, we need to invest in the necessary systems, in Washington and worldwide, that will enhance our ability to gather development information and experience, and share it with our clients.'

He did not see lending alone as achieving poverty reduction. Instead, he believed that knowledge sharing of 'know how' on project implementation internally within the World Bank and with external partners was more likely to have a greater impact. Knowledge was clearly seen as more powerful in poverty reduction than simply providing financial loans. This was a radical step away from former perceptions of the role of the World Bank and called for a radical change in mindsets of all employees. Information technologies and the internet were seen as useful catalysts for tapping into the vast store of dispersed knowledge within the World Bank and mobilising this knowledge for local initiatives.

At this time, Washington was the central locus of World Bank activities. Anything of any importance had to be sanctioned through the Washington HQ. Often when field officers contacted Washington offices over development assistance, the problem would be resolved on the ground before any response was forthcoming. Typically, it could take a month simply for documents to go backwards and forwards between Washington and the field site. The effectiveness of these centralised operations was being questioned.

James Wolfensohn recognised that technology could provide an answer to some of their challenges, but he was mindful that in many client countries there was a lack of basic infrastructure such as electricity and telecommunications capabilities. Following an in-depth analysis of the various technological options, the World Bank selected satellite technology as the most appropriate global communications technology particularly given the deficiencies of basic infrastructure in many countries. But this didn't come without its fair share of costs and a measure of resistance from some countries. India and Pakistan were initially reluctant to have a satellite network in their countries hosted by an external party. Also, satellite dishes and equipment were prone to damage from the harsh climates and interference by animals.[1]

In order to become a 'knowledge bank', the World Bank adopted the notion of 'communities of practice' as a key strategy. They called these 'thematic groups' and saw them as the best way of creating and sharing knowledge. The thematic groups were informal groups that had some work-based social connection. The informality of the groups allowed trust to develop and a greater propensity for colleagues to engage in dialogue and discussion over work-related issues. This often resulted in individuals freely sharing their knowledge and expertise and, at times, the creation of new knowledge from the dialogue and interaction. The World Bank provided modest funding for communication such as creating intranets and newsletters and some funding for face-to-face meetings. Soon there were more than 100 thematic groups recognised by the bank.[2] The combination of web-based satellite technology and the thematic groups meant that people could interact with one another in a way that had never been possible before.

Stories and storytelling were important tools in the thematic groups. Dr Steve Denning, the former Head of Knowledge Management at the World Bank, saw stories as agents for mobilising knowledge and action. 'Perhaps the most powerful role of stories today is to ignite and drive changes in management policy and practices.' He recognised that stories engaged listeners as participants to share in the experiences and to co-create the story, which changed on each occasion it was retold. Stories often spell out a predicament and are often filled with drama, crises and conflicts before they reach some form of conclusion. Dr Steve Denning acknowledged that stories are integral to our everyday understanding of the world around us.

'The way we share and jointly shape stories is important for three fundamental reasons. This is how we create a sense of who we are, our sense of self or identity, it is how we socially construct reality, and it is how we co-ordinate actions. Facts and figures are only small parts in a storied understanding that communicates to us far more important issues such as: character, causality, motive, morality, tension, drama, success and failure. The story brings the meaning to facts and figures in a way that tells us how we should act.'[3]

A noteworthy example of the power of satellite communication technology and thematic groups came from Nigeria. A team leader sent an e-mail to a thematic group asking advice on good practice for a national transport strategy in Nigeria. The first response arrived in 20 minutes and there were detailed responses from eleven countries with 24 hours. These responses included transport strategy reforms in other countries and working papers on strategy development. The consequence of this query was to reduce the technical assistance costs and speed up development of the national transport strategy.[4] Cross-border knowledge sharing requires a considerable investment in time, money and people to generate the necessary levels of trust and cultural sensitivity, particularly between individualistic and more family-oriented cultures.[5]

In terms of technological advances to aid knowledge sharing, the World Bank had instigated a Development Gateway website as a platform for the development community. This portal included help-desk and advisory services, knowledge repositories on the web, tacit knowledge debriefings and sites for the thematic groups.[6] There were more than 20 advisory groups acting as knowledge intermediaries on all aspects of the bank's business. In addition, the satellite technology allowed videoconferencing around the world, interactive TV, online learning applications such as WebCT, web-based video casting and online discussion forums and newsletters. There was some resistance and scepticism to these interventions by staff. The cynics viewed knowledge management as the latest fad with the 'techies' taking over the organisation.

In 2003 the bank decided to conduct an independent evaluation of its knowledge management activities through the Operations Evaluations Department (OED).[7] Internal staff surveys were generally positive indicating favourable responses to having sufficient knowledge and information to conduct their work (83 per cent). Also, externally the World Bank had received accolades through the MAKE (Most Admired Knowledge Enterprise) awards and named as Best Practice Partner with the American Productivity & Quality Center. But the evaluation did recognise some areas for growth. The evaluation recognised that the Bank could do more in applying its KM tools to core business processes such as support for its task teams in their operational work. Also, regional units, country teams and task managers could do more to apply their knowledge services more strategically to clients.

Bruno Laporte finished his cup of coffee. By coincidence, Karen Millet, Director of Knowledge Programmes walked by. 'Ah, Karen, can I have a word? I want to pick your brains over some new KM proposals. Can we pencil a time to meet in our diaries?'

References

1 Regani, S. (ed.) (2004) *Knowledge Sharing Initiatives at the World Bank: Creating a 'Knowledge Bank'*, Hyderabad, India, ICFAI Centre for Management Research.

2 Laporte, B. (2004) 'The evolution of the knowledge bank', *Inside Knowledge*.

3 Dearlove, D. (2003) 'The power of fairy tales', *The Times*, London.

4 Laporte, B. (2004) 'The evolution of the knowledge bank', *Inside Knowledge*.

5 McMahon, M. (2006) 'Best practice: knowledge management – Moving knowledge across borders', *Financial Times*, London.

6 Laporte, B. (2003) 'Knowledge sharing at the World Bank: The fad that would not go away', *Inside Knowledge*.

7 Ash, J. (2005) 'Running on empty? Maintaining momentum as KM matures', *Inside Knowledge*.

Questions

1 What advice would you give Bruno Laporte on potential interventions for the next phase of growth in the World Bank's knowledge management activities?

2 How could knowledge management activities be applied more centrally to the World Bank's core business?

3 What interventions would allow the World Bank's knowledge to be used strategically for the aid of clients in developing countries?

Summary

This chapter has elaborated four main themes:

1 The development of western philosophy with its perpetual quest for an understanding of knowledge underlies many contemporary justifications of the term. Broadly, western philosophy has created a distinction between the idealist philosophers who view knowledge as an entity within our minds and empirical philosophers who view knowledge as arising from our senses.

2 The notions of 'knowing that' and 'knowing how' arising from Gilbert Ryle and Michael Polanyi are considered to exist along a continuum rather than as separate entities. The current typologies of knowledge within the literature are expressed as a reworking of this form of logical behaviourism.

3 The competing philosophical positions are explored using Burrell and Morgan's framework, especially the more common perspectives of positivism, constructivism, postmodernism and realism in knowledge management research.

4 A realist theory of the structure of knowledge is presented based on 'past experience' to underpin the processes of 'knowing how' and the outcomes of 'knowing that'. It is argued that a reflection phase is primary in transforming organisational routines to double-loop learning in the underlying structure of knowledge.

Questions for further thought

1 Do you agree with the idealist notion that knowledge can only exist in our heads? If not, what alternative can you provide to our current conception of knowledge?

2 What are the strongest arguments against an empiricist perspective of knowledge?

3 Using Hegel's notion of the dialectic process, which one of the competing perspectives is likely to provide a credible antithesis to the dominant positivist paradigm in management research?

4 From Husserl's perspective, knowledge is linked to a directed mental content called 'intentionality' in our consciousness. What are the merits and drawbacks of this perspective in knowledge management?

5 What are the likely consequences of an almost total lack of regard of issues concerning language in knowledge management research?

6 How could a philosophical understanding of knowledge improve worker performance?

7 Philosophical debates are often excluded and denigrated as being esoteric and inappropriate for management. Can this position be defended in the further quest for knowledge?

8 If knowledge is not purely about what we can say, how can we incorporate other forms of communication such as non-verbal cues into our theory of knowledge?

9 What is the difference between data, information and knowledge in an organisation? How can a manager effectively transform data and information into effective knowledge? How can organisations manage competing and often conflicting interpretations of the same data and information? What are the drawbacks of relying on position power in these circumstances?

10 If the underlying structure of knowledge is past experience, what are the drawbacks of considering intuitions, hunches and insights as part of one's past experience?

Further reading

1 Magee, B. (2000) is an excellent introduction to the thinking of western philosophers in the form of a dialogue between Magee and academics who have spent a lifetime studying particular philosophers.

2 Ryle, G. (1949) acts as the basis for much of the philosophical assumptions around the notion of 'knowledge' in the current literature.

3 Jashapara (2007) articulates a realist and practice-based perspective of organisational knowledge that acknowledges the key roles of organisational memory and consciousness.

References

Abrahamson, E. and Eisenman, M. (2001) 'Why management scholars must intervene strategically in the management knowledge market', *Human Relations*, 54, 67–75.

Ash, J. (2005) 'Running on empty? Maintaining momentum as KM matures', *Inside Knowledge*.

Argyris, C. and Schon, D.A. (1978) *Organizational Learning: A Theory of Action Perspective*, Addison-Wesley, Reading, MA.

Aristotle (1998) *The Metaphysics*, H. Lawson-Tancred, translator, Penguin Books, London.

Baudrillard, J. (1988) *Selected Writings*, Polity Press, Cambridge.

Berger, P.L. and Luckmann, T. (1966) *The Social Construction of Reality: A Treatise in the Sociology of Knowledge*, Penguin, New York.

Bhaskar, R. (1975) *A Realist Theory of Science*, Leeds Books, Leeds.

Bhaskar, R. (1978) *A Realist Theory of Science*, Harvester Wheatsheaf, Hemel Hempstead.

Blackler, F. (1995) 'Knowledge, knowledge work and organizations: An overview and interpretation', *Organization Studies*, 16, 1021–46.

Brown, J.S. and Duguid, P. (1998) 'Organizing knowledge', *California Management Review*, Vol. 40, No. 3, 90–111.

Burrell, G. and Morgan, M. (1979) *Sociological Paradigms and Organizational Analysis*, Heinemann, London.

Cohen, W. M. and Levinthal, D. (1990) 'Absorptive capacity: A new perspective on learning and innovation', *Administrative Science Quarterly*, 35, 128–52.

Collier, A. (2003) *In Defence of Objectivity and Other Essays: On realism, existentialism and politics*, Routledge, London.

Cook, S. D. N. and Brown, J. S. (1999) 'Bridging epistemologies: The generative dance between organizational knowledge and organizational knowing', *Organization Science*, 10(4), 381–400.

Davenport, T. H. and Prusak, L. (1998) *Working Knowledge: How Organizations Manage What They Know*, Harvard Business School Press, Boston, MA.

Dearlove, D. (2003) 'The power of fairy tales', *The Times*, London.

Descartes, R. (1996) *Meditations on First Philosophy*, J. Cottingham, ed., Cambridge University Press, Cambridge.

Dewey, J. (1990) *The School and Society and the Child and the Curriculum*, P. W. Jackson, ed., University of Chicago Press, Chicago.

Dewey, J. (1991) *The Later Works, 1925–1953*, J. A. Boydston, ed., Southern Illinois University Press, Carbondale, Il.

Drucker, P.F. (2002) *The Effective Executive*, HarperCollins Publishers, New York.

Foucault, M. (1980) *Power/Knowledge*, Pantheon, New York.

Gherardi, S. and Nicolini, D. (2000) 'To transfer is to transform: the circulation of safety knowledge', *Organization*, 7, 329–48.

Gioia, D. and Pitre, E. (1990) 'Multi-paradigm perspectives on theory building', *Academy of Management Review*, 15(4), 584–602.

Goles, T. and Hirschheim, R. (2000) 'The paradigm is dead, the paradigm is dead ... long live the paradigm: The legacy of Burrell and Morgan', *Omega – The International Journal of Management Science*, 28, 249–268, reprinted with permission from Elsevier.

Gourlay, S. (2006) 'Conceptualising knowledge creation: a critique of Nonaka's theory', *Journal of Management Studies*, 43, 1415–36.

Grimshaw, J. (1996) 'Philosophy, feminism and universalism', *Radical Philosophy*, 76, 19–28.

Hansen, M. T. and Haas, M. R. (2001) 'Competing for attention in knowledge markets: Electronic document dissemination in a management consulting company', *Administrative Science Quarterly*, 46, 1–28.

Haraway, D. J. (1991) *Simians, Cyborgs, and Women: The Reinvention of Nature*, Free Association Books, London.

Harding, S. (1991) *Whose Science, Whose Knowledge? Thinking from Women's Lives*, Oxford University Press, Oxford.

Hassard, J. and Kelemen, M. (2002) 'Production and consumption in organizational knowledge: The case of the "paradigms debate"', *Organization*, 9(2), 331–355.

Hegel, G. W. F. (1997) *On Art, Religion, and the History of Philosophy*, J. G. Gray, ed., Hackett Publishing Co., Cambridge, MA.

Heidegger, M. (1978) *Being and Time*, Blackwell Publishers, Oxford.

Hume, D. (2000) *A Treatise of Human Nature*, D. F. Norton and M. J. Norton, eds, Oxford University Press, Oxford.

Husserl, E. (2001) *The Shorter 'Logical Investigations'*, D. Moran and M. Dummett, eds, Routledge, London.

James, W. (1990) *Pragmatism and the Meaning of Truth*, Harvard University Press, Cambridge, MA.

Jashapara, A. (2007) 'Moving beyond tacit and explicit distinctions: A realist theory of organizational knowledge', *Journal of Information Science*, 33, 752–66.

Kant, I. (1999) *Critique of Pure Reason*, P. Guyer and A. W. Wood, eds, Cambridge University Press, Cambridge.

Kogut, B. and Zander, U. (1992) 'Knowledge of the firm, combinative capabilities and the replication of technology', *Organization Science*, 5, 383–397.

Laporte, B. (2003) 'Knowledge sharing at the World Bank: The fad that would not go away', *Inside Knowledge*.

Laporte, B. (2004) 'The evolution of the knowledge bank', *Inside Knowledge*.

Locke, J. (1998) *An Essay Concerning Human Understanding*, Wordsworth Editions Ltd, Ware, Herts.

Lyotard, J. F. (1984) *The Postmodern Condition: A Report on Knowledge*, G. Bennington and B. Massumi, translators, University of Minnesota Press, Minneapolis.

Macmurray, J. (1933) *The Philosophy of Communism*, Faber, London.

Macmurray, J. (1957) *The Form of the Personal: The Self as Agent* (Vol. 1), Faber, London.

Macmurray, J. (1961) *The Form of the Personal: Persons in Relation* (Vol. 2), Faber, London.

McMahon, M. (2006) 'Best practice: knowledge management – Moving knowledge across borders', *Financial Times*, London.

Magee, B. (2000) *The Great Philosophers*, Oxford University Press, Oxford.

Nelson, R. and Winter, S. (1982) *An Evolutionary Theory of Economic Change*, Harvard University Press, Cambridge, MA.

Newell, S., Robertson, M., Scarbrough, H. and Swan, J. (2002) *Managing Knowledge Work*, Palgrave, Basingstoke, Hampshire.

Nonaka, I. (1994) 'A dynamic theory of organizational knowledge creation', *Organization Science*, 5(1), 14–37.

Orlikowski, W. J. (2002) 'Knowing in practice: Enacting a collective capability in distributed organizing', *Organizing Science*, 13, 249–73.

Orlikowski, W. J. (2007) 'Sociomaterial practices: Exploring technology at work', *Organization Studies*, 28, 1435–48.

Peirce, C. S. (1998) *The Essential Peirce: Selected Philosophical Writings, 1893–1913* (Vol. 2), N. Houser, ed., Indiana University Press, Bloomington, IN.

Pfeffer, J. and Sutton, R. I. (1999) 'Knowing "what" to do is not enough: turning knowledge into action', *California Management Review*, 42, 92–3.

Plato (1992) *Theaetetus*, B. Williams and M. F. Burnyeat, eds, Hackett Publishing Co, Cambridge, MA.

Polanyi, M. (1967) *The Tacit Dimension*, Doubleday, New York.

Regani, S. (ed.) (2004) *Knowledge Sharing Initiatives at the World Bank: Creating a 'Knowledge Bank'*, Hyderabad, India, ICFAI Center for Management Research.

Ryle, G. (1949) *The Concept of Mind*, Hutcheson, London.

Sartre, J. (1968) *Being and Nothingness*, Routledge, London.

Sayer, A. (1992) *Method in Social Science: A Realist Approach*, Routledge, London.

Sayer, A. (2000) *Realism and Social Science*, Sage, London.

Searle, J. R. (1999) *Mind, Language and Society: Philosophy in the Real World*, Basic Books, New York.

Skinner, B. F. (1938) *The Behaviour of Organisms: An Experimental Analysis*, Appleton-Century-Crofts, New York.

Sole, D. and Edmondson, A. (2002) 'Situated knowledge and learning in disperse teams', *British Journal of Management*, 13, S17–S34.

Spender, J. C. (1996) 'Organizational knowledge, learning and memory: Three concepts in search of a theory', *Journal of Organizational Change*, 9, 63–78.

Spender, J. C. (1996) 'Making knowledge the basis of a dynamic theory of the firm', *Strategic Management Journal*, 17, 45–62.

Spender, J. C. (1998) 'Pluralist epistemology and the knowledge-based theory of the firm', *Organization*, 5(2), 233–56.

Stones, R. (1996) *Sociological Reasoning: Towards a Post-Modern Sociology*, Macmillan, London.

Tsoukas, H. (1996) 'The firm as a distributed knowledge system: A constructionist approach', *Strategic Management Journal*, 17, 11–25.

Weick, K. E. (1995) *Sensemaking in Organizations*, Sage Publications, Thousand Oaks, CA.

Weick, K. E., Sutcliffe, K. M. and Obstfeld, D. (2005) 'Organizing and the process of sensemaking', *Organization Science*, 16, 409–21.

Wittgenstein, L. (1953) *Philosophical Investigations*, G. E. M. Anscombe, translator, Basil Blackwell, Oxford.

Wittgenstein, L. (2001) *Tractatus Logico-philosophicus*, Routledge, London.

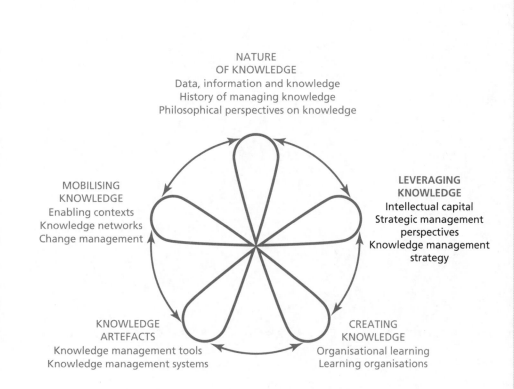

Part 2

LEVERAGING KNOWLEDGE

NATURE
OF KNOWLEDGE
Data, information and knowledge
History of managing knowledge
Philosophical perspectives on knowledge

**LEVERAGING
KNOWLEDGE**
Intellectual capital
Strategic management
perspectives
Knowledge management
strategy

MOBILISING
KNOWLEDGE
Enabling contexts
Knowledge networks
Change management

KNOWLEDGE
ARTEFACTS
Knowledge management tools
Knowledge management systems

CREATING
KNOWLEDGE
Organisational learning
Learning organisations

Chapter 3

Intellectual capital

Learning outcomes

After completing this chapter the reader should be able to:

- understand the differing conceptions and frameworks of intellectual capital;
- evaluate the need to have non-financial measures of intellectual capital to supplement traditional financial measures;
- apply concepts of intellectual capital in practice;
- appreciate the different aspects of intellectual property such as patents and copyrights.

Management issues

The measurement and management of intellectual capital implies these questions for managers:

- Are intellectual capital accounts likely to help a firm gain competitive advantage and how can they enable a firm to critically review its practices and processes?
- What aspects of 'knowing how' and 'knowing that' can be reliably measured to be meaningful for an organisation and its external stakeholders?
- How can intellectual capital accounts be produced using existing organisational processes. If new processes are needed, what form should they take?
- How can a firm strategically manage its intellectual property?

Links to other chapters

Chapter 4   helps to understand the implications of intellectual capital measurement and reporting on strategic development.

Chapters 7 and 9 recognise the implications of knowledge management systems and communities of practice on organisational and human capital.

A little knowledge is deadly dangerous   FT

It is the 'unknown knowns' that can kill you. But this was the category of information which Donald Rumsfeld, the former US defence secretary, left off his famous list ('known knowns', 'known unknowns') a few years ago.

A pity. One of the lessons of the September 11 2001 hijackings, as well as the recent attempt to blow up an aircraft on Christmas day, is that organisations may already possess the information they need to avoid disaster. It is just that they do not know that they know.

In criticising his security services last week, Barack Obama summed up this management dilemma well. 'This was not a failure to collect intelligence,' he said. 'It was a failure to integrate and understand the intelligence that we already had.' His colleagues had neglected to 'connect the dots', he observed.

This is a familiar story to business leaders. 'If only Unilever knew what Unilever knows,' went the old lament. And you can substitute the name of almost any other company into that last sentence.

It was this lingering sense of unconnectedness, of dots not being joined up, that led to the emergence of 'knowledge management' as a business discipline two decades ago. It was based on the idea that all sorts of valuable information – about customers' preferences or what employees knew – was simply disappearing into the cracks that separated teams and business units. People within their silos could not or would not share knowledge.

Tom Stewart, chief marketing and knowledge officer for consultants, Booz, moved the debate on with his 1997 book, *Intellectual Capital: The New Wealth of Organizations*, which described what properly managed knowledge could do for businesses. Surely things were about to change? Maybe knowledge management was too drab a label to hold people's attention. Perhaps it all sounded too much like hard work. But 'KM' soon fell prey to the curse of the management fad. It was talked about, popularised, then – too often – forgotten. Today too few compa-

nies can be confident that their employees share the knowledge and information that they need. Do their people know what they know?

The events over Detroit this Christmas confirmed the danger of ignoring the information that circulates, whether unprocessed or imperfectly understood, within organisations. In a blog post last week, Harvard Business School's Rosabeth Moss Kanter said that dispatching e-mails or entering comments into databases is not enough. Only 'relentless follow-up' would hold colleagues accountable for what they were supposed to be doing.

Smart knowledge management involves spotting useful patterns in the data that you have. Leaders should reward 'pattern recognisers', she said. They should also 'stress the importance of passing on items of value to others'.

But while Prof Kanter is hopeful that social networking technology will lead to a greater sharing of information, others are not so sure. Morten Hansen, professor at Berkeley and Insead and author of last year's well-regarded book, sees other factors at play. The failure of colleagues to communicate effectively 'requires a change in culture and incentive systems, not an IT fix', he says.

It is not always easy to recognise the value of the information you have. The father of the alleged Detroit bomber, a former banker from Nigeria, warned US officials about his concerns over his son. For whatever reason – fatigue, overwork – the crucial tip-off was ignored. Too casual by half. The son's name was even mis-spelled by one official, confusing his identity.

But information must be taken seriously. Managers need more than gut instinct and past experience to help them make good decisions. This means that knowledge has to be seen as an asset, something to be both respected and exploited.

This is why the collective corporate memory is so important. People forget – or just never get to learn – crucial details about the markets they are operating in. Veteran CIA officers understand this. As one former field operative, Bob Baer, told the BBC last week, it is no wonder his former colleagues seem 'clueless' about where the next threat is coming from. 'You're seeing the price the CIA is paying for getting rid of so many people in the 1990s,' he said. 'We fired people or let them retire.'

If we didn't know then how unwise that approach was, we know now.

Source: from A little knowledge is deadly dangerous, *The Financial Times*, 12/01/2010 (Stern, S.), copyright © The Financial Times Ltd.

Questions

1 How do you get colleagues to 'connect the dots' in organisations?

2 What can be done to improve the 'silo' mentality in organisations?

3 How can organisations harvest the knowledge of former employees?

Introduction

In an international survey conducted in 1998, 82.3 per cent of the 1,300 firms questioned named intellectual capital as the critical factor for their future business success (Bertels and Savage 1998). National governments have also recognised intellectual capital as a major factor in their country's future prosperity. For example, the UK government's (1999) White Paper, *Our Competitive Future: Building the Knowledge Driven Economy*, clearly recognises the power of knowledge to transform economic growth and performance. An interesting trend of the so-called 'knowledge-driven economy' is that shareholders are becoming better informed from a variety of financial and non-financial sources (often from the internet) and becoming more critical in their analyses of companies. Jean-Claude Paye, Secretary General of the OECD, reinforced the importance of knowledge for economic performance (Skyrme and Amidon 1997):

> 'Knowledge is now a critical factor underpinning economic growth. Producing goods and services with high value-added is at the core of improving economic performance and international competitiveness [...] Increasing investment [...] has become a major issue for enterprises and governments.'

A great deal of the current literature on intellectual capital is about how we measure this elusive entity. Measurement of any entity needs to consider its overriding purpose and its likely market of recipients. This can raise a number of key questions:

● Is measurement purely for internal consumption to improve management practices?

● Is measurement for external consumption by analysts, brokers, banks, customers or any other stakeholders?

● Are there dangers in predominantly measuring the more easily accessible explicit knowledge base of the firm at the expense of the potentially more valuable tacit knowledge or 'know how'?

● What is the time frame for such measures to be meaningful? Are snapshots annually likely to be meaningful in highly fluctuating capital markets?

● Commonly accepted frameworks of intellectual capital are likely to lend themselves to benchmarking among organisations. Are there likely dangers of benchmarking? Are firms likely to reveal their sensitive knowledge assets for external monitoring purposes?

We start this chapter by considering the nature of intellectual capital from a variety of perspectives as well as its historical background. The dangers of adopting a purely financial approach to intellectual capital are highlighted and the need to build in non-financial measures is explored. A multitude of intellectual capital frameworks are presented and the notions of human capital and organisational capital are examined in greater depth. We illustrate how intellectual property can be managed, especially through the use of smart patents. An interesting recent development of intellectual capital as a narrative is forwarded as well as a practical approach to the process of knowledge auditing.

What is intellectual capital?

'Intellectual capital' is a relatively new academic endeavour that is grounded in practice and has its origins in consultancy and industry. There are currently no universally accepted definitions of this term. A simplistic definition would be: 'The difference between the market value of a publicly held company and its official net book value is the value of its intangible assets' (Svieby 1997). One argument for existence of intellectual capital is the marked way in which stock prices change in response to changes in management of an enterprise. A general characteristic of knowledge-intensive organisations such as Microsoft, Oracle and SAP is that their market-to-book-value ratio is often several times higher than that of traditional organisations. From a financial perspective of intellectual capital, one recognises that intellectual capital can be a highly volatile entity and dependent on daily fluctuations of capital markets. The inherent potential of rapidly changing values of intellectual capital may create tangible risks for investors and other stakeholders, such as witnessed by the collapse of some dotcom companies with high market-to-book values.

Stewart (1997) has proposed that intellectual capital is the 'intellectual material – knowledge, information, intellectual property, experience – that can be put to create wealth'. Some authors have used the term expressively 'to refer to the knowledge and knowing capability of a social collectivity, such as an organisation, intellectual community, or professional practice' (Nahapiet and Ghoshal 1998). Other scholars have associated the term more closely with human resources (Boudreau and Ramstad 1997) or with information technology (Davenport and Prusak 1998). A workable definition of intellectual capital has been offered by the Organisation for Economic Co-operation and Development (OECD 1999):

> 'The economic value of two categories of intangible assets of a company: organisational ('structural') capital and human capital.'

There can be some confusion between intellectual capital and intangible assets. The OECD definition treats intellectual capital as a subset of the overall intangible base of an organisation such as its reputation. Structural capital refers to the tangible elements within an organisation such as software and supply chains that remain after employees go home at night. Human capital is what remains in employees' heads when they go home at night, such as customer relationships, know how and their creativity. A

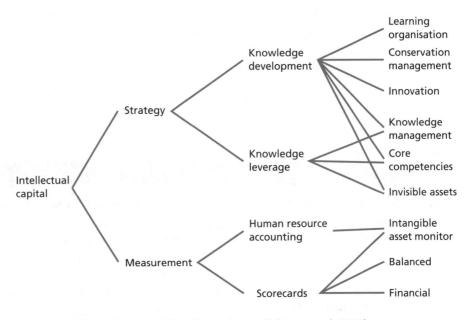

Figure 3.1 **Conceptual roots of intellectual capital** (Roos *et al.* 1997)

useful map of the intellectual capital terrain is proposed by Roos *et al.* (1997) who make a distinction between efforts focused on a strategic perspective or a measurement perspective, as shown in Figure 3.1. A strategic perspective is interested in the management of intellectual capital to increase value of the organisation, whereas a measurement perspective focuses on reporting mechanisms of a quantitative or qualitative nature.

A critical aspect of these definitions is that intellectual capital is not an object or a stable entity (such as knowing that) but rather a consequence of certain elements of collectivity. In this conception, intellectual capital is a dynamic entity and closely linked with the processes and practices of knowledge management.

Critical thinking and reflection

Reflect on your personal knowledge assets. How would you describe your personal intellectual capital? Do you believe this is a function of your academic or professional qualifications or more concerned with your general skills and experience? How far would you factor the strength of your contacts and relationships into your intellectual capital? How would you ascribe a market value to your intellectual capital?

There have been considerable efforts to capture the concept of intellectual capital, with a number of frameworks forwarded to encapsulate the term. In its current stage of development, it is important to recognise the shortcomings of the different schemas proposed by asking the 'so what?' questions (Andriessen 2002). For example:

- As an employee, what does it mean to be told that the share of employees with higher degrees has gone up and line manager satisfaction rating has gone down?
- As a senior manager, how would an instrument of intellectual capital assist you in your change management programmes or strategic development plans?
- As an investor, how would the notion of an intellectual capital account help you to decide whether or not to invest in a company?

History of intellectual capital

Intellectual capital has emerged from the accounting discipline in a quest to find more comprehensive measures of organisational performance. The roots of the accounting profession can be traced back to its father, Luca Pacioli, whose starting point in 1494 was to measure tangible assets linked to factors of production. However, the interest in intellectual capital is much more recent. In the 1980s James Tobin's q ratio highlighted the major differences between the market value and book value of firms as they entered the information age. During this time, there was a recognition of the inadequacy of traditional financial measures and a search began to incorporate non-financial measures into the analysis. The first major turning point in intellectual capital came from Skandia, the Swedish financial services firm, which in 1990 appointed Leif Edvinsson as 'Director of Intellectual Capital' and published an intellectual capital supplement to its annual accounts in 1994. A rough history of intellectual capital is depicted in Table 3.1 with a number of milestones presented.

Problems of measuring organisational performance

Conventional measures of organisational performance tend to favour the more widely available financial information. This has arisen due to requirements in law where companies must disclose specific financial information annually. For instance in the UK, a public limited company has to disclose a profit and loss account, a balance sheet and a funds flow statement. From these accounts, analysts can calculate a number of financial performance ratios such as return on capital employed (ROCE), return on investment (ROI) and so on.

Table 3.1 **History of intellectual capital**

Period	Milestones
1969	Tobin's q ratio established to compare a firm's market to book ratio.
1969	John Kenneth Galbraith first coined phrase 'intellectual capital' in a letter to economist Michael Kalecki: '*I wonder if you realise how much those of us in the world around have owed to the intellectual capital you have provided over these past decades.*'
Early 1980s	Accounting profession uses the term intangible assets predominantly in the form of goodwill.
Mid 1980s	Gap between market and book values widens for many IT-related firms.
1988	Establishment of the European Foundation for Quality Management promoting non-financial indicators of excellence.
1989	Attempts by Svieby to measure intellectual capital in the form of an 'invisible balance sheet'.
1990	Leif Edvinsson is appointed 'Director of Intellectual Capital' at Skandia AFS.
1992	Kaplan and Norton introduce concept of 'balanced scorecard'.
1994	Skandia and Rambøll publish a supplement on intellectual capital to their company's annual accounts. Went on to develop an instrument for measuring intellectual capital called 'Skandia Navigator'. Dow Chemical collaborates with Skandia and pursues an intellectual capital framework forwarded by Petrash.
1995	World Trade Organization (WTO) negotiates agreement on Trade Related Aspects of Intellectual Propert Rights (TRIPS). Celemi uses a 'knowledge audit' to provide a detailed assessment of its intellectual capital.
1997	Roos *et al*. propose a single 'intellectual capital' index to group the different indicators. Stewart develops an instrument called the 'Intellectual Capital Navigator'.
1998	'Method of doing business' (MDB) is given right to be patented under US case law. Danish Agency for Trade and Industry sponsors a report on the preparation of 'intellectual capital accounts' based on the experience of ten companies. UK government publishes White Paper entitled *Our Competitive Future: Building the Knowledge Driven Economy*. In Spain, 23 companies form 'Club Intellect' to promote measurement of intellectual capital.
1999	OECD co-sponsors an international symposium on intellectual capital in Amsterdam. Danish Confederation of Trade Unions proposes a framework for intellectual capital. European Union funds research project 'MERITUM' to examine intellectual assets.
2000	Launch of academic *Journal of Intellectual Capital* dedicated to an international exchange of research and best practice on all aspects of managing intellectual capital in organisations.
2002	Mouritsen *et al*. propose the addition of a narrative to intellectual capital accounts.

However, these conventional measures are not free from accounting manipulations, as witnessed by the collapse of the US giant Enron. For example, Smith (1992) identi-fied 45 leading UK companies that used five or more debatable 'financial engineering' techniques to massage financial figures and present a spurious reflection of the firm's performance. These financial engineering techniques included questionable approaches to undervaluation of assets, provisions, capitalisation of costs, depreciation, goodwill, brands and off-balance-sheet finance. For instance, BAA increased the economic life of its terminals and runways from 16 and 23.5 years respectively to 50 and 100 years. This resulted in the reduction of annual depreciation costs and a subsequent major increase in profits with comparatively little change in its organisational practices.

Despite the potential for accounting manipulations, one financial method for eval-uating intellectual capital from an external perspective is Tobin's q derived from the Nobel Prize winner and economist James Tobin (1969). The Tobin q ratio compares the market value of an asset with its replacement cost (book value). If the quotient q (known as the 'market-to-book value') is less than 1, the market value of the product or service is lower than its cost of reproduction. If the firm enjoys a high q, it is likely to generate higher profits and income. Assuming that similar sized firms have compar-able tangible assets, the difference in competitive performance can be said to arise from intellectual capital.

There are hazards in measuring intellectual capital from the market-to-book value. In high-growth markets the intellectual capital may become inflated purely due to spec-ulation by investors. For instance, Bill Gates lost $5 billion during the 'Russia crises' between August and September 1998 even though the 'intellectual capital' of Microsoft remained relatively unchanged (Reinhardt *et al.* 2001). Additional external influences that can affect Tobin's q are the interest rates, inflation rates, money supply and cycli-cal shifts from bonds and shares. The book value of a firm can be distorted and is not entirely free of accounting manipulations. Hence, even though knowledge manage-ment practices and processes may increase within a firm, they may not be supported by external perceptions of the firm through such ratios.

There has been an increasing call to supplement the small set of traditional financial performance measures with non-financial indicators that provide an understanding of the processes behind them (Eccles and Nohria 1992). In addition, there has been a rec-ognition that a new paradigm of performance measurement is required that regards it as an ongoing evolving process. The European Foundation for Quality Management (EFQM), formed by 14 leading European companies in 1988, has established an annual European Quality Award for the most successful exponent of Total Quality Management (TQM) in Europe. It is revealing that the performance categories deemed critical for excellence in organisational performance are rather lacking in financial measures, as shown in Figure 3.2.

The measurement of intellectual capital can be viewed as a continuation of the historical approaches used to measure human resource performance. Morgan (1992) identified three dominant approaches to measuring human resource performance. The first approach attempts to identify meaningful and reliable human resource measures of greatest concern to the organisation. This approach can be costly, time-consuming and may result in no clear guidelines for action. There is also the danger of creeping

+1

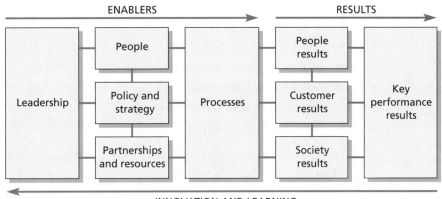

Figure 3.2 EFQM excellence model

numeration, as every measure deemed relevant is turned into the official measurement system (Eccles and Nohria 1992).

The second approach is to develop measures whose potential benefits outweigh the expense or difficulty of data collection. The rationale is to keep things simple and to avoid information overload by developing a few measures to help managers gauge the state of affairs. This approach runs the risk of being too superficial as it does not tell a manager why an outcome may have occurred and how to incorporate the lessons learnt into the system.

The third approach to human resource performance is the use of benchmarking. This involves a comparison of selected performance indicators with other firms in the same industry. It can help managers to establish whether certain human resource practices are within or outside a given norm in a particular sector so that they can take appropriate action. The most common form of human resource benchmarking is salary surveys. Benchmarking does have its limitations. There can be a difficulty in finding standard and acceptable indicators and a reluctance within companies to divulge sensitive information. It can be a time-consuming and expensive process and may promote a culture of imitating competitors' practices rather than encouraging innovative 'leading-edge' practices. Also, the data collected does not provide the highly prized (qualitative) information of the processes that enabled certain outcomes to occur. Clearly the same issues are likely to be apparent if a common benchmarking framework for intellectual capital is developed. At the current time, a number of frameworks for intellectual capital have been forwarded but none has been universally accepted.

Frameworks of intellectual capital

When considering various frameworks and indices to measure intellectual capital, one has to be mindful of the old adage that what gets measured gets managed but what is not understood is ignored. Some key questions in determining the effectiveness of various frameworks and indices includes:

- Does it add value to the customers?
- Can it offer potential for the future?
- How can one interpret it during a recession?
- Does it provide a unique competitive advantage?
- Is it sustainable over some years?
- Is it firmly anchored within the organisation?
- Does it engender a proactive transformative approach?

In 1992 Robert Kaplan and David Norton (1992) developed the first approach to intellectual capital that took into account a number of perspectives apart from the traditional financial one. They suggested that a 'balanced scorecard' that included a customer perspective, a financial perspective, an internal business perspective and an innovation and learning perspective was likely to provide senior managers with a fast single report on organisational performance. This approach has become popular, as shown in Figure 3.3, since it provides management with extra internal indicators to establish cause-and-effect relationships and examine performance drivers. However, it is less appropriate for external reporting.

Critical thinking and reflection

Using the balanced scorecard approach, how would you go about measuring the less tangible dimensions such as the 'internal business process' perspective in your organisation? What do you see as potential difficulties in comparing these measures historically? In your opinion, how realistic is the use of the balanced scorecard to report performance across an industry? What are the pitfalls of an industry benchmarking exercise in this area?

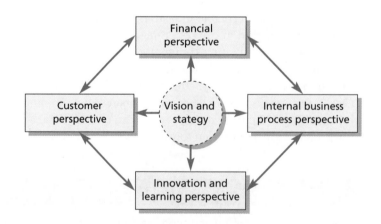

Figure 3.3 **The balanced scorecard** (from Kaplan and Norton 1992)

In 1993, Leif Edvinsson reported the 'hidden' intellectual assets of Skandia AFS as a supplement to the annual report. It was the first time that the term 'intellectual capital' was used rather than the accounting term 'intangible assets' (Edvinsson and Malone 1997). Using the intellectual capital framework shown in Figure 3.4, Skandia went on to develop the 'Skandia Navigator' for managing intellectual capital. The aim of managing these invisible assets was to create further sustainable value for the organisation. The intellectual capital reports published subsequently in the accounts provided concrete display of different indicators of intellectual capital:

- financial focus;
- customer focus;
- human focus;
- process focus;
- renewal and development focus.

Dow Chemical was another pioneering company to measure intellectual capital at this time and its efforts were based on a similar framework forwarded by Petrash (1996). The dotted lines between the three major forms of intellectual capital (see Figure 3.4) depict the dynamic management of these assets. Dow Chemical collaborated with Skandia and based its definition of intellectual capital on this simple formula:

Intellectual capital = human capital + organisation capital + customer capital

There has been a growing trend towards developing a single index for intellectual capital rather than reporting a multitude of differing indicators. Roos *et al.* (1997) found Skandia used 24 different indicators to measure intellectual capital. They proposed grouping the different indicators together into an 'intellectual capital' index. Such an index would encourage managers to discuss any areas that were uncertain and enable benchmarking to occur.

Lowendahl (1997) provides an alternative perspective of intangible assets based on competence and relational resources, as shown in Figure 3.4. He further divides these entities into individual or collective resources depending on their specific focus. Competence is the ability of the individual or firm to do things. In contrast, relational resources are based on the reputation, client loyalty and reputation of the firm or individual.

As shown in Figure 3.4, Sullivan (1998) develops a model primarily based on human capital. He defines human capital as the capabilities of employees, contractors and suppliers to solve customer problems. This capability is based on collective experience, know how and skills of employees. The human capital is supported by structural capital such as computers, information systems and physical buildings. Effective management of the human capital is likely to lead to increased intellectual assets and intellectual property. Another similar framework is proposed by Annie Brooking (1996) based on four aspects of intellectual capital: market assets (such as brands, customers, distribution channels and backlog), human-centred assets (problem-solving abilities), intellectual property assets (such as patents, trademarks and copyrights) and infrastructure assets (such as culture, processes, databases and communication systems).

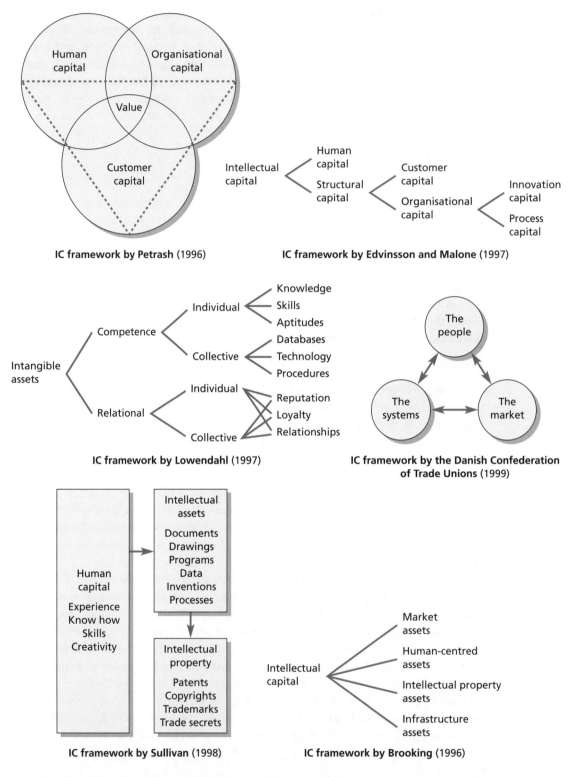

Figure 3.4 **Sample of varying intellectual capital frameworks**

In comparing the different frameworks forwarded, one needs to be mindful of the assumptions underlying them. For instance, is the goal of the measurement framework (such as Sullivan) to enable managers to extract value from the know how of human capital and possibly lead to higher profits? Or is the goal focused on value creation which is concerned with the creation of knowledge through managing training and development, developing relationships and managing organisational culture?

Human and social capital

Human capital theory has its roots in the 1960s (Becker 1964; Schultz 1961). The pre-occupation at the time was the levels of investment required in education and the likely returns on this investment in the form of economic growth and profitability. Becker defined the development of human capital as:

> *'activities that influence monetary and psychic income by increasing the resources in people.'*

The 'black box' notion of human capital with certain inputs leading to prescribed outputs has lingered, with more recent attempts to link individual competences with organisational competences. In their theory of core competences, Hamel and Prahalad (1994) argue that the success of any company lies in the optimal utilisation and development of its core competences rather than its products or services or current markets. The core competences consist of a combination of intangible assets which flourish in a given culture. The problem of considering core competences as intangible assets is that they do not fit the traditional accounting transaction-based model. Intangible assets can increase or decrease without a transaction taking place. Intangible assets are difficult to identify and do not lend themselves to simple addition of their separate values. The benefits of intangible assets are uncertain and their competitive advantage can be lost almost overnight (Andriessen 2002).

A human capital approach to intellectual capital needs to take into account three considerations (Reinhardt *et al.* 2001). First, that economic theory has not dealt adequately with the problem of knowledge creation (Machlup 1984). Secondly, human capital flows and their transformations are predominantly discussed from an individual or organisational learning perspective. Lastly, there is a distinction between human embodied knowledge (human capital) and non-embodied knowledge (organisational capital).

A closely related aspect of human capital is social capital. This concept has its roots in community studies examining the functioning of city neighbourhoods and the relationships inherent in the development of young children. In an organisational context, this concept is based on the premise that a firm's capabilities are best developed through cooperating individuals. It has its organisational origin in Barnard's (1956) conception of an organisation as a cooperative entity made up predominantly of relationships. This view has resulted in the notion of organisations as social communities (Kogut and Zander 1996; Nahapiet and Ghoshal 1998). There are intrinsically three dimensions to social capital:

● *structural dimension* showing the linkages and connections between actors such as the density and hierarchy of networks;

- *relational dimension* that provides the history of interactions between individuals resulting in certain levels of trust, norms and expectations;
- *cognitive dimension* that leads to shared meanings, interpretations, mental models and alignment of views.

Critical thinking and reflection

Given the diversity of individual personalities in a team, what measures could you take to maintain or increase your team's social capital? For example, how would you get more introverted colleagues to develop social networks across and outside your organisation? In addition, how could you promote shared understanding of problems and alignment of views? How would you gauge whether the level of your team's social capital has risen or decreased from one year to the next?

Organisational capital

The roots of the concept of organisational capital lie in research exploring ways of increasing efficiencies in organisations where employee effort was considered to be sub-optimal (Tomer 1987). Hence, organisational capital has been seen as an extension of human capital, as it contains both organisational and behavioural variables (Reinhardt *et al.* 2001). It is based on the level of knowledge sharing, cooperative effort and conflict resolution within organisations.

Tomer (1998) identified two types of organisational capital: a pure form (such as its organisational structure) and a hybrid form (embodied in individuals through investment in activities such as socialisation). The assumption underlying this concept is that investment in organisational capital will lead to a range of benefits in terms of worker productivity. The types of intervention may include (Tomer 1987):

- changing formal and informal relationships and patterns of activity within the organisation;
- changing certain attributes key to organisational effectiveness;
- developing information to match the optimal worker to a given situation.

It is clear that the literature on organisational capital is closely linked with the concept of structural capital within the intellectual capital literature. However, there is a danger of the hybrid conception of organisational capital creeping into intellectual capital frameworks and resulting in confusion between human and organisational capital.

Intellectual property and smart patents

The collective experience, skills and general know how of a firm lead to the development of intellectual assets. These intellectual assets may be in the form of documents, drawings, software programs, data, inventions and processes (Sullivan 1998). As these explicit assets are codified, tangible or contain physical descriptions of a firm's knowledge and processes, a firm has the right to claim ownership to this intellectual property in the form of patents, copyrights, trademarks and trade secrets. In an increasingly knowledge-based economy, strategic management of intellectual property may well lead to competitive advantage where value is generated from protecting the knowledge, skills, processes and ideas of a firm. It can no longer be left purely as a technical or legal imperative in successful organisations.

Patents are a common form of intellectual property and provide a high level of protection. They can enable firms to gather valuable sources of revenue through licensing agreements. In the US, there has been a marked growth in software patents and, since 1998, a 'method of doing business (MDB)' has been given the right to be patented under case law. Hence, a firm can provide an effective barrier to entry if it owns a software patent and an MDB patent for at least the twenty-year life of the patent (Lang 2001). However, the real life of patents is typically 15–17 years from the original date of application. MDB patents can include information systems, investment systems, e-commerce systems, insurance systems and training methods. Maxwell (2002) shows that the life of the patent can be extended almost indefinitely by using a smart patent in the form of a continuation patent, as shown in Table 3.2. This has the benefit of rewarding honest innovation and discouraging competitors who may try to exploit a patent's weakness.

The process of securing a patent involves filing a patent application at a Patent Office. The proposed patent undergoes an 'examination period' often lasting a few years where the examiner enters into a dialogue with the inventor about the precise language to be used in the patent. Once the patent is issued, it has a life of twenty years. However, if the inventor files an application for a continuation patent (child of the original patent) before the original patent (parent) issues, the examination period for the patent is extended to allow the inventor to make changes that may take into account competitor offerings. This process can be continued for generations, creating grandchildren patents and so on where each continuation patent is filed just before its parent issues (Maxwell 2002), as shown in Figure 3.5.

Copyright is primarily concerned with the rights to the owner in the distribution medium to prevent infringements on copying, distributing, performing or displaying material. It protects the original works for a longer period of 100 years. In the case of the creator's death, copyright lasts for 70 years. However, in our age of digital networks, because of the ease of distribution and the minimal cost of making perfect copies on digital printers, there is a pertinent threat to copyright unless digital information can be encrypted.

Table 3.2 **Characteristics of patents and continuation patents**

Patent	*Continuation patent*
• Description of invention	• Allows changes to original patent
• Citations of 'prior art'	• Can add new 'claims'
• Related publications and patents	• Can add newly discovered 'prior art'
• 'Claims' – descriptions of exclusive rights of patent holder	• Can be modified taking into account competitor's product

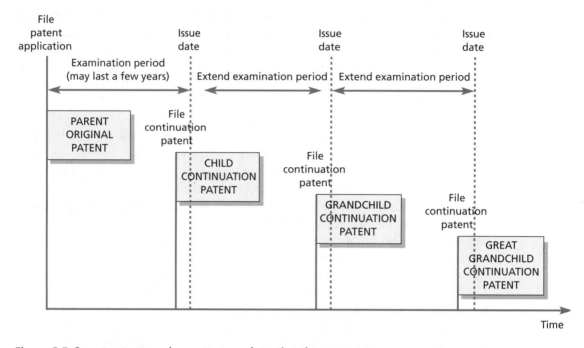

Figure 3.5 **Smart patents: using patents and continual patents**

Ignoring or mismanaging intellectual property rights can have disastrous results for firms. One example illustrating the minefield of intellectual property rights is the case of Kodak in 1975. Polaroid had erected vast patent barriers in the high-growth instant camera market. Kodak was well aware of these patents but it was advised by its lawyers that they were invalid. Kodak took a calculated risk but was found to have infringed Polaroid's patents soon after it launched a line of instant cameras and films. Kodak was ordered to pay $925 million in damages to Polaroid, shut down its manufacturing plant and retrieve the 16 million cameras sold to consumers between 1976 and 1985 (Rivette and Kline 2000). This example illustrates the strategic importance of intellectual capital and how it can result in the potential demise of a company.

There can be considerable differences in laws on intellectual property and their enforcement in countries worldwide. There have been attempts by the World Trade Organization to promote harmonisation of intellectual property laws. In 1995 the WTO negotiated an agreement on Trade Related Aspects of Intellectual Property Rights. This agreement establishes the right of member states to impose sanctions on TRIP signatories that do not fulfil their obligations under TRIPS. It is interesting to note that TRIPS protects computer programs as literary works under the Berne Convention.

Critical thinking and reflection

What might you consider patenting in your organisation? How would you decide on the strategic importance of a patent? How would you scan the competitive environment to ensure that your intellectual property rights were not being infringed? From your experience, how effective do you find patents as a barrier to entry for competitors?

FInancial reporting of intellectual capital

The basic problem for international accounting bodies has been how one captures the present value of a highly volatile asset, namely, intellectual capital. Conventional reporting methods are not sufficiently responsive and may lead to risky investments from unreliable reports. This risk could lead to reduced economic growth resulting from the increased cost of capital and reduced liquidity in the markets. The Financial Accounting Standards Board (FASB) has got together with a number of international accounting bodies to take action. They have concluded that the measurement of financial instruments such as intangible assets needs to be tackled with the notion of fair value (Kossovsky 2002). The FASB (1999) describes fair value as:

> *'an estimate of the price an entity would have realized if it had sold an asset or paid if it had been relieved of a liability on the reporting date in an arm's-length exchange motivated by normal business conditions.'*

The European Commission (2000) describes fair value as:

1 *a market value, for those items for which a reliable market can readily be identified. Where a market value is not readily identifiable for an item but can be identified for its components, the market value of that item may be derived from that of its components; or*

2 *the value resulting from establishing valuation models and techniques, for those items for which a reliable market cannot be readily identified. Such valuation models and techniques should ensure a reasonable approximation of the market value.*

It is worthy of note that traditional intangibles such as brand equity, patents and goodwill could not be reported in financial statements until recently unless they met strict recognition criteria (International Accounting Standards Committee (IASC) 1998; International Federation of Accountants (IFAC) 1998). In these circumstances, it is not surprising that more novel forms of intangibles such as customer loyalty, staff competences and computer systems have not received the recognition they merit. There may be a sea change in the pipeline as the Securities and Exchange Commission in the US has indicated that it would like to see an intellectual capital supplement to companies' annual accounts.

Intellectual capital as a narrative

If one accepts that the aim of measurement of intellectual capital is to grasp the knowledge management processes that underlie this unstable entity, our focus needs to be directed to a qualitative understanding of this term. Roos *et al.* (1997) suggest the notion of 'intellectual capital as a language for thinking, talking and doing something about the drivers of companies' future earnings'. Intellectual capital comprises relationships with customers and partners, innovation efforts, company infrastructure and the knowledge skills of organisational members. In this sense, knowledge may be usefully presented and interpreted in the form of a narrative (Mouritsen *et al.* 2002). This

insight was gained from the experience of Danish firms working to develop intellectual capital statements. They found the notion of knowledge as a narrative most useful
when it was centred around the 'value to a user'.

A narrative is seen as a plot of a certain phenomenon that leads one through a
sequence of events and highlights the linkages between the events. The narrative may
highlight 'positive' things that happen along the way as well as 'problems and pitfalls'
to allow the narrative to succeed (Boland and Schultze 1996; Czarniawska 1997). A
narrative is more than a story and provides a real-life example of the trials and tribula-
tions of an organisation. It is deeply embedded in the culture and identity of the firm
and presents the raison d'être of its decisions, processes and activities (Mouritsen *et al.*
2002). To complement the notion of knowledge as 'value to the user', the strategy for
managing knowledge is organised around a knowledge narrative that explains the relevance of a firm's knowledge to a group of users. Mouritsen *et al.* (2002) suggest three
elements to a narrative:

- a product/service;
- an account of value to user;
- presentation of firm's 'intellectual production function'.

In each of the cases examined, a simplistic map is provided of the intellectual capital
statement containing the knowledge narrative or value proposition, management challenges, efforts and indicators, as shown in the example in Figure 3.6.

The difficulty in this approach arises where one may have multiple potentially
conflicting value propositions in a large organisation engaged in a highly turbulent environment where the simplicity of these maps may not provide the necessary
value to the user nor aid investors in their decision making. Also, how much would
the knowledge narrative reveal about the firm's potential with new and challenging

Figure 3.6 **Example illustrating framework for key components of an intellectual
capital statement** (adapted from Mouritsen *et al.* 2002)

environments rather than a historical review of the past year? Are there likely to be biases in this approach where the positive aspects of the narrative are embellished and the negative aspects are played down or even not reported at all? Who would take on the role of the independent storyteller and narrator of the firm's knowledge narrative? How could one determine the reliability of the narrative?

Knowledge auditing in practice

It has been argued that traditional tools of financial reporting are losing relevance in a world where the most valuable assets are information, expertise, technology and skill (Svieby 1997). The problem for companies is how they can identify these elusive knowledge assets when they often don't know what they know. There has been a tendency in earlier attempts at mapping knowledge assets to concentrate on the explicit knowledge and produce long inventories that are difficult to use. An important characteristic of any knowledge audit is that it needs to capture the explicit as well as the more dynamic tacit knowledge within organisations.

From consultancy experience in knowledge management, Truch (2001) has proposed a 'value-based knowledge management' approach to auditing a firm's intellectual capital based primarily on an information-processing perspective. He suggests that the evaluation of knowledge assets is most effective when linked to a firm's key processes and aligned to its strategic development. This approach comprises three stages, as shown in Figure 3.7:

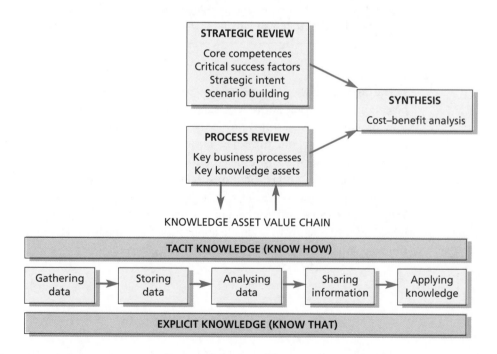

Figure 3.7 **Process of knowledge auditing** (adapted from Truch 2001)

1 *Strategic review.* This comprises a top-down review of business strategy including the critical success factors as well as the core competences required for success in the business. The stage may include capturing the strategic intent of the senior managers and developing potential scenarios for the future.

2 *Process review.* This comprises a bottom-up identification of key business processes and the knowledge assets they produce in terms of tacit and explicit knowledge. Existing process maps formed as part of a quality assurance system such as ISO 9000 can be used to map key business processes. Each knowledge asset is analysed further in terms of the 'knowledge value chain', as shown in Figure 3.7. This allows a better understanding of the tacit and explicit assets which may follow different but inter-linked value chains. A knowledge inventory of tacit and explicit knowledge is developed at this stage.

3 *Synthesis.* This comprises of an evaluation of the knowledge inventory (Stage 2) in the context of the core competences and critical success factors (Stage 1) and conducting a cost–benefit analysis of current and potential knowledge assets.

Critical thinking and reflection

Imagine you were asked to produce an intellectual capital account for your organisation. How would you go about reporting such an account in practice? What forms of data collection would you adopt? How cost intensive is your approach? How far could your intellectual capital accounts be used for external reporting? How valuable do you think shareholders would consider these accounts to be over and above conventional financial reporting and material available through other sources such as the internet? How could you guard against potential filtering of bad news from senior executives in such accounts?

During the synthesis stage, Truch (2001) suggests that a cost–benefit analysis can be conducted on each knowledge asset by identifying the additional value or leverage they provide to key business processes. The value may be derived from new synergies in areas such as revenue from new business opportunities, new markets and efficiency gains. In contrast, the cost of each knowledge asset needs to consider factors such as training people, IT infrastructure, special software, external data, expert consultants and any other resources. Each knowledge asset can then be plotted on a 2 × 2 grid of value of knowledge asset (or benefit) against cost of knowledge asset (high or low). This would allow decisions to be made about future knowledge investments or divestments from a company's knowledge portfolio.

Infosys (India)

Kris Gopalakrishnan put the phone down after a final word with Mark Hunter, the founder and former Chairman of Axon.[1] The £407m acquisition of Axon had fallen through to a higher bidder. Mr Gopalakrishnan paused and reflected on Infosys' current and future strategy; organic growth or growth through acquisitions on the international stage.

Axon represented the first attempt at a foreign takeover by Infosys. Both companies were involved in implementing back-office functions designed by SAP. There were potential overlaps between the two businesses and this opportunity signified greater exposure to the UK market. The rationale behind the acquisition was similar to that of other large players in the Indian domestic market, developing reputable names in the global market. Recently, Tata had acquired Land Rover for £1.1bn and Apeejay Surendra had acquired Typhoo for £80m.[2]

Mr Gopalakrishnan was one of seven engineers to set up Infosys in 1981. From its inception it relied heavily on overseas business. It recruited many early employees from the Indian Institute of Technology in Chennai and trained them in proprietary software systems linked to a variety of industries including banking, retail and telecommunication.

Soon Infosys recognised that its knowledge and expertise was its most valuable resource and started to encourage employees to share their knowledge with one another. In 1992 Infosys embarked on the development of the Body of Knowledge (BoK)[3] to allow employees to share their on-the-job learning on software development, methodologies, new technologies and cultural tips on living abroad. However, there were difficulties in getting people to share their precious knowledge to these corporate repositories. Contribution rates were low. Initial attempts were made to link rewards with knowledge sharing. But early results were not encouraging.

Learning was central to all Infosys' operations. The Education & Research Department instigated a wide variety of induction and training courses to meet the diverse training needs of employees. In 1996 Infosys introduced a corporate intranet named Sparsh which incorporated a central repository as well as virtual classrooms and discussion forums. The virtual classrooms and e-learning interventions allowed employees to learn at their own rate and increased the efficiency of training delivery. People could log on to a wide spectrum of e-learning modules and have access to online tutors when it suited them.

To encourage greater sharing of knowledge on projects, Infosys instituted an organisation-wide system named 'Process Assets'. This was owned by project managers who had responsibility for reporting on project learning at the conclusion of projects. The emphasis was more on procedural rather than experiential knowledge. An online library gave employees access to explicit knowledge and ideas from outside the firm in the form of trade magazines and journals relevant to their work. An expertise database ('Yellow Pages') was set up to help employees find one another with the necessary expertise particularly in a large and dispersed firm.

By 1999 many of these technological interventions were seen as piecemeal and there was a pressing need to develop a more coherent approach to managing knowledge at Infosys that would allow it to leverage its learning and knowledge. Infosys set up a steering committee and a dedicated knowledge management group of nine employees to provide oversight over cultural, leadership and technological elements that would allow knowledge to be managed effectively. There was no blueprint on how to go about doing this but senior executives recognised the importance of this venture in the firm's survival.

The initial deliberations of the new KM group centred around how best to re-use existing knowledge particularly in highly competitive markets. Infosys' generic strategy was one of cost leadership where price of services was its major selling point and there was little room for error. This thinking led to the introduction of a new knowledge portal, KShop, in 2000. The idea behind the KShop was to provide a space to create, disseminate and re-use knowledge. This central repository was sub-divided into four core areas: people, content, process and technology. Each department was encouraged to contribute their knowledge to these areas and asked to specify their knowledge along these dimensions:

- knowledge area – one of 2000 areas;
- the nature of knowledge: project learning, publications, case studies, industry knowledge (trends, key players, regulatory frameworks), consultancy reports and so on;
- target audience: software programmers, managers, directors and so on;
- source of knowledge: internal or external.

Each 'knowledge asset' was screened to ensure there was no infringement of intellectual property rights particularly from external sources. The KM Steering Committee soon realised that there were two high order levels of knowledge within Infosys: domain-specific knowledge relating to particular industries, and technological knowledge relating to software engineering. They set up two internal consultancy groups to help facilitate the creation and sharing of this knowledge: the 'Domain Competency Group' with industry-specific knowledge, and the 'Software Engineering & Technology Laboratories' with specific technical knowledge.

However, contribution rates to KShop were still low. In 2001 the steering committee introduced a reward system named Knowledge Currency Units (KCUs) for employees to contribute to KShop as well as review content in terms of its quality. The contributions to KShop rose significantly as KCUs were linked to monetary rewards. An unforeseen consequence of the reward system was that employees saw KCUs as a way of making money rather than openly sharing their knowledge. The system was adapted with a rating scale to focus more on the usefulness of the contributions to actual users to determine rewards. By 2006 more than 4,000 'knowledge assets' were downloaded from KShop each day.

Mr Nilekani, another co-founder of Infosys, recognised the firm had three unique selling points[4] to leverage their global outsourcing delivery model.[5] The first was to provide cost-effective, front-office consultancy services with technological solutions directly to boardrooms.[6] The second was to integrate its non-Indian workforce as it expands its reach to new countries. For example, Infosys had acquired an IT unit of 300 staff in Australia. And last, to re-organise itself into vertical lines of business activity with staff who understand each line of business and can provide appropriate technological solutions to changing needs and demands.

In 2006 Infosys launched its Global Talent Programme[7] to recruit and train UK and US graduates in India prior to them operating in their home countries. This allowed Infosys to present a local face when dealing with clients on business processes and their information systems. This is a shift away from purely back-office functions to more strategic consultancy roles where Infosys can show clients how they can transform their businesses using technological solutions. This drive for international recruitment is also to redress the imbalance of only 3 per cent of Infosys' employees being non-Indian. The challenge is to retain these international recruits rather than grooming them only to finding them poached by rival competitors. There is additional rivalry from international competitors, as firms such as IBM and Microsoft look at setting low-cost bases in India with highly educated workforces.

But now with the global economic downturn, Mr Gopalakrishnan is reconsidering the strategic focus and direction of Infosys; growth through acquisition of cheap market assets or consolidation of Infosys' market position. He has no plans for any lay-offs but is considering how far to honour current recruitment goals above Infosys' 100,000 workforce.[8] He decides to reflect on the matter over lunch.

References

1 Dunkley, J. (2008) 'Axon leaps as Infosys confirms £407m deal', *Daily Telegraph*, London: 4.

2 Hawkes, S. (2008) 'Infosys swoops for British IT company as Indian acquisition drive gathers pace', *The Times*, London: 37.

3 Indu, P. (2006) 'Infosys' knowledge management initiatives', ICFAI Center for Management Research, Cranfield University, UK, ECCH: 1–14

4 Merchant, K. (2004) 'Golden statues mark progress: Asian Case Study – Infosys', *Financial Times*, London: 5.

5 Hell, I. (2005) 'The interview: Narayana Murthy – "The power of money is to give it away": Infosys' yogi has a mantra for our times', *The Independent on Sunday*, London: 4.

6 Leahy, J. (2007) 'Infosys no longer the big boys' fixer. Company offers the kind of strategic consulting services once the preserve of IBM and Accenture', *Financial Times*: 14.

7 Leahy, J. (2006) 'Programmers' passage to India. Recruitment: Infosys is bringing western graduates to Mysore in a reversal of the usual pattern of outsourcing', *Financial Times*, London: 10.

8 Leahy, J. (2009) "Worst I have seen", says Infosys chief', *Financial Times*, London: 3.

Questions

1 Discuss critically Infosys' current and future strategy. What advice would you give Kris Gopalakrishnan?

2 KShop has resulted in information overload among staff. What operational measures would you suggest to overcome such challenges?

3 If Infosys is committed to providing strategic consulting services internationally, what cultural changes would you recommend over and above those currently instigated?

Summary

This chapter has elaborated five main themes:

1 An international consensus among firms, governments and regulatory bodies that intellectual capital is the critical factor in future growth and prosperity.

2 Traditional financial measures cannot capture the richness and diversity of intellectual capital within an organisation.

3 Intellectual capital frameworks used in practice tend to centre around the notions of human capital, organisational capital and customer capital.

4 Increased importance of firms to manage their intellectual property strategically.

5 The use of narratives for reporting intellectual capital accounts.

Questions for further thought

1 David Bowie has undergone several transformations from Ziggy Stardust to the Thin White Duke over three decades in the music industry. The capital markets have seen considerable value in his talents. He became the first person in the music industry to float a bond issue for a total cost of $50 million. The entire issue was sold within one hour. Can we consider David Bowie's talents as intellectual capital? How would you have reliably valued his talents earlier in his life when he was Ziggy Stardust?

2 How does one identify an emerging knowledge process and add a value to it when one may not know whether it will contribute to the future success of an organisation or not? Is developing scenarios enough?

3 What are the likely positive and negative consequences of 'method of doing business' patents? How would patent offices be able to distinguish between two MDB patents such as toasting a piece of bread?

4 How could you determine the shelf life of intellectual capital? For example, is any attempt to measure intellectual capital valid for only three months?

5 How can we reliably account for the depreciation in intellectual assets in a firm?

6 How can the manipulation of intangible assets be curtailed?

7 What are the dangers of high levels of social capital within an organisation?

8 Are intellectual capital accounts likely to increase spurious reporting and financial engineering of company accounts?

9 What are the advantages and disadvantages of an international agreement on intellectual capital accounts led by the WTO or OECD?

10 If an intellectual capital narrative is based on a company's culture and values, how can an analyst make meaningful comparisons between firms in the same industry or other industries?

Further reading

1 Stewart (1997) provides a well-researched and readable book on intellectual capital.

2 Edvinsson and Malone (1997) shows how intellectual capital was first used in Skandia's annual report and how the 'Skandia Navigator' was developed for managing a firm's intellectual capital.

References

Andriessen, D. (2002) 'Weightless wealth: Four modifications to standard IC theory', *Journal of Intellectual Capital*, 2(3), 204–214.

Barnard, C. I. (1956) *The Functions of the Executive*, Harvard University Press, Cambridge, MA.

Becker, G. S. (1964) *Human Capital*, University of Chicago Press, Chicago.

Bertels, T. and Savage, C. M. (1998) 'Tough questions on knowledge measurement', *Knowing in Firms. Understanding, Managing and Measuring Knowledge*, G. von Krough, J. Roos and D. Kleine, eds, Sage, London.

Boland, R. J. and Schultze, U. (1996) 'Narrating accountability: Cognition and the production of the accountable self', *Accountability. Power, Ethos and the Technologies of Managing*, R. Munro and J. Mouritsen, eds, Thomson Business Press, London.

Boudreau, J. W. and Ramstad, P. M. (1997) 'Measuring intellectual capital: Learning from financial history', *Human Resource Management*, 36(3), 343–56.

Brooking, A. (1996) *Intellectual Capital*, Thomson Business Press, London.

Czarniawska, B. (1997) *Narrating the Organization: Dramas of Institutional Identity*, University of Chicago Press, Chicago.

Danish Confederation of Trade Unions (1999) 'Your knowledge – can you book it?', *International Symposium Measuring and Reporting Intellectual Capital: Experiences, Issues and Prospects*, Amsterdam.

Davenport, T. H. and Prusak, L. (1998) *Working Knowledge: How Organizations Manage What They Know*, Harvard Business School Press, Boston, MA.

Eccles, R. and Nohria, N. (1992) *Beyond the Hype: Rediscovering the Essence of Management*, Harvard Business School Press, Cambridge, MA.

Edvinsson, L. and Malone, M. S. (1997) *Intellectual Capital: Realizing Your Company's True Value by Finding its Hidden Brainpower*, Judy Piatkus (Publishers) Ltd, London.

European Commission (2000) *Proposal for a Directive of the European Parliament and the Council amending Directives 78/660/EEC as regards the valuation rules for the annual and consolidated accounts of certain types of companies*, 24 February.

FASB (1999) 'Preliminary views on major issues related to reporting financial instruments and certain related assets and liabilities at fair value', *Financial Accounting*, Series No. 204–B (December 14).

Hamel, G. and Prahalad, C. K. (1994) *Competing for the Future*, Harvard Business School Press, Boston, MA.

International Accounting Standards Committee (IASC) (1998) *IAS 38 Intangible Assets*, International Accounting Standards Committee, London.

International Federation of Accountants (IFAC) (1998) *The Measurement and Management of Intellectual Capital: An Introduction*, International Federation of Accountants (IFAC), New York.

Kaplan, R. S. and Norton, D. P. (1992) 'The balanced scorecard as a strategic management system', *Harvard Business Review*, 70(1), 71–9.

Kogut, B. and Zander, U. (1996) 'What firms do? Coordination, identity and learning', *Organization Science*, 7, 502–518.

Kossovsky, N. (2002) 'Fair value of intellectual property', *Journal of Intellectual Capital*, 3(1), 62–70.

Lang, J. C. (2001) 'Managerial concerns in knowledge management', *Journal of Knowledge Management*, 5(1), 43–57.

Lowendahl, B. (1997) *Strategic Management of Professional Service Firms*, Handelshojskolens Forlag, Copenhagen.

Machlup, F. (1984) *Knowledge: Its Creation, Distribution, and Economic Significance: Vol. 3. The Economics of Information and Human Capital*, Princeton University Press, Princeton.

Maxwell, R. (2002) 'Smart patents: Is your intellectual capital at risk?', *Harvard Business Review*, March/April, 18–19.

Morgan, J. (1992) 'Human resource information: A strategic tool', *Strategies for Human Resource Management*, M. Armstrong, ed., Kogan Page, London.

Mouritsen, J., Bukh, P. N., Larsen, H. T. and Johansen, M. R. (2002) 'Developing and managing knowledge through intellectual capital statements', *Journal of Intellectual Capital*, 3(1), 10–29.

Nahapiet, J. and Ghoshal, S. (1998) 'Social capital, intellectual capital, and the organizational advantage', *Academy of Management Review*, 23(2), 242–66.

OECD (1999) 'Guidelines and instructions for OECD symposium', *International Symposium Measuring and Reporting Intellectual Capital: Experiences, Issues and Prospects*, Amsterdam.

Petrash, G. (1996) 'Dow's journey to a knowledge value management culture', *European Management Journal*, 14(4), 365–73 reprinted with permission from Elsevier.

Reinhardt, R., Bournemann, M., Pawlowsky, P. and Schneider, U. (2001) *Intellectual Capital and Knowledge Management: Perspectives on Measuring Knowledge*, M. Dierkes, A. B. Antal, J. Child and I. Nanaka, eds, Oxford University Press, Oxford, 794–820.

Rivette, K. G. and Kline, D. (2000) 'Discovering new value in intellectual property', *Harvard Business Review*, 78(1), 54–66.

Roos, J., Roos, G., Edvinsson, L. and Dragonetti, N. C. (1997) *Intellectual Capital: Navigating in the New Business Landscape*, Macmillan Business, Houndsmills.

Schultz, T. W. (1961) 'Investment in human capital', *American Economic Review*, 51(1), 1–17.

Skyrme, D. J. and Amidon, D. M. (1997) *Creating the Knowledge-based Business*, Business Intelligence, London.

Smith, T. (1992) *Accounting for Growth*, Century Business Books, London.

Stewart, T. A. (1997) *Intellectual Capital: The New Wealth of Organizations*, Doubleday/Currency, New York.

Sullivan, P. H. (1998) *Profiting from Intellectual Capital: Extracting Value from Innovation*, Wiley, London.

Svieby, K. (1997) *The New Organizational Wealth: Managing and Measuring Knowledge-based Assets*, Berrett-Koehler, San Francisco.

Tobin, J. (1969) 'A general equilibrium approach to monetary theory', *Journal of Money, Credit and Banking*, 1, 15–29.

Tomer, J. F. (1987) *Organizational Capital: The Path to Higher Productivity and Wellbeing*, Praeger, New York.

Tomer, J. F. (1998) 'Organizational capital and joining-up: Linking the individual to the organization and to society', *Human Relations*, 51, 825–46.

Truch, E. (2001) 'Knowledge management: Auditing and reporting intellectual capital', *Journal of General Management*, 26(3), 26–40.

Chapter 4

Strategic management perspectives

Learning outcomes

After completing this chapter the reader should be able to:

- explain the differences between the industrial organisation tradition and the institutionalist perspective in strategic thinking;
- understand the contribution of the resource-based view and the knowledge-based view of the firm to strategic management;
- discuss the development of IS strategy and its influence on knowledge management strategies;
- apply different knowledge management strategies appropriately to different contexts.

Management issues

The use and application of knowledge management systems implies these questions for managers:

- How far do you plan a knowledge management strategy or do you allow it to emerge through the everyday processes of organisational learning?
- What are the core competences of your organisation and how do you exploit them for competitive advantage?
- How do you manage the conflicting interests of the IS/IT department and HR department to develop a coherent knowledge management strategy?

Links to other chapters

Chapter 5   provides an insight into organisational learning that contributes to our current understanding of knowledge management strategies as a flux between codification (exploitation) and personalisation (exploration) strategies.

Chapter 7   describes many of the technology tools used for sharing and storing knowledge inherent in many KM strategies.

Chapter 8   considers the KM systems that may be necessary to support codification strategies.

Chapter 10   assesses the human resource issues necessary to implement a successful KM strategy.

A hunger for knowledge is China's real secret weapon   FT

On a flight last week from San Francisco to Beijing I was seated next to a bright young Chinese software engineer, currently employed in Silicon Valley. Somewhere over the Bering Sea, conversation turned to the way some countries have a knack for certain types of business. Thus Italy does luxury better than anyone. Japan is the master of quality. America, we decided, has a gift for the new.

'And what of China?' I asked. 'At what do Chinese companies excel?'

'Learning,' came the unhesitating reply.

A few days spent at the Beijing office of Lenovo, China's largest personal computer maker, confirmed the wisdom of this off-the-cuff remark. Forget the notion that China's competitive advantage lies only in cheap labour and protectionist trade policies, though these certainly play a part. The PCs Lenovo builds for the Chinese market are every bit as sleek and sexy as the best that Sony, Hewlett-Packard or Toshiba can offer. The Dell laptop I was toting looked overweight and frumpy by comparison.

With the acquisition earlier this year of IBM's PC division, Lenovo is now preparing to step on to the world stage. Will the acquisition prove successful? More on that another day. For now, suffice to say that the deal was driven not only by a hunger for scale but also by a desire among Lenovo's Chinese executives to keep climbing the learning curve as fast as humanely possible.

There is ambition, to be sure. But there is also a 'we can really learn from these people' enthusiasm that is rarely in evidence among US or European acquirers.

Now, the idea that the ability to learn can be a source of competitive advantage is nothing new. Management researchers Chris Argyris and Donald Schon started writing about 'organisational learning' in the 1970s. Peter Senge's *The Fifth Discipline*, one of the management blockbusters of the early 1990s, was an influential guide to creating companies that learn fast and embrace change.

These days, however, you don't hear much about the topic. Most managers in the US and Europe seemed to lose interest in the organisational learning agenda somewhere around 2001.

There were a couple of reasons for this. First, recession struck. The focus in most executive suites moved from growth and development to cost-cutting and survival. Some of the easiest budgets to cut were those labelled 'training' and 'organisational development'. Since there was no immediate effect on the business, a dollar trimmed from the training budget was a dollar added to the bottom line.

Second, the organisational learning movement took a wrong turn. A quick browse through the website of the Society for Organizational Learning (www.solonline.org) reveals that much of what gets written on the topic in the US these days has a distinctly New Age feel.

'Virtually all indigenous or native cultures have regarded nature or the universe or Mother Earth as the ultimate teacher. At few points in history has the need to rediscover this teacher been greater,' write Prof Senge and a triumvirate of organisational learning luminaries in *Presence: An Exploration of Profound Change*, published last month.

Overall, the movement has adopted an agenda that has less to do with organisational effectiveness and more to do with personal growth and social salvation. These are noble objectives – important, even. British management guru Charles Handy addresses many of the same themes, laced with his own peculiar brand of folksiness.

But it is easy to see why these ideas fail to generate much enthusiasm in today's execution-oriented boardrooms. Asked to stake your business career on either Jack Welch or Mother Earth as ultimate teacher, which would you choose?

Back in Beijing, there was plenty of talk of profound change, but not of the hippy-dippy variety. The management style at Lenovo is decisive, results-oriented and fiercely competitive. There is no time for ersatz philosophy. The desire to learn arises instead from a potent mix of greed and fear, laced with considerable intelligence and a sprinkling of humility. It is the classic entrepreneurial cocktail.

Is the Confucian respect for education also at work, as some amateur Sinologists have claimed? Will the gift for learning demonstrated by China's entrepreneurs extend beyond mimicry of best practice to world-beating innovation? Will Beijing-based companies deal any better than their rivals in Berlin or Buffalo with the management problems that come with international scale? A few days in Beijing hardly qualifies me to judge. But the rate of progress demonstrated by the likes of Lenovo, Haier (in white goods) and Sina (in online media) already demands serious attention. Contrary to what you might expect, these companies have prospered in spite of, not because of, China's economic system. The flair for learning and adaptation is striking.

In the 1980s, remember, western companies turned back the tide of imports from Japan by learning from the Japanese approach to quality.

The management tools that arose in this period – Total Quality Management, Lean Production and, latterly, Six Sigma – have transformed the way many companies are run.

Learning to learn as fast as the new breed of entrepreneurial Chinese companies may turn out to be equally important in the decade to come.

And what of my friend, the Chinese software engineer? He is planning to relocate from Silicon Valley to Beijing to start a company – taking with him everything he has learned.

Source: from A hunger for knowledge is China's real secret weapon, *The Financial Times*, 05/10/2005, p. 12 (London, S.), copyright © The Financial Times Ltd.

Questions

1 How can learning increase the competitive advantage of Chinese firms?

2 What issues do firms need to consider when adapting to their external environment?

3 What is important when 'learning to learn'?

Introduction

The underlying assumption within the knowledge management literature is that actions arising from KM practices will result in some form of competitive advantage. But how is this likely to happen? One of the implications is that firms may need some form of knowledge management strategy to achieve these goals. But what is the nature of a KM strategy and how does it change over time? The two dominant pillars of knowledge management are technology and human resource considerations. What are the likely configurations of technology and human aspects to make such strategies effective? The current situation is unclear as the literature on KM strategy is relatively young and has been developing in the last few years.

An important starting point is to explore how KM strategies may relate to a firm's business strategy. Similar to philosophical perspectives, there is a diverse range of viewpoints and schools of thought on the nature of strategy and competitive change. This chapters begins by exploring the meaning of strategy in terms of deliberate and emergent strategies as our goals and plans may not be realised as expected. Then three dominant schools of strategic thought are examined showing their theoretical and economic foundations. These schools are the industrial organisation tradition, excellence and turnaround literature, and the institutionalist perspective. In the last decade, this perspective has developed greater prominence as scholars have explored the resource-based view (RBV) and knowledge-based view of the firm. A number of recent publications have explored the notion of a 'knowledge management strategy' and the resulting debates and arguments are considered towards the end of the chapter. There is a distinction between codification strategies which are technology led and innovation strategies that are people led. It is not surprising that this can give rise to confusion in the KM literatures where articles are either technology-oriented or human-resource oriented. Both types of literature are important in our understanding of the interplay between them in KM strategies.

Strategic management: schools of thought

What is a strategy? Many people may say it is a plan of action linked to achieving one's goals. The assumption is that in any given situation, be it a football match, a war between nations or a product launch, the strategy or plan will deliver the desired outcomes. However, it does not often happen that the intended or deliberate strategy becomes the realised strategy. There may be some aspects of the strategy or plan that are unrealised and get overlooked (or swept under the carpet!). The notion of strategy as a plan gives much greater power to those in authority such as managers and executives to determine the effective plan/strategy for the organisation. But how often do strategies achieve corporate goals and visions? The problem is that we live in dynamic environments prone to change where sudden economic forces, competitor behaviour and maybe even loss of key players can require a response from organisations that is at odds with the intended strategy.

On the other hand, if you ask a group of people about their firm's strategy in the past year or five years, they will tend to describe a pattern of actions and behaviours which have converged over time into a certain consistency. This is referred to as an 'emergent strategy' and is likely to have arisen through the firm's learning over time (Mintzberg and Waters 1985). The notion of strategy as a plan is more about control whereas a pattern is more about learning. In reality, it is likely that executives will respond to changing circumstances with a mixture of these two notions, as shown in Figure 4.1.

The dominant school of thought in strategic management treats strategy as a plan and is known as the 'industrial organisation' or microeconomic tradition. In contrast, an alternative school of thought is concerned with the dynamics of competitive processes and the contribution of learning and uncertainty in strategy. This school is referred to as the institutionalist perspective. A new strategy literature developed in the 1980s in response to the Japanese threat to the west (see Chapter 8 on drivers of KM systems) became known as the 'excellence and turnaround' school of thought in strategy. This school was high on generic recipes and prescriptions but relatively low on empirical foundations. Nevertheless, the excellence and turnaround movement has had considerable influence on senior management thinking on strategy.

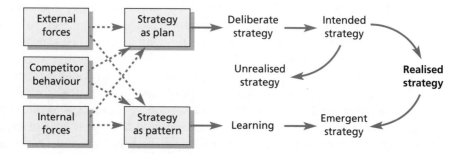

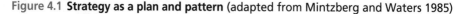

Figure 4.1 **Strategy as a plan and pattern** (adapted from Mintzberg and Waters 1985)

Critical thinking and reflection

Reflect on the strategy in your organisation. Describe how you perceive the corporate strategy of your organisation. To what extent were you consulted in the preparation of it? In relation to your organisation, what do words such as 'mission', 'vision' and 'strategy' mean to you? How alive are those words in informing your everyday actions? How typical are your views compared with those of colleagues in the organisation? Is there any advice you would give to senior managers in the preparation of annual strategies?

Industrial organisation tradition

In the industrial organisation (IO) tradition, the relationship between the firm and industry is central. The performance of a firm is determined by the structure of the industry and its market structures. Many of the principal models about market structure and competition come from rational microeconomic theory. At its most basic level, the market is concerned with the supply and demand of goods and services and the elasticity or inelasticity of the demand curve. Ideally, firms want elastic demand curves where price falls can still lead to revenue increases. Without labouring over the intricacies of microeconomics, the market structure can lead to perfect competition (large number of buyers and sellers), a monopoly (allowing the firm with the monopoly to earn abnormal profits) or an oligopoly (competition among a few firms). The dominant form of market structure in many countries is an oligopoly where firms tend to fluctuate between intensely competitive and often unstable collusive behaviours.

The nature of competition in this school is determined by the number and relative size of firms and the barriers to entry to that market (Bain 1956). From this perspective, the raison d'être of the firm is to reduce the level of competition either by collusion, creating higher barriers to entry, greater differentiation of their products and services, or lowering costs. The intended consequence is to reduce the number of firms in the market and lead to greater profits. The notion of differentiation has its roots in Chamberlinian economics which recognises the unique capabilities of a firm, such as its know how and reputation, and tries to exploit the firm's uniqueness through its strategies (Chamberlin 1933; Pettigrew and Whipp 1991).

The industrial organisation tradition has been influenced by a design model and a planning model of strategy (Ansoff 1965; Chandler 1962; Porter 1980). In the design model, the central technique is to use a SWOT (strengths, weaknesses, opportunities and threats) analysis in order to design a unique response following the dictum that structure follows strategy (Chandler 1962). In the planning model, different generic strategies are forwarded to respond to certain market conditions (Porter 1980):

- *cost leadership* – reducing the cost of product and services relative to competitors with a drop in quality;

- *differentiation* – providing products or services which are unique or different and valued by customers;

- *focus* – providing high perceived value justifying higher prices in certain market segments such as traditional corner shops compared with supermarkets.

In the planning model, adopted by most MBA students and executives, the traditional approach to strategy is along the following rather mechanical lines (Johnson and Scholes 2002):

- Conduct a PESTEL (political, economic, social, technological, environmental and legal) analysis at a macro level within the external environment and its likely effect on the firm.

- Conduct a SWOT (internal – strengths, weaknesses; external – opportunities and threats) analysis and look at half a dozen critical success factors in a particular industry.

- Analyse the competitive environment using Porter's (1980) five-force framework exploring the threat of entry of new players, the power of buyers and suppliers, the threat of substitutes and the extent of competitive rivalry.

- Analyse the impact of the industry lifecycle such as growth markets that require strategies to fight to increase market share compared with mature markets that require strategies to maintain market share.

- Use scenario planning techniques to determine how different scenarios may affect your strategy.

- Analyse resources in terms of Porter's 'value chain analysis' where activities are isolated that have a perceived value to the customer. Linkages between different activities are seen as competitive, particularly where competitors cannot imitate them.

- Examine strategic options such as generic strategies and whether to follow different directions for strategy development such as withdrawal, consolidation, market penetration, market development, product development or diversification.

- Evaluate the strategic options and check for their suitability in terms of organisational structure and cultural fit. Use a BCG matrix (cash cows, stars, question marks and dogs linked to a plot of market share and market growth) to determine which products or services to divest or invest. Consider a strategic planning or financial control style of operation.

- Manage strategic change through forcefield analysis to identify forces for and against change and adopt suitable management styles to circumstances.

Despite the popularity of the industrial organisation tradition, it does have its shortcomings. The drawbacks of this approach include the following (Mintzberg *et al.* 1998; Pettigrew and Whipp 1991):

- Only 10 per cent of formulated strategies get implemented.

- Separating thought from action by isolating the formulation and implementation processes.

- Assuming that firms and individuals have perfect knowledge of market changes when in reality there may be considerable ignorance leading to questioning of the rationalist tenets of the microeconomic tradition.

- No real conception of competition as a process over time.

- Environments assumed to be predominantly stable.

- Detachment of management from everyday actions and processes.
- Focused more on large businesses.
- Denial of internal social and political influences on strategy.

Excellence and turnaround

With the Japanese beating US competition in terms of design features, price, reliability, speed to market and quality in the 1980s, there was an enormous need to show managers how to respond effectively to these threats. This gave rise to an extensive literature in excellence and turnaround based on a wide range of managerial remedies and recipes of successful companies (Grinyer *et al.* 1988; Peters and Waterman 1982). Many of these publications became bestsellers in airport lounges and made a considerable impact on management strategy.

In Search of Excellence (Peters and Waterman 1982) prescribed eight attributes that characterised excellent and innovative companies: 'a bias for action, close to the customer, autonomy and entrepreneurship, productivity through people, hands-on/value driven, stick to the knitting, simple form/lean staff, simultaneous loose-tight properties.' Many similar books defined half a dozen or so prescriptions for success, with amusing anecdotes to support them, and offered glib platitudes and panaceas in easy-to-read form (Newstrom 2002). They confirmed the beliefs and attitudes of the typical managers, providing them with simple lists for success where they were in control and promoting universal application of their prescriptions across different sectors and environments (Huczynski 1992). The effective management of cultural change often plays an important role in these prescriptions. In order to win hearts and minds, ordinary people are espoused to do extraordinary things thanks to the strength of corporate cultures (Peters and Waterman 1982):

> 'The top performers create a broad, uplifting, shared culture, a coherent framework within which charged-up people search for appropriate adaptations. Their ability to extract extraordinary contributions from very large numbers of people turns on the ability to create a highly valued sense of purpose. Such purpose invariably emanates from love of product, providing top-quality services, and honouring innovation and contribution from all.'

This literature continues to play a role in strategic development, particularly where managers require ideas for quick-fix solutions. For example, a recent remedy to turnaround situations suggests the following prescription for managers (Reisner 2002):

- Don't miss your moment – the importance of timing in strategic initiatives.
- Connect change initiatives to your core business.
- Don't mistake incremental improvements for strategic transformation (a call for double-loop learning?).
- Be realistic about your limits and the pace of change.

The shortcoming of this school of thought is the overemphasis on the firm and internal processes rather than on competitive changes in the external environment.

There is also often a lack of empirical evidence to support the remedies prescribed. In fact, it is hard to see how the excellence and turnaround literature has contributed to further theory development in strategic thinking. In the face of objective scientific inquiry, the remedies offer little evidence of reliability, validity, practicability and integrating with a firm's existing knowledge base (Argyris 2001). Ultimately, many of the successful companies cited as following many of these bestseller prescriptions have often declined in performance or in some cases ceased trading.

Institutionalist perspective

The institutionalist perspective draws heavily on Schumpeter's (1934; 1950) stream of microeconomics which argues against the rational and stable notions of competitive forces and the external environment. Instead, this perspective suggests that competitive forces are inherently unstable and in a continual process of 'creative destruction' (Schumpeter 1950). As one can imagine, this perspective does not sit comfortably with strategic planners following the industrial organisation form of analysis.

Institutional economics places greater emphasis on agents (individuals) and suggests that their economic relations are determined through their experience and learning over time rather than through some form of rational maximisation behaviour. In this explanation, economic activity is dynamic and is informed by social institutions that interact with agents. In turn, competition is viewed as dynamic, impermanent and a continual process informed by people's day-to-day learning. This uncertainty in competition contrasts directly with the industrial organisation tradition that treats it as a steady-state affair. For strategic planners, their rational conjectures of competition led to considerable shock waves in the 1970s when their assumptions of incremental change were severely challenged as a result of an oil crisis. Subsequently, the notion of discontinuous (uncertain) change has come into mainstream thinking and many strategic planners have tried to rationalise it through the process of scenario planning. This attempts to create a number of plausible scenarios and considers effective management responses to them. However, one wonders how many scenario planners predicted the consequences of discontinuous changes, such as the September 11 attacks in America, the fall of the Berlin Wall in Germany and the end of apartheid in South Africa.

In the case of September 11, the events leading to it may be considered wholly unpredictable in terms of location and timing, even though some may argue that conceptually this was not the case. In this instance, we can deal only with the consequences of the event. However, with the fall of the Berlin Wall and the end of state socialism in Eastern Europe, a wide range of scenarios had been predicted with reasonable accuracy. Similarly, the end of apartheid was not entirely unexpected, though few scenario planners would have envisaged the peaceful transition to democracy and multiculturalism.

Strategy from an institutionalist perspective is seen as a process over time and considered synonymous with strategic change. Strategic change is informed by the managers' (or other agents) understanding and learning of a situation over time. This includes their subjective and objective understandings of the competitive environment in relation to their firm as well as the political dimensions pertaining to both. In this respect, competition and strategic change are viewed as intimately linked (Pettigrew and Whipp 1991). A contrast between the industrial school tradition and the institutionalist perspective in terms of their approach to thought and action is shown in Figure 4.2.

Mintzberg (1991) has provided a major strategic framework from an institutionalist perspective that examines the dynamics of competitive forces in an organisation. This framework doesn't provide a blueprint for organisations but rather an understanding of the interplay between competitive forces, as shown in Figure 4.3. The underlying assumption of this model is that there is the potential for one or more of seven forces to dominate an organisation at any given time:

- the force for *direction* is concerned with strategic vision and may relate to organisations in startup or turnaround situations;
- the force for *efficiency* is concerned with standardisation and formalisation of processes and may relate to bureaucratic organisations where rationalisation and restructuring are a major focus;
- the force for *proficiency* is concerned with tasks requiring high levels of knowledge and skills and may relate more to professional organisations;
- the force for *concentration* is concerned with concentrating efforts on serving certain markets, particularly in large diversified firms;
- the force for *innovation* is concerned with discovering new things for the customer and may relate to adhocracies comprising skilled experts or multidisciplinary projects.

Figure 4.2 Strategic thought and action: industrial organisation tradition and the institutionalist perspective

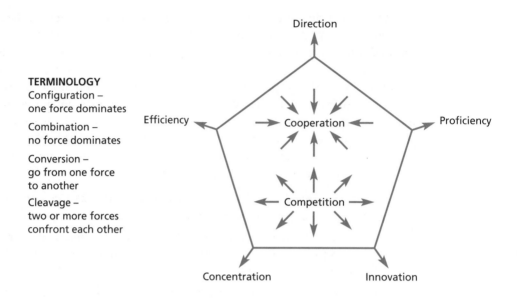

TERMINOLOGY

Configuration –
one force dominates

Combination –
no force dominates

Conversion –
go from one force
to another

Cleavage –
two or more forces
confront each other

Figure 4.3 Dynamic forces in organisations (adapted from Mintzberg 1991)

The internal catalytic forces comprise forces of cooperation and competition. The force for cooperation is concerned with the pulling together of ideology such as norms, beliefs and values. At one extreme, dominant forces of cooperation may result in ideological organisations such as an Israeli kibbutz. The force for competition is concerned with the pulling apart of politics and may relate to political organisations where in-fighting is rife. There may be limits to levels of cooperation as ideology discourages change and if individuals perceive a need for change, they may be forced to challenge the ideology which breeds politics. From the industrial organisation perspective, the force for efficiency and innovation could be seen as similar to generic strategies of 'cost leadership' and 'differentiation' respectively.

In line with an institutionalist perspective, there is a recognition that these forces are rarely static but rather tend to vary continuously over time. A state of 'configuration' occurs when one force dominates and the organisation is drawn towards a coherent established form. However, configuration can lead to the problem of 'contamination' where the dominant force undermines other equally valid forces. For instance, a firm dominated by the force of efficiency may be hindered from following the force for innovation in response to critical changes in the marketplace.

In some periods, an organisation may go through states of 'combination' of different forces where no single force dominates. This may result in periods of 'conversion' from one form to another. For example, an adhocracy may develop a highly successful product or service and settle down into a bureaucracy to exploit it. The state of 'combination' may result in problems of 'cleavage' where two or more forces may confront each other and eventually paralyse the organisation. One can imagine only too well the consequences of boardroom battles where different factions try to pull the organisation in different directions based on their understanding of competitive changes. The internal forces of competition and cooperation can act as useful catalysts to manage the problems of 'contamination' and 'cleavage'. Is this continual flux of forces a 'dialectical interplay between actions (practices and structures), meanings, and actors' (Zilber 2002)?

Two important concepts within this perspective are core competences and strategic intent (Hamel and Prahalad 1989; Prahalad and Hamel 1990). The premise is that strategy is based on learning and learning depends on capabilities (dynamic? See Chapter 5). The core capabilities or competences arise from collective learning in organisations, especially from the coordination of skills and the integration of technologies. By nature, core competences do not diminish in value but need to be nurtured as knowledge and skills are lost over time. They are identified as roots of competitive advantage and the idea of core competence is developed using the analogy of a tree (Prahalad and Hamel 1990):

> 'The diversified corporation is a large tree. The trunk and major limbs are core products, the smaller branches are business units; the leaves, flowers and fruit are end-products. The root system that provides nourishment, sustenance and stability is the core competence. You can miss the strength of competitors by looking only at their end-products, in the same way you miss the strength of a tree if you look only at its leaves.'

As firms respond to competitive pressure, there may be an anomaly between their resources and their aspirations. If a firm has considerable resources but low aspirations, this could be considered as a low 'stretch' circumstance (Hamel and Prahalad 1993). On the other hand, a firm may have very low resources but very high 'stretch' aspirations driven by high ambitions. Such high aspirations or 'stretch' are insufficient to gain competitive advantage and firms require leverage. Leverage entails (Hamel and Prahalad 1993):

- concentrating resources effectively around a strategic focal point;
- accumulating resources more efficiently by extracting knowledge from experience and grafting knowledge from other sources;
- complementing one resource with another to create synergy and higher value;
- conserving resources by recycling and partnering resources from other firms;
- resources from the market in the shortest possible time.

An additional drive to stretch and leverage is 'strategic intent' (Hamel and Prahalad 1989). Strategy is seen as revolution and strategic intent is a firm's obsession with winning in the short or long term. It is stable over time and provides the major driver for organisational commitment and motivation from employees. Strategic intent requires the following demands of senior management (Hamel and Prahalad 1989):

- create a sense of urgency;
- develop a competitor focus at every level through widespread use of competitive intelligence;
- provide employees with the skills they need to work effectively;
- give the organisation time to digest one challenge before launching another;
- establish clear milestones and review mechanisms.

Resource-based view of the firm

In situations of perfect competition, there is a competitive price for products and services. However, in reality, firms may generate 'superprofits' or 'rents' for a variety of reasons. The difference between the actual price of a product or service and its competitive price is known as an 'economic rent'. Rents are payments to assets that exceed their competitive price (Ricardo 1817). This provides firms with their source of competitive advantage. The key question in strategic management is how firms can do this and sustain the competitive advantage over time.

One institutionalist response to increasing rents in firms is to suggest that it is the firm's resources that lead to competitive advantage, arising from a 'resource-based theory of the firm' (Barney 1991; Wernerfelt 1984). Resources are the tangible and intangible assets a firm uses to choose and implement its strategies (Barney 2001). One of the historic tools used in strategic management has been the SWOT analysis where attempts are made to give equal attention to the internal (strengths and weaknesses) and external (opportunities and threats) factors affecting a firm. One could argue that the industrial organisation has shifted the balance in this analysis more towards the external industrial, market-based perspective (Porter 1980). The resource-based view of the firm is an attempt by institutionalists to shift the balance back to the internal aspects of the firm. A seminal paper in this area suggests a number of characteristics of resources to achieve competitive advantage (Barney 1991):

- Resources are distributed heterogeneously across firms.
- Resources have a 'stickiness' and cannot be transferred from firm to firm without a cost.
- Resources are rare – not widely held.
- Resources are valuable – they promote efficiency and effectiveness.
- Resources are not imitable and cannot be replicated easily by competitors.
- Resources are not substitutable – other resources cannot fulfil the same functions.
- Resources are not transferable and cannot be bought in resource markets.

A wide variety of resources that follow the above conditions has been suggested to lead to sustainable competitive advantage in the current literature. These include information technology, strategic planning, human resource management, top management skills, trust and organisational culture (Priem and Butler 2001). One of the highly influential concepts arising from the resource-based view is the notion of core competence described earlier (Prahalad and Hamel 1990).

Critical thinking and reflection

Many companies adopt the rhetoric that 'people are our greatest assets'. What is your experience of the difference between rhetoric and reality in your organisation? If knowledge was considered the most critical resource in organisations, how would you suggest that it was developed among colleagues and work teams? What role do social networks play in your organisation for developing and sharing your knowledge base?

An outcome of the resource-based view of the firm is the development of the 'knowledge-based view' of the firm which assumes that knowledge (know how and know what) is the firm's most important resource (Grant 1996; Spender 1996). This view revisits many of the tenets of individual knowledge (Polanyi 1967; Ryle 1949), organisational learning (Huber 1991), conversion of one form of knowledge to another (Nonaka 1991) and organisational routines (Levitt and March 1988) as potential sources of competitive advantage. Knowledge sharing is seen as vital to this perspective and there is a recognition of the difficulty of sharing tacit knowledge which may be primary to competitive advantage. The principal role of the firm is to integrate the knowledge resident in individuals into their goods and services (Grant 1991). Hence, the primary task of management is to coordinate the process of knowledge integration. One potential aid in this integration process is to treat the firm as a dynamic sociotechnical and self-regulating system (Spender 1996).

There are a number of criticisms aimed at the resource-based view of the firm (Priem and Butler 2001):

- How can resources be obtained?

- How and in which contexts do resources contribute to competitive advantage?

- How do resources interact and compare with other resources?

- How can a firm operate successfully through the denial of market context?

Information systems strategy

In our quest to develop knowledge management strategies, one can learn a great deal from the more mature literature on information systems (IS). It is important at this stage to make a distinction between information systems (IS) and information technology (IT). IT is purely about technology such as hardware and software. In contrast, IS is concerned with the effective interaction between technology and social phenomena (people). It is possible for some IS to have no technology (where information is exchanged verbally between people) whereas other IS may be totally reliant on technology. The importance of the IS is how they can aid effective action and decision making (Checkland and Holwell 1998).

Organisations can become overwhelmed by technology where IT and IS become synonymous terms. IT is not a strategy on its own and the purchase of hardware and software without recourse to organisational issues and activities is unlikely to lead to competitive advantage. It is easy to be seduced by applications (software designed to meet certain business processes or activities) rather than examining whether they will address key business problems in an effective manner and taking into account the competence of the existing workforce.

The past decade has seen the dominance of e-commerce – conducting business electronically using internet technologies. This gave rise to the boom (and subsequent collapse) of dotcom companies and there was a stage a few years ago where the mere announcement of a firm's name change to a dotcom company sent its share price soaring without necessarily any other change in its business. E-commerce did exist in the 1980s when electronic data interchange (EDI) was used to exchange documents between firms at a much reduced cost. Subsequently, financial EDI allowed the customer into the loop by enabling them to issue electronic payment instructions to the supplier directly. More recently the appearance of WAP (wireless application protocol) has allowed individuals to use mobile devices (such as mobile phones and personal digital assistants) to browse the net and make purchases directly while on the move (Ward and Peppard 2002). The use of mobile devices for conducting business transactions has been termed m-commerce.

In the 1960s the dominant IS/IT strategy was focused on 'data processing' (DP) where the emphasis was to use technology to automate tasks. The rationale was to produce twice as many products in half as much time through automation leading to greater efficiency and profits. This data-processing approach did not change the business processes or alter the overall corporate strategy. Modern-day examples of the data-processing approach are the computerised reservation systems (CRS) used among airlines and the electronic point of sale (EPOS) systems used in retailing. The aim of both these systems is to increase the overall efficiency in the business process through efficient transaction handling and resource control. The users of the data-processing approach tend to be operators, clerical staff or first-line supervisors (Ward and Peppard 2002).

In the 1970s and 1980s there was a development in IS/IT towards management information systems (MIS). The objective was to provide middle and senior managers with information for monitoring and controlling business processes and to aid decision making. The focus became the information needs of the users and there was a development of information centres in many organisations to meet this need. The linkages between MIS and organisational performance became much harder to justify than the data-processing approach. The development of large databases characterised this approach but they were not necessarily integrated between different parts of the firm. The contributions of DP and MIS are (Strassman 1985):

● IS/IT has increased the efficiency of information-based activities;

● returns on investment likely to be around 5–10 per cent;

● in terms of managerial effectiveness, good managers get even better, bad managers get worse!

● IS/IT can speed up the mess if used inappropriately.

A further development of information systems and one that builds on DP and MIS is known as strategic information systems (SIS) (Galliers and Somogyi 1987). The aim of SIS is to improve the firm's competitiveness through the effective deployment of IS/IT. SIS is business driven in terms of competitors, suppliers and customers and links directly to the firm's corporate strategy. The four main types of strategic systems (Ward and Peppard 2002) are those that:

● change the nature of the relationship with customers and suppliers by sharing information through technology-based systems. This may include e-procurement, web-based ordering systems and customers tracking their orders online through work-flow management systems;

- produce effective integration of information linked to a firm's value-adding processes. This has often been achieved through customer relationship management systems or enterprise resource planning systems;

- enable a firm to develop and market new products or services based on information. These have included online banking, online support and order-tracking initiatives;

- provide executive management with information (internal and external) to support development and implementation of strategy. An example of this is the use of executive information systems for tracking market, customer and industry changes through external databases as well as key internal indicators of performance.

Critical thinking and reflection

Imagine you were given the position of IS manager in your organisation. What would be your approach to strategy? Think of data processing, management information systems, strategic information systems and information systems capability as potential options for IS strategy. Given the nature of your organisation, which option or combination of options would you adopt and why? How would you integrate and justify your approach with your company's strategy?

The most recent development in the IS/IT strategy literature is the notion of 'IS capability' (Bharadwaj 2000) that is likely to enhance a firm's competitiveness. Instead of a fixation on external changes, the focus of IS strategy becomes more internal. The suggestion is the desire to embed IS capability into all the various practices and processes within the organisation. IS capability takes on a resource-based theory of the firm and appears to be reminiscent of the notions of dynamic capabilities and double-loop learning (Argyris and Schon 1978; Zollo and Winter 2002). Similar to March's (1991) distinction between exploitation and exploration, there may be a tidal swing in the direction of exploration and looking at things differently. As Hamel (2000) asserts about the key factor affecting the competitiveness of e-commerce:

> 'The real story of Silicon Valley is not 'e' but 'i', not electronic commerce but innovation and imagination ... It is the power of 'i' rather than 'e' that separates the winners from the losers in the twenty-first century economy.'

Developing a knowledge management strategy

As industrialised economies have moved from natural resources to intellectual assets, it has been argued that the most important asset that a firm possesses is its knowledge. In terms of economic theory, we are looking for strategies that will produce Ricardian rents (or super profits) (Ricardo 1817) where the effective use of knowledge will enable firms to sustain competitive advantage. There are other forms of rent, such as luck, chance and history, but these rents cannot be managed (Liebeskind 1996). It is assumed that knowledge in its tacit and explicit manifestations can be managed. But how do we develop knowledge management strategies to effectively utilise this valuable resource? Also, how do we protect the valuable knowledge from expropriation and imitation?

The KM strategy literature is relatively young and the forms of strategy proposed can be characterised as a dialectic between the forces of efficiency and innovation (Mintzberg 1991), as shown in Figure 4.4. Firms are never static and are moving in one or another direction towards efficiency or innovation given a certain set of market conditions. In this manner the firm's KM strategy becomes aligned with the overall business strategy. It is likely that a crisis or discontinuity will trigger the firm to move from one force, say, efficiency to innovation. Discontinuities may arise from sudden deregulation of markets, economic downturns or aggressive competitor behaviour resulting in drastic loss of market share.

Among management consultants, the most common forms of knowledge management strategies are codification strategies and personalisation strategies (Hansen *et al.* 1999) as shown in Figure 4.5. For example, Andersen Consulting and Ernst & Young have pursued codification strategies. Codification strategies are heavily based on technology and use large databases to codify and store knowledge. The rationale of a codification strategy is to achieve 'scale in knowledge reuse'. After completion of

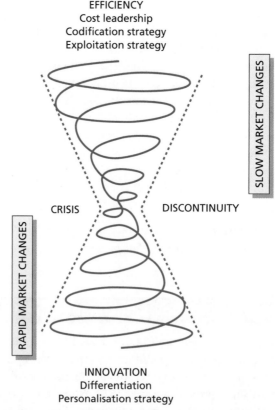

Figure 4.4 The dialectic of knowledge management strategies

CODIFICATION STRATEGY	PERSONALISATION STRATEGY
Technology-led	People-led
Explicit knowledge orientation	Tacit knowledge orientation
Codify knowledge	Engage in dialogue
Use databases	Channel expertise
High turnover	High profits

Figure 4.5 **Codification and personalisation strategies**

a project, consultants will retrieve key pieces of knowledge from the assignment and create 'knowledge objects' to store valuable knowledge such as key industry information, market segmentation analyses, presentations, interview guides, programming documents and change management programmes. This knowledge is stored in a knowledge repository so that others in the firm can use the same material for their assignments. Put crudely, consultancy reports for clients become little more than a 'cut and paste' affair from knowledge and templates found in the repository. Of course, there is significant input from consultants about the specifics of the case, but the tools, techniques and background knowledge come from the knowledge repositories. There is little room for creativity and innovation in this approach and they are likely to be discouraged. Instead, the tried and tested methods of consultancy are promoted. This is what the clients are paying them for: a solid consultancy approach based on previous knowledge without the potential risks of innovation. In this case, codification strategies are clearly aligned with the consultancy firm's business strategy focused on efficiency, cost savings and cost leadership. What the clients value from such consultants is their reduced fees (half or a third) compared with other consultants in the field.

Critical thinking and reflection

Think of the way knowledge is managed in your organisation. How would you assess the level of personalisation or codification strategies involved? Has the emphasis towards one or the other strategy changed over the past few years? What is your involvement with strategy development? On a theoretical level, which one of these strategies do you consider most appropriate for small organisations? Do you consider personalisation strategies as the ultimate knowledge management strategy if companies can afford them?

Other consultants such as Bain or McKinsey tend to favour knowledge management strategies focused on 'personalisation' strategies. These strategies are less about technology and more about people. Bain and McKinsey are more interested in developing people through brainstorming exercises and face-to-face communication and gaining deeper insights into problems. They place considerable emphasis on knowledge sharing, either face to face, over the phone, by e-mail or via videoconferences (Hansen *et al.* 1999). In terms of KM technology, they tend to use expertise databases or internal 'yellow pages' to find consultants with the right set of knowledge and skills for their problem. The focus is on networking within the organisation and through dialogue developing creative solutions for unique problems in their assignments. Knowledge sharing, mentoring and the use of creative and analytical skills are key to this approach. As certain clients value this approach, they are prepared to pay substantially higher fees for this personalised and unique service. In this sense, a personalisation strategy is in alignment with the business strategy focused on differentiation through innovative solutions.

Similar knowledge management strategies have been found in other industries where firms have followed a codification strategy if they were led by efficiency or cost leadership concerns and personalisation strategies where innovation forces and differentiation concerns were foremost. In the US pharmaceutical industry, the knowledge management strategies firms followed a similar pattern of codification strategies ('exploiters' and 'loners') and personalisation strategies ('explorers' and 'innovators') (Bierly and Chakrabarti 1996). Codification strategies rely on large investments in knowledge repositories and proprietary search engines and use incentives to encourage people to codify and store their knowledge in these large databases. On the contrary, personalisation strategies require low levels of technology such as expertise databases but high levels of reward for knowledge sharing and dialogue with their colleagues. Firms that try to pursue both strategies simultaneously tend to fail, as with the problems of 'cleavage' in business strategy where the forces of efficiency and innovation confront each other in the boardroom and can paralyse the firm if there are major divisions in competitive response (Hansen *et al.* 1999; Mintzberg 1991).

Given the dominance of codifying knowledge, what is the best way of codifying explicit knowledge that can be useful and valuable? For example, Ernst & Young has a three-level hierarchy in its knowledge repositories. There is an 'elite' database that has its best knowledge on a topic. In the next level there are specific 'knowledge objects' containing consultancy reports, templates, market analyses and so on from previous assignments. Finally, there are 'holding tanks' for a variety of materials (Hansen *et al.* 1999). A similar framework for mapping knowledge is to classify it under three levels of core knowledge, advanced knowledge and innovative knowledge (Zack 1999):

- Core knowledge is the minimum knowledge required to function in any business or public arena.
- Advanced knowledge is knowledge in process, cost or quality that enables a firm to compete in a particular market and allows some knowledge differentiation between firms.
- Innovative knowledge is knowledge that is substantially differentiated and allows the firm to lead the industry through doing things differently.

An alternative codification of strategic knowledge distinguishes between four types of business knowledge and the tools associated with them (Drew 1999):

- What we know we know: knowledge sharing, access and inventory. Tools include benchmarking and communities of practice.
- What we know we don't know: knowledge seeking and creation. Tools include R&D, market research and competitive intelligence.

- What we don't know we know: uncovering hidden or tacit knowledge. Tools include knowledge maps, audits, training and networks.

- What we don't know we don't know: discovering key risks, exposures and opportunities. Tools include creative tension, audits, dilemmas and complexity science.

Once we have codified knowledge in an appropriate manner, how do we acquire, integrate, store, share and apply the knowledge to achieve competitive advantage? It has been argued that the key drivers and creative tension for strategic action arise from a knowledge gap and strategic gap (Zack 1999). A knowledge gap is the difference between what a firm must know and what it actually knows. Similarly a strategic gap is the difference between what a firm must do and what a firm can do given its resource base. From this gap analysis, there are two potential orientations to knowledge strategy (Zack 1999):

- pursue a conservative knowledge strategy of exploiting past internal knowledge (similar to a codification strategy);

- pursue an aggressive knowledge strategy that integrates exploration and exploitation of internal and external knowledge (a combination of a codification and personalisation strategy). Whereas personalisation or exploration strategies may provide a useful alternative in their own right, firms need to be mindful of the dangers of pursuing both strategies at the same time (Hansen *et al.* 1999). This has often resulted in failure.

A knowledge management strategy needs to contribute to a firm's bottom-line performance. But who takes responsibility for knowledge management in an organisation? If the firm pursues a codification strategy, should the IS/IT department take the lead? Alternatively, if a personalisation strategy is pursued, should the human resource department provide the necessary direction? Our argument is that knowledge management strategies need to be developed in consultation and partnership with both IS/IT and human resource departments. We would go further to include the finance department in these consultations as the benefits of a knowledge management strategy will affect the firm's financial performance and its intellectual capital. The relationship between KM strategy and performance is shown in Figure 4.6.

Figure 4.6 **KM strategy and performance**

Innovation and personalisation strategies

It appears that in times of crisis – rapid market changes or economic decline – many firms may need to reconsider their position and move more towards personalisation or innovation strategies. Their traditional codification or efficiency-related strategies may not be enough. But how do we innovate, particularly if we are used to a totally different way of working? This could be a wake-up call for many firms to change their ways and look more closely at their processes of innovation.

Most people think of innovation as starting with an idea, an 'aha' feeling in the bath, or as an invention. But ideas are not enough in themselves. They need to be nurtured to prevent them from decay and need to be implemented in an organisational context. A useful definition of innovation is as follows (Van de Van 1986):

> *'The process of innovation is defined as the development and implementation of new ideas by people who over time engage in transactions with others within an institutional context.'*

Research in organisational innovation shows that the results from different studies are inherently inconsistent and do not provide us with a clear road map of the best way to proceed (Wolfe 1994). Ideas come from people and need champions to take them forward. People carry, develop and marshal their ideas in a socio-political process of dialogue and discussion with other people before they gain legitimacy and currency. Ideas may go through a number of stages over time (Van de Van 1986):

- appreciation – a threatening, disruptive event leading to the idea;
- articulation – ideas may surface as solutions;
- adoption – ideas may galvanise through networks and political debate;
- institutionalisation – ideas gain legitimacy and are taken for granted;
- decay – ideas become outmoded.

This research has focused predominantly on what are the determinants of organisational innovation. Effectively the determinants fall into a variety of organisational, innovation, managerial and environmental characteristics. The studies have followed quantitative regression models where innovation is measured in terms of its magnitude and speed of adoption. Parallel studies have focused on diffusion of innovation in organisations. These studies have explored the pattern, extent and rate of diffusion of innovation across an organisation. Again these studies have used cross-sectional surveys looking at organisational, innovation and managerial characteristics of the promoter of the innovation. Lastly, research has looked at innovation as a process to see how it emerges, develops, grows and terminates over time. This has been done in a qualitative manner by conceptualising innovation as a series of stages over time. The common stages in the innovation cycle among many studies are (Wolfe 1994):

- idea conception;
- awareness;
- matching;

- appraisal;
- persuasion;
- adoption decision;
- implementation;
- confirmation;
- routinisation;
- infusion.

These processual innovations have had a profound effect on many organisations and have occurred in forms such as business process re-engineering, lean production and customer requirements management. They are affected considerably by cognitive, social and organisational factors. The political dynamics, interests and power bases can also considerably influence the innovation. By their nature, innovations can be irrational, unpredictable and uncertain and fail to follow rationalised management processes. These can lead to frustrations among managers about how to effectively manage innovation. An alternative conceptualisation to the stages of innovation shown above is the notion of innovation as four 'episodes', as shown in Figure 4.7. The four episodes emphasise that the different stages are overlapping and may not occur in a linear manner.

The agenda formation episode is principally about knowledge creation and acquisition. Firms can acquire knowledge internally through congenital or experiential learning or externally through vicarious learning, grafting, searching and noticing (Huber 1991). Given that many new ideas come from external sources, the firm's ability to acquire new ideas from external sources becomes critical. This is normally achieved through individuals engaging in external networks, acquiring new ideas and sharing them across the firm (knowledge diffusion). It is argued that weak ties in these networks provide the most productive source of ideas as they are more likely to

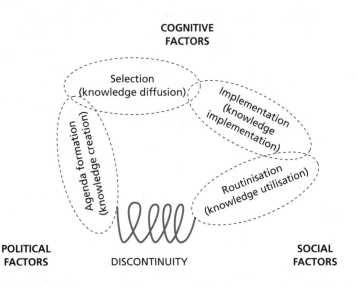

Figure 4.7 **Episodes in the innovation process** (Clark and Fujimoto 1992; Newell *et al.* 2002)

challenge conventional thinking rather than conform to it (Hansen 1999; Newell *et al.* 2002). The strength of networking is measured as a form of social capital (Adler and Kwon 2002) and determines the level and quality of new ideas coming into the organisation from external sources.

New ideas on their own do not create innovation. They need to be developed and merged into local conditions through organisational processes, practices and political environments. The culture of the organisation can significantly influence whether these ideas are accepted or rejected. Strong ties between organisational members are important as they allow greater facility to engage in discussion and dialogue leading to a greater opportunity for the idea to be implemented in a practice or process as an innovation (Hansen 1999). These phases are part of the implementation and selection episodes. The last episode in the innovation cycle is the routinisation episode concerned with the utilisation of knowledge and its efficient reuse. This episode has parallels with the codification strategy where knowledge codification, storage and retrieval mechanisms are developed. To be successful, an innovation starts as an irrational idea but turns into a codified, constrained and routinised form of knowledge. Exploration leads back to exploitation. It needs a discontinuity to kick-start the innovation process again.

Exploitation strategies require 'discipline' in collecting knowledge for any given situation, developing alternatives and evaluating the one most likely to increase the value of the firm. A form of convergent thinking towards a problem. In contrast, exploration strategies require 'imagination' to go beyond the conventional methods of thinking and promote divergent thinking towards a problem. The primacy of imagination in the long term is illustrated by Einstein (Szulanski and Amin 2001):

'Imagination is more important than knowledge. For knowledge is limited, whereas imagination embraces the entire world, stimulating progress, giving birth to evolution.'

Social networks are essential for the success of innovations as they rely heavily on social interactions between different interests. These networks may exist within (intra) or between (inter) organisations, through educational and professional networks and increasingly through virtual networks such as Facebook. They may be formal or informal (see communities of practice in Chapter 9) but need to encompass different aspects of knowledge processes: creation, diffusion, integration and implementation. Material artefacts such as mobile technologies can play an important role as 'boundary objects' in linking together different groups and interests.

CASE STUDY

Unilever (UK/Netherlands)

Two weeks after Paul Polman had been appointed as Chief Executive, he asked for a review meeting with Cathy Bautista, Head of Unilever's Knowledge Management Group. At the meeting they discussed Unilever's achievements in establishing communities of practice and various knowledge repositories. However, he was concerned about the extent to which Unilever's knowledge creation and transfer processes were aligned to corporate objectives and strategies. His fear was while there may be a lot of learning and knowledge within Unilever, it might be insufficiently focused towards delivering better products and services. He asked Cathy to re-evaluate current knowledge management activities from a strategic perspective and to put forward recommendations that would move Unilever towards a more purposeful approach to its learning and knowledge.

Unilever is one of the largest consumer goods companies in the world with an annual turnover of over €40bn. The company employs around 250,000 people based in over 100 countries. It has a large and varied portfolio of foods, home and personal care products including such well-known brands as Flora, Omo, Ragu, Calvin Klein and Dove. Uniliver invests around 2.5 per cent of its annual turnover in research and development leading to continuous product innovations and filing of patents each year. It takes learning and knowledge seriously and believes that transferring this knowledge into its products and services is a key source of competitive advantage. The organisation has ambitions to be 'multi-local' through understanding and anticipating local needs around the world and producing products and services that fulfil these needs. Internally Unilever aspires to be a networked learning organisation with its diverse and dispersed workforce and often questions whether it has become more of a top-down 'teaching organisation'.

Unilever's Knowledge Management Group has aimed at delivering the learning organisation vision through a number of targeted interventions. They have developed a framework of organisational knowledge processes and focused their efforts on locating, capturing, sharing, transferring and creating knowledge. Cathy Bautista sees two clear reasons for this approach: 'Firstly, as a group it is helpful to have a structured way of organising the what and the how of knowledge acquisition. Secondly, the team knows that to be able to give better advice and support to their customers, they must excel at what they do'. She recognises the benefits of learning from mistakes and 'error harvesting' but appreciates that it is more of an aspiration in some parts of the organisation. 'Learning from success is relatively easy as we can actively promote and help embed lessons derived from successful experiences. Learning from failure is more sensitive but just as important. We are promoting a culture of being willing to learn as you go and to embrace and apply learning both from successes and failures. This is what I would call a "wholesome way of learning".'

Unilever started its knowledge management activities in 1996. A key strand of its activities has been the development of several dozen communities of practice (CoP). To initiate these informal networks, they organised 'Knowledge Workshops' to bring together key experts and practitioners from around the world. The purpose of the workshops was to focus efforts in a functional domain and to ascertain what people did and didn't know about the area. The domain had to be core to Unilever's strategy. This allowed a shared vocabulary and terminology to develop as well as identifying any knowledge gaps. Each workshop generated a 'Knowledge Domain' for each community of practice. This comprised handbooks, manuals, presentations and any information deemed valuable to that domain. There was also a list of key people and groups within Unilever who had long-term experience in that domain such as meal sauces.[1]

Each CoP had a champion to help coordinate and mobilise the network. The champion held a relatively senior position to encourage commitment and focus to the CoP. The aim of the CoP was to encourage collaboration between geographically dispersed plants and to cross functional boundaries. The CoPs were built around four key principles: deliverables, people, operations and leverage. The deliverables could be business deliverables such increasing efficiencies in organisational processes or they could be knowledge deliverables such as new insights or producing best-practice guidelines. The people aspect ensured that there was a right mix of experts from diverse geographical and functional backgrounds. An 'activist' role was articulated in each CoP. The activist position rotated around the group and was introduced to ensure that there was strategic alignment with community activities. The operations element of each CoP was around creating a safe and trusting environment where people felt comfortable to contribute and co-create new knowledge. The leverage dimension was to create linkages between the different communities rather than having lots of isolated communities within such a large organisation. Each community developed their own identity and brand and engaged in two-way dialogue with other communities.[2]

External feedback was provided to each CoP after it had been in operation for some time. This took the form of a health-check questionnaire and identified strengths and gaps in the persistence of the community. Each CoP also tried to classify the value of their activities in a variety of ways. This included a list of success stories, quotes from satisfied community 'customers' and use of the balanced-scorecard framework.

Another major strand in Unilever's knowledge management endeavours was the development of an intranet portal. The aim of the portal was to aid knowledge sharing and increase collaboration across the organisation. The portal held a knowledge repository with a search engine covering different CoP projects, a CRM database as well as key procedures and practices. The knowledge repositories were supported by 'chat groups' who provided hints, tips and guidance on how best to use the material. Community interactions were maintained using community software such as e-groups and Geocrawler. A 'yellow pages' database was created to help identify experts.

The main challenge was getting experts to maintain and update their profiles regularly.[3]

Unilever has tried to capture the knowledge and learning of retiring employees through narrative accounts called 'learning histories'. They used two game-show formats, 'Blind Date' to match people with the necessary expertise and 'Mastermind' to help people question a departing expert. The learning histories served as a form of organisational memory to help employees think through what they might do in similar situations.[4]

Learning from projects was captured in 'Knowledge Debriefs' to help prevent recurrent mistakes 're-inventing the wheel' on each project. The debriefing focused on process and technical learning. Interviews were conducted with project participants to capture the five best and worst aspects of the project. These were discussed with all participants and documented as a form of process learning. Technical learning came from comparing key product attributes and consumer attributes set at the beginning of the project. Two delegates from new related projects attended the project debriefs to ensure that mistakes weren't repeated and any learning was transferred to the new project.[5]

Cathy reflected on her earlier meeting with Paul Polman and smiled at his perceptive remarks around knowledge management. She recalled her own affirmation in this area through organisational circulars:

> 'Knowledge management needs to be aligned with CEO's strategy. It will be essential to define how KM can support the business strategy, as well as build and/or strengthen KM competencies across the business. Professional competencies need to focus not only on what people do, but also on what they need to know in order to deliver. In that sense the discussion shouldn't be as to whose responsibility it is, either the CKO, CIO or HR function, but rather of how to ensure that those needs are deliberately identified and addressed'.

It was time to move some of this rhetoric into reality. Cathy called her knowledge management team together to discuss the way forward.

References

1 von Krogh, G., I. Nonaka *et al.* (2001) 'Making the most of your company's knowledge: a strategic framework', *Long Range Planning* 34: 421–39.
2 Poss, A., K. Linse *et al.* (2005) 'Unilever: Leveraging community value', *Inside Knowledge* 8(4).
3 Iske, P. L. (2002) 'Building a corporate KM community', Ibid, 6.
4 Higgison, S. (2007) 'The Knowledge: Sam Marshall', Ibid, 27 June.
5 von Krogh, G. (2002) 'The communal resource and information systems', *Journal of Strategic Information Systems*, 11(2): 85–107.

Questions

1 What advice would you give Cathy Bautista on improving the strategic focus of Unilever's knowledge management activities?

2 What changes, if any, would you make to Unilever's communities of practice?

3 How could 'learning histories' be further developed to capture organisational memory?

Summary

This chapter has elaborated five areas that need to be considered when developing a knowledge management strategy:

1 Realised strategies may emerge from the way a firm develops through experience rather than as an outcome of a deliberate plan or strategy. Many deliberate strategies may be unrealised.

2 A clear understanding of strategy needs awareness of the different schools of thought and their underlying assumptions. The dominant schools of thought in the knowledge management literature are the industrial organisation tradition, the excellence and turnaround literature, and the institutionalist perspective.

3 The resource-based and knowledge-based view of the firm place greater emphasis on the firm's resources (tangible and intangible assets) to achieve competitive advantage.

4 Information systems and information technology strategies have developed from operational data-processing approaches to management information systems and strategic information systems. More recently, IS/IT strategies have adopted a resource-based view of the firm and suggest that IS capabilities are the primary source of competitive advantage.

5 Knowledge management strategies occur as a dialectic between codification (exploitation) strategies and personalisation (exploration) strategies. Firms that follow both strategies simultaneously are likely to fail. The dialectic or change between strategies is likely to occur following a crisis or discontinuity.

Questions for further thought

1 At the extremes of KM strategy, is a codification strategy purely an IS/IT strategy and a personalisation strategy a human resource (HR) strategy? What is the importance of the IS/IT department and HR departments talking to one another for the development of a KM strategy?

2 Given the institutionalist perspective's preoccupation with learning, how do we know that the organisation is learning about the right things and responding to market changes in the appropriate manner?

3 If only 10 per cent of formulated strategies ever get implemented, why do firms bother with elaborate planning processes?

4 Why do people knock books and publications from the excellence and turnaround literature when they have probably had more impact and influence on managers than literature from the industrial organisation and institutionalist perspective put together?

5 Core competences are described using the analogy of the roots of a tree. How effective are these core competences in times of discontinuity when the environment changes the soil nourishing the roots of competence into sand?

6 Is there potential in development of strategic thinking by a synthesis of the best ideas from the industrial organisation and institutionalist perspective?

7 What lessons can managers take from the innovation literature when the results of several studies are inconsistent? Could literature hinder the very creative and innovative processes it is trying to describe?

8 If we cannot predict the future, what is the point of codifying strategic knowledge into 'what we don't know we know' and 'what we don't know we don't know' (Drew 1999)? Is this the same as the use of scenario planning in the industrial organisation tradition?

9 Is KM strategy development the domain of the finance director, the IS/IT director or the HR director? If you propose a joint body, how do you overcome the communication difficulties between the different areas, their interests and different languages?

10 What is the likelihood of codification strategies developing superficial learning and personalisation strategies developing a deeper insight on any subject.

Further reading

1 Mintzberg *et al.* (1998) is an excellent exploration of the different strategy schools and their underlying assumptions. The authors distinguish ten schools of strategic thought rather than the three described in this chapter.

2 Johnson and Scholes (2002) is a classic strategy text for MBA students. The main caution is that it comes from a predominantly industrial organisation background and needs to be read in this context.

References

Adler, P. S. and Kwon, S. (2002) 'Social capital: Prospects for a new concept', *Academy of Management Review*, 27(1), 17–40.

Ansoff, H. I. (1965) *Corporate Strategy*, McGraw Hill, New York.

Argyris, C. (2001) *Flawed Advice and the Management Trap*, Oxford University Press, New York.

Argyris, C. and Schon, D. A. (1978) *Organizational Learning: A Theory of Action Perspective*, Addison-Wesley, Reading, MA.

Bain, J. S. (1956) *Barriers to New Competition*, Harvard University Press, Cambridge, MA.

Barney, J. B. (1991) 'Firm resources and sustained competitive advantage', *Journal of Management*, 17(1), 99–120.

Barney, J. B. (2001) 'Is the resource-based "view" a useful perspective for strategic management research? Yes', *Academy of Management Review*, 26(1), 41–56.

Bharadwaj, A. (2000) 'A resource-based perspective on information technology and firm performance: An empirical investigation', *MIS Quarterly*, 24(1), 169–96.

Bierly, P. and Chakrabarti, A. (1996) 'Generic knowledge strategies in the U.S. pharmaceutical industry', *Strategic Management Journal*, 17 (Winter Special Issue).

Chamberlin, E. H. (1933) *The Theory of Monopolistic Competition*, Harvard University Press, Cambridge, MA.

Chandler, A. D. (1962) *Strategy and Structure. Chapters in the History of the Industrial Enterprise*, The MIT Press, Cambridge, MA.

Checkland, P. B. and Holwell, S. (1998) *Information, Systems and Information Systems: Making Sense of the Field*, John Wiley & Sons, Chichester.

Clark, K. and Fujimoto, T. (1992) *Product Development Performance*, Harvard Business School Press, Boston, MA.

Drew, S. (1999) 'Building knowledge management into strategy: Making sense of a new perspective', *Long Range Planning*, 32(1), 130–36.

Galliers, R. D. and Somogyi, E. K. (1987) 'From data processing to strategic information systems: A historical perspective', *Towards Strategic Information Systems*, R. D. Galliers and E. K. Somogyi, eds, Gordon & Breach Publishing Group, Reading, 5–25.

Grant, R. M. (1991) 'The resource-based theory of competitive advantage: Implications for strategy formulation', *California Management Review*, 33(3), 114–135.

Grant, R. M. (1996) 'Toward a knowledge-based theory of the firm', *Strategic Management Journal*, 17, 109–22.

Grinyer, P., Mayes, D. and McKiernan, P. (1988) *Sharpbenders: The Secrets of Unleashing Corporate Potential*, Basil Blackwell, Oxford.

Hamel, G. (2000) *Leading the Revolution*, Harvard Business School, Boston, MA.

Hamel, G. and Prahalad, C. K. (1989) 'Strategic intent', *Harvard Business Review*, May–June, 63–76.

Hamel, G. and Prahalad, C. K. (1993) 'Strategy as stretch and leverage', *Harvard Business Review*, 71(2), 75–84.

Hansen, M., Nohria, N. and Tierney, T. (1999) 'What's your strategy for managing knowledge?' *Harvard Business Review*, March–April, 106–16.

Hansen, M. T. (1999) 'The search-transfer problem: The role of weak ties in sharing knowledge across organization subunits', *Administrative Science Quarterly*, 44, 82–111.

Huber, G. P. (1991) 'Organizational learning: The contributing processes and the literatures', *Organization Science*, 2, 88–115.

Huczynski, A. (1992) 'Management guru ideas and the 12 secrets of their success', *Leadership & Organization Development Journal*, 13(5), 15–20.

Johnson, G. and Scholes, K. (2002) *Exploring Corporate Strategy: Text and Cases*, Prentice Hall, Harlow, Essex.

Levitt, B. and March, J. G. (1988) 'Organizational learning', *Annual Review of Sociology*, 14.

Liebeskind, J. P. (1996) 'Knowledge, strategy, and the theory of the firm', *Strategic Management Journal*, 17 (Winter Special Issue), 93–107.

March, J. G. (1991) 'Exploration and exploitation in organizational learning', *Organization Science*, 2(1), 71–87.

Mintzberg, H. (1991) 'The effective organization: Forces and forms', *Sloan Management Review*, Winter edition, 54–67.

Mintzberg, H., Ahlstrand, B. and Lampel, J. (1998) *Strategy Safari*, Pearson Education Limited, Harlow, Essex.

Mintzberg, H. and Waters, J. A. (1985) 'Of strategies, deliberate and emergent', *Strategic Management Journal*, 6(3), 257–72.

Newell, S., Robertson, M., Scarbrough, H. and Swan, J. (2002) *Managing Knowledge Work*, Palgrave, Basingstoke, Hampshire.

Newstrom, J. W. (2002) 'In search of excellence: Its importance and effects', *Academy of Management Executive*, 16(1), 53–56.

Nonaka, I. (1991) 'The knowledge-creating company', *Harvard Business Review*, 69 (November–December), 96–104.

Peters, T. J. and Waterman, R. H. (1982) *In Search of Excellence: Lessons from America's Best Run Companies*, Harper & Row, New York.

Pettigrew, A. and Whipp, R. (1991) *Managing Change for Competitive Success*, Blackwell Publishers, Oxford.

Polanyi, M. (1967) *The Tacit Dimension*, Doubleday, New York.

Porter, M. (1980) *Competitive Strategy*, Free Press, New York.

Prahalad, C. K. and Hamel, G. (1990) 'The core competence of the corporation', *Harvard Business Review*, 68(3), 79–91.

Priem, R. L. and Butler, J. E. (2001) 'Is a resource-based "view" a useful perspective for strategic management research?', *Academy of Management Review*, 26(1), 22–40.

Reisner, R. A. F. (2002) 'When a turnaround stalls', *Harvard Business Review*, 80(2), 45–52.

Ricardo, D. (1817) *Principles of Political Economy and Taxation*, Murray, London.

Ryle, G. (1949) *The Concept of Mind*, Hutcheson, London.

Schumpeter, J. (1934) *The Theory of Economic Development*, Harvard University Press, Cambridge, MA.

Schumpeter, J. A. (1950) *Capitalism, Socialism, and Democracy*, Harper, New York.

Spender, J. C. (1996) 'Making knowledge the basis of a dynamic theory of the firm', *Strategic Management Journal*, 17, 45–62.

Strassman, P. A. (1985) *The Information Payoff*, Free Press, New York.

Szulanski, G. and Amin, K. (2001) 'Learning to make strategy: Balancing discipline and imagination', *Long Range Planning*, 34, 537–56.

Van de Van, A. H. (1986) 'Central problems in the management of innovation', *Management Science*, 32(5), 590–607.

Ward, J. and Peppard, J. (2002) *Strategic Planning for Information Systems*, John Wiley & Sons Ltd, Chichester.

Wernerfelt, B. (1984) 'A resource-based view of the firm', *Strategic Management Journal*, 5, 171–180.

Wolfe, R. A. (1994) 'Organizational innovation: Review, critique and suggested research directions', *Journal of Management Studies*, 31(3), 427–53.

Zack, M. (1999) 'Developing a knowledge strategy', *California Management Review*, 41(3), 125–45.

Zilber, T. (2002) 'Institutionalization as an interplay between actions, meanings and actors: The case of a rape crisis center in Israel', *Academy of Management Journal*, 45, 234–54.

Zollo, M. and Winter, S. G. (2002) 'Deliberate learning and the evolution of dynamic capabilities', *Organization Science*, 13(3), 339–51.

Part 3

CREATING KNOWLEDGE

NATURE
OF KNOWLEDGE
Data, information and knowledge
History of managing knowledge
Philosophical perspectives on knowledge

LEVERAGING
KNOWLEDGE
Intellectual capital
Strategic management
perspectives
Knowledge management
strategy

MOBILISING
KNOWLEDGE
Enabling contexts
Knowledge networks
Change management

CREATING
KNOWLEDGE
Organisational learning
Learning organisations

KNOWLEDGE
ARTEFACTS
Knowledge management tools
Knowledge management systems

Organisational learning

Learning outcomes

After completing this chapter the reader should be able to:

- understand cognitive and behavioural approaches to learning;
- contrast single-loop and double-loop learning;
- present the nature of organisational learning from an information-processing perspective;
- explain how organisational routines are changed and transformed to dynamic capabilities;
- describe the role of politics in organisational learning.

Management issues

An understanding of individual learning, team learning and organisational learning implies these questions for managers:

- What learning environments can be developed to promote effective learning?
- How can complacency from successful ventures and defensive routines from failures be managed effectively?
- When is it appropriate to maintain stability or challenge status quo to promote organisational learning?
- Is an autocratic or participative leadership style more suitable for organisational learning?

Links to other chapters

OPENING VIGNETTE

Recruits fired up by virtual rivalry

FT

Global companies are deploying a new tool to reinforce their brands with students, build links with universities and management schools, find talent and deliver management education. Corporate games, costing up to €1m ($1.3m, £900,000) each to run, are increasingly seen by faculty as an 'experiential learning' device that can improve educational quality and even count towards course credits.

Recently, the aircraft manufacturer Airbus and bank BNP Paribas have joined existing players such as cosmetics group L'Oréal and technology consultants IBM in launching global games for undergraduates, attracting in the process thousands of players.

Peter Cardwell, a director at the business simulation design company, Learning Dynamics, says these multi-player online team games are a powerful way to teach business skills. Learning Dynamics, he says, defines them as a 'multimedia experience that immerses the participant in a realistic business situation or management role which requires decision-making in a risk-free environment – so learning is accelerated'.

Moreover, corporate business games designed for building brand awareness are starting to spawn siblings used for employee education or even targeted at high school students. Certainly, corporate games seem to be weaving a growing number of participating business schools into their web.

A record 240 teams took part in the 2008/9 IBM University Business Challenge in the UK. Finalists included teams from Imperial College Business School in London and Exeter University. There were also teams from University of Liverpool Management School, University of Abertay Dundee Business School, Bournemouth University Business School and Ashcroft International Business School in Cambridge and Cheltenham.

Business schools also dominated the finals of BNP Paribas's Ace Manager game. The competition was won by a team from WHU–Otto Beisheim School of Management in Koblenz, Germany, with a team from Bocconi Business School in Italy and a team from Moscow's Financial Academy among the finalists.

At BNP Paribas, Antoine Sire, director of brand, communication and quality, says the banking group is spending €1m on its Ace Manager game, launched in October to extend awareness among French graduates and college-leavers worldwide. The bank, which counts more than half its staff outside France, worked with consultants to create a game that builds on international awareness arising from its role as the world's leading tennis sponsor.

The fact-based Ace Manager game requires teams of four students to assume banking roles in a virtual tennis 'industry', covering the group's three main business lines. Retail banking teams must help a tennis federation develop a tournament; for asset management, they must manage a tennis champion's assets and, for corporate and investment banking, they must help a racket maker to expand through acquisition.

The game has attracted 1,000 teams from 106 countries, with strong representation from the bank's main markets that include India, Turkey, France, China, Ukraine, Italy, Russia, Germany, Hong Kong, the UK and Algeria. The game website has had 90,000 visitors. BNP Paribas recruitment and marketing staff use the game as a tool in campus campaigns. But Mr Sire says it is, above all, designed to develop awareness of the brand and positive association such as creativity and diversity. 'We think the cost is reasonable in relation to the benefits,' he says.

BNP Paribas has launched a staff-only online business game, Starbank, to help recruits understand its businesses. As companies launch more games, the objectives are becoming more diverse. The Airbus Fly Your Ideas Challenge includes the classic elements of building brand awareness among students, spotting potential recruits and deepening connections with academia. But it is also a search for ideas relevant to its business.

Airbus, based in Toulouse, France, challenges students from all disciplines to come up with ideas that will improve environmental efficiency in both its aircraft and in the aviation industry.

Rachel Schroeder, head of project, says the involvement of Airbus experts was important in winning the commitment of academics. 'Universities say they want students to have real contact with companies,' she says. Projects under development range from cabin materials and engine technology to taxiing efficiencies and 'green' leasing.

The Challenge is likely to cost Airbus at least €100,000 in cash – including €50,000 in prize money and the cost of hosting the five short-listed teams attending final presentations before a jury at the Paris Airshow in June. But Ms Schroeder says the company already sees the benefits and regards its Challenge as an ongoing commitment.

IBM, meanwhile, is one of the oldest players in the student game market. Its University Business Challenge has been running in the UK for more than three annual editions, with 1,200 participants from 80 universities. It is designed by Learning Dynamics and is part of a vast global strategy to update perceptions of its business and also plug a perceived skills gap among graduates.

Half of IBM's revenues now derive from consultancy rather than computer hardware and software, so it needs to attract articulate, technically competent graduates who are able to analyse businesses. Kevin Farrar, a programme manager at IBM Academic Initiative in the UK and Europe, says its latest online game, Innov8, is designed to 'help students acquire the skills we need in services science'.

Players enter a 3D virtual call centre as a business consultant and interview game characters about its problems, gather data to understand the business process, then design solutions using modelling tools, dealing with unexpected business events as they go along. IBM also provides real enterprise tools to professors for use in their seminars.

A complementary classroom tool

Alison Wride, deputy head of University of Exeter Business School and an associate professor in economics, is a strong believer in the benefits of business simulations for course participants. The school entered 15 teams in the 2008/9 University Business Challenge, of which two reached the finals.

'I think these business simulations are fantastically useful,' she says. 'We have found there is value in each stage. These games help students practise the theory we teach and they force them to apply it against a deadline.'

Benefits include sharpening participants' decision-making, presentation, teamworking and marketing skills. Teaching techniques in the games reflect and complement increased use of classroom simulations by professors, says Prof Wride.

Peter Bollen, senior lecturer in the faculty of economics and business administration at Maastricht University, uses a game from US group Innovative Learning Solutions to teach undergraduates. Teams tackle an online simulation of running a global company as economic and business conditions change. Lecturers provide support. Mr Bollen uses the game on MBA programmes but it is a complementary tool, not a substitute for a professor, he warns. 'There must be a coach or a lecturer to spot repeated mistakes and provide guidance,' he warns.

Source: from Recruits fired up by virtual rivalry, *The Financial Times*, 04/05/2009 (Tieman, R.), copyright © The Financial Times Ltd.

Questions

1 What is the value of business simulation games for organisational learning?

2 What are the drawbacks of business simulation games for organisational learning?

3 What other forms of virtual reality could help organisational learning?

Introduction

There is considerable fragmentation in the field of organisational learning and no single framework has successfully encapsulated the diversity of its offerings. The discipline of organisational learning has its roots in a number of wider disciplines of psychology, management science, sociology, strategy and cultural anthropology (Easterby-Smith 1997). The literature of organisational learning is much more mature than the relatively recent literatures of the 'learning organisation' and 'knowledge management' and provides an essential cornerstone for the emerging knowledge management literature.

This chapter begins by looking at how we learn as individuals and how we learn in groups. It examines the role of success and failure in organisational learning and forwards the proposition that moderate levels of failure may act as important drivers in the learning process. The notion of organisational learning is explored in terms of single- and double-loop learning and two commonly cited frameworks are investigated – one from an ethnomethodology background and the other from an information-processing one. The information-processing perspective (Huber 1991) of organisational learning is further developed by considering the processes of knowledge acquisition, information distribution, information interpretation and organisational memory.

The role of 'unlearning' is examined together with its importance in preventing stagnation and inertia in organisations. A common response to familiar problems in organisations is to develop routines based on existing knowledge. Learning in the form of organisational routines is explored and how these routines change in response to performance gaps or new possibilities. It is assumed that many of these routines contain tacit knowledge and are stored as procedural memory in organisations. A recent conceptual development of organisational routines is the concept of 'dynamic capabilities'. The theoretical nature of these dynamic capabilities is explored and their role in highly volatile environments. A much neglected area of organisational learning is the impact of politics on learning. A model is forwarded showing a dialectic of cooperative and competitive environments linked to potential asymmetry of power relations, emotions and self-identities.

Individual learning

In an organisation's infancy or in micro-firms comprising a few members, organisational learning could be considered synonymous with individual learning. However, as organisations grow, a clear distinction develops between individual and organisational learning. But are they one and the same? Argyris and Schon (1978, p. 9) articulate this dilemma as follows:

> 'There is something paradoxical here. Organisations are not merely collections of individuals, yet there are no organisations without such collections. Similarly, organisational learning is not merely individual learning, yet organisations learn through the experience and actions of individuals. What, then, are we to make of organisational learning? What is an organisation that it may learn?'

The current theories of individual learning come from various branches of behaviourism and cognitive psychology. Some of the early behaviourist theories of individual learning were based on a stimulus-response model of behaviour (Gutherie 1935; Skinner 1938). These simplistic notions were extended by examining changes in response probabilities from various stimuli in the learning process. Further behavioural research in the 1950s was conducted on mechanisms of learning where learning became connected with an acquisition of associations, conditioned reflexes and stimulus–response bonds. Subsequent behavioural research explored the role of memory to understand the process of strengthening and weakening associations through rote verbal learning (Underwood 1964). Behaviorists assume that behaviour is a function of its consequences. Hence positive reinforcement such as praise or a reward is likely to result in the desired behavioural outcome. Negative reinforcement such as punishment can weaken certain behaviours but research shows this tends to occur in the short term. Burns (1995) observes that much competency-based training is based on this approach. Competence approaches are useful for repetitive tasks but can be rigid and mechanical and lack higher-order learning.

Another branch of learning theory came from cognitive psychology, which saw learning as a change in states of knowledge rather than a change in the probability of response (Bruner *et al.* 1956). This information-processing perspective laid an emphasis on problem solving. Further research in this area moved to investigate memory structures, processing of information, organisation of knowledge and the process of problem solving (Klahr and Wallace 1976). The advent of the information-processing perspective has led to wide acceptance of computer simulation and modelling of the learning process. The emphasis is on understanding the different levels of experience, meaning and insights within individuals.

The constructivist perspective sees learning as a process where individuals develop new ideas based on their current and past knowledge and experiences. Learning occurs when individuals engage in social activity and conversations around shared tasks and problems. Bandura (1977) argues that learning would be extremely arduous on one's own. Instead, he suggests that most human behaviour occurs through observing and interacting with others. Social learning theory explains human behaviour as continuous interaction between cognitive, behavioural and environmental factors. The process underlying social learning are:

- characteristics of the learner such as their sensory capacities and past reinforcement. This includes the attention ability of the learner to discern the distinctiveness, complexity and value of a given behaviour;
- learner reproducing a cognitive map illustrating the elements and linkages underlying a behaviour;
- learner motivation including external and self-reinforcement.

Social learning theory develops Vygotsky's (1978) framework that social interaction plays a vital role in the development of cognition. Lave and Wenger (1990) extend this notion by arguing that all learning is situated in activity, context and culture. Learners engage in a 'community of practice', an informal network of learners, and the social interaction embodies the beliefs and behaviours to be acquired.

A model of the learning process that is widely used in teaching, training and management is the Lewinian experiential learning model (Kolb 1984), as shown in Figure 5.1. Individual learning can be defined as (Kim 1993):

'increasing one's capacity to take effective action.'

The basic learning cycle from the experiential school of thought has appeared in a variety of different management guises: Deming's (1986) plan–do–check–act cycle, Schein's (1987) observation–emotional reaction–judgement–intervention cycle and Argyris and Schon's (1978) discovery–invention–production–generalisation cycle. Each of the four aspects of the learning process have been developed into learning styles to help individuals understand their strengths and weaknesses in the learning process. An instrument commonly used by trainers is the Learning Styles Questionnaire devised by Honey and Mumford (1986). This instrument provides individual profiles against the four learning styles, activist, pragmatist, reflector and theorist, which are directly related to the Lewinian learning model.

One of the main criticisms against this learning model is that it ignores the learner's motivation to learn. Without this motivation, or 'fire under the belly', it is unlikely that the individual will have any incentive to learn. How do we ignite this fire in individuals to foster learning in organisations? Also, learning models assume that feedback and reflection are central to the learning process. However, in many organisations, there can be a tendency towards an action-fixated, non-learning cycle (Garratt 1987) where the reflection stage is ignored. People don't necessarily have time to think and reflect, being bombarded by urgent problems and pressing deadlines. Are there serious consequences for individual learning in the 'busy-busy' cultures and environments we inhabit? How is the space and time for reflection managed in organisations?

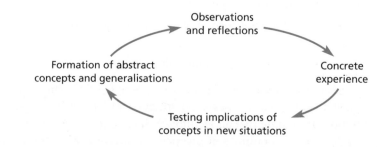

Figure 5.1 **The Lewinian experiential learning model** (Kolb 1984)

The traditional goals of the learning process are acquisition of knowledge (know what), development of skills (know how) and a change in attitudes of the individual learner. However, through introspection, a learner can also learn about their strengths and weaknesses as a learner. Bateson (1987) coined the phrase 'deutero-learning' for individuals who became effective at 'learning to learn' and more skilled at problem solving. Defensive routines can create blockages in deutero-learning and inhibit further learning. This is particularly evident among smart and professional people where there may be a disparity between what they say (their 'espoused theories') and what they believe (their 'theories in use') (Argyris 1991). The defensive reasoning often arises from smart people's high aspirations for success and their equally high fear of failure which may lead to embarrassment and feelings of vulnerability and incompetence.

Reg Revans (1977) developed the notion of 'action learning' from observing managers and recognising that their learning entails taking effective action rather than purely recommending or making an analysis of a given situation. He stressed the need to integrate cognition and action and theory and behaviour. Revans based his notion of learning on the simple mathematical equation:

$$L \text{ (Learning)} = P \text{ (Programmed Learning)} + Q \text{ (Questioning Insight)}$$

Team learning

Team learning can be viewed as the capacity of a group to engage appropriately in dialogue and discussion (Senge 1990). There are three characteristics of effective team learning:

- ability to think insightfully about complex issues and bring together the collective intelligence of the team rather than the insight of the dominant individual;
- ability to provide innovative and coordinated action. This implies alignment of minds between team members and a conscious awareness of other team members and their actions. The example of great jazz ensembles provides a useful metaphor for spontaneous and coordinated action;
- ability to share practices and skills between teams in organisations.

Dialogue is the free and creative exploration of complex issues involving active listening and suspending one's own view. The purpose of dialogue is to go beyond one's own understanding and become an observer of one's own thinking. This means suspending one's own assumptions and playing with different ideas. Dialogue means letting go of power differentials between team players and treating each member equally. It means exploring our assumptions behind our closely held views. Dialogues are particularly useful for divergent thinking where we want a richer grasp of a complex issue rather than fostering agreement. All the early western philosophers such as Socrates, Plato and Aristotle used dialogue in their development of knowledge. Isaacs (1993) provides a useful analogy of the dialogue process when it works well:

'A flock of birds suddenly taking flight from a tree reveals the potential coordination of dialogue: this movement all at once, a wholeness and listening together that permits individual differentiation but is still highly interconnected.'

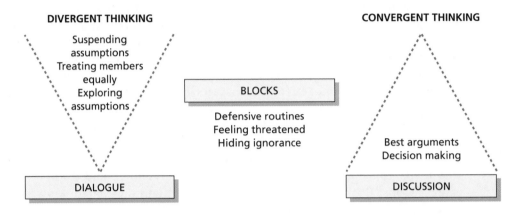

Figure 5.2 **Team learning** (Senge 1990)

Discussion is complementary to dialogue and is best employed in situations of convergent thinking and decision making, as shown in Figure 5.2. In discussion, different views are presented and defended and there is the search for the best view and arguments to support the decision that needs to be made (Senge 1990). Discussions converge to a conclusion and a course of action. The assumption is that the best argument tends to win in discussions. However, it can be the best arguer using rhetoric or emotive language rather than logic that wins as objective criteria against which the quality of and validity of an argument are rarely tested.

However, there can be defensive routines that can block effective team learning, especially if an individual digs in their heels with their own perspective. This can lead to team conflict, entrenched views and a block of energy flow in a team. Often the defensive routines can arise from individuals not wishing to confront their own thinking to save themselves from threat or embarrassment. This enables them to maintain an air of confidence in a situation based on past judgements and obscures their ignorance.

The distinction between discussion and dialogue can be seen as the difference between decision making and sense making. Weick (2002) describes how a leading firefighter makes this distinction clear:

> 'If I make a decision it is a possession, I take pride in it, I tend to defend it and not listen to those who question it. If I make sense, then this is more dynamic and I listen and I can change it. A decision is something you polish. Sense making is a direction for the next period.'

Drivers of organisational learning: success or failure?

Is failure a prerequisite to organisational learning? If it is, many organisations do little to cultivate it and learn the important lessons from it. Instead, we live in a dominant culture where failure and mistakes are often not tolerated, leading to behaviours where people don't talk about them, dissociate themselves from them and never freely admit to such experiences. Yet failures and mistakes occur on a daily basis in organisations and they can be costly if there isn't a culture of 'error harvesting' where people share their mistakes and hard-won lessons with fellow colleagues. In large organisations, this could prevent costly mistakes from recurring due to blame cultures that may be dominant. Successful forms of 'error harvesting' cultivated in organisations have included groups or work teams coming together on a regular basis and discussing problems, issues and collective appraisals on remedial measures and future actions. Such reflective groupings have been called 'quality circles' or 'action learning groups' in the past.

What is the problem with success? Surely it provides a secure and reliable basis for future action? If certain practices, procedures and routines have worked in the past, why discard them for something new? Success tends to maintain the status quo and short-term stability as people are rewarded for their successes and follow their tried and tested ways. The danger is that success can lead to complacency, restricted search and attention, risk aversion and homogeneity (Sitkin 1992).

Success can lead to little motivation to change our ways as existing behaviours are reinforced. The tendency is towards risk-averse and conservative behaviours connected with innovation or decision making. Managers want to guard themselves against the embarrassment and dangers of undertaking risky options that may backfire. Firms prefer to pursue the traditional ways that have worked in the past and have led to their success. Given the nature of dynamic external environments, such 'play it safe' behaviours can provide reliable performance only in the short term. Some of the characteristics of success and failure in organisations are shown in Figure 5.3.

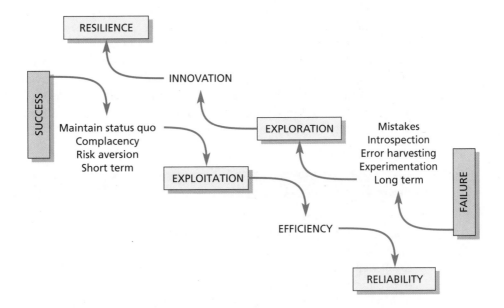

Figure 5.3 **Success and failure in organisations**

Failure allows organisations to learn through experimentation and making adjustments from their mistakes. Major failures are to be avoided as they can lead to the ultimate demise of any firm. However, modest failures could be tolerated to enhance the levels of risk taking and foster experimentation. Failure challenges traditional norms and promotes greater introspection and analysis of what went wrong. People tend to focus on the inconsistencies of the outcome and draw attention to problems that may have been overlooked. This stimulates much greater experimentation with new strategies, procedures and processes. Such varied outcomes and resulting capabilities can lead organisations to be more adaptable to unexpected environments. Hence, moderate levels of failure can lead to increased innovation and improve an organisation's resilience to adapt to differing environments. As Shakespeare reminds us in *Measure for Measure*:

'They say best men are moulded out of faults and, for the most, become much more the better for being a little bad.'

It is clear that organisations can be weighed down by their history, their past experiences and traditions laid down by their founding fathers. But how far is history a driver for organisational learning? Organisational learning from history may be restricted to small samples of experience in any given situation (March et al. 1991). If an organisation's experience was successful in the past, the learning and behaviours may become embedded in its actions. If there are different perspectives and cultures in an organisation, this may lead to several different lessons being learnt from the same experience and increasing an organisation's repertoire of interpretations.

Single-loop and double-loop learning

The nature of organisational learning will depend to a large extent on one's definition of an organisation. If one views the organisation as a political entity, the level of organisational learning will depend on political theory and theory of socio-political movements. In a similar way, if one views the organisation as a culture, the level of organisational learning will depend on studies connected with anthropology, ethnomethodology and phenomenology. If one takes a cognitive school approach, organisational learning may be viewed as a distinction between cognition development and behavioural development (Fiol and Lyles 1985). These conceptions of organisational learning as a mental process have become embedded within the literature through the notions of single-loop learning (behavioural) and double-loop learning (cognitive) (Argyris and Schon 1978).

Single-loop learning refers to the process that maintains the central features of the organisation's 'theory-in-use' by detecting and correcting errors within a given system of rules. This means that, given any set of problems, an organisation is likely to act in the same traditional ways and patterns. In contrast, the higher cognitive level of double-loop learning is where current organisational norms and assumptions are questioned to establish a new set of norms. Firms do not continue with their age-old patterns but question their assumptions and values. This often leads to new ways of working and acting.

For example, a firm may be faced with the problem of drastically diminishing sales. The firm may place the blame for the problem on the poor sales force and introduce measures to make them work harder or face redundancy. This would be an example of single-loop learning where the firm responds in a tried and tested manner but assumes it can accomplish its goals by pushing harder. An example of double-loop learning would be if the firm tried to assess the problem more closely and look at the underlying assumptions. It might discover that the customers find its products or services dated, unappealing and poor value for money compared with competitive offerings. In this situation the firm might decide to innovate its product or service by engaging the collective talents of its marketing, design and operations teams. The new product or service might compete more effectively in the changing competitive markets. Such measures would be an example of double-loop learning.

This example illustrates the difference between exploration and exploitation in organisational learning (March *et al.* 1991). Exploration behaviours (double-loop learning) are where organisations engage in risk taking, play with ideas, experiment, discover and innovate. In contrast, exploitation behaviours (single-loop learning) are concerned with the refinement of existing processes and emphasise efficiency goals. Both behaviours are important for an organisation, depending on the context. If efficiency is the driving force in the competitive environment, single-loop or exploitation behaviours become important. However, there can be a continual flux between exploitation and exploration as they compete for a firm's scarce resources.

As exploration behaviours require risk taking and experimentation, their outcomes can be less certain and have much longer time horizons. The exploration of new ideas, markets and relationships and their likely outcomes are much more ambiguous than exploiting and imitating current methods and relationships. It has been argued that as firms adapt to the changing environments by refining exploitation behaviours more rapidly than exploration ones, they are likely to be effective in the short term but self-destructive in the long term.

Sensemaking

Sensemaking is concerned with making sense of ambiguous situations of high complexity and uncertainty. It involves the process of 'situational awareness' where individuals and organisations can understand the complex linkages between people, places and events to allow them to make inferences of future scenarios and act accordingly. Situational awareness is an understanding of the interrelationships between information, events and actions and how they influence present and future goals and objectives. It is the perception and understanding of different elements in the environment and how they may project into the near future (Endsley 1995). A lack of situational awareness is the primary factor affecting human error in accidents. Hence, situational awareness is vitally important in situations where poor judgement of environmental factors and inferences of their future changes can lead to adverse consequences. Examples include aviation, critical paramedic interventions and threats of nuclear attack or war. Mental models are critical to situational awareness. They provide highly organised and dynamic knowledge structures gained through years of experience. People with high levels of situational awareness are not overwhelmed by information overload in complex environments but are able to process new data using their mental models from previous experiences (Klein *et al.* 2006).

Sensemaking occurs when individuals or organisations realise that their mental models and frames of reference are inadequate for understanding events in situations of complexity or uncertainty. Sensemaking is best conceived as the process that leads to the outcome of situational awareness. It is an iterative process between mental models and changing data to find the best fit between the two. At the individual level, Dervin (2003) suggests sensemaking arises when an individual notices a gap between their point of view from previous experiences and new observations that do not fit this world view. Sensemaking is about bridging the 'cognitive gap' between these two situations to develop a changed and more refined mental model of the observed phenomena.

At the organisational level, sensemaking is 'a way station on the road to a consensually constructed, coordinated system of action' (Taylor and Van Every 2000, p. 275). The 'way station' is like the cognitive gap where new circumstances are comprehended in words to inform future action. The current state of the world is different from expectations. There is normally an interruption where people search for reasons to resume their disrupted activity. If resumption of activity is difficult, sensemaking moves towards alternative action or further deliberation. Meaning in sensemaking arises through labelling and categorisation. Labelling is articulating cognitive representations of certain interdependent events that suggest some form of managerial action. These representations can be placed into categories that are socially defined. Categories need a certain level of plasticity to respond to changing circumstances and uncertainty. Sensemaking is not about truth and accuracy, but about updating plausible stories and narratives that incorporate new observations. These arise from dialogue, bargaining, persuasion and negation created through new actions.

Identity (who we think we are) shapes our mental models and actions in organisations. External parties can stabilise or destabilise identity by their images of the organisation. Identity can be conceived as sensegiving through external parties (present and future images) and through a combination of insider and outsider images (Gioia and Chittipeddi, 1991). When organisations are sensemaking in uncertain times, they may ask the following searching questions linked to their identity: 'Who are we? What are we doing? What matters? Why does it matter?' (Weick *et al.* 2005, p. 416). Sensemaking processes are shown in Figure 5.4.

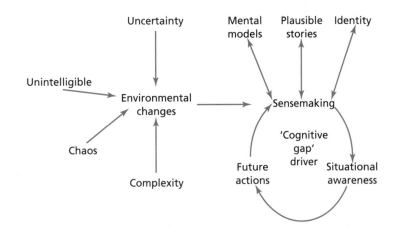

Figure 5.4 Sensemaking and situational awareness

Organisational learning frameworks

In the organisational learning literatures, there is an underlying assumption that learning will improve a firm's performance. In contrast, a key premise in the strategy literatures is that this will be achieved by close alignment of the firm to its environment. A definition of organisational learning based on action that encompasses such assumptions is proposed by Fiol and Lyles (1985):

> *'Organisational learning means the process of improving actions through better knowledge and understanding.'*

A number of studies have investigated the disparate literatures of organisational learning and tried to chart its varied terrain (Crossan *et al.* 1999; Easterby-Smith 1997; Fiol and Lyles 1985; Huber 1991; Levitt and March 1988; Shrivastava 1983). Each examination has provided a somewhat different map of the landscape depending on the epistemological perspectives and backgrounds of the researchers. A recent ethnomethodology framework of organisational learning (Bontis *et al.* 2002; Crossan *et al.* 1999) builds on the tension between exploration and exploitation in organisations and places these notions at the heart of strategic renewal. Renewal is based on organisations exploring and learning new ways while at the same time exploiting what they have already learnt. This framework considers organisational learning at three levels: individual, group and organisational, as shown in Table 5.1. There are four learning processes that flow naturally from one to another without any clear distinction of where they begin or end. Also, there may be feedback loops from the learning processes between the three levels.

Table 5.1 **Organisational learning framework** (Crossan *et al.* 1999)

Level	Process	Inputs/outcomes
Individual	Intuiting	Experiences Images Metaphors
	Interpreting	Language Cognitive map Conversation/dialogue
Group	Integrating	Shared understandings Mutual adjustments Interactive systems
Organisation	Institutionalising	Routines Diagnostic systems Rules and procedures

The four learning processes entail:

- *Intuiting*. This is largely a subconscious process that often requires some form of pattern recognition. For instance, an expert may be able to foresee a pattern in a problem that a novice may not. This pattern recognition will support exploitation. However, intuition is also important for exploration to help generate new insights and novel applications. Metaphors and the use of imagery can help provide the language to communicate one's insight to someone else.

- *Interpreting*. This is the process of explaining through words and/or actions an insight or an idea to one's self or to another person. We develop our own cognitive map of a domain and can interpret the same stimulus differently thanks to our established cognitive maps. In a group situation, this can result in multiple and potentially conflicting interpretations of the best course of action.

- *Integrating*. This learning process is about developing shared understanding and taking coordinated action through mutual adjustment. Group dialogue and storytelling are seen as major tools for developing new and deeper shared understandings.

- *Institutionalising*. This learning process is to ensure that routinised actions occur. Successful actions over time often become embedded in organisational routines. Such routines have an effect on the systems, structures and strategies of an organisation. One characteristic of institutionalisation is the endurance of the behaviour over a period of time.

This model proceeds to suggest a dynamic between the four learning processes through 'feedforward' and feedback loops. It does not elaborate on how these processes assist organisations to find the balance between exploration and exploitation behaviours which are seen as critical for strategic renewal. Most of the innovation in this 4I framework rests on the entrepreneurial intuiting in the first individual phase. Without the 'feedforward' loops, it is unlikely that the institutionalised organisational routines would be challenged, with a consequence of exploitation behaviours predominating within any organisation. How could managers balance the wisdom of their experts with the uneasy flair of the entrepreneurs? What effect would culture have on strategic renewal? Dialogue may be valuable for developing divergent thinking but what are the implications for actions requiring convergent thinking and decision making?

One criticism of this 4Is model is the tendency in management literature towards prescriptions related to certain characters of the alphabet: 4Ps in marketing and 4Is in action learning (Mumford 1991). What distinguishes the effectiveness of Mumford's model based on 4Is of interaction, integration, implementation and iteration over the Crossan *et al.* one? There appear to be similarities between interaction in one model and interpreting in another, integration occurs in both models, and iteration could be seen as a form of the feedback loops leading to institutionalisation.

Most empirical research in organisational learning tends to be qualitative in nature and it is relatively uncommon to find many quantitative studies. This is mainly related to the difficulties of developing valid instruments that measure organisational learning. One can always develop a multitude of items from pilot interviews and theoretical frameworks related to organisational learning. From statistical analysis one can demonstrate the strength of reliability of these constructs relatively easily. However, we still don't know whether what we are measuring is really organisational learning. Evidence for validity of these instruments is often found wanting. The main reason is that there isn't a singular valid instrument in the public domain that has the consensus of this academic community. If this was the case, one could develop new instruments confidently, knowing that an element of a valid instrument was contained within the questionnaire for empirical testing.

The second major issue is around sampling. Who do you send your questionnaires to? How many people need to be sampled within a firm to get a reliable sample? Assuming that the research has limited resources, do you sample many people in a few firms or a few people in lots of firms to get greater generalisations from the results? Some researchers have surveyed a single senior executive from each firm, assuming that their position is likely to give them a 'helicopter view' of the organisation. Given the complexity of these methodological issues, can the results from quantitative studies of organisational learning be meaningful?

One of the seminal papers in this discipline comes from Huber (1991) who attempts to understand and evaluate the diverse literatures of organisational learning under four constructs, as shown in Figure 5.5. He adopts an information-processing perspective defining organisational learning as follows:

> 'An entity learns if, through its processing of information, the range of its potential behaviours is changed.'

This framework adopts a behavioural rather than a cognitive perspective of learning and assumes that the four constructs are interrelated. No attempt is made to show how the processes in each construct integrate with one another. Knowledge acquisition is seen as the process by which knowledge is obtained. Information distribution is the process by which information is shared, which can often lead to new information or understanding. Information interpretation is the process by which information is given one or more interpretations. Organisational memory is the means by which knowledge is stored for future use (Huber 1991).

Figure 5.5 **Organisational learning framework** (Huber 1991)

The main criticisms of this perspective are around the problems of implementing organisational learning (Easterby-Smith 1997):

● Political behaviours in organisations are not considered in the framework and can lead to distortion and suppression of information. The political climate can also lead managers to make decisions based on irrational grounds. The framework could be considered as politically naïve.

● As the framework adopts a behavioural rather than a cognitive perspective, there is a danger that it may lead to a tendency towards exploitation rather than exploration in organisations.

● Behavioural perspective may create a tendency to hold on to old views and practices rather than questioning them.

Knowledge acquisition

Organisations acquire new knowledge through the processes of congenital learning, experiential learning, vicarious learning, grafting, and searching and noticing (Huber 1991), as shown in Figure 5.6. Congenital learning is the learning influenced by the founding fathers of the organisation. This inherited knowledge can affect the way a firm acts and interprets new knowledge. Experiential learning is acquired from direct experience and can be found in a number of guises:

● Organisational experiments may take the form of pilot studies with feedback of findings and recommendations to the organisation.

● Move from behavioural learning to cognitive learning through questioning key assumptions and values.

● Enhancing adaptability as an experimenting organisation with a greater emphasis on exploration rather than exploitation.

● Unintentional learning through the haphazard and multi-faceted lives of workers.

● Learning curves or 'learning by doing' show that as an organisation produces more of a product, the unit cost of production decreases at a decreasing rate. The beauty of this experiential learning is that performance over time can often be predicted using a mathematical model. Such learning can be explained through individuals learning over time as well as the organisation, such as the effective use of technology (Yelle 1979). Effective decisions can be made by managers on how best to balance technology against working practices (Epple *et al.* 1996).

Figure 5.6 **Knowledge acquisition constructs** (Huber 1991)

Often organisations don't have the time to gain certain knowledge to meet competitive pressures. They may seek to borrow competitors' strategies, practices and technologies. Such learning is termed vicarious learning and it adopts imitation or mimicry of other firms. Gaining the 'know how' of other firms is termed 'corporate intelligence' and can be gained from consultants, professional meetings and publications.

Knowledge can also be acquired by 'grafting' or employing new members with the knowledge and skills lacking within the organisation. This may be seen as preferable to developing the knowledge and skills in-house through various human resource interventions. On a bigger scale, firms engage in acquisitions of other companies where the acquisition may have core competences lacking within the parent firm.

Critical thinking and reflection

Benchmarking is all the rage in some organisations. What do you think are the problems of this form of vicarious learning? Similarly, what are the advantages and limitations of using off-the-shelf solutions compared with building them in-house? From your experience in organisations, what do you feel hinders them from learning? Many organisations seem to make the same mistakes over and over again. What do you believe could help organisations break such detrimental cycles?

Firms also acquire knowledge through intentional search and unintentional noticing behaviours. Organisational search can take a number of forms (Huber 1991):

● scanning – a monitoring behaviour of organisations often conducted by senior managers searching for non-routine but relevant information;

● focused search linked to a particular organisational problem;

● performance monitoring of internal targets and measures as well as satisfying the needs of external stakeholders.

Information distribution

In small organisations, information distribution may remain at a very informal level. However, the quality of information distribution may lead to new or more broadly based organisational learning. Such information sharing can enable the development of new information as well as new understanding (Krone *et al.* 1987). Information distribution highlights the role of organisational communication and the nature of the internal political environments (Jashapara 1993) which may aid or hinder such communication. There are technological aspects (see Chapter 7) of knowledge storage and retrieval as well as social capital aspects such as the relationships between employees (see Chapter 3) that will have an impact on the nature of information distribution within an organisation.

Information interpretation

Information interpretation can be seen as the process by which information is given meaning and the development of shared understanding (Daft and Weick 1984; Huber 1991). Is the goal to develop similar understandings or diverse understandings within organisations? Would similar understandings result in greater cooperation and coherence whereas more diverse understandings would lead to greater strife and conflict? The shared understandings and interpretations of new information are affected by cognitive maps and framing, media richness, information overload and unlearning, as shown in Figure 5.7.

A person's existing cognitive map determines how a piece of information is interpreted. They may be influenced by their position within an organisational hierarchy, previous experience and their current working team and environment. To establish uniformity of shared interpretation, there needs to be uniformity in cognitive maps among the team. This is easier when new information is framed in a consistent and familiar manner. If new information is framed in a different manner around different divisional units, it is likely that there will be a diversity of shared understandings of the information.

Media richness is the communication medium's capacity to change mental representations within a specific time interval (Huber 1991). Managers often explore the most effective media to communicate their message to develop shared meaning. For example, the use of e-mail as opposed to face-to-face meetings to transmit a message may convey very differing messages. Face-to-face communication has much greater richness as it displays the person's tone of voice and body language as well as the words, unlike the monotone nature of e-mails.

Information overload has a direct effect on an individual's capacity to interpret information. In group situations, information overload may result in disparities of shared understandings due to different levels of overload within the same group. Even if there are consistencies in the levels of overload within a group, there are likely to be diverse interpretations of the same message as individuals respond more to their own internal state and perceptions than to the external stimulus.

Figure 5.7 **Information interpretation constructs** (Huber 1991)

Critical thinking and reflection

We live in a world where we are bombarded with information and countless e-mails every day. From your experience, describe your perceptions of information overload on your job. How do you manage large quantities of information? If you discard much of this information, how do you know what to discard? How does information overload affect your emotions and reasoning? What practical strategies have you developed to cope with information overload?

Unlearning is the process by which individuals discard obsolete or misleading knowledge (Hedberg 1981). At an organisational level, unlearning can have the effect of blocking the firm in areas where it used the misleading knowledge or behaviours. It can also activate a firm to search for knowledge or behaviours to replace the obsolete ones and encourage it to become more open to new forms of learning and knowledge. Further elaboration of unlearning is provided below.

Organisational memory

The old oral traditions utilised the human memory and highlighted its limitations. Long periods of time were spent memorising information, leaving little room for critical evaluation. In an organisational context, organisational memory may reside in people's minds as repositories of organisational knowledge. However, as people leave a firm, this precious organisational memory may be lost for ever. This 'soft' form of organisational memory can be invaluable in a variety of circumstances:

- diagnosing an error in a complex piece of technology;
- knowledge of organisational skills, experts and resources;
- locating non-traditional information sources.

In the psychology literature, a distinction is made between semantic (general) and episodic (context-specific) memory (Stein and Zwass 1995). Semantic memory comes from shared interpretations of significant events that are not personally experienced and may take the form of handbooks and procedural manuals. Episodic memory is shared interpretations and collective understandings of personally experienced events.

The 'hard' forms of organisational memory relate to storage and retrieval processes and computer-based organisational memory, as shown in Figure 5.8. The latest KM component technologies related to effective storage and retrieval and data warehouses are discussed in Chapters 7 and 8. Such notions of organisational memory treat the construct as a set of repositories of stored information from an organisation's history. The repositories may contain knowledge about individuals, culture, transformations, structure and ecology (Walsh and Ungson 1991).

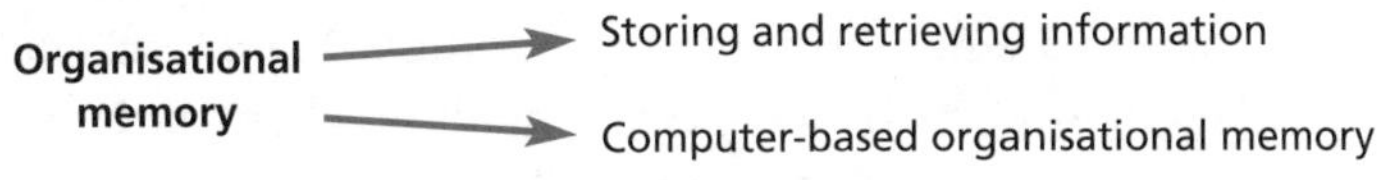

Organisational memory → Storing and retrieving information
→ Computer-based organisational memory

Figure 5.8 **Organisational memory constructs**

Unlearning

Do organisations exist in closed or open systems? Often the tendency among decision makers is to treat their subsystems and environments as closed systems, leading to a perception of stability in organisational learning. This is fine if environmental changes are low, stable and predictable. Typically after some delay, organisations will respond to environmental changes by adjusting their goals and expectations and modifing their decision-making behaviours. In benevolent environments, there is little incentive for organisations to change their ways, which ultimately can lead to inertia and stagnation.

However, if the environmental changes are more substantial and discontinuous, the traditional responses may need to be reconsidered, deleted and replaced to ensure organisational survival. This is known as unlearning.

'Unlearning is a process through which learners discard knowledge. Unlearning makes way for new responses and mental maps.' (Hedberg 1981)

Successful behaviours in the past may no longer provide a valid response to future levels of environmental uncertainty. This requires organisations to pull down obsolete mental maps showing the correct ways of doing things and starting afresh. If they don't do this, the environmental discontinuities may threaten an organisation's survival. The effective response in these circumstances is to unlearn old behaviours and learn new ones.

Unlearning is a difficult and cumbersome process as it threatens the organisation's way of doing things. To external observers, organisations undergoing unlearning can appear incompetent and ineffectual. On the inside of organisations, unlearning can lead to disorientation and upheaval where traditional benchmarks are lost. Unlearning has three modes of operation (Hedberg 1981):

- challenge and negate (disconfirmation) processes for selecting and identifying stimuli. People and organisations unlearn their world views;
- challenge and negate (disconfirmation) any connections between stimuli and responses so that people don't know what responses to make to particular stimuli;
- challenge and negate (disconfirmation) any connections between responses so that people no longer know how to assemble responses to new situations.

Unlearning can be unnerving at an individual level as the traditional points of reference are lost. So what can act as useful triggers for unlearning in organisations? Effective triggers include problems, which can arise from cashflow shortages, declining revenues and profits, financial losses and criticisms from stakeholders. Problems typically arise from the gap between performance and expectations. Organisations do not respond in new ways to all problems. The deviation between performance and expectations needs to be large before any adjustments or reorganisations are likely to occur, as shown in Figure 5.9.

Problems are not the only triggers, otherwise problem-ridden organisations would be the best innovators (Hedberg 1981) and this is clearly not the case. The dilemma for many organisations undergoing major problems and crises is that they cannot afford to take the

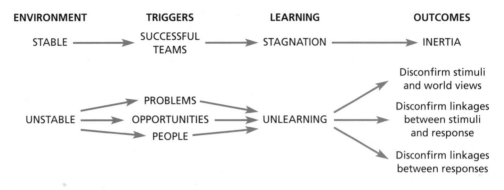

Figure 5.9 **Environments and unlearning**

necessary risks implied in the unlearning process. Opportunities in the external environment such as development of niche markets can also provide triggers for unlearning.

The third trigger for unlearning is people, particularly when key individuals leave the organisation, taking with them the experiences of procedures and processes from the organisational memory.

Organisational routines

Organisational routines are an important aspect of organisational learning as they help us to understand the interplay between an organisation's structure, its processes and its actions. Originally, routines were associated with an organisation's operating procedures and resembled the mechanical notions of computer programs with their routines and subroutines (Cyert and March 1963; March and Simon 1958). This included an organisation's norms, conventions, rules and procedures and the way it operates on a daily basis. They helped contribute to an organisation's stability. These routines were embedded in the organisation's culture, beliefs and frameworks and could often contradict rules found in operating manuals. In general, the routines were seen as independent of individual actors and capable of surviving significant turnover in personnel (Levitt and March 1988). Routines also explained the inertia within organisations through repeated patterns of behaviour bound by rules and customs (Nelson and Winter 1982). Such routines were seen as regular and predictable patterns of behaviour. In new circumstances, an organisation might draw from a pool of alternative routines (Levitt and March 1988).

Routines can be communicated through a variety of channels such as imitation, socialisation, education and personalisation processes, and become part of the collective memory. It was initially assumed that organisational routines did not change, but increasing empirical research shows that routines *are* subject to change (Feldman 2000; Pentland and Rueter 1994). A number of definitions of this phenomenon are forwarded in the literature:

'An executable capability for repeated performance in some context that has been learned by an organization in response to selective pressures.' (Cohen *et al.* 1996)

'An organizational routine is not a single pattern but, rather, a set of possible patterns – enabled and constrained by a variety of organizational, social, physical and cognitive structures – from which organizational members enact particular performances.' (Pentland and Rueter 1994)

'Recurring patterns of behaviour of multiple organizational members involved in performing organizational tasks.' (Feldman and Rafaeli 2002)

Cohen and Bacdayan (1994) have argued that organisational routines are stored as procedural memory. They make a distinction between 'procedural' memory and 'declarative' memory arising in the psychology literature. Procedural memory stores the cognitive and motor skills associated with an individual's skilled actions and could be considered as the individual 'know how'. By nature, it is tacit, relatively automatic and difficult to articulate. In contrast, declarative memory is the repository of facts, propositions and events and similar to an individual's 'know what' or explicit knowledge. The difference is similar to the more static notion of 'organisation' compared with the more dynamic process of 'organising' (Weick 1979).

Routines are an important part of an organisation's competence and without them organisations would lack efficient methods of collective action. However, routines can have detrimental consequences if they are automatically transferred to inappropriate new situations. Working routines are seen as much more than standard operating procedures as official documents may or may not be followed. What happens in reality is similar in distinction between espoused theories and theories-in-use in organisations (Argyris and Schon 1978). They are produced gradually over time through multi-actor learning engaged in a particular routine. The tacit and multi-actor nature of organisational routines makes them difficult to research effectively as the problem entails surfacing, verbalising and externalising an organisation's 'unconscious' memory (Cohen and Bacdayan 1994). Changes in habitual routines in groups can be triggered in a number of ways (Gersick and Hackman 1990):

- encountering a novel state of affairs;
- experiencing a failure;
- reaching a milestone in the life or work of the group;
- receiving an intervention that calls members' attention to their group norms;
- having to cope with change in the structure of the group itself.

Critical thinking and reflection

As human beings, we have been considered as creatures of habit. Such habits in organisational terms may be considered as routines. How do you believe that such stable patterns of behaviour or organisational routines can aid or hinder organisations? From your experience, do you feel that all processes, no matter how new or innovative, inevitably lead to organisational routines? Is it worth actively discouraging such routines in organisations? If so, how?

An alternative conception of organisational routines is one that resembles a set of possible patterns that are neither fixed nor automatic. A novel representation of routines is to use a grammatical model (Pentland and Rueter 1994). The 'grammar' analogy to routines allows actors to use a set of possibilities to accomplish a task without specifying a fixed outcome. This model acknowledges the importance of both the structure and agency (actor) within routines rather than the earlier fixation on operating procedures and the traditional elements of stimulus and automatic response. This approach concurs with social theory that regards routines in social activity as achieved through considerable effort (Giddens 1984).

A similar metaphor which demonstrates the stability and adaptability of routines is the ballroom dance (Feldman and Rafaeli 2002). Individual actions in dances are scripted beforehand but dances can allow flexibility depending on the context. Dancers will adapt their styles to this context depending on the number of other dancers on the floor, any obstructions in the floor, the competence of their partner and whether or not they have danced the particular number before. Communication between the dancers (similar to organisational routines) will allow flexibility in the dance to occur. Empirical research suggests that changes in organisational routines can occur due to a number of reasons (Feldman 2000):

- *Repairing* routines so that participants can produce intended and desired outcomes. This occurs when actions do not produce the intended outcome or produce an undesirable outcome.

- *Expanding* routines so that participants can produce new possibilities from outcomes. The changed routine takes advantage of new possibilities.

- *Striving* routines so that participants can respond to outcomes that fall short of ideals. This attempts to attain something that is difficult by nature.

Success and failure in outcomes can have a major impact on routines. Favourable performance with an inferior routine can lead to its perpetuation and the denial of a superior routine can lead to a competency trap (Levitt and March 1988). Sub-optimal performance may persist with the use of familiar procedures, practices and technologies. Success reinforces successful routines whilst inhibiting other routines. As outlined earlier in this chapter, failure or significant performance gaps may be the necessary determinant to change organisational routines as organisations search for ones that can match their desired outcomes.

Recent research has tried to unravel the processes that contribute to the stability and change of organisational routines (Feldman and Rafaeli 2002). The starting point in this theory is that organisational routines are a form of coordination used in organisations. The routines make 'connections' where connections are defined as the interactions between people that enable them to transfer information. The outcomes of the connection process are social support and information transfer (note the similarity to social capital and knowledge transfer). The encounters in connections create variations in strong and weak ties between organisational members.

The connections enable shared understandings to occur. These arise through verbal as well as non-verbal communication. The coming together of people in a routine allows different interpretations to be explored and the development of a common

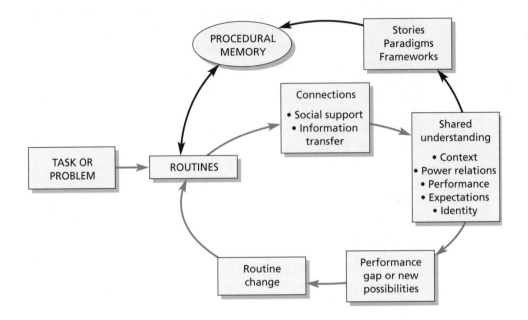

Figure 5.10 **Organisational routines** (adapted from Cohen and Bacdayan 1994; Feldman and Rafaeli 2002)

understanding. These understandings include aspects of the organisational context, performance expectations, power relations and organisational identity. The organisational context concerns what an organisation does and why, as well as who are the critical stakeholders. The power relations allow participants to understand the hierarchy and their status within the organisation. This theory assumes a time delay between routines and their development of connections and shared understandings and rather like the same notion in social theory needs to be worked on over time. A model providing a synthesis of the organisational routine literature is shown in Figure 5.10 (Cohen and Bacdayan 1994; Feldman and Rafaeli 2002). A useful anology to describe organisational routines was expressed vividly by an anonymous reviewer as follows:

> 'Routines are like ruts in a well-travelled road. They do not exactly determine where the next wagon will go, but neither do they merely describe where past wagons have gone.' (Pentland and Rueter 1994)

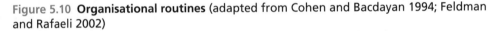

Dynamic capabilities

Dynamic capabilities as a concept is a relatively new phenomenon and has evolved from research on organisational routines. In fact, there is confusion within the literature about where organisational routines end and dynamic capabilities begin. It is fair to say that the literature on dynamic capabilities is based more on theoretical developments rather than empirical research. On a simplistic level, dynamic capabilities have been considered as 'routines to learn routines', similar to the notion of deutero-learning (learning to learn). The following definitions of dynamic capabilities illustrate some of the variations in the field:

'Firm's ability to integrate, build, and reconfigure internal and external competences to address rapidly changing environments.' (Teece *et al.* 1997)

'The firm's processes that use resources – specifically the processes to integrate, reconfigure, gain and release resources – to match and even create market change. Dynamic capabilities thus are organizational and strategic routines by which firms achieve new resource configurations as markets emerge, collide, split, evolve, and die.' (Eisenhardt and Martin 2000)

'A dynamic capability is a learned and stable pattern of collective activity through which the organization systematically generates and modifies its operating routines in pursuit of improved effectiveness.' (Zollo and Winter 2002)

So are organisational routines and dynamic capabilities synonymous concepts? The key distinction appears to be the level of change encountered as a factor of market dynamism. In stable or static environments and market conditions, organisational routines predominate, characterised by stable patterns of behaviour. The routines can be complex but are predictable and build on existing knowledge. They evolve slowly over time and exhibit qualities of single-loop learning. However, in moderately dynamic or highly volatile markets, the use of organisational routines can prove hazardous in their automatic response to changed stimuli. Organisations can learn to adapt their routines to the changed circumstances, which leads to the development of dynamic capabilities. If this does not occur, core competences can become core rigidities (Leonard-Barton 1992).

The fine line between organisational routines and dynamic capabilities arises due to models that highlight similar stable and predictable modes of activity for each phenomenon (Zollo and Winter 2002). In this conception, dynamic capabilities can be viewed as modified operating routines following predictable mathematical arrangements, as shown in Table 5.2. The primary distinction is systematic learning, which implies a stable pattern of learning not dissimilar to single-loop learning. What happens in highly volatile market conditions when organisations cannot rely on systematic learning and existing knowledge? Do organisations fall back on their old tried and trusted learning mechanisms in the vain hope of achieving desired outcomes?

Experience accumulation is perceived as occurring from learning investments aimed at developing a collective understanding of action–performance linkages. A principal aspect of the learning process is 'knowledge articulation' when groups of people come together in a variety of circumstances such as meetings and debriefing sessions and make their understandings and interpretations of a situation explicit.

Table 5.2 **Dynamic capabilities** (adapted from Zollo and Winter 2002)

Dynamic capabilities	=	Systematic learning + Organisational routines
Systematic learning	=	Experience accumulation + Knowledge articulation + Knowledge codification

This does not imply that there needs to be agreement within the group, but through a process of dialogue and discussion, a shared understanding is developed. Given that much of the knowledge is likely to be tacit, this process of externalisation is important to make the knowledge explicit. Knowledge codification as part of the systematic learning allows further reflection on existing routines to help understand which routines work, which don't work, and why (Zollo and Winter 2002). Knowledge codification may take the form of developing manuals, decision-support systems and blueprint guides of best practice.

Eisenhardt and Martin (2000) provide a clearer distinction between organisational routines and dynamic capabilities. They suggest that in stable and moderately dynamic market conditions, collective organisational activity resembles traditional predictable routines where managers rely heavily on their existing tacit knowledge. However, in high-velocity and volatile markets, organisational activity tends towards dynamic capabilities where managers rely much less on existing knowledge due to the ambiguity of the situation and more on situation-specific new knowledge. In these uncertain environments, the dynamic capabilities are composed of simple routines consisting of very few rules and a greater tendency towards improvisation. Flexibility of response becomes an important determinant. Dynamic capabilities possess a number of key attributes (Eisenhardt and Martin 2000):

- *equifinality* – firms develop similar dynamic capabilities even though they may have different starting points and take unique paths;
- *commonality of dynamic capabilities* – such routines are transferable between contexts and industries;
- *idiosyncrasy* – firms may have commonalities in their dynamic capabilities but differ in their levels of detail (firm specific) which leads to competitive advantage;
- *prototyping* – often used to test and gain new knowledge quickly through small losses and feedback;
- *real-time information* – to allow adjustment and adaptation to occur due to changing circumstances;
- *multiple options* – parallel consideration of alternatives to allow managers to act confidently and quickly;
- *path dependent* – a firm's investments in certain routines historically tend to constrain its future behaviour.

Dynamic capabilities can lead to competitive advantage if they are valuable, rare, inimitable and non-substitutable (VRIN attributes). However, it has been argued that they are necessary, but not sufficient, conditions for sustainable competitive advantage (Eisenhardt and Martin 2000). Their idiosyncratic nature may give them short-term competitive advantage, but this cannot be sustained as they are substitutable due to their equifinality and commonality characteristics.

Absorptive capacity

Many innovations occur through the acquisition and application of new knowledge from external sources. Absorptive capacity is the extent to which organisations can absorb and apply new knowledge such as scientific and technological advances. Cohen and Levinthal (1990, p. 128) introduced the concept and defined absorptive capacity as

'the ability of a firm to recognize the value of new external information, assimilate it, and apply it to commercial ends is critical to innovative capabilities.'

There is a lack of uniformity in defining absorptive capacity. One view is that absorptive capacity is a range of skills needed to deal with imported tacit knowledge and its application in organisations (Mowery *et al.* 1996). Another view is that it is the firm's capacity to learn and solve problems (Kim and Mauborgne 1998). Zahra and George (2002) make a distinction between potential and realised absorptive capacity. Lane, Koka and Pathak (2006, p. 856) critically reviewed the absorptive capacity literature and provided a reconceptualised definition:

'Absorptive capacity is a firm's ability to utilize externally held knowledge through three sequential processes: (1) recognizing and understanding potentially valuable new knowledge outside the firm through exploratory learning, (2) assimilating valuable new knowledge through transformative learning, and (3) using the assimilated knowledge to create new knowledge and commercial outputs through exploitative learning.'

This definition is in keeping with Easterby-Smith *et al.* (2008) who define absorptive capacity as

'the ability to locate new ideas and to incorporate them into an organization's process'.

Figure 5.11 shows the three key processes related to absorptive capacity. Absorptive capacity is based on cognitive structures and learning and increases with higher levels of knowledge and problem-solving capabilities. It is the ability of a firm to store past experiences as memory and retrieve this memory to apply to new knowledge and circumstances. The more diverse the knowledge base, the greater the likelihood for more learning, as there are increased linkages between past and present knowledge.

A firm's absorptive capacity depends on individual capacities and its ability to transfer knowledge across organisational boundaries. Gatekeepers are important in this respect to promote knowledge flows across unit boundaries. Individuals can network across these boundaries and learn about other people's complementary knowledge and capabilities. A diverse knowledge base is more likely to develop novel linkages leading to innovation. However, there is a balance between diversity and commonality of knowledge. If the knowledge base lacks commonality, application of new knowledge is unlikely to be fruitful.

Research & Development (R&D) departments can provide firms with strong absorptive capacities. They have the capacity to evaluate and incorporate new technological knowledge into the firm through their prior training and professional networks. This becomes important when new knowledge is highly complex and lacks fit with the firm's knowledge base. One way of increasing absorptive capacity is through exploiting competitor spillovers such as vicarious learning from competitor R&D departments. A number of scholars are suggesting that absorptive capacity may be closely linked with dynamic capabilities or be a component of this concept (Todorova and Durisin 2007; Wang and Ahmed 2007).

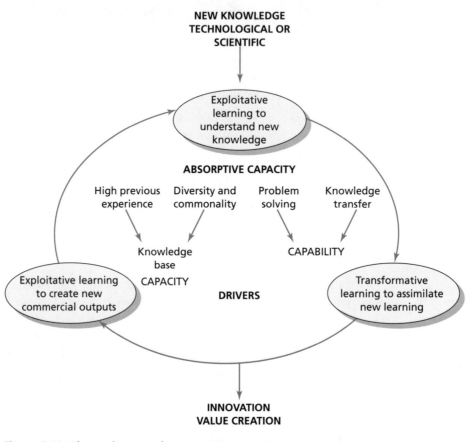

Figure 5.11 Absorptive capacity processes

Politics and organisational learning

The impact of politics and power relations has received relatively little attention within the literature (Coopey and Burgoyne 2000; Knights and McCabe 1998; Nissley and Casey 2002; Vince 2001). Organisations exist in dynamic contexts where power relations may vary considerably, resulting in internal environments fluctuating between polarities of cooperative, consensual coalitions at one end and conflictive in-fighting from deep political manoeuvrings at the other (Jashapara 2003).

In a broad societal context, politics can be seen as a way of ruling divided societies based on conciliation rather than on coercion or undue violence (Crick 1982). Linked with societal political structures is the notion of rights in most democracies: political rights, social rights and civil rights (Coopey and Burgoyne 2000). As organisations do not exist in a vacuum, the values and beliefs associated with these rights have a bearing on organisational political processes. Organisations also have a variety of leadership styles encompassing highly autocratic and highly participative ones. There is an interplay between top-down power relations and bottom-up ones. The leadership and management styles as well as day-to-day relationships will have a bearing on

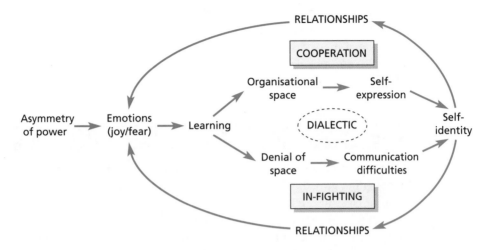

Figure 5.12 **Politics and organisational learning** (adapted from Coopey and Burgoyne 2000; Jashapara 2003; Vince 2001)

assymetrical power relations within an organisation. An individual may not have position power but may have power gained through self-confidence and authority in their relationships. A model showing the interplay between power, emotions, identity and the dialectic of learning is provided in Figure 5.12.

The asymmetry of power relations gives rise to a variety of emotions such as joy or fear. Often our learning in organisations is driven purely by anxiety and the way we relate to people around us (Vince 2001). Such emotions and power relations will have an important bearing on the nature of learning spaces created in organisations. At an individual level, positive emotions are more likely to lead to greater self-expression in discussions and dialogue with other group members, leading to a more self-assured identity. Even though there may be disagreements between organisational members, these organisational spaces are more likely to foster cooperative and partnership forms of working. In contrast, anxiety-driven emotions are more likely to result in the denial of organisational learning space where individual views and opinions become marginalised. This can lead to communication difficulties where individuals knowingly collude, censor and subvert organisational processes to meet their own goals (Coopey and Burgoyne 2000). This behaviour has a direct impact on a person's self-identity and is likely to breed political infighting. The cycle of fear can perpetuate indefinitely as relationships reinforce an individual's emotional make-up. For organisational learning, this can invoke the politics of remembering or forgetting (Nissley and Casey 2002). The politics of remembering are often associated with positive experiences whereas the politics of forgetting involve discarding painful and negative experiences from a firm's history.

Recent empirical research shows that effective organisations tend to fluctuate between cooperative and competitive phases rather than becoming fixated on an idealised form (Jashapara 2003). This provides a creative dialectic between opposites. There may be limits to the levels of cooperation as ideology discourages change and if individuals perceive a need for change they may be forced to challenge the ideology which breeds politics. Cooperation is more likely to foster single-loop learning where existing routines are maintained and go unchallenged. In contrast, political environments are more likely to foster double-loop learning as underlying assumptions and values are questioned more frequently. Empirical research shows the need for a dialectic in the central ground between cooperation and competition to promote short-term stability and a healthy upheaval in underlying norms and patterns of behaviour.

Critique of organisational learning

There are numerous criticisms of organisational learning in the literature. Despite the exponential growth of the literature, there is little agreement on the definition of the term or clear research-based guidelines for managers. Is the term about organisational processes or merely a metaphor for them? The literature lacks cumulative development or synthesis and integration of prior research. This has led to conceptual divergence, uncertainty about the term and difficulty in translating the term into a measurable construct. The term 'organisational learning' has become ambiguous and conceptually complex with a wide variety of disciplinary perspectives placing claims to the term – from psychology, sociology, to economics and political science (Friedman *et al.* 2005). In short, the concept is highly elusive even though it is extremely popular.

The behavioural approach to organisational learning (Cyert and March 1963) promotes human characteristics of learning to a non-human entity, the organisation. This anthropomorphism does not look at the 'black box' of organisational learning directly but rather at its antecedents such as its structures, routines, systems and technologies. Behaviourists are more interested in how incremental or radical environmental changes affect a firm's strategies, processes and structures.

In contrast, the cognition school is more interested in the 'black box' of organisational learning and asks the more vexed question: 'what is an organisation that it may learn?'. The emphasis is on how organisations reflect on their assumptions and values which affect individual and collective action. These actions become embedded in the psyche of the organisation – in their cognitive maps termed 'theories-in-use' which can be found functioning in their procedures, strategies and structures.

The practice-oriented school is high on rhetoric but low on actual guidance for managers. The literature provides expressions on what managers need to do such as 'being open to discordant information', 'avoid losing critical knowledge', but not on how managers can actually achieve these ambitions. The practice school is criticised for its evocative use of metaphors and the visionary nature of its prescriptions.

Postmodernists have criticised organisational learning as either a dreamlike ideal or a nightmare for employees (Driver 2002, p. 34). The nightmare scenario is viewed as a way to exploit employees by trapping them in a utopian vision by those in power within organisations. Postmodernists argue that organisational learning is really a rhetorical device to increase employee productivity and represents a Machiavellian subterfuge where the true intentions of management are not made clear (Armstrong 2000, p. 359).

CASE STUDY

Toyota (Japan)

Akio Toyoda, Executive Vice President with responsibilities for Toyota's North American operations,[1] rocked back in his chair and reflected on what his great-grandfather would have done in the current circumstances. Sakichi Toyoda had started Toyota in 1897. Toyota had been hard hit by the steep downturn in the global car industry. Akio Toyoda had a decision to make. He was considering the various options in relation to Toyota's truck plants in San Antonio and Princeton where they manufacture Toyota Tundra trucks. In the course of two years, they had manufactured over 226,000 trucks from scratch. However, the global demand had shifted from trucks to smaller cars. Sales had been down by 53 per cent.

Hidehiko Tajima, President of Toyota Texas, had been proud appointing Don Jackson as Vice President for quality and production at Toyota's new San Antonio pick-up plant. Mr Tajima recognised Jackson's talent

'The best thing I like about him is his passion to build the best quality truck for the customer. Without knowledge or experience it may be difficult to pursue a good job. Not only knowledge or experience will bring you to a good result. It's all based on the passion people have.'

After graduation in industrial technologies, Don Jackson was gripped with the Toyota Way even though he worked with a supplier for Ford, General Motors and Chrysler. The Toyota Way was based on five principles: Challenge (to provide employees with a realistic stretch vision), *Kaizen* (continuous improvement), *Genchi Genbutsu* (hands-on experience or 'go and see' or 'have you seen it yourself?'), Respect and Teamwork. Jackson had been involved with implementing Toyota's new global body line at their Kentucky plant. He lived and breathed the experience for 18 months including many weekends

'The best way to describe it is like Lego blocks. We would take apart part of the old body line and move it out of the assembly line with the old technology. Then we would carry the parts to the line, creating space as we went. The new technology is a smaller line, more compact.'

The production line had to be fully functioning by each Monday morning.[2]

Learning had been embedded as a strong part of Toyota's culture. New recruits got hands-on experience on production lines next to highly trained managers. After their initial training they would join older worker groups and engage in the weekly quality circles forums. Here workers would spend time analysing their performance – any potential problems and explore solutions for implementation the following week. The consequence was an improvement in overall quality and a reduction in errors. Rather than losing the learning from their problem solving, each team contributed to the Yokoten System, a method of documenting and distributing learning from a library of problems to others within the organisation. Toyota used a web-based tool called Analytical Problem Solving (APS) for distributing this problem-based learning around the world. The system looked for underlying causes of problems and tried to identify any general trends for wider analysis. An everyday tool for hands-on learning was the Toyota suggestion-screening system. Anyone could ask a question by typing the question on a terminal which would be flashed on a large screen in the plant. Anyone on the plant floor could then answer the question.[3] A continual mantra from senior executives was 'Never be satisfied' and 'There's got to be a better way!'.

Toyota also formalised its learning through the development of a Toyota University. The University provided over 400 courses for its employees around the world. Many of these courses were transmitted over the internet through e-learning. A Learning Management Solution (LMS) was provided to train its 50,000 dealers on a variety of online courses. In 2002 Toyota launched the Global Knowledge Center to help distribute and share its sales and marketing knowledge. In 2003 Toyota established the Global Production Center (GPC) to help train its middle managers on production best practices.

A certain tension existed within Toyota as it fostered contradictory viewpoints to help drive its experimentation and continual improvement. For example, Toyota's operations were highly efficient, but its use of human resources in meetings could appear wasteful especially when few employees actively participated in discussions. Each employee belonged to several committees, self-study groups and other social groups. The company was known for taking small steps and improvements through *kaizen* but also for taking great leaps with the development of its hybrid car, Prius in 1997.[4] This was the world's first hybrid vehicle run on both petrol and an electric motor. Even though hybrid technology was very crude at this time, Toyota was able to reach production within 15 months of inception and try out 80 hybrid engine designs concurrently within this period. From the outside, Toyota could appear frugal with practices such as switching off its office lights at lunchtimes and yet it spent huge sums on its manufacturing facilities and human resource-development activities. Toyota's internal communications was kept simple to a single side of paper in most cases, yet it had created a complex web of horizontal and vertical linkages across functional and geographical boundaries. Even though Toyota had a strong hierarchy, employees were encouraged to provide constructive criticism and contrary views to their bosses. Zenji Yasuda, a former Toyota executive, highlighted the broad nature of goal setting at Toyota:

'If he makes (the goal) more concrete, employees won't be able to exercise their full potential. The vague nature of this goal confers freedom to researchers to open new avenues of exploration; procurement to look for new and unknown suppliers who possess needed technology; and sales to consider the next steps needed to sell such products.'[5]

Toyota's supplier networks had been vital in helping the organisation deliver its lean production and just-in-time (JIT) manufacturing systems. The Operations Management Consulting Division (OMCD) played a pivotal role in coordinating its suppliers and offering a problem-solving role. There was a high deal of openness in problem-solving between Toyota and its suppliers. In some cases, there were employee transfers between the two organisations if it was deemed necessary. The strength and openness of the supplier network can be attested from the crisis that resulted from a fire at Aisin Saiki in 1997, Toyota's sole supplier of P-valves. There was little reserve stock of P-valves due to their JIT system. Aisin Saiki faxed the design of these P-valves to a number of suppliers and within three days over 200 suppliers had engaged in close collaboration and successfully manufactured the P-valve sharing their successes and failures with one another. Toyota was up and running to normal capacity within a week.

Akio Toyoda was mindful that his founding family wielded much influence within Toyota even though it had only 2 per cent of the company stock. His decision over Toyota's Tundra plants in North America would certainly get endorsement from Toyota's President, Katsuaki Watanabe. There were already a large number of 2008 trucks amassed on American dealer forecourts without the introduction of 2009 stock.[6] He was aware that Toyota weathered the Asian financial storm in 1996 where Toyota Thailand had experienced four years of losses. The Toyota President at the time, Hiroshi Okuda, was adamant 'Cut all costs, but don't touch any people.' At that very moment, the phone rang. It was Katsuaki Watanabe who wanted to have lunch with him and discuss the Tundra plants.

References

1 Maynard, M. (2008) 'New leader expected at Toyota next year', *New York Times*.
2 Wood, S. M. (2006) 'Toyota VP in charge of production has fire within for companies', *San Antonio Express-News (Texas)*.
3 Chaturvedi, R. (2005) *Knowledge Management Practices at Toyota Motors*, Hyderabad, ICFAI Center for Management Research (ICMR).
4 Schachter, H. (2008) 'Toyota success driven by contradictions', *The Globe and Mail (Canada)*.
5 Takeuchi, H., Osono, E. and Shimizu, N. (2008) 'Contradictions, are the drivers of Toyota's success', *Business Day (South Africa)*, Management Review editorial.
6 Wood, S. M. (2008) 'Last 2008 Tundra rolls off S.A. line', *San Antonio Express-News*, State & Metro Edition editorial.

Questions

1 What advice would you give Akio Toyoda about the Toyota Tundra plants in North America?

2 How could you help improve Toyota's learning and human capital?

3 What are the benefits and shortfalls of having contradictory viewpoints at Toyota?

Summary

This chapter has elaborated and argued five major themes associated with organisational learning:

1 Individual learning – the differences between a behavioural and a cognitive science perspective on learning. The central role of motivation in individual learning that is often overlooked in the traditional learning cycle. The importance of 'deutero-learning' or 'learning to learn'.

2 Team learning as a distinction between discussion and dialogue and its function in convergent or divergent thinking.

3 Organisational learning conceived as single-loop and double-loop learning and driven by moderate levels of failure and unlearning.

4 Adoption of an information-processing perspective linking organisational learning to knowledge acquisition, information distribution, information interpretation and organisational memory.

5 The development of organisational routines in stable environments and dynamic capabilities in more volatile market conditions.

Questions for further thought

1 Most individual learning theory tends to focus on how we can change the external environment to promote greater learning. How could we synthesise cognitive and behavioural approaches to better understand our internal learning mechanisms?

2 By nature, some team members may be more argumentative whereas others may be more reflective and deeper thinkers. How does one manage these two groups without developing defensive routines in specific circumstances where discussion or dialogue may be required?

3 What measures can be taken to promote 'error harvesting' and sharing mistakes in organisational environments where mistakes are concealed and never discussed?

4 What are the advantages of a 'dialectic' between single-loop and double-loop learning rather than a preoccupation with double-loop learning for organisational success?

5 In what circumstances is it most appropriate to use vicarious learning or grafting in organisations?

6 How can a diversity of interpretations be managed effectively in an organisation?

7 What issues need to be considered when transferring organisational routines within the same organisation or between organisations? How would global factors affect the transfer of these routines?

8 What managerial competences are required to manage dynamic capabilities?

9 It has been argued that competitive advantage occurs from the unique resource configurations and linkages between organisational routines. Given that routines are predominantly tacit in nature, how can managers develop them to ensure they possess VRIN attributes (valuable, rare, inimitable and non-substitutable)?

10 Knowledge sharing assumes a certain level of openness and cooperation between organisational members. What are the dangers of highly cooperative environments for organisational learning?

Further reading

1 Fiol and Lyles (1985) and Levitt and March (1988) are two classics in the field of organisational learning and a good starting point.

2 Cohen and Sproull (1996) provides a good overview of the debates and thinking in the field of organisational learning.

3 Dierkes *et al.* (2001) offers a more theoretical perspective on some of the current debates in organisational learning and knowledge.

References

Argyris, C. (1991) 'Teaching smart people how to learn', *Harvard Business Review*, 69(3), 99–109.

Argyris, C. and Schon, D. A. (1978) *Organizational Learning: A Theory of Action Perspective*, Addison-Wesley, Reading, MA.

Armstrong, H. (2000) 'The learning organization: Changed means to an unchanged end', *Organization*, 7, 355–61.

Bandura, A. (1977) *Social Learning Theory*, Prentice-Hall, London.

Bateson, G. (1987) *Steps to an Ecology of Mind*, Jason Aronson, San Francisco, CA.

Bontis, N., Crossan, M. M. and Hulland, J. (2002) 'Managing an organizational learning system by aligning stocks and flows', *Journal of Management Studies*, 39(4), 437–69.

Bruner, J. S., Goodnow, J. J. and Austin, G. A. (1956) *A Study of Thinking*, Wiley, New York.

Burns, R. (1995) *The Adult Learner at Work*, Sydney, Business & Professional Publishing.

Chaturvedi, R. (2005) *Knowledge Management Practices at Toyota Motors*, ICFAI Center for Management Research (ICMR), Hyderabad.

Cohen, D. and Bacdayan, P. (1994) 'Organizational routines as stored procedural memory: Evidence from a laboratory study', *Organization Science*, 5(4), 554–68.

Cohen, M. D., Burkhart, R., Dosi, G., Egidi, M., Marengo, L., Warglien, M. and Winter, S. (1996) 'Routines and other recurring action patterns of organizations: Contemporary research issues', *Industrial and Corporate Change*, 5(3), 653–98.

Cohen, M. D. and Sproull, L. S. (1996) *Organisational Learning*, Sage, London.

Cohen, W. M. and Levinthal, D. (1990) 'Absorptive capacity: A new perspective on learning and innovation', *Administrative Science Quarterly*, 35, 128–52.

Coopey, J. and Burgoyne, J. (2000) 'Politics and organizational learning', *Journal of Management Studies*, 37(6), 869–85.

Crick, B. (1982) *In Defence of Politics*, Penguin, Harmondsworth.

Crossan, M. M., Lane, H. and White, R. (1999) 'An organizational learning framework: From intuition to institution', *Academy of Management Review*, 24(3), 522–37.

Cyert, R.M. and March, J. G. (1963) *A Behavioural Theory of the Firm*, Prentice-Hall, Englewood Cliffs, NJ.

Daft, R. L. and Weick, K. E. (1984) 'Toward a model of organizations as interpretation systems', *Academy of Management Review*, 9, 284–95.

Deming, W. E. (1986) *Out of the Crisis*, MIT Press, Boston, MA.

Dervin, B. (2003) 'Audience as listener and learner, teacher and confidante: The sense-making approach', in Dervin, B., Foreman-Wernet, L. and Launterbach, E. (eds) *Sense-making Methodology Reader: Selected Writings of Brenda Dervin*, Hampton Press, Inc., Cresskill, NJ.

Dierkes, M., Antal, A. B., Child, J. and Nanaka, I. (2001) *Handbook of Organizational Learning and Knowledge*, Oxford University Press, Oxford.

Driver, M. (2002) 'The learning organization: Foucauldian gloom or Utopian sunshine?', *Human Relations*, 55, 33–53.

Easterby-Smith, M. (1997) 'Disciplines of organizational learning: Contributions and critiques', *Human Relations*, 50(9), 1085–1116.

Easterby-Smith, M., Graca, M., Antonacopoulou, E. and Ferdinand, J. (2008) 'Absorptive capacity: A process perspective', *Management Learning*, 39, 483–501.

Eisenhardt, K. and Martin, J. (2000) 'Dynamic capabilities: What are they?', *Strategic Management Journal*, 21, 1105–1121.

Epple, D., Argote, L. and Devadas, R. (1996) 'Organizational learning curves: A method for investigating intra-plant transfer of knowledge acquired through learning by doing', *Organizational Learning*, M. D. Cohen and L. S. Sproull, eds, Sage Publications Inc., Thousand Oaks, CA, 83–100.

Endsley, M. R. (1995) 'Toward a theory of situation awareness in dynamic situations', *Human Factors*, 37, 32–64.

Feldman, M. (2000) 'Organizational routines as a source of continuous change', *Organization Science*, 11(6), 611–29.

Feldman, M. and Rafaeli, A. (2002) 'Organizational routines as sources of connections and understandings', *Journal of Management Studies*, 39(3), 309–31.

Fiol, C. and Lyles, M. (1985) 'Organizational learning', *Academy of Management Review*, 10(4), 803–13.

Friedman, V. J., Lipshitz, R. and Popper, M. (2005) 'The mysification of organizational learning', *Journal of Management Inquiry*, 14, 19–30.

Garratt, B. (1987) *The Learning Organization*, Gower, Aldershot.

Gersick, C. J. and Hackman, R. (1990) 'Habitual routines in task-performing groups', *Organizational Behaviour and Human Decision Process*, 47, 65–97.

Giddens, A. (1984) *The Constitution of Society: Outline of the Theory of Structure*, University of California Press, Berkeley, CA.

Gioia, D. A. and Chittipeddi, K. (1991) 'Sensemaking and sensegiving in strategic change initiation', *Strategic Management Journal*, 12, 433–48.

Gutherie, E. R. (1935) *The Psychology of Learning*, Harper & Row, New York.

Hedberg, B. L. T. (1981) 'How organizations learn and unlearn', *Handbook of Organizational Design*, P. C. Nystrom and W. H. Starbuck, eds, Oxford University Press, Oxford.

Honey, P. and Mumford, A. (1986) *The Manual of Learning Styles*, Peter Honey, Maidenhead.

Huber, G. P. (1991) 'Organizational learning: The contributing processes and the literatures', *Organization Science*, 2, 88–115.

Isaacs, W. H. (1993) 'Dialogue, collective thinking, and organizational learning', *Organization Dynamics*, 22(2), 24–39.

Jashapara, A. (1993) 'The competitive learning organization: A quest for the Holy Grail', *Management Decision*, 31(8), 52–62.

Jashapara, A. (2003) 'Cognition, culture and competition: An empirical test of the learning organization', *The Learning Organization*, 10(1), 31–50.

Kim, D. H. (1993) 'The link between individual and organizational learning', *Sloan Management Review*, Fall, 37–50.

Kim, W. C. and Mauborgne, R. (1998) 'Procedural justice, sttrategic decision making, and the knowledge economy', *Strategic Management Journal*, 19, 323–38.

Klahr, D. and Wallace, J. G. (1976) *Cognitive Development: An Information Processing View*, Halsted Press, New York.

Klein, G., Moon, B. and Hoffman, R. F. (2006) 'Making sense of sensemaking I: Alternative perspectives', *IEEE Intelligent Systems*, 21, 70–73.

Knights, D. and McCabe, D. (1998) 'When "life is but a dream": obliterating politics through business process reengineering?', *Human Relations*, 51(6), 761–98.

Kolb, D. A. (1984) *Experiential Learning: Experience as the Source of Learning and Development*, Prentice Hall, Englewood Cliffs, NJ.

Krone, K. J., Jablin, F. M. and Putnam, L. L. (1987) 'Communication theory and organizational communication: Multiple perspectives', *Handbook of Organizational Communication*, F. M. Jablin, L. L. Putnam, K. H. Roberts and L. W. Porter, eds, Sage, Newbury Park, CA.

Lane, P. J., Koka, B. R. and Pathak, S. (2006) 'The reification of absorptive capacity: A critical review and rejuvenation of the construct', *Academy of Management Review*, 31, 833–63.

Lave, J. and Wenger, E. (1990) *Situated Learning: Legitimate Peripheral Participation*, Cambridge University Press, Cambridge.

Leonard-Barton, D. (1992) 'Core capacities and core rigidities: Paradox in managing new product development', *Strategic Management Journal*, 13, 111–125.

Levitt, B. and March, J. G. (1988) 'Organizational learning', *Annual Review of Sociology*, 14.

March, J. G. (1991) 'Exploration and exploitation in organizational learning', *Organization Science*, 2(1), 71–87.

March, J. G. and Simon, H. A. (1958) *Organizations*, Wiley, New York.

March, J. G., Sproull, L. S. and Tamuz, M. (1991) 'Learning from samples of one or fewer', *Organization Science*, 2(1), 1–13.

Maynard, M. (2008) 'New leader expected at Toyota next year', *The New York Times*.

Mowery, D. C., Oxley, J. E. and Silverman, B. S. (1996) 'Strategic alliances and interfirm knowledge transfer', *Strategic Management Journal*, 17, 77–91.

Mumford, A. (1991) 'Learning in action', *Personnel Management*, July, 34–37.

Nelson, R. and Winter, S. (1982) *An Evolutionary Theory of Economic Change*, Harvard University Press, Cambridge, MA.

Nissley, N. and Casey, A. (2002) 'The politics of the exhibition: Viewing corporate museums through the paradigmatic lens of organizational memory', *British Journal of Management*, 13, S35–S45.

Pentland, B. T. and Rueter, H. H. (1994) 'Organizational routines as grammars of action', *Administrative Science Quarterly*, 39, 484–510.

Revans, R. W. (1977) *The ABC of Action Learning*, Action Learning Trust, Luton.

Schachter, H. (2008) 'Toyota success driven by contraindications', *The Globe and Mail (Canada)*.

Schein, E. H. (1987) *Process Consultation: Lessons for Managers and Consultants*, Addison-Wesley, Reading, MA.

Senge, P. M. (1990) *The Fifth Discipline: The Art and Practice of the Learning Organisation*, Doubleday Currency, New York.

Shrivastava, P. (1983) 'A typology of organizational learning systems', *Journal of Management Studies*, 20(1), 7–28.

Sitkin, S. B. (1992) 'Learning through failure: The strategy of small losses', *Research in Organizational Behaviour*, B. M. Staw and L. L. Cummings, eds, JAI Press, Greenwich, CT.

Skinner, B. F. (1938) *The Behaviour of Organisms: An Experimental Analysis*, Appleton-Century-Crofts, New York.

Stein, E. W. and Zwass, V. (1995) 'Actualizing organizational memory with information systems', *Information Systems Research*, 6, 2(85–117).

Takeuchi, H., Osono, E. and Shimizu, N. (2008) 'Contradictions are the drivers of Toyota's success', *Business Day (South Africa)*, Management Review editorial.

Taylor, J. R. and Van Every, E. J. (2000) *The Emergent Organization: Communication as Its Site and Surface*, Erlbaum, Mahwah, NJ.

Teece, D. J., Pisano, G. and Shuen, A. (1997) 'Dynamic capabilities and strategic management', *Strategic Management Journal*, 18, 509–33.

Todorova, G. and Durisin, B. (2007) 'Absorptive capacity: Valuing a reconceptualization', *Academy of Management Review*, 32, 774–86.

Underwood, B. J. (1964) 'The representativeness of rote verbal learning', *Categories of Human Learning*, A. W. Melton, ed., Academic Press, New York.

Vince, R. (2001) 'Power and emotion in organizational learning', *Human Relations*, 54(10), 1325–51.

Vygotsky, L. S. (1978) *Mind in Society*, Harvard University Press, Cambridge, MA.

Walsh, J. P. and Ungson, G.R. (1991) 'Organizational memory', *Academy of Management Review*, 16, 57–91.

Wang, C. L. and Ahmed, P. K. (2007) 'Dynamic capabilities: A review and research agenda', *International Journal of Management Reviews*, 9, 31–51.

Weick, K. E. (1979) *The Social Psychology of Organizing*, Addison-Wesley, Reading, MA.

Weick, K. E. (2002) 'Puzzles in organizational learning: An exercise in disciplined imagination', *British Journal of Management*, 13, S7–S15.

Weick, K. E., Sutcliffe, K. M. and Obstfeld, D. (2005) 'Organizing and the process of sensemaking', *Organization Science*, 16, 409–21.

Wood, S. M (2006) 'Toyota VP in charge of production has fire within for companies', *San Antonio Express-News (Texas)*.

Wood, S. M. (2008) 'Last 2008 Tundra rolls off S.A. line', *San Antonio Express-News*, State & Metro Edition editorial.

Yelle, L. E. (1979) 'The learning curve: Historical review and comprehensive survey', *Decision Sciences*, 10, 302–328.

Zahra, S. A. and George, G. (2002) 'Absorptive capacity: A review, reconceptualisation, and extension', *Academy of Management Review*, 27, 185–203.

Zollo, M. and Winter, S. G. (2002) 'Deliberate learning and the evolution of dynamic capabilities', *Organization Science*, 13(3), 339–51.

Chapter 6

The learning organisation

Learning outcomes

After completing this chapter the reader should be able to:

- contrast the differences between organisational learning and the learning organisation;
- explain the characteristics of the dominant conceptual models in the field;
- describe the differences between a static, teaching and learning organisation;
- outline the different strategic dimensions of a learning organisation.

Management issues

The use and application of the learning organisation implies these questions for managers:

- What is the most appropriate model of a learning organisation to adopt in your organisation?
- How can a shared vision of a learning organisation be developed?
- How can trust and commitment be developed to promote a true learning organisation rather than a teaching organisation?

Links to other chapters

Chapter 4   expands on institutionalist perspectives of the competitive learning organisation.

Chapter 5   explores the similarities and distinctions between different forms of organisational learning.

Teaching materials: From pen and paper to wikis and video FT

When it comes to teaching materials for executive education, it seems that the only limitation is the school's or client's imagination.

Options range from the traditional case studies and lectures to modern technology such as web-based computer applications or other media, such as video. Action learning, where participants work together on role plays, simulations and other group activities, is also common.

The choice of appropriate materials is generally dictated by the overall objectives of the customer. Content designed for open programmes, where the emphasis is on individuals, is not always transferable to customised offerings, which focus on change at an organisational level. Striking the right balance of academic rigour and practical relevance is also important.

Typically students on open programmes are more diverse. They come from different companies, often specialising in different functions of business and bring differing perspectives to the classroom. Indeed, the participants themselves are an important element of the programme – the opportunity to network as well as listen to feedback from other students is an invaluable part of the experience.

It is with this in mind that Bettina Buechel, dean of programmes and professor of strategy and organisation at IMD, describes open programmes as 'a mini-MBA'. The diversity of participants should be reflected by the content, she says: 'Ideally, programmes should not only be case based, but include variety.'

Attendees of LESE's advanced management programme, a four-week course run in four instalments over a six-month period, are 'given a window into all aspects of management', according to Professor Mike Rosenberg, director of executive education at the Barcelona-based school.

Teaching is based on cases, augmented by the use of simulations and the recent introduction of the 'executive challenge'. As part of this exercise, participants are put into groups and asked to put forward a particular 'live issue' they face in their workplace. Each group is then tasked with selecting one issue, presenting their proposed solution to the class, before receiving comments. 'The case study itself is not that important but the participants' feedback is extremely valuable,' explains Prof Rosenberg.

In contrast to this approach, custom programmes, tailored to the needs of companies rather than individuals, tend to be more specific.

Mike Canning, executive vice-president for client relations at Duke Corporate Education, says that development of a new customised programme typically takes eight to 12 weeks. This involves an extensive period of 'discovery and diagnostics', where the school builds up a deeper understanding of the client's strategy and goals. This knowledge is then used to identify learning needs and devise company-specific cases.

As with open programmes, the content needs to mix real problems with academic rigour: 'Theory is terrific, however it needs to be relevant. Development of tools for customers, where the theory is applied, is also important,' says Mr Canning. Getting people to work together more effectively is fundamental.

During one particular programme, developed by Duke for the top 500 leaders of a global pharmaceutical company, video was used as a feedback mechanism. Colleagues of participants were asked to comment on their strengths and weaknesses as a manager, a powerful tool for improving performance and re-enforcing other messages from the rest of programme. At the end of the course, participants were invited to record a statement detailing how they would integrate the new knowledge into the workplace, including setting objectives.

Despite the extensive choice of available options, some tried and tested classroom techniques are hard to beat, according to Dr Mark Pegg, director of *Ashridge*. 'Global trends we might expect are towards more virtual learning … We see striking growth in websites, e-sharing sites and online discussion fora. But paper for reading, writing and working out ideas is still very much with us and the flip chart is still one of the best ways of capturing and sharing ideas in discussion.'

Source: from Teaching materials: From pen and paper to wikis and video, *The Financial Times*, 11/05/2009 (Jacobs, M.), copyright © The Financial Times Ltd.

Questions

1 What are the key elements to consider when developing executives?

2 What are the advantages of wikis and video as learning tools over pen and paper?

3 What are the advantages of executive development through business schools rather than other sources?

Introduction

The external environment for many organisations nowadays is characterised by turbulence associated with globalisation, deregulation of markets, changing customer and investor demands and increasing product–market competition (Jashapara 2003; Mitroff *et al.* 1994). There is a growing need in organisations to move beyond solving existing problems to improving continuously in the face of changing conditions (Hamel and Prahalad 1994). Knowledge has emerged as the most strategically significant resource of the firm (Grant 1996) and the ability of a firm to learn faster than its competitors as the only sustainable form of competitive advantage (de Geus 1988).

These assumptions have given rise to the notion of a learning organisation. Much of the literature tends to be conceptually based and prescriptive in nature with little empirical work to support its assertions. There is also confusion between the terms 'learning organisation' and 'organisational learning' as some authors use the terms synonymously and interchangeably. A useful distinction is to consider organisational learning as the processes or activities in an organisation, whereas a learning organisation can be considered as the end state. Some authors suggest that the learning organisation exists only in an ideal form, creating an unattainable tension: a holy grail (Jashapara 1993). Some major distinctions between organisational learning and the learning organisation are shown in Table 6.1.

Table 6.1 **Distinctions between organisational learning and the learning organisation**

Organisational learning	*Learning organisation*
• Means	• End
• Process or activity	• Idealised form
• Attainable	• Easily lost due to changes
• Descriptive research	• Prescriptive research
• Inductive	• Deductive (normative)
• Academic and scholarly orientation	• Practitioner and consultancy orientation
• Predominantly qualitative research	• Predominantly quantitative research (little empirical evidence so far)
• Theoretical orientation	• Action orientation

The learning organisation literature gained in popularity in the mid-1990s but interest has declined as the concept of knowledge management has taken over (Swan *et al.* 1999). Despite the fact that knowledge is often the output of the learning process, many key contributors in knowledge management fail to acknowledge the processes of organisational learning or the learning organisation in their considerations (Davenport and Prusak 1998; Svieby 1997). In the same way, exponents of the learning organisation literature say relatively little about the pervasive use of information systems and technology to achieve competitive advantage in contemporary organisations. There currently exists an opportunity to synthesise these two emerging literatures and bring together the technological and human dimensions into a coherent whole (Loermans 2002).

This chapter shall attempt to forward the major conceptual and empirical advances in the learning organisation literature. It begins by examining the major US contribution of *The Fifth Discipline* by Peter Senge that popularised the notion of the 'learning organisation' in the early 1990s. It continues to explore some of the British contributions to the concept in the early 1990s (Garratt 1990; Honey 1991; Pedler *et al.* 1991). The Japanese contribution of Nonaka (1991) is recognised for its elucidation of transformation processes involved in converting tacit and explicit knowledge from one form to another. None of these idealised forms of learning organisations shows explicitly how they will lead to competitive advantage. Instead a model of a 'competitive learning organisation' (Jashapara 1993; Jashapara 2003) is forwarded showing how learning can be aligned to changes in the competitive environment. The problems of ideology, power and politics in learning organisations and the potential exploitation of the workforce are highlighted towards the end of the chapter to show how the concept could be misused by organisations. As empirical research on the learning organisation is limited and has suffered from widespread anecdotes and assertions, the current position of empirical research is examined (Jashapara 2003; Örtenblad 2002).

US contribution: the fifth discipline

Peter Senge was instrumental in popularising the concept of the 'learning organisation', especially among consultancy and business school circles, and placing it firmly on the academic agenda. He saw organisations as a product of how we think and how we interact. His definition of a learning organisation was (Senge 1990):

> *'Learning organizations [are] organizations where people continually expand their capacity to create the results they truly desire, where new and expansive patterns of thinking are nurtured, where collective aspiration is set free, and where people are continually learning to see the whole together.'*

He considered the quality movement as the first wave of the true learning organisation and believed that the building blocks for such organisations revolve around practising five distinct disciplines, as shown in Figure 6.1: personal mastery, team learning, systems thinking, mental models and shared vision.

Personal mastery is seen as developing our capacity to clarify what is important to us in terms of our personal vision and purpose. This helps to develop a 'creative tension'

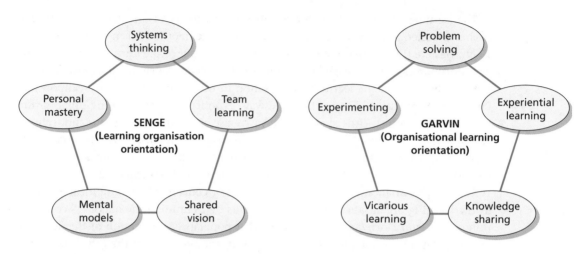

Figure 6.1 **The learning organisation** (Garvin 1993; Senge 1990)

between our current reality and our future vision. The qualities of perseverance and patience become guiding principles. This assumes that individual commitment to one's own growth and a supportive environment are prevalent in the organisation. Cynics often opposed to personal mastery are recognised as 'frustrated idealists' disappointed when reality falls short of their high ideals.

Team learning is deemed to develop our capacity for conversation and balancing dialogue and discussion. In many decision-making processes there can be a tendency towards engaging in 'discussion' where different views are presented and defended. This is useful in instances of convergent thinking where a quick decision needs to be made and the best argument prevails. However, in many other instances that require divergent thinking, engaging people in 'dialogue' is considered primary where different views are presented as a means to discovering a new view. People are more receptive to new and different views and willing to change their own views.

Systems thinking is seen as developing our capacity for putting the pieces together and seeing wholes rather than disparate parts. This is the conceptual cornerstone of the fifth discipline as it provides the incentive and means to integrate disciplines and recognise the whole. This is seen as the major drawback with traditional management approaches to problems that produce simplistic frameworks to understand complex and dynamic systems and processes.

Mental models is our capacity to reflect on our internal pictures. This discipline involves balancing our skills of inquiry and advocacy as well as understanding how our mental models influence our actions. An example of mental models is the increasing use of scenario planning which forces managers to examine how they would manage under different conditions in the future.

Shared vision is concerned with building a sense of commitment in a group based on what they would really like to create. In this respect, leaders and managers play an important role in developing learning organisations through building shared visions rooted firmly in personal visions.

There are a number of questions and reservations that arise from this notion of the learning organisation. These are predominantly linked to the prescriptive nature of the model. How did these disciplines arise? What empirical or theoretical background underpins this model? Why not have another five equally valid disciplines such as training, mentoring, participation, partnerships and feedback? How realistic is the development of a shared vision given the inherent difficulty of aligning individual goals and organisational goals? Also, many organisations are unlikely to want to relinquish management control to the extent suggested by this model in the quest for employee empowerment. The internal political environments have been ignored. Instead, the lasting contribution of this model has been the promotion of 'dialogue' in team learning and recognising the importance of systems thinking for understanding complex and dynamic situations.

In response to the prescriptive and idealistic nature of the five disciplines, the significant other US contribution (Garvin 1993) took the notion of a learning organisation back to various aspects of organisational learning. Hence, it is not surprising that confusion has persisted between these two related concepts to this day. The definition of a learning organisation from this perspective is (Garvin 1993, p. 80):

> 'A learning organization is an organization skilled at creating, acquiring, and transferring knowledge, and at modifying its behavior to reflect new knowledge and insights.'

Here we have an operational perspective of the learning organisation where learning can be measured, is actionable and provides guidelines for practice. Given the fact that often what gets measured gets managed in organisations, are the right forms of learning being measured? Are there dangers that measures may show high levels of learning that are misdirected? As shown in Figure 6.1, the five forms of organisational learning or activities construed as important in this model are (Garvin 1993):

- systematic problem solving;
- experimentation;
- learning from past experiences and mistakes;
- learning from others – including vicarious learning and benchmarking;
- transferring and sharing knowledge across the organisation.

UK contribution: the learning company

Apart from the above US contributions, much of the activity in the learning organisation literature has occurred in the UK. This began with Bob Garratt (1987) who proposed a model based on a three-level hierarchy, as shown in Figure 6.2. Garratt was influenced by the principles of action learning (Revans 1977) and was critical of the 'action-fixated non-learning cycle' found in many organisations. He argued that there was a tendency to ignore the reflection phase in this action orientation with a consequence of people trying harder rather than thinking smarter on problems.

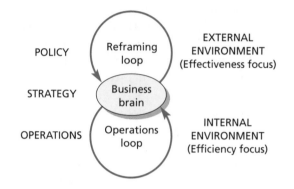

Figure 6.2 **A three-level hierarchy for the learning organisation** (Garratt 1987)

There are also important cultural dimensions related to a reflection orientation. For example, in Japan, a manager sitting on his own in his office is less likely to be interrupted due to the assumption that he is reflecting on important organisational problems and matters. The fact that he may be thinking about lunch is immaterial! This valuing of reflection is less common in the West.

This model of the learning organisation is based on a three-level hierarchy of policy, strategy and operations. Organisational learning occurs at these three levels in the form of double-loop learning with multiple feedback loops from information flows, direction giving and monitoring environmental changes. The model provides a means of processing and integrating these information flows by positioning the direction givers (business brain) at the centre of organisational learning. This places a large responsibility for learning on direction givers, even though senior executives can often exhibit major defences to learning (Argyris 1991). This model suggests that organisational learning is highly dependent on executive learning but fails to consider the political dimensions of learning at this level.

Similar to Garvin's model, another UK model was more focused on organisational learning and valued experimentation highly (Easterby-Smith 1990). This central quality of experimentation was promoted in a number of ways. The proposed model suggested experimenting in people to generate creativity and innovation, experimenting in organisational structures to introduce flexibility, experimenting in reward systems so that risk takers were not disadvantaged, and experimenting in information systems by focusing on unusual variations. The difficulty is that experimentation can be costly, especially when it does not lead to any clear signs of creativity or innovation and lessons learnt from mistakes are not passed around the organisation.

Another UK perspective on the learning organisation saw the concept much more simply as encouraging wanted behaviours in organisations and suppressing unwanted behaviours. The role of managers from this behaviourist perspective was to discover the triggers and reinforcers for wanted behaviours and suitable mechanisms to discourage unwanted behaviours. Examples of potential wanted and unwanted behaviours in a learning organisation are shown in Table 6.2 (Honey 1991).

Table 6.2 Potential wanted and unwanted behaviours in a learning organisation (Honey, 1991)

Wanted behaviour	Unwanted behaviour
• Asking questions	• Acquiescing
• Suggesting ideas	• Rubbishing ideas
• Exploring alternatives	• Going for expedient, quick fixes
• Taking risks/experimenting	• Being cautious
• Being open about the way it is	• Telling people what they want to hear/filtering bad news
• Converting mistakes into learning	• Repeating the same mistakes
• Reflecting and reviewing	• Rushing around keeping active
• Talking about learning	• Talking anecdotes (i.e. what happened, not what was learnt)
• Taking responsibility for own learning and development	• Waiting for other people to do it
• Admitting inadequacies and mistakes	• Justifying actions/blaming other people or events

Critical thinking and reflection

Imagine you were tasked with initiating a company-wide programme for surfacing people's mistakes and learning from them. How would you instigate such an 'error harvesting' programme where mistakes were surfaced and errors were discussed? What do you see as the primary difficulties in implementing such a programme? What cultural factors would you need to consider and how could they be overcome?

The most telling UK contribution has come from two conceptual models of a 'learning company' (Pedler *et al.* 1991). The definition of a learning organisation from this perspective is:

'*The Learning Company is a vision of what might be possible. It is not brought about simply by training individuals; it can only happen as a result of learning at the whole organization level. A Learning Company is an organization that facilitates the learning of all its members and continuously transforms itself.*'

The first proposed blueprint of a learning company was composed of five components, as shown in Figure 6.3. The authors were highly influenced by action learning, double-loop learning and the quality movement (Argyris 1999; Deming 1986; Revans 1977) in their proposed model. They suggested that the five key clusters in a learning organisation are:

● *strategy* includes a learning approach to strategy with small-scale experiments and feedback loops to enable continuous improvement and participative policy making;

● *looking in* includes using IT to help individuals understand what's going on and using formative accounting and control to assist learning and delighting internal

Figure 6.3 The learning company (Pedlar *et al.* 1991)

customers. In addition, this cluster includes developing an environment of collaboration between internal departments and exploring assumptions and values behind the reward systems;

● *structures* implies the need for roles and careers to be flexibly orientated to allow for experimentation, growth and adaptation;

● *looking out* includes regularly scanning and reviewing the external environment and developing joint learning with competitors and other stakeholders for 'win:win' learning;

● *learning opportunities* includes a climate of continuous improvement where mistakes are allowed and encouraged together with self-development opportunities for all.

The original model above can appear somewhat mechanical and lifeless. In order to convey a greater dynamic to this model, Pedler, Burgoyne and Boydell (1991) went further to propose an energy-flow model based on four components: ideas and actions at the individual level and policy and operations at the collective level. All of these four components are connected through four figures of eight to represent double-loop learning. There is little elaboration of the potential drivers and retarders of this energy flow in organisations or recommendations if the energy becomes stuck in organisations.

Japanese contribution: the knowledge-creating company

Instead of learning being the critical success factor in organisations, Nonaka (1991) argues that it is knowledge that is more primary and the lasting source of competitive advantage. He forwards the notion of a knowledge-creating company based on continuous innovation through knowledge creation. Despite the fact that knowledge is the output of learning, the major contribution in this model is the transformation process of tacit knowledge to explicit knowledge and vice versa to create new knowledge, as shown in Figure 6.4. He looks at six successful Japanese companies to discern the different dimensions of innovative processes. He uses the distinction of tacit and explicit knowledge (Polanyi 1967) and incorporates an individual's mental models and beliefs into the difficult-to-articulate concept of tacit knowledge.

Figure 6.4 **The knowledge-creating company** (Nonaka 1991)

Critical thinking and reflection

Imagine that you have been asked to manage the development of a new product or service in your organisation. Describe how you could use metaphors, slogans, symbols and other figurative forms of language to fire the imagination of your team. What interventions could you make if your initial approaches were not well received? Can you think of any alternative approaches that could spark the creative spirit of your team?

The knowledge-creating company uses four processes for creating knowledge. However, it is only when one form of knowledge is transformed into another, such as tacit to explicit or vice versa, that new knowledge is created. The four processes as shown in Figure 6.4 are as follows:

- *Socialisation* allows tacit knowledge from one person to be passed to the other. For example, this is traditionally how knowledge is passed in a master–apprentice relationship. Such knowledge does not become explicit and, hence, cannot be leveraged and used by the whole organisation.

- *Combination* is about combining discrete pieces of explicit knowledge held by individuals. Such explicit to explicit knowledge transfer does not expand the organisation's knowledge base.

- *Articulation* is the conversion of tacit knowledge to explicit knowledge. Here new knowledge is formed and made explicit in a form that can be shared around the organisation.

- *Internalisation* allows individuals to broaden their knowledge base and create knowledge by converting explicit knowledge to tacit knowledge.

In all the companies studied, articulation was a primary process for successful innovation. This involved using people's imagination, playing with abstract ideas and moving them towards a model of logical thinking that could be exploited by the organisation. To get the tacit knowledge and ideas moving in a group, there was considerable recourse to figurative language. This allowed hunches, intuitions and insights in the group to surface. For the development of a new car, Honda used the slogan 'Theory of Automobile Evolution' with its design team. Such creative tension allowed the design team to consider a car as a living organism and explore how it would evolve. Metaphors were also used to express the inexpressible, even though they might have multiple meanings and appear contradictory. The tension in meanings was seen as a valuable resource in the creative process. Once the knowledge creation process was triggered through figurative language and the use of imagination, there were two additional steps to get those ideas into a workable solution. The first was the use of analogy to reconcile differences and make clear distinctions between ideas. The second was to create a model of the ideas to give them a logical coherency.

Nonaka (1991) sees the continual challenge of knowledge-creating companies as re-examining what they take for granted. In terms of organisational design, he promotes a 'redundant organisation' to encourage knowledge sharing and dissemination. By redundancy, he means the conscious overlapping of company information, business activities and responsibilities. This can be achieved by individuals and groups overlapping information and responsibilities to allow greater dialogue and communication to occur. Another approach is to promote job rotation so that employees can see the business from a wide range of perspectives. In addition, internal competition between groups on the same project is encouraged so that the merits and shortcomings of different approaches and perspectives are aired and the most effective solution is chosen.

Nonaka and Takeuchi (1995) have received criticism for their theory from a number of quarters. Jorna's (1998) critique focused on the use of past research and claimed that Nonaka had overlooked learning theory, misread organisational theorists and had failed to engage in philosophical debates over knowledge. Instead, knowledge was defined as a manager's belief and their authority became central when deciding whether new knowledge was created. Bereiter (2002) argued that Nonaka's model failed to explain how new ideas or understandings were created in organisations and how they could be applied to other contexts.

Gourlay (2006) provides alternative explanations of what happened in the four processes. In 'socialisation', he suggests that there was a misattribution of reasons for 'tasty bread' which could have been due to a lengthy development process. No evidence is provided such as cognitive mapping to show that customer ideas influenced manager ideas. Nonaka claims that 'externalisation' proceeds from the use of metaphor and analogy but this hypothesis remains untested. In 'combination', Nonaka uses MBA education as a good example of moving explicit to explicit knowledge. Gourlay (2006) argues that MBA education is more than the transfer of explicit knowledge and includes the development of tacit knowledge and skills through case studies and group work. For 'internalisation', Nonaka claims that reading promotes the conversion of explicit to tacit knowledge even though there is no body of research to support this claim.

The competitive learning organisation

The major shortfall in many models of the learning organisation is the lack of emphasis on the competitive performance of the organisation. This remains implicit in the models and there is little discourse on how such learning organisations would lead to sustainable competitive advantage. The organisational learning and operational aspects are articulated but the strategic dimensions appear to be missing.

One dynamic model that pursues the strategic nature of organisational learning is the 'competitive learning organisation' (Jashapara 2003), as shown in Figure 6.5. The model adopts an institutionalist perspective where competition and strategic change are seen as intimately linked (Pettigrew and Whipp 1991). This means that organisational learning cannot be viewed separately from competition and the key to success is alignment between an organisation and its environment (Fiol and Lyles 1985). Competition is regarded as a process through people's day-to-day learning rather than as a steady state of affairs. The model rejects the planning school approach to competition as the dynamic processes of competition are never explored. Instead, it assumes that strategy formation is adaptive, incremental and a complex learning process where ends and means are either specified simultaneously or are intertwined (Jashapara 2003). A competitive learning organisation is defined as:

'a continuously adaptive enterprise that aligns itself to the environment by focusing its learning on the major competitive forces at a given time.'

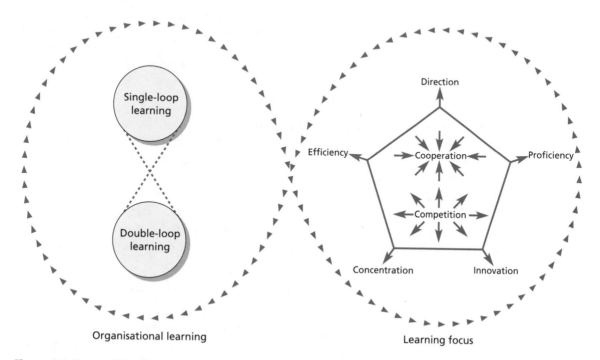

Figure 6.5 **Competitive learning organisation** (Jashapara 2003)

This model comprises two aspects: an organisational learning one and a strategic one. Organisational learning can be considered as a distinction between cognitive and behavioural development. Behavioural development can be seen as new responses or actions based on existing interpretations. In contrast, cognitive development can be regarded as organisational changes that affect the interpretation of events and development of shared understanding among organisational members. The behavioural learning is referred to as 'single-loop learning' in the model and the cognitive level as 'double-loop learning' (Argyris and Schon 1978). Another way of looking at single-loop learning is 'doing things better' in organisations whereas double-loop learning is 'doing things differently or doing different things' (Hayes and Allinson 1998).

The model of a 'competitive learning organisation' argues that learning by itself is not enough to achieve competitive advantage. What if the learning is misdirected? Instead, the emphasis in the model is on how best to focus the learning. Would sending senior executives on Japanese flower-arranging courses be suitable? Is sending all prospective senior managers on MBA programmes the best way forward? The problem with any prescriptive approach is that the external environment and competitive changes tend to be left out of the equation. Instead, this model argues that any learning needs to be focused on the predominant competitive force acting on an organisation at any given moment. Undoubtedly, these forces are dynamic and change over time.

Critical thinking and reflection

As a manager, how can you ensure that the collective learning of your team is responding to changes in the competitive environment? How would you manage your team learning in an uncertain and turbulent environment? What time frames do you consider most workable for managing learning in your teams? How would you influence your team to be more proactive and take greater responsibility for their learning?

The learning focus for a competitive learning organisation is based on a system of seven forces identified in effective organisations (Mintzberg 1991), as shown in Figure 6.5. There are five generic forces that act externally on an organisation and two diametrically opposite internal forces. At any given time, one of these forces tends to dominate and learning is focused on responding to this force as best as possible. For example, if innovation is the dominant force, learning efforts may be driven towards creativity through articulation of tacit knowledge and the use of figurative language (Nonaka 1991). The dominant external forces impacting on an organisation due to changes in the competitive environment are as follows:

● *The force for direction* is concerned with strategic vision and may relate to organisations in start-up or turnaround situations.

● *The force for efficiency* is concerned with standardisation and formalisation of processes and may relate to bureaucratic organisations where rationalisation and restructuring are a major focus.

- *The force for proficiency* is concerned with tasks requiring high levels of knowledge and skills and may relate to professional organisations.

- *The force for concentration* is concerned with concentrating efforts on serving certain markets, particularly in large diversified firms.

- *The force for innovation* is concerned with discovering new things for the customer and may relate to adhocracies comprising skilled experts or multidisciplinary projects.

There are also two internal cultural forces that have an impact on a firm's learning and effectiveness: the forces of cooperation and competition. In this conception, organ-isational culture is viewed as a product of continual struggles by groups of organisational members to impose values and identities on the role of others (Carroll 1995). If the forces of cooperation are dominant in an organisation, this may result in an ideological organisation such as a kibbutz. In contrast, if the forces of competition are dominant, this may result in the pulling apart of politics and a highly political organisation where conflicting in-fighting takes over. There may be limits to the levels of cooperation in an organisation as ideology discourages change and if individuals perceive a need for change, they may be forced to challenge the ideology which breeds politics.

As competitive forces are rarely static and vary continuously over time, a state of 'configuration' may occur where one of the external forces described above dominates and the organisation is drawn towards a coherent form (Mintzberg 1991). However, configuration may lead to the problem of 'contamination' where the dominant force undermines equally valid forces. For example, a firm may be so fixated on improving its efficiency over five years that it fails to recognise that it needs to focus on innova-tion given the market changes with new products and services.

In some periods organisations may go through states of 'combination' where no single force dominates. This may result in periods of 'conversion' from one form to another. The state of 'combination' may result in problems of 'cleavage' where two or more forces may confront each other and eventually paralyse the organisation. For instance, half the management board of an organisation may wish to focus organis-ational energies and learning on efficiency whereas the other half may see innovation as a much greater priority. The internal forces of competition and cooperation can be important catalysts for managing these problems of 'contamination' and 'cleavage'.

The competitive learning organisation is seen as an ideal rather than an end state. Metaphorically, such organisations can be seen as in a 'continual quest for the Holy Grail' (Jashapara 1993). The Holy Grail represents a search for improved methods of learning at all levels and an understanding of the changing nature of competitive bases which act as a focus for organisational learning. The fluctuating nature of the com-petitive environment and the fragility of competitive bases means that organisations are likely to maintain their 'competitive learning' phase for very limited periods before they slip into either a 'teaching' phase, or a 'static' phase as shown in Table 6.3.

Table 6.3 **Development of a competitive learning organisation** (Jashapara 1993)

	Static organisation	*Teaching organisation*	*Competitive learning organisation*
Level of organisational learning	Poor	Fair	High
Rate of learning	Poor	Fair	High
Learning focus	None	Limited	High
Level of communication	Poor	Fair	High
Flow of communication	None	One-way	Two-way
Organisational performance	Poor	Fair	High

The static organisation is characterised by a lack of learning. Such organisations may view their workforces as costs to be minimised rather than assets to be developed. It is inevitable that such organisations will face an internal crisis through lack of responsiveness to the external environment. This crisis may act to inhibit learning or result in a transformation into a 'competitive learning' phase. Such crises can be seen as opportunities for growth or can herald the beginning of the eventual decline of an organisation.

The competitive learning organisation places high value on the learning of all its employees at individual, group and organisational levels. Double-loop learning is encouraged, with an emphasis on questioning underlying assumptions. The distribution of learning is facilitated through open channels of two-way communication throughout the organisation. Each employee is committed to focused learning that responds to forces in the external environment.

However, the problems of contamination and cleavage may become more evident or major cultural changes (fluctuation in forces of cooperation or competition) may dominate an organisation, forcing it to slip towards a 'teaching organisation' where the overarching role of senior managers as teachers becomes important. Learning can become prescriptive and the domain of human resource departments rather than the responsibility of each learner. As these organisations are characterised by one-way communication from senior managers to employees, there is little scope for an equal exchange of ideas and knowledge. The role of learning focus is left solely to organisational strategists and human resource departments. Learning becomes parochial and employees may feel blocked due to a lack of challenge and responsibility for their learning. In such circumstances, firms may slip into static organisations. This model promotes the nature of adaptive enterprises responding to the ideal of continuous improvement similar to the quest for the Holy Grail. Each time they feel they have arrived at this elusive destination, the goal posts change due to the dynamics of the competitive environment.

Power, politics and the learning organisation

The concept of a learning organisation conveyed in this chapter has been conceived as a Utopian ideal, but could it be a Foucauldian nightmare instead (Coopey 1998)? Is the concept of the learning organisation prone to exploitation of workers by managers in more devious ways to attain their own goals? Let's explore the nature of reality in many organisations nowadays. Directors are under increasing pressure to satisfy the short-term profit goals of shareholders and more concerned about potential underperformance which may lead to predatory action. This nervousness often results in tight organisational controls where employees can be reduced to mechanical objects in a performance-driven system. Employees don't have the same voice through their representatives (traditionally the trade unions), as the balance of power has moved more towards employers in many western countries through successive government interventions and diminishing trade union membership.

There are two perspectives of the learning organisation. One is of a Utopian sunshine forwarded by practitioners and consultants, the other a Foucauldian gloom promoted by academics (Denton 1998; Driver 2002). From the Foucauldian gloom perspective, human resource management can be seen as a device to organise and control the work process. Any deviation from the norm is a cause for concern. Individuals lose their personal identity in the workplace as they are subsumed in an overarching ideology of enterprise and competition. People are disempowered and maintain the 'them and us' attitude. This hides the crucial element of trust, as employees have little confidence that their personal interests and goals will be honoured by their line managers. If trust is in short supply, this will have a direct influence on employee commitment to organisational learning or the Utopian goal of a learning organisation. Under the Foucauldian gloom perspective, we have a teaching organisation where senior managers learn and win. This contrasts with a Utopian sunshine perspective where everyone learns and wins along the lines espoused in a competitive learning organisation.

Critical thinking and reflection

Reflect on any organisational situation where you feel power has been misused by your line manager. Describe your general feelings and impressions over the situation. What impact did the incident have on your performance and commitment to learning? How could the incident have been handled differently? What lessons have you learnt in the use of power as a manager?

The dangers of the learning organisation concept is that organisations can use it as an ideology to disguise control but phrased in an emancipatory rhetoric. The consequences are that employees may be manipulated through coercive controls or outright exploitation (Driver 2002). In these teaching organisations, dominant coalitions may form and decide on the nature and form of learning. True learning is discouraged as it could disrupt established norms and become harder to control. Learning becomes radical and a challenge to those in power. There is little room for dissent or questioning organisational values and assumptions. The power dynamics of such a scenario mean that the organisation is caught in a perpetual single-loop learning cycle leading to its eventual decline. Double-loop learning is considered too disruptive to the balance of power in such organisations.

Group norms can also play a negative role on indoctrination and coercive persuasion (Schein 1999). This can result in a suppression of conflict and diversity and greater conformity to the rhetoric of the dominant powerful coalitions in an organisation. In its extreme form, there may be participatory control through group surveillance of an individual's behaviour. There is little room for dissent and personal identity is reduced to a psychic prison from which employees may be unable to escape due to fear of job losses or impact on career progression (Driver 2002).

Are there ways out of this Foucauldian nightmare scenario of the teaching organisation? How can diversity and conflict be managed effectively in learning organisations? One suggestion is to move from an adversarial to an inclusive approach with stakeholders (Coopey 1998). This implies greater employee involvement and a loss of management control which may be unpalatable to some parties comprising the dominant coalitions in organisations. In 1995 British Airways created a post of a 'court jester' reminiscent of the medieval courts with kings (chief executive) and senior courtiers (executives). The jester's role was to provide unorthodox criticism couched as harmless jest in an environment where questioning was not the norm. Being a fool allows the jester to play with ideas and ask basic questions about buried assumptions and ways of thinking.

A more challenging suggestion is to use theatre to explore roles, discourses and power dynamics in organisations (Coopey 1998). This is about getting people to take different roles that allow them to play out various perspectives, including their own, and to explore different ways of approaching everyday scenarios. It is about giving 'oppressed' employees a voice and reducing their sense of powerlessness. An influential form of this radical theatre is the 'Theatre of the Oppressed' or 'Forum Theatre' (Boal 1979). This has been used to elicit employee views by commissioning live theatre by a British local authority to solve communication difficulties. Drama stimulates the power of imagination and allows people to play different roles from everyday scenarios and explore different options and solutions to their problems. Such theatre celebrates diversity and difference in social groups, though it can be seen to challenge hierarchy and established norms. The central political problem is how organisations can explore issues of power imbalances and their negative impacts on organisational learning. If they succeed, they become a Utopian sunshine learning organisation. Otherwise, the Foucauldian gloom of a teaching or static organisation beckons.

Empirical research and the learning organisation

Empirical research on the learning organisation and the role of knowledge within the firm and links with a firm's strategy has suffered from widespread reliance on anecdotes and assertion rather than statistical evidence. Apart from small-scale, in-depth studies of a few organisations, there is virtually no empirical work in this area. Even the related discipline of organisational learning is characterised by qualitative research with a few handful of studies involved with hypotheses development and testing. These tend to be around earlier research on learning curves in organisations.

A recent inductive study with a small sample of ten Swedish people showed that their understanding of a learning organisation arose from four perspectives, as shown in Figure 6.6 (Örtenblad 2002). The first perspective is that the learning organisation is synonymous with organisational learning and is purely 'old wine in new bottles'. The second perspective is that the learning organisation is learning at work and connected with experiential and action learning. The third perspective is an association with a learning climate. This is concerned with positive attitudes and beliefs towards learning. The last perspective is that a learning organisation is a learning structure where the ideal is an organic, flatter structure.

Apart from this small-scale inductive study, there is currently only one empirical study that has engaged in hypothesis testing of the concept of a learning organisation (Jashapara 2003). This study used a large stratified random sample of 180 construction executives in the UK and developed an instrument of a 'competitive learning organisation' and organisational performance. Much of this research was developmental as no scales of the learning organisation existed. The questionnaire was composed of ten constructs comprising 125 items with at least eight items per construct. As individuals may be prone to give socially desirable answers of their learning, this was controlled using a shortened form of the Marlowe–Crowne social desirability scale (Ballard 1992).

Each construct in this study demonstrated high levels of reliability and there was considerable evidence for convergent, discriminant, nomological and known groups validity. The results showed that organisational learning in the form of double-loop learning does lead to competitive advantage and provides support to the assumptions underlying the learning organisation literature (de Geus 1988). The results also showed that cooperative cultures are more likely to achieve competitive advantage. However, an anomaly arose in the results showing that competitive or political cultures are more likely to lead to double-loop learning. Hence, successful organisations are more likely to have a flux between cooperative and competitive cultures rather than either extreme. At the time of the study, the competitive dynamics showed that learning focused on efficiency and proficiency led to increased performance in the UK construction industry.

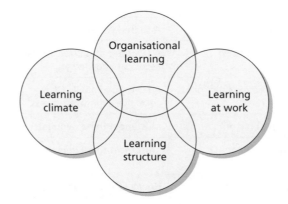

Figure 6.6 **Inductive typology of a learning organisation** (Örtenblad 2002)

The results of the stratified sample in this study could be developed into benchmarks related to company size. However, this is to be discouraged as benchmarking can lead to organisations developing imitative strategies more akin to single-loop learning rather than strategies to align themselves to changing environments. Also, it is unlikely that executives would engage in benchmarking exercises on a regular basis due to the strategic and sensitive nature of the information supplied. In addition, the information gathered in benchmarking exercises can have a very short shelf life if the competitive environments are highly volatile. The greatest challenge in future quantitative studies is to provide sufficiently large representative samples from within an organisation as well as large representative samples across organisations. This may be a pipe dream and it is not surprising that most studies in this area are of a qualitative nature. In current studies, the assumption is that executives can accurately assess levels of organisational learning given that they have a 'helicopter view' of their organisations. From our discussions of power and politics in organisations, this may prove to be insufficient.

The learning organisation and knowledge management

In the mid-1990s there was a shift in the literature away from the learning organisation towards the new notion of knowledge management. This shift built on existing themes of people management but there was an increased call to integrate emerging themes of IS/IT and intellectual capital. Lena Aggestam (2006) has examined the two literatures looking for similarities and differences between them. Her analysis based on keywords is shown in Table 6.4.

Table 6.4 **Keywords in the learning organisation and knowledge management literatures** (Aggestam 2006)

Keyword	LO: 'an entity', which requires KM	KM: 'a process', which assumes a LO
Culture	A LO has a learning culture. (e.g. Personal Mastery, Team Learning, Mental Models)	Culture constrains the efficient use, because KM is carried out by individuals
Leadership/management	Leadership fosters the culture	Management has a central role, but acts within a culture
Vision	A shared vision is necessary	KM must have a vision
Work processes	A LO integrates attention to every aspect of knowledge	KM must be integrated
Organisational learning	A LO is good at OL, OL is a collective cognitive process	Knowledge is the result of OL
External factors	Must meet these demands	–
Internal factors	Must meet these demands	Constrains the efficient use, e.g. culture and IT
System's thinking	How a LO thinks about the world	–
Organisational memory	–	E.g. data repository
Technical	–	Is a prerequisite

The learning organisation is conceptualised as managing external factors such as customers and competitors, whereas knowledge management is about managing internal factors within an organisation. In this sense, the learning organisation exists at a higher level of abstraction, whereas knowledge management exists at the level of work processes. The learning organisation is the overall organisational system whereas knowledge management is a sub-system within it.

Organisational memory has a much greater prominence in the knowledge management literature. In its explicit form it is captured in a variety of information systems and, in its tacit form, it resides in stories and narratives within organisational communities. The learning organisation literature places less emphasis on organisational memory except as a subset of organisational learning.

The learning organisation literature does not really engage with the information systems aspects of learning and consequent development of intellectual capital. This oversight may be historical. Much of the theoretical underpinnings of the learning organisation started way before information systems and Web 2.0 technologies gained prominence as important artefacts to mobilise knowledge and aid learning. A useful theoretical contribution to the literature would be an integration of human and technical perspectives at the level of a learning organisation.

CASE STUDY

Honda (Japan)

Takeo Fukui, CEO of Honda, met Masaaki Kato, CEO of Honda R&D, along the corridor. They hadn't seen each other for over a month even though their offices were less than 50m apart. 'Have you got time for a quick tea and a chat?' asked Mr Fukui. 'Yes of course, my morning meeting's been cancelled! How serendipitous!' replied Mr Kato. 'What's the latest in battery technology? I'm mindful that General Motors have invested heavily in battery technology especially with their new Chevrolet Volt,' enquired Mr Fukui. Mr Kato was clear about the use of 100-volt Nickel Metal Hydride batteries on Honda's new 'Insight' petrol-electric hybrid car. He added 'But though lithium-ion batteries pack more energy than the nickel-metal hydride power sources found in hybrids like Toyota's Prius, they would not satisfy most consumers because they are costly. Lithium-ion batteries still hold less than half the energy of gasoline as measured by weight.[1] Mr Kato insisted that the major challenge with electric and hybrid cars was the range, power and reliability of batteries. He joked that if their Honda Accord was purely electrically driven, it would require more than two tons in batteries. He saw the future of Honda in inexpensive hybrid compact vehicles rather than the more expensive electric vehicles favoured by their competitors. As ever, Mr Fukui was clear that Honda's future competitiveness lay in its knowledge and ability to learn. At present, this learning was focused on battery technology with predictions that different types of electric vehicles might command between 10–25 per cent of the global automotive market by 2020. He asked Mr Kato to reflect on their overall knowledge and learning processes at Honda and if there were any grounds for improvement.

Honda is the world's leading manufacturer of motorcycles and power products and a global leader in automotive manufacturing. The company has over 23 million customers globally and produces a diverse range of products from scooters to cars and humanoid robots. Honda has revenues of $94.8 billion and margins of around 9 per cent. It had spent $9.5 billion on research and development in 2008 and intended to increase this to $10 billion in 2009. There is a ➡

distinct 'Honda Way' in terms of the firm's values and ways of doing things. This is typified by their entry into the car market from the motorcycle market in 1963 in Japan despite opposition from many government departments. There is a certain air of defiance in their attitude. Another example is their entry into the US car market in 1969. They capitalised on their Honda Civic in the oil crisis of 1973 when there was a greater demand for fuel efficiency rather than traditional gas-guzzling American cars. They took the risk of manufacturing their cars in the US with a small group of suppliers who lacked their own US plant. Subsequently, the US has become their largest and most profitable market. There is a commitment in Honda to create products of the highest quality at an acceptable price. At most meetings, workers will reflect on 'What would the customer want us to do?'.[2]

An interesting aspect to Honda's approach is their use of slogans. In 1978 they had used the slogan 'Let's Gamble' for the development of a concept car when they felt that their Accord and Civic cars were becoming outdated. A young design team, with an average age of 27, was charged with coming up with a concept car that was fundamentally different from previous Honda offerings at an inexpensive (but not cheap) price. The team coined another slogan 'Theory of Automobile Evolution' to help them explore how cars may evolve if they were like organisms. The team answered this slogan with another slogan 'Man-maximum, machine-minimum' to show that they wanted to transcend conventional perceptions of cars. They transformed this slogan into a sphere, as the sphere gave the customer the greatest level of comfort and used the least space on the road. Soon this figurative language and reasoning led to the formation of the Honda City, an innovative urban car.[3] At a global level, Honda brands its products with a slogan 'Power of Dreams'.

Honda's success has been in its ability to allow its engineers to play with and experiment with products and ideas. On one level, this can appear entrepreneurial, and on another quite quirky. For example, Honda's engineers have developed a four-foot humanoid robot called 'Asimo' that can balance on one foot, recognise faces and distin-guish between different sounds. The assumption is that these robotic features may have applications in other parts of their business. Honda's R&D engineers are fiercely independent and tend to avoid engaging in alliances with other organisations. Even though they are a subsidiary of Honda Motors, they have provided CEOs for the main organisation since its inception in 1948.

The lack of direct consumer orientation at Honda R&D has led it astray on the odd occasion. For example, Honda launched a hybrid car called 'Insight' in 1999 and was the first car to market in the US. However, it was the Toyota Prius that captured the giant share of the hybrid market, selling over 180,000 cars in 2007. Toyota Prius was a conventional small car whereas the Honda Insight had a bizarre appearance and lacked a back seat. In 2006 Honda's Insight was withdrawn from production.[4]

Training is combined with personal coaching at Honda under the corporate guise of 'talent management'. The rationale is to improve the potential of each employee rather than just the stars. It is ultimately about behavioural change rather than attendance at training courses. In the UK, talent management is based on a structure of 10:20:30:40. Each figure represents the quantity of resources to be expended on talent management activities.

- Ten per cent of resources are to be spent on finding the right coaches with high levels of persistence and passion to avoid future failures.

- Twenty per cent of resources to be spent on training employees on coaching and allowing them to take responsibility for change and their own training.

- Thirty per cent of resources to be spent on coaching after their training courses to ensure behavioural change. Also, for coaching the next batch of corporate coaches in order to dispense with the need for external coaches.

- Forty per cent of resources to be spent on integrating learning into mainstream activities.[5]

Mr Fukui reflected that much of Honda's early success was a mixture of miscalculation, serendipity and organisational learning. In the 1960s it was all about the Honda 50 under their ad slogan

'Nifty, Thrifty, Honda Fifty'. The bigger bikes came much later. He asked Mr Kato if it was time for Honda to have a new slogan given that times and consumers had changed to become more environmentally and internet savvy: the 'twitter generation'. Mr Kato rose to leave and said that he would place that task with a young team of his R&D engineers and see what they came up with. They shook hands and parted company.

References

1 Van Praet, N. (2009) 'GM to open battery factory in U.S.: Move raises its bet on viability of electric Volt', *National Post's Financial Post & FP Investing (Canada)*, p. FP5
2 Chappell, L. (2009) 'The Honda Way is unpredictable, contrarian – and successful: Automaker's go-it-alone attitude serves it well', *Automotive News*, p. H004.
3 Nonaka, I. and H. Takeuchi (1995) *The Knowledge Creating Company*, New York: Oxford University Press.
4 Taylor, A. (2008) 'Inside Honda's brain', *Fortune*, 157(5), pp. 64–5.
5 Johnston, D. (2006) 'Thought leader: A model for coaching at Honda', *Inside Knowledge*, 10(3).

Questions

1 How can Honda improve their learning and competitiveness of battery technologies?

2 What role do slogans play in the innovation process at Honda?

3 How can Honda improve its 'talent management' processes in the UK?

Summary

This chapter has explored the latest thinking around the concept of a learning organisation and elaborated five key themes:

1 The distinction between organisational learning and a learning organisation. Organisational learning is seen as a process and means in an organisation, whereas a learning organisation is an end and an idealised state.

2 The popular conception of a learning organisation by Peter Senge as five disciplines of personal mastery, team learning, systems thinking, mental models and shared vision.

3 Different models of a learning organisation were articulated, some emphasising organisational learning, some knowledge creation, some structures and others strategy.

4 The problems of the learning organisation ideology were highlighted where the concept could be used for management manipulation and control. Various approaches such as the use of 'court jesters' and radical theatre were suggested as ways of overcoming power imbalances and generating trust and commitment to learning in organisations.

5 The paucity of empirical research to test various assumptions in the conceptual frameworks. Apart from some small sample inductive studies, there is little statistical evidence to support the assertions of the various models of learning organisations.

Questions for further thought

1 What are the main differences between organisational learning and the learning organisation? Is the notion of a learning organisation little more than 'old wine in new bottles'?

2 How can an idealised notion of a learning organisation help organisations succeed?

3 What are the problems of high-stretch goals?

4 What are the advantages and drawbacks of a prescriptive approach to a learning organisation?

5 How can a shared vision be achieved in organisations?

6 What are the dangers of clusters of learning and equal clusters of non-learning in organisations?

7 In what ways can imagination be mobilised in organisations?

8 How can cooperative cultures be a liability for organisations?

9 What are the dangers of a Foucauldian nightmare conception of a learning organisation?

10 What are the advantages and limitations of quantitative empirical research on the notion of a learning organisation?

Further reading

1 Senge (1990) is a must-read if only because it placed the concept of the learning organisation firmly on the academic and consultancy agenda.

2 Pedler *et al.* (1991) is the dominant UK contribution in this field and contains many useful organisational development exercises to complement the conceptual models developed.

3 Nonaka and Takeuchi (1995) is useful from a knowledge management perspective as the book elaborates on the whole knowledge-creation process.

References

Aggestam, L. (2006) 'Learning organisation or knowledge management – Which came first, the chicken or the egg?' *Information Technology and Control*, 35, 295–302.

Argyris, C. (1991) 'Teaching smart people how to learn', *Harvard Business Review*, 69(3), 99–109.

Argyris, C. (1999) *On Organizational Learning*, Blackwell, Oxford.

Argyris, C. and Schon, D. A. (1978) *Organizational Learning: A Theory of Action Perspective*, Addison-Wesley, Reading, MA.

Ballard, R. (1992) 'Short forms of the Marlowe–Crowne social desirability scale', *Psychological Reports*, 71, 1155–60.

Bereiter, C. (2002) *Education and Mind in the Knowledge Age*, Mahwah, NJ, Lawrence Erlbaum Associates.

Boal, A. (1979) *Theatre of the Oppressed*, Pluto Press, London.

Carroll, C. (1995) 'Rearticulating organizational identity: Exploring corporate images and employee identification', *Management Learning*, 26(4), 463–82.

Chappell, L. 'The Honda Way is unpredictable, contrarian – and successful; Automaker's go-it-alone attitude serves it well,' *Automotive News*.

Coopey, J. (1998) 'Learning to trust and trusting to learn: A role of radical theatre', *Management Learning*, 29(3), 365–82.

Davenport, T. H. and Prusak, L. (1998) *Working Knowledge: How Organizations Manage What They Know*, Harvard Business School Press, Boston, MA.

de Geus, A. (1988) 'Planning as learning', *Harvard Business Review*, 66 (March/April), 70–4.

Deming, W. E. (1986) *Out of the Crisis*, MIT Press, Boston, MA.

Denton, J. (1998) *Organizational Learning and Effectiveness*, Routledge, London.

Driver, M. (2002) 'The learning organization: Foucauldian gloom or Utopian sunshine?', *Human Relations*, 55(1), 33–53.

Easterby-Smith, M. (1990) 'Creating a learning organisation', *Personnel Review*, 19(5), 24–28.

Fiol, C. and Lyles, M. (1985) 'Organizational learning', *Academy of Management Review*, 10(4), 803–13.

Garratt, B. (1987) *The Learning Organization*, Gower, Aldershot.

Garratt, B. (1990) *Creating a Learning Organization: A Guide to Leadership, Learning & Development*, Director Books, Cambridge.

Garvin, D. A. (1993) 'Building a learning organization', *Harvard Business Review*, 71(4), 78–91.

Gourlay, S. (2006) 'Conceptualising knowledge creation: a critique of Nonaka's theory', *Journal of Management Studies*, 43, 1415–36.

Grant, R. M. (1996) 'Toward a knowledge-based theory of the firm', *Strategic Management Journal*, 17, 109–22.

Hamel, G. and Prahalad, C. K. (1994) *Competing for the Future*, Harvard Business School Press, Boston, MA.

Hayes, J. and Allinson, C. W. (1998) 'Cognitive style and the theory and practice of individual and collective learning in organizations', *Human Relations*, 51(7), 847–71.

Honey, P. (1991) 'The learning organisation simplified', *Training and Development*, July, 30–33.

Jashapara, A. (1993) 'The competitive learning organization: A quest for the Holy Grail', *Management Decision*, 31(8), 52–62.

Jashapara, A. (2003) 'Cognition, culture and competition: An empirical test of the learning organization', *The Learning Organization*, 10(1), 31–50.

Johnston, D. (2006) 'Thought leader: A model for coaching at Honda,' *Inside Knowledge*, 10.

Jorna, R. (1998) 'Knowledge management is really about representations', *The Semiotic Review of Books*, 9, 5–8.

Loermans, J. (2002) 'Synergizing the learning organization and knowledge management', *Journal of Knowledge Management*, 6(3), 285–94.

Mintzberg, H. (1991) 'The effective organization: Forces and forms', *Sloan Management Review*, Winter edition, 54–67.

Mitroff, I. I., Mason, R. O. and Pearson, C. M. (1994) 'Radical surgey: What will tomorrow's organizations look like?', *Academy of Management Executive*, 8, 11–22.

Nonaka, I. (1991) 'The knowledge-creating company', *Harvard Business Review*, 69 (November–December), 96–104.

Nonaka, I. and Takeuchi, H. (1995) *The Knowledge-Creating Company: How Japanese Companies Create the Dynamics of Innovation*, Oxford University Press, New York.

Örtenblad, A. (2002) 'A typology of the idea of learning organization', *Management Learning*, 33(2), 213–30.

Pedler, M., Burgoyne, J. and Boydell, T. (1991) *The Learning Company: A Strategy for Sustainable Development*, McGraw-Hill, London.

Pettigrew, A. and Whipp, R. (1991) *Managing Change for Competitive Success*, Blackwell Publishers, Oxford.

Polanyi, M. (1967) *The Tacit Dimension*, Doubleday, New York.

Revans, R. W. (1977) *The ABC of Action Learning*, Action Learning Trust, Luton.

Schein, E. H. (1999) 'Empowerment, coercive persuasion and organizational learning: Do they connect?', *The Learning Organization*, 6(4), 163–72.

Senge, P. M. (1990) *The Fifth Discipline: The Art and Practice of the Learning Organisation*, Doubleday Currency, New York.

Svieby, K. (1997) *The New Organizational Wealth: Managing and Measuring Knowledge-Based Assets*, Berrett-Koehler, San Francisco.

Swan, J., Scarborough, H. and Preston, J. (1999) 'Knowledge management – the next fad to forget people?', *Proceedings of the 7th European Conference on Information Systems*, Copenhagen.

Taylor, A. (2008) 'Inside Honda's brain', *Fortune*, 157, 64–5.

Van Praet, N. (2009) 'GM to open battery factory in U.S.: Move raises its bet on viability of electric Volt', *National Post's Financial Post & FP Investing (Canada)*.

KNOWLEDGE ARTEFACTS

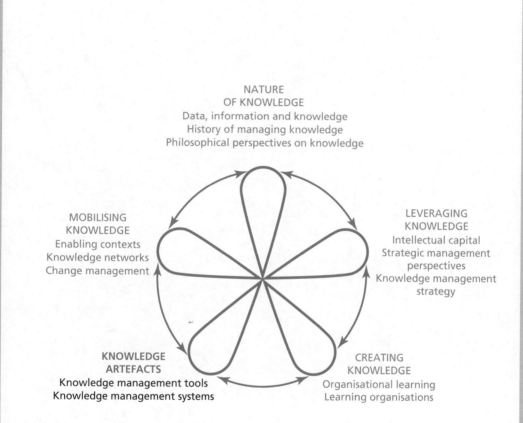

NATURE
OF KNOWLEDGE
Data, information and knowledge
History of managing knowledge
Philosophical perspectives on knowledge

MOBILISING
KNOWLEDGE
Enabling contexts
Knowledge networks
Change management

LEVERAGING
KNOWLEDGE
Intellectual capital
Strategic management
perspectives
Knowledge management
strategy

KNOWLEDGE
ARTEFACTS
Knowledge management tools
Knowledge management systems

CREATING
KNOWLEDGE
Organisational learning
Learning organisations

Chapter 7

Knowledge management tools: component technologies

Learning outcomes

After completing this chapter the reader should be able to:

- describe different component technologies found in knowledge management;
- explain the different technologies for capturing, organising, storing and sharing new knowledge;
- contrast the functions of different component technologies;
- feel confident about selecting appropriate knowledge management technologies for particular needs.

Management issues

The use and application of knowledge management tools and technology implies these questions for managers:

- What KM tools are most appropriate for a given business problem?
- What is the nature of different KM tools and technologies?
- How do these technologies help capture and share the valuable tacit knowledge or 'know how' in an organisation?

Links to other chapters

Chapter 3	looks at strategic perspectives for integrating technology and human aspects of knowledge management.
Chapter 8	explains how the various KM component technologies are configured into a variety of knowledge management systems.
Chapter 10	examines the difficult aspects of implementing technological solutions within organisations.

Business starts to take Web 2.0 tools seriously   FT

At each stage in its extraordinary development, the internet has encountered scepticism and resistance in boardrooms. Alarms have greeted each internet-based technology: would it distract employees or, worse, create unacceptable risks?

Over time, internet tools have been accommodated and have delivered huge benefits. But the same questions are now being asked about the latest generation of internet technologies, such as social networking tools.

Much attention has been lavished on the poster children of the Web 2.0 phenomenon – Facebook, YouTube, Twitter and the like – but for many business leaders, such consumer-led innovations seem frivolous, and have little to do with developing new products, increasing market share or streamlining clunky business processes. Some ban Web 2.0 tools. They need to be aware, however, that a quiet revolution is taking place. That's the message from Soumitra Dutta and Matthew Fraser, academics at the Insead business school in France and authors of *Throwing Sheep in the Boardroom*.

They detail how companies, including **General Electric**, **Procter & Gamble**, **Shell** and **Airbus**, are busy integrating social networking into their corporate strategies. These companies, say the authors, are showing that the use of blogs, wikis, widgets and other Web 2.0 tools 'encourages horizontal collaboration and harnesses the power of collective intelligence to boost productivity, foster innovation and create enhanced value'.

'We set out to explore, in an objective and rigorous way, whether the concept of Enterprise 2.0 could deliver real business benefits,' they say. They found plenty of evidence that it could, although conceding that the biggest obstacles to its acceptance may be cultural, overcoming the scepticism of business leaders and their fears about the free flow of information in their companies.

Mr Fraser says the current economic crisis could force Web 2.0 into the business mainstream: 'A downturn raises questions about how organisations are structured and how they tap into the knowledge and expertise of employees, suppliers and customers. Enterprise 2.0 has already been shown to provide valuable answers, where it is used intelligently.'

Silicon Valley venture capitalist Gordon Ritter of Emergence Technologies believes the value proposition of Enterprise 2.0 tools is that they make the benefits of social networking more palatable to businesses by offering audit trails, access control, version control, authentication, provisioning and back-up. 'The aim is to replicate the immediacy and ease-of-use of Web 2.0 in a way that imposes highly customised best practices on customers to create real productivity gains,' he says.

Oliver Young, an analyst with Forrester Research, says there are two key areas: tools to boost collaboration and productivity, both internally and with trusted partners; and tools used by companies to provide a forum for dialogue between them and their customers.

'The first camp is the best established,' says Mr Young. Corporate knowledge management initiatives have seen a steady rise in the use of wikis, for example, with groups of experts working together, pooling ideas and solving problems. This is where SocialText, a key company in the Enterprise 2.0 movement, made its start in 2002.

Ross Mayfield, SocialText's chairman, president and co-founder, says: 'Our belief has always been that, when technology doesn't get in the way, people are eager to share and collaborate, and wikis are a great way to do that. But a corporate customer needs a tool that can accommodate the hierarchies, norms of behaviour and levels of accountability and control that exist already within its culture.'

Where that has been achieved, it has proved powerful in such areas as product development, says David Bailey, head of the manufacturing practice at PA Consulting. 'It's hardly surprising that organisations are interested in technologies that can shorten product development cycles.'

The collaborative approach is also delivering gains in customer support. If frontline employees use wikis when dealing with customers, average call times can be cut by between 10 and 30 per cent, says Mr Mayfield.

The second area – public-facing communities – is less established but likely to grow, says Mr Young. He says social networking tends to be cheaper than other forms of marketing and has the advantage of supporting two-way conversations.

'Customers are talking about your organisation and its products online anyway. A social networking community offers corporates the chance to participate in these conversations and have more control over them,' says Lyle Fong, chief executive of Lithium Technologies. 'Those that do are discovering the benefits of reduced customer service costs,' he adds.

Enterprise 2.0 tools are now being offered by the big IT companies, most notably **Microsoft**, with new social media add-ons to its Sharepoint collaboration platform, and **IBM**, with its Lotus Connections product.

'We have signed such customers as **Colgate-Palmolive** and **HSBC**, partly on the demonstrable value that IBM has delivered to itself using social software,' says Bob Picciano, general manager of IBM's Lotus Software group.

In September 2008 the company established its Center for Social Software, a research hub based in Cambridge, Massachusetts, where IBM staff are working alongside academics from the Massachusetts Institute of Technology (MIT) and Harvard, as well as researchers from companies including Dow Jones and Thomson Reuters' healthcare division, to explore the impact of Enterprise 2.0 on the workplace.

But for many organisations, Enterprise 2.0 represents a chance to preserve existing investments in technology by liberating the data contained in back-end systems and making it available to users over the internet through the use of 'widgets'.

Ness, a technology consulting firm, for example, has built a widget using tools from Worklight, an Israel-based company, that enables its consultants to input details of billable hours via the internet on a regular basis, rather than at month-end. The widget feeds directly into Ness's core SAP system.

'When we take into account the hours of employee time saved in this way, we've calculated that we'll get an ample return on the project cost of $100,000 within a year,' says Andres Kukawka, Ness chief executive. The company plans a similar widget for capturing employee expenses information.

'Mash-ups and widgets may sound like the Wild West to more conservative companies but, to a large extent, it's a question of extracting more value from the services they already provide, by mixing them with external services and presentation methods to create new markets, new revenues and new products,' says Andy Mullholland, chief technology officer at IT consultant **CapGemini**.

In any case, many executives may find that Enterprise 2.0 is already happening at their organisation without them knowing, so they may as well embrace it, says John Newton, chief technology officer and chairman at Alfresco, an open-source content management company. He says: 'Any scepticism will not be overcome by technology vendors, but by employees.' As the next generation of employees enters the workplace, he adds, their demands are likely to become more strident, making the provision of social networking tools critical to businesses looking to attract the best and brightest.

Source: from Business starts to take Web 2.0 tools seriously, *The Financial Times*, 28/01/2009 (Twentyman, J.), copyright © The Financial Times Ltd.

Questions

1 Why are Web 2.0 tools important for business?

2 What are the different forms of Web 2.0 tools?

3 How can you overcome the scepticism of boardrooms towards Web 2.0 tools?

Introduction

For any aspiring purchaser of KM systems or technologies, the internet provides a multitude of vendors promising to transform your business. But where do you start? How do you understand the complexity of the offering and its effectiveness with your business problem? In the highly volatile market of software engineering, it is likely that many of these so-called 'market leaders' will cease trading in a few years' time. As an experiment in this book, it was found that fourteen 'market leaders' in KM tools (Mertins *et al.* 2000) had ceased trading in a two-year time frame.

So how can we decipher the offerings of the multitude of technologies in the marketplace? The approach adopted in this chapter is to examine the component technologies that make up a knowledge management system or suite. The analogy of a hi-fi purchase is used where each item has a certain function and purpose. I have grouped various technologies in their ability to perform a knowledge function such as organising, capturing, analysing, storing and sharing knowledge, as shown in Figure 7.1. The multitude of KM systems on offer in the marketplace is seen as a composite variation of a number of these component technologies. Firms may decide to buy different components off-the-shelf or develop their own tools to meet their needs.

As with purchasing hi-fi systems, one can purchase cheap or expensive KM technologies. Rather than becoming mesmerised by the power of these technologies, it is important to remain focused on the organisational needs that are driving the procurement of these technologies and whether an alternative may suffice; dare I say a telephone and e-mail! As a rule of thumb, experience shows that no more than one third of a knowledge management budget should be committed to technology (O'Dell

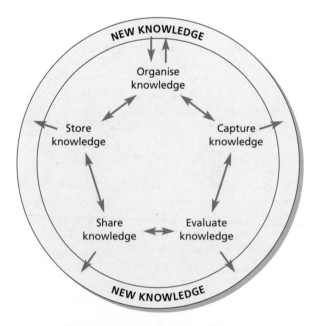

Figure 7.1 **A typology of knowledge tools and component technologies**

et al. 2000). Often the focus of technology is on hardware and software and managers can underestimate the value of knowledge content such as news feeds from Reuters. In a 1997 Ernst & Young survey business managers indicated that the most important types of knowledge that would help them act effectively were (Smith and Farquhar 2000):

● knowledge about customers (97 per cent);

● knowledge about best practice and effective processes (87 per cent);

● knowledge about competences and capabilities of their company (86 per cent).

In the same survey, it is noteworthy that 46 per cent of the 431 US and European executives felt that their organisations were good at generating new knowledge but only 13 per cent of the respondents agreed that their organisations were good at transferring existing knowledge (Ruggles 1998). The most common technologies employed by organisations were:

● creating an intranet (47 per cent);

● creating data warehouses (33 per cent);

● implementing decision-support tools (33 per cent);

● implementing groupware to support collaboration (33 per cent).

Since this survey, there have been a multitude of technologies developed linked to Web 2.0 platform. There has been a mini-revolution where power has shifted to the user rather than so-called 'experts'. The emphasis in these technologies has been involvement and engagement of users and development of online communities, real or virtual. Online social network sites such as Facebook, MySpace and Twitter have gained in popularity. Businesses and universities have started engaging in virtual worlds such as Second Life. People have started publishing their personal journals through blogs. RSS feeds have allowed people the opportunity to connect directly with others with whom they share a connection. Wikis have allowed the collective knowledge of groups to be articulated and shared on a website. And the participation rates are astonishing. Every type of media is being engaged from text, audio to video.

Organising knowledge tools

▶ Ontology and taxonomy

Knowledge can come in a variety of forms: structured, semi-structured or unstructured, as shown in Figure 7.2. In order to organise this knowledge, one starts by gathering knowledge and working out a way to group, index or categorise it in some way. One could present a schema conceptualising a vocabulary of terms and relationships to represent the knowledge. This is called a 'knowledge map' or an 'ontology'. If each one of us tried to organise the same knowledge, we might come up with wide variations depending on our understanding and perspective on the subject. In an attempt to prevent this situation from occurring, we have developed 'ontologies' to improve our level of information organisation, management and understanding. Gruber (1993) defines ontology as:

'a formal, explicit specification of shared conceptualisation.'

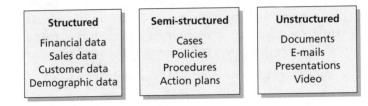

Structured	Semi-structured	Unstructured
Financial data Sales data Customer data Demographic data	Cases Policies Procedures Action plans	Documents E-mails Presentations Video

Figure 7.2 **Different forms of knowledge**

This implies that a domain ontology provides us with a formalised vocabulary for describing a given domain. This is not the same as a philosophical understanding of 'ontology' which refers to our perceptions of 'the nature of being' and our assumptions of the nature of reality. In the context of KM tools, the term ontology is often used interchangeably with taxonomy as this may be the operational conceptualisation of a domain chosen by a user. To clarify the distinction, it is important to recognise that an ontology is an overall conceptualisation whereas a taxonomy is a 'scientifically based scheme of classification', as shown in Figure 7.3. An ontology may have non-taxonomic conceptual relationships such as 'has part' relations between concepts. In contrast, knowledge taxonomies generate hierarchical classification of terms that are structured to show relationships between terms. These ontologies and taxonomies have a significant impact on our ability to deal with vast amounts of information such as that found on the internet or corporate intranets.

The current norms are to generate ontologies manually. The English language comprises over half a million words and there is an almost infinite array of terms to convey the same concepts. This can present semantic complications and ambiguities in classifying, locating and retrieving knowledge. The scope of most ontologies is to provide a clear, consistent and coherent conceptualisation that is extensible and easily reusable.

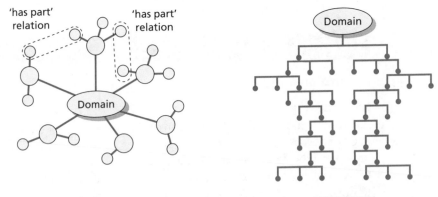

Figure 7.3 **Ontology and taxonomies**

One doesn't want to reinvent the wheel each time new knowledge is added to a particular domain. Uschold and Gruninger (1996) have provided a useful approach to build ontologies manually to achieve these aims:

1 Identify purpose and scope.

2 Build the ontology via a three-step process.

 (a) ontology capture – identify key concepts and relationships;

 (b ontology coding – commit basic terms such as class, entity and relations and choose a representation language or write the code;

 (c) integrate existing ontologies.

3 Evaluate ontologies.

4 Document ontologies.

5 Provide guidelines for previous phases.

However, apart from being time consuming, manually generated ontologies have the added problem of being prone to errors and can pose difficulties in maintaining and updating them (Ding and Foo 2002). If there are significant delays in updating ontologies, this can cause problems in their usefulness and hinder their development. Some of these factors have driven the current impetus towards semi-automated and fully automated ontology generation systems.

Critical thinking and reflection

Reflect on all the different aspects of your knowledge that you use in everyday life. Spend five minutes drawing a map showing the diversity of your knowledge and the relationships between the various stands. You may find the analogy of a knowledge tree useful, with major branches and smaller branches of your knowledge. How could you replicate such an approach to develop an ontology for an organisation? What may be some of the limitations of this ontology? How could you get staff to cooperate in the development of your organisational ontology?

The current state-of-the-art ontology generation technologies still use some seed words provided by domain experts as the basis of ontology generation and have not yet reached their ultimate goal of using learning ontologies. Concepts are extracted from raw data using a variety of relatively mature techniques such as:

● 'part-of-speech (POS)' tagging to extract high-frequency words or phrases that could be used to define concepts and may perform a syntactic analysis;

● 'word sense disambiguation' to extract relations such as 'is-a' and 'associated with' where the distinction lies in the linguistic property of the nouns;

● 'tokenisers' to break strings into a series of tokens between two delimiting characters (such as the spacing between words) and determine the length of each string;

● 'pattern matching' – for example, a system may learn a semantic lexicon of paired words with their meanings and have the ability to extract phrase-meaning pairs from a document.

In recent years, automatic ontology generation or classification tools have advanced to such a point that they are comparable to manual classifiers of ontology in a well-organised operation. For example, the degree of accuracy of the best performing algorithms in automatic classifiers can exceed 85 per cent on good quality data (Marwick 2001). This degree of accuracy may be acceptable for many applications. A fundamental aspect of the current generation of automatic classifiers is their use of 'machine learning' to train themselves from example data which can give rise to refined distinctions given a wide variety of training data. Also, the new generation of classifiers have a high level of reuseability, enabling easy application to new domains and reducing overall costs of ontology generation.

Ontologies have been represented in a variety of ways depending on the technology. In their most simplistic form, they can be represented as a conceptual hierarchy similar to their related taxonomy. However, some classification tools use an algebraic extraction technique to generate a graph structure with thesaurus entries for all words. Others store the results of text processing into annotations using XML-tagged text (Ding and Foo 2002).

Current ontology generation tools are not free from problems. In part, this helps drive the next generation of tools. For example, there can be problems with the sense of a word in different contexts or the recognition of different phrases referring to the same concept. Machine-learning techniques that enable the classifier tool to learn patterns can be helpful, but many of these learning relationships are highly complex. A general problem can be the 'shallow' semantics generated which can hide the richness and depth of any domain. Also, there may be differences between the automatic generation of ontologies and the schematic conceptions of a community or a group of experts. An almost classical conflict may arise from a group of artists who may have a loose and highly visual conception of their domain and the ontology engineer, who may represent their ontology in a highly mathematical or hierarchical framework.

Ontologies are dynamic. Concepts and schemas do change their meaning and sense relations over time. How can we reuse existing ontologies and incorporate new meanings, relations, domains and knowledge over time? Given the overwhelming production of knowledge in organisations each year, there is likely to be a need to integrate existing ontologies with new domains. However, this can create numerous problems, such as semantic inconsistencies and differences in knowledge formats. Ontology mapping has developed as an area of research to address these problems. The current approaches for integrating a number of ontologies (see Figure 7.4) include (Sofia Pinto *et al.* 1999):

- reusing available ontologies linking different domains;
- aligning ontologies by establishing links between them through some form of translation function using agent technology;
- merging ontologies to create a single ontology;
- integrating ontologies through clustering on the basis of similarities.

These approaches recognise that successful integration of ontologies requires a good understanding of semantics to reconcile semantic similarities, discrepancies, compatibilities, relevance and relativity. Semantics are concerned with the meanings

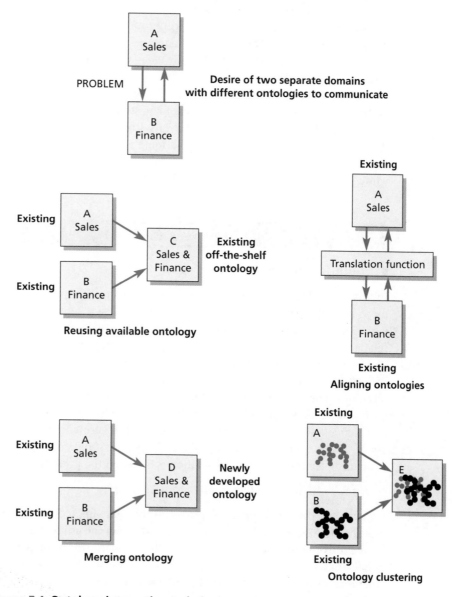

Figure 7.4 Ontology integration techniques

individuals or groups give to a particular term or concept. It is understandable that confusion may easily arise from different communities associating different meanings or nuances of meaning with the same term. For example, the term 'elegance' may have connotations of aesthetics and beauty to an architect, whereas the same term may imply optimal use of materials to an engineer.

Given the continual information overload problem in many organisations, there is a need to maintain and improve an existing ontology as it changes over time. Manual maintenance of ontologies can be tedious and time consuming. Hence, a variety of tools have been developed to assist the 'ontology editor' to semi-automate the tasks. Certain tools exist to acquire new concepts and place these within the domain ontology and some of these are based on machine-learning techniques. It is notable that Tim Berners-Lee, inventor of the World Wide Web, believes that the information overload problems on the existing Web will lead to a second generation which he calls a 'Semantic Web'. This will make explicit the semantics underlying all resources on the Web and create a form of 'global' ontology. It is unclear whether this future 'global' ontology will be reused to create local ontologies by standardising concepts and the relations between them. An alternative route may be to use a universal classification system such as Dewey to represent a 'global' ontology in order to comprehend the whole of human knowledge, including that which is not yet known.

Capturing knowledge tools

▶ Cognitive mapping tools

In any given area of knowledge, each one of us has our own ontology or 'cognitive map' of that particular domain. The map is a visual representation of the domain which makes explicit mentally the concepts that exist within that domain and the relationships between them. In many cases, this map is likely to be tacit and unarticulated within an individual or an organisation. This tacit knowledge is a key source of competitive advantage as it is difficult to articulate, imitate, is context specific and has direct practical relevance (Ambrosini and Bowman 2002; Barney 1991; Grant 1996). Cognitive mapping provides a valuable tool to represent an individual's knowledge and experience and their view of reality (Eden and Ackermann 1998; Weick and Bougon 1986). The mapping process is based on Kelly's personal construct theory (1955). The structuring technique of idea generation is based on the premise:

'How do I know what I think until I hear what I say?'

Currently, the main application for cognitive mapping tools is in the area of mapping strategic knowledge (Huff and Jenkins 2002) through the use of causal maps. Causal maps are cognitive maps that can establish multiple relationships between entities through causal links. For example, entity A may 'cause' entity B and D and the complexity of other relationships can be depicted graphically, as shown in Figure 7.5. The advantage of causal mapping tools is that they provide a way of ordering and analysing something that is 'fuzzy' and vague and allow us to impose a structure on the fuzziness and visualise the relationships between concepts (Ambrosini and Bowman 2002; Weick and Bougon 1986).

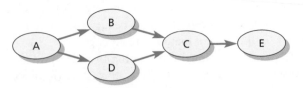

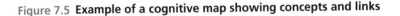

Figure 7.5 **Example of a cognitive map showing concepts and links**

In terms of strategic management, it is not the individual tacit maps but rather the organisational tacit knowledge that is likely to result in competitive advantage or greater effectiveness. If one views an organisation as a social system with interdependent parts (Gharajedaghi and Ackoff 1994), tacit organisational knowledge can be conceived as residing in a set of organisational routines (Grant 1996; Nelson and Winter 1982; Spender 1996). Nelson and Winter (1982) argue that these formal and informal routines are embedded in organisational activities and organisations remember them through action. These tacit routines are not codified and do not follow standard rules and operating procedures. They are related to their specific context and, by implication, there are limits to the extent to which they can be articulated (Grant 1991). However, cognitive mapping tools allow us to reveal 'collective maps' of tacit routines from a process of group dialogue and discussion.

The most developed application of cognitive mapping tools has been in the field of strategy making to help surface and explore tacit knowledge, assumptions, assertions, values, beliefs, aspirations and concerns within a management team or board of directors (Eden and Ackermann 1998). This technique allows the important processes of 'sharing meaning' and 'making sense' to be facilitated and misunderstandings from implicit assumptions to be minimised. In a group situation the technique supports important group processes such as negotiation and anonymity (Eden and Ackermann 2002). The resulting cognitive map comprises the collective thinking of a group of individuals which may contain conflicting views from a variety of perspectives.

The most common method of creating a cognitive map is through the 'oval mapping technique' and software that aids the mapping process (Decision Explorer™ www. Banxia.com) with effective representation, retrieval and analytical support, as shown in Figure 7.6. These visual thinking tools allow ideas and their relationships with other ideas to be made explicit. The process of oval mapping is as follows:

- Facilitator to ask group to focus on a question or issue.

- Ask participants to cover the working space such as a wall with flip chart paper.

- Give participants a set of 'oval' cards and encourage them to focus on their expertise and record their views for public display.

- Ask participants to write one idea per oval preferably.

- Inform participants that no ovals will be removed (except in cases of total agreement by group) and they need to make disagreements explicit.

- Facilitator to organise ideas into clusters and subclusters. A 'dump' cluster can be used to give facilitator time, particularly where themes or patterns may not be self-evident.

- Facilitator to elicit linkages between different ideas and clusters of ideas by looking at 'means and ends' or 'options and desired outcomes'. In essence, whether one idea causes or leads to another idea or cluster.

This public procedure, where each idea is considered equally valid, allows participants to look at the issues from alternative viewpoints and possibly change their position without the need to defend their own viewpoint. The process encourages social negotiation and greater commitment to the outcomes.

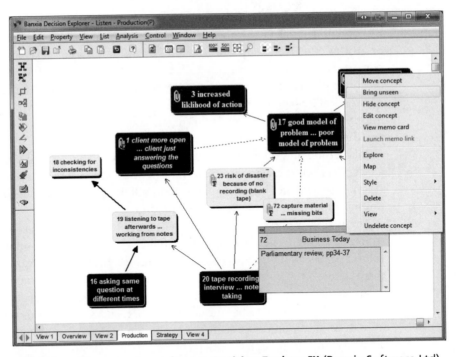

Figure 7.6 Cognitive mapping software: Decision Explorer™ (Banxia Software Ltd)

In strategy development, the causal maps are reorganised into clusters following a 'tear drop' model where aspirations and goals are at the top of the model (Eden and Ackermann 1998), as shown in Figure 7.7. These are the concepts with 'heads' but no 'out-arrows' in terms of consequences. The next layer of clusters are the issues or possible strategies supporting the aspirations and underlying them are the more detailed strategic options that impact on the potential strategies. Further analyses can be conducted on the cognitive map using the computer software such as:

- identifying the busiest concepts;
- calculating the centrality of a concept in the overall structure;
- exploring feedback loops.

In this example, cognitive mapping tools allow us to see how a business model or a livelihood scheme (for not-for-profit organisations) can be realised with the necessary intellectual and emotional commitment from key players. The logic and coherence of different parts of the map can be shared across the organisation to facilitate the change process by reducing the ambiguity of action programmes and demonstrating the impact of singular tasks on multiple objectives.

▶ Information-retrieval tools

The key goal in information retrieval is to retrieve knowledge that may be useful or relevant to a user. Traditionally, there have been two processes involved in information retrieval. First is the creation of an index that enables the location of a text and

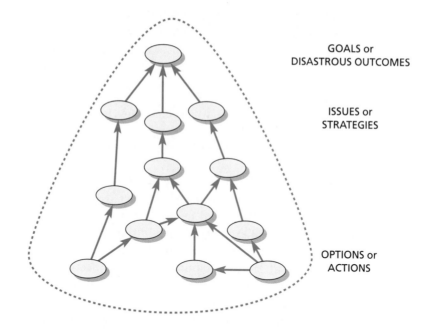

GOALS or
DISASTROUS OUTCOMES

ISSUES or
STRATEGIES

OPTIONS or
ACTIONS

Figure 7.7 **Strategy development 'tear drop' model**

document structure. Textual data can be loaded into the system and en route it undergoes transformation such as the removal of common words. This is often referred to as
a 'logical' view of a document. An index has the advantage of speeding up the retrieval
process and reducing the computational costs. Otherwise each record would have to be
searched individually. All information-retrieval systems have an index which helps to
locate the full text records. Generally, they use an inverted file approach. The second
process is solving a user's information needs in the form of a query through algorithms
and ranking the results in some form of relevance to the user.

One recent trend has been the development of compression technology that allows
direct indexing and searching on compressed text with high compression and decom-
pression speeds. Text can be compressed to 30–35 per cent of its original size. This can
be a critical consideration as text collections are increasingly becoming huge. A typical
process of indexing a text database is shown in Figure 7.8.

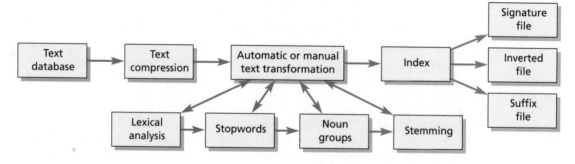

Figure 7.8 **Indexing a text database**

Critical thinking and reflection

From your experience, what role has serendipity played when you've been trying to find information? Can you describe these experiences and see any patterns within them? How valuable have you found formal methods of information retrieval? What informal methods do you use to find information? If search engines or your traditional sources fail to provide you with your required information, what alternative strategies do you adopt?

Individual records such as full texts, news stories or market reports can be indexed using a structured taxonomy of terms generated from the text, with the indexed terms being attached to the record to enable retrieval. This approach has a long history in library sciences. An example of such indexing is the addition of SIC (standard industry classification) codes to documents. Another example of an index is the Dewey Decimal Classification, a bibliographic classification system that is used in many libraries to classify knowledge domains into 999 classes, each having a multitude of divisions to cater for the subtleties of any knowledge domain. The index terms are often a collection of selected keywords or concepts whose semantics helps us find the document's main themes. Indexing can be performed either manually by a specialist or automatically with text-classification tools. The accuracy of automatic text classification is improving and in some cases can be comparable to human indexers. The steps involved in the automatic classification process can utilise one or more of the following technologies (Baeza-Yates and Ribeiro-Neto 1999):

- Lexical analysis is used to identify the words in the text from a stream of characters including numerical digits, punctuation marks and hyphens.

- Stopwords that occur too frequently in a collection of documents are eliminated as they do not provide good discriminators for the purposes of retrieval. An advantage is that it results in compression of the index, though it may subsequently reduce the level of recall.

- As nouns tend to carry most of the semantics in a given sentence, they are often used as index terms rather than verbs, articles, adjectives, adverbs or connectives. Nouns that appear near to one another in the text can be clustered into a single indexing component called a 'noun group' (e.g. human resource management). This can make retrieval much more efficient.

- Stemming is the removal of the affixes (prefixes and suffixes) of a word to improve retrieval performance. The premise is that a user may specify a variant of a word in a search that may not successfully retrieve the necessary document. For example, the word *construct* is a stem for the variants *constructing, construction, constructions* and *constructed*.

In lexical analysis and clustering of noun groups, there may be the additional association with terms not found in the document index but which act as alternative descriptors in the retrieval process. This can be done manually or automatically. Once the text classification, if any, has been conducted, the three most common index structures are as follows:

- **Inverted files**. These are currently the best choice for most applications. An inverted index is composed of the *vocabulary* or different words in the text and their occurrences in terms of their precise storage location.

- **Suffix trees**. These form a tree data structure of the text rather than assuming the text is a sequence of words. These indices are particularly helpful for answering complex queries for non-word-based applications such as genetic databases.

- **Signature files**. These are index structures that divide text into blocks for analysis. They help reduce the size of documents to speed retrieval but impose a sequential mode of searching from one text block to another. The inverted file outperforms the signature file in most applications.

After the text database has been indexed, the retrieval process can commence. This comprises the user specifying their knowledge needs in the form of search terms on a user interface, as shown in Figure 7.9. The search terms may have the same 'text-classification' tools applied to form a query. Once a query is entered, this is processed to produce a representation such as terms and structures. These tend to involve co-occurrence, frequency, position of terms and possibly semantic and syntactic processing. Similarly, documents in the database are processed and essentially the representation of the query is matched with the representation of the document. The query can be expressed in a variety of forms:

- Boolean operators (such as OR, AND and BUT) have precise semantics and are used most commonly by commercial systems. This is the most popular approach. The main drawback is that exact matching of Boolean expressions may result in too few or too many documents.

- Vector expressions assign weights to index terms according to their frequency in a document. The premise is that the lower frequency of an index term is likely to have much greater relevance in a search than a highly occurring index term.

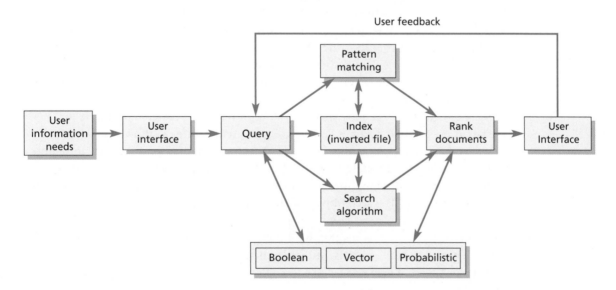

Figure 7.9 **Information retrieval process**

- Probabilistic expressions try to assign probabilities to documents that it assumes users will find relevant. This approach is problematic as it is almost impossible to compute probabilities of relevance without the necessary feedback loops and learning from the user.
- Fuzzy expressions use a thesaurus to expand the query into related terms to allow additional documents to be retrieved.

The retrieved documents are subsequently ranked according to their likelihood of relevance based on a Boolean, vector or probabilistic notion of the query. Following this, some systems enable the user to interact with the search process by specifying whether a certain text is relevant. The information-retrieval system redefines the search algorithm and, hopefully, retrieves similar texts. This is known as relevance feedback.

As databases grow at exponential levels in most organisations, there is a need to develop search technologies that will enable retrieval of information efficiently and speedily. One technique is to use parallel computing where several processors are used simultaneously in the retrieval process, with each processor focusing on a different aspect of the problem. An alternative is to use a distributed computing technique whereby different computers connected to a common network are used to tackle a search problem.

▶ Search engines

The above information-retrieval principles are applied in a wide range of environments and for a range of purposes. Search engines work on a similar process. You search an index and not the full text document. One of the main distinctions between traditional information retrieval techniques and the Web is that queries do not have access geographically to the full text of documents. Simply, it would cost too much to have every page on the Web stored locally and the retrieval times would be extremely slow, even with the most powerful networks. In addition, the Web contains highly volatile and redundant data. It is estimated that 40 per cent of data on the Web changes monthly and 30 per cent of Web pages are almost duplicates (Baeza-Yates and Ribeiro-Neto 1999). An intrinsic characteristic of the Web is the diverse variety of data types and the poor quality of the data as there are no editorial processes for publication. This can result in the problem of search precision where most documents retrieved are irrelevant to a user's needs (Marwick 2001).

Search engines are the most common form of retrieving material on the Web. They are based predominantly on a crawler-indexer architecture, as shown in Figure 7.10. Crawlers are software programs using agent technology that send requests to remote Web servers looking for new or updated pages. The results of the crawling are subsequently indexed centrally in the search engine. Most indices on the Web use a variant of the inverted file. The second part of the search engine deals with user needs in the form of a query. The most common query on the Web is two words and the average query length is 2.3 words (Marwick 2001). The search engine processes the index through a variety of algorithms and ranks the results. It is suggested that this crawler-indexer architecture may not be able to cope with the exponential growth of the Web in the future.

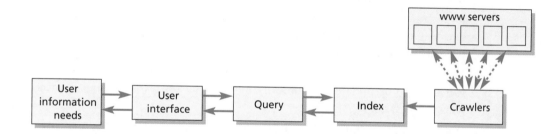

Figure 7.10 **Search engine: crawler-indexer architecture**

An alternative to the crawler-indexer architecture is a distributed approach using several networked Web servers to act either as 'gatherers' (similar to crawlers) or 'brokers' (providing the query and index interface) in a distributed mode of operation. There are also 'metasearchers' on the Web that work by sending a query to numerous search engines and collating and ranking the replies for a user.

◗ Agent technology

To the uninitiated, agent technology can appear like something from science fiction where certain computer systems act like robots (autonomously) to deliver the best solution in terms of their original design. In effect, agents are computer systems that are capable of *autonomous* action in a given environment in order to fulfil their design objective. These systems can act without intervention from humans and take control over their actions and internal state (Jennings and Wooldridge 1998). Agents are similar to crawlers that identify specific material in terms of semantic content, structure and properties. 'Tailored' crawlers can learn and mutate in terms of results and user feedback.

An advancement on agent technology is the development of intelligent agents. These computer systems are capable of *flexible* autonomous action where their *flexibility* derives from their responsiveness to the environment, their opportunistic and proactive behaviour, and their ability to interact with other agents or humans to optimise their problem-solving abilities.

Agents are particularly powerful tools for dealing with complex systems. They manage complex systems by making them *modular*. In essence agents take a large complex problem and divide it into smaller, simpler and more manageable components. This allows each agent to use the appropriate techniques to solve the smaller problem at hand. The other technique used by agents in complex systems is *abstraction*. This allows the complex system to be conceptualised as a series of cooperating autonomous agents. Agent technology has had a wide range of applications including the following:

● Electronic mail filtering agents observe every action a user performs and treat it as a lesson. After some time, the agents begin to predict the user's behaviour based on a history of patterns. As the agent becomes more successful in its predictions, it provides suggestions for the user to help manage their e-mail. This is particularly valuable for users experiencing information overload problems where they desire to focus clearly on their information needs rather than wasting time (Maes 1994).

- In business process management, agents negotiate for services on behalf of departments or divisions with other agents for a mutually acceptable price, time and degree of quality. This allows services in an organisation to be scheduled in a just-in-time manner (Jennings *et al.* 1996).

- In large organisations 'agent wrappers' are built to enable critical organisational functions to be updated periodically by allowing software to interact with other parts of the system.

- Summarisation includes processing text in documents to identify key sentences.

- Business news feeds in organisations filter, cluster, summarise and deliver relevant news to users.

Nevertheless, agent technology does have its limitations which include (Jennings and Wooldridge 1998):

- no overall system controller;

- good optimal solutions locally but a lack of globally optimal decisions;

- quite a learning curve before people can feel comfortable trusting them and delegating some responsibility for decision making over to them;

- problem of relevance in terms of the changing profile of users.

❱ Personalisation

Agent technology has led to a more proactive push technology that can be personalised. The primary goal of all personalisation technology is to provide the needs and wants of every user perfectly. Without being asked, the technology tailors itself to fulfil the user's desire at any time. In information retrieval, personalisation technology may be used to restrict a search to particular categories most often sought by the user or to assign higher weights to documents from those categories. The technology can learn to refine the search specifications by examining keywords used in browsed documents or derived from profiles from communities of interest linked to the user. In addition, personalisation technology can analyse patterns of queries and query results in terms of relevance to the user (Mack *et al.* 2001).

Personalisation technology has been exploited by marketers to gain better knowledge of their customers' behaviours and preferences. The commonly adopted tools are called 'cookies'. These cookies are small data files that are planted on an end user's computer to allow websites to identify them. Cookies infringe a user's privacy and can allow retrieval of their preferences from a database. Typically cookies store an identification number and details of the last visit to a site. However, companies can associate personal information gained in different ways to the user's computer. There are privacy concerns that cookies may contain sensitive personal details as well as credit card information that could be exploited. It is possible to block cookies but this can be a difficult exercise for the average user. In many cases, users are unaware that their privacy has been infringed.

Evaluating knowledge

❱ Case-based reasoning (CBR)

One of the subfields of artificial intelligence is case-based reasoning (CBR). CBR offers a technique for acquiring and storing past problems, their solutions and the reasoning behind them in a retrieval system. Users can type various problem descriptors and check whether cases from the past can throw insights into their current problem. If the case is able to help, the new case is tagged outlining the current problems, evaluations and solutions with the original case for future retrieval. For example, the CBR framework developed to assist effective delivery on a construction project had the following case descriptors (Ribeiro 2001):

- *problems* – client requirements, client capabilities, project specifications, project environment, allocation of risk factors and relationships;
- *project delivery solutions* – procurement methods, contract structure, forms of contract and project management structure;
- *project outcomes* – schedule variance, budget variance, conformance with specifications, safety, servicing during operation, administrative burden, sustainability of facility and project return.

CBR applications have been particularly successful for help desk and call centre applications where users often face repetitive problems. The user can retrieve past solutions and learning and utilise or adapt them for their own problem solving and add their experiences and actions to the changing circumstances encountered.

Critical thinking and reflection

What do you consider to be the main strengths and limitations of case-based reasoning systems in organisations? How often do you use past lessons and experiences to solve current problems? What would you consider to be the time limits, if any, of past experience? Some managers may believe that past experiences hinder progress. How would you answer such managers on the benefits of CBR systems?

❱ Online analytical processing (OLAP)

Spreadsheets can become limited when an individual wants to analyse a large set of data from a variety of perspectives. They can be valuable for analysing data along two dimensions and provide tools to display the results as graphs or pie charts. However, let's explore an organisation that has 30 products in five regions and wishes to analyse all this data in terms of sales, expenses and profits. For such cases, online analytical processing (OLAP) comes into its own. It provides a multidimensional tool to analyse and manipulate the data into various categories. The OLAP Council defines OLAP as enabling the user:

'to gain insight into data through fast, consistent, interactive access to a wide variety of possible views of information that has been transformed from raw data to reflect the real dimensionality of the enterprise as understood by the user.'

OLAP uses the notion of a hypercube or a cube with more than three dimensions as a central aspect of this technique. The most common form of reporting multidimensional analysis is to rotate a cube by 90 degrees to show different analyses using the multidimensional variables. The technique of rotating the cube is sometimes called 'slice and dice'.

▶ Knowledge discovery in databases – data mining

The commonly used term 'data mining' can be misleading as the intention of the process is to produce knowledge from structured data. From a young age, we are used to observing and searching and discovering new things. The data mining or knowledge discovery process is similar, including an iterative progression of data cleaning, data analysis, model interpretation and integration of results. The development of knowledge discovery in databases (KDD) or data mining over the past twenty years can be charted in the following manner (Klösgen and Zytkow 2002):

- First generation (1980s): focused on single tasks such as building classifiers, finding clusters in data and visualising data using one approach.

- Second generation (around 1995): led to data mining 'suites' which supported data preprocessing and cleaning and performed multiple discovery tasks.

- Third generation: tightly integrated domain knowledge into discovery process to provide solutions in areas such as marketing, fraud detection, production control and the web.

Knowledge Discovery in databases is 'the non-trivial process of identifying valid, novel, useful and ultimately understandable patterns in the data' (Fayyad *et al.* 1996). It provides deeper insights than traditionally obtained from reports, queries, executive information systems and OLAP. However, investigations in organisations collecting large data sets such as NASA show that only 5–10 per cent of the data ever gets analysed.

Large organisations such as Walmart, the largest retailer in the US, have a strong urge to tap the hidden knowledge that may lie within their huge customer databases (43 tera-bytes at the time of writing). The resulting analysis may provide the key basis for improving their competitive advantage in their market.

Statisticians believe that every time the amount of data increases by a factor of ten we should rethink how we analyse it (Friedman 1997). This is a primary challenge in knowledge discovery where complexity has increased with the large number of cases and the high dimensionality or numbers of variables.

The tools used in knowledge discovery are simple, concise and easy-to-use algorithms that model non-random (statistically significant) relationships or patterns. These tools may include one or more ideas from the following models (Gargano and Raggad 1999):

- **Expert systems** tend to mimic the reasoning of experts whose knowledge is assumed to be deep in a narrow domain. The expert system consists of a knowledge base of rules and data and a logic inference engine that creates new rules and data based on accumulated knowledge. The weaknesses of expert systems are their narrow domain of application, their reliance on the knowledge of the expert, their poor clarity and internal inconsistencies. Attempts to resolve some of these problems have been made by using fuzzy expert systems where the truth or falsity of a fact can be captured on a scale from 0 to 1 rather than traditionally assuming a fact had to be either true or false.

- **Decision trees** are based on a simple tree model where every branch in the tree represents different classes and subclasses. Decision trees are effective when the user wants an exploratory understanding of the data to get a gut feel.

- **Rule induction** uses statistical techniques to discover rules which relate to the frequency of correlation, the rate of accuracy and the accuracy of prediction. Rules are most commonly developed using IF/THEN statements.

- **Genetic algorithms and genetic programming** evolve complex data structures and are based on biological mechanisms of natural selection. They are useful for finding solutions to hard optimisation problems. The main weakness is the non-explanatory aspect of these models.

- **Neural networks or back-propagation** are tools designed to imitate the physical thought processes of a biological brain in the form of neurons or nerves. The model adapts weights for the interconnections among neurons to allow learning and memory creation to take place. These neural network problems are particularly suited to problems where a great deal of historic data exists for training purposes. Their strength is that they can handle multidimensional and 'noisy' data. However, neural network models do not provide much explanatory power and their training periods may be long.

- **Associative memories** are where pairs of associated data are memorised using a long-term memory network model. These associations can be retrieved at a later date and may provide creative data associations for creative solutions in response to novel stimuli.

- **Clustering techniques** are ideal for classification and category prediction problems. They tend to group together closely related data in a database. They can handle noisy multidimensional data sets but can suffer from long training times.

The knowledge discovery tasks to extract patterns from large datasets can be divided into the following taxonomy (Shaw *et al.* 2001):

- dependency analysis – looking at associations and sequences;
- class identification – examining the mathematical taxonomies and clustering of concepts;
- concept description – attempting to summarise, discriminate and compare different concepts;
- deviation detection – exploring anomalies and changes in the data;
- data visualisation – reporting the data analysis.

The key challenge in knowledge discovery is to provide intelligent systems that improve the selectivity of a search and the ability to understand and respond to a user's needs.

◗ Machine-based learning

Machine learning has been singled out as a vital tool in knowledge discovery in databases applications due to its ability to focus on complex representations, ill-defined problems and search-based methods (Domingos 2002). The flexibility of machine learning methods makes them well suited to problems where little is known about a particular domain. The theory in this area has produced highly successful algorithms such as 'boosting' (Littlestone 1997) and 'support vector machines' (Scholkopf *et al.* 1998). Machine learning has further developed into the realm of biases as biases are what remain in the absence of generalised assumptions in ill-defined problems. It is noteworthy that machine learning techniques are prolific and have found compelling applications in many large databases.

Sharing knowledge

◗ Internet, intranets and extranets

The start of the internet can be traced back to 1969 when the Advanced Research Projects Agency conducted research on networking to link scientists and academics around the world. These networks were configured either as local area networks (LANs) to connect computers via cables over short distances or as wide area networks (WANs) to connect computers over longer distances using transmission lines similar to phone systems. The internet was designed to connect these different networks (LANs and WANs) across the world and performed this task using special computers called routers. In essence, it became similar to a postal system and it needed a common system or set of rules whereby computers could transmit and receive data. This common system or *protocol* was called TCP/IP (transmission control protocol/internet protocol). The IP breaks any data or information into sizeable packets to be sent to a computer across the network and the TCP reassembles the packets of information when they reach their destination. Each computer on the internet has a unique IP address and allows each packet of information to know its sender's and destination address. A major application of the internet is using electronic mail (e-mail). This is the modern postal system of the internet. It also allows text, sound, video and image files to be sent with the e-mails as attachments.

All software used on the internet is based on client/server technology. This means that the software either acts as a server offering services to other computers on the network or acts as a client requesting a service from the server. All the data such as e-mails and Web pages are stored on servers. Client software requests information from a server on a distant computer and server software sends the requested information to the client via the internet.

The basic document on the Web is a page with its own particular location. This location or URL (uniform resource locator) is simply a Web identifier starting with a string such as 'http' or 'ftp'. When you click on a link, your Web browser (client) sends off a packet to that address asking for the URL and, subsequently, the server sends back the requested page to your computer. In the past, most pages have been written in a mark-up language called HTML (hypertext mark-up language). Each HTML page contains a number of tags or instructions on how text, video, graphics and sound are placed on the page and how links to other documents can be created.

A recent development to markup languages has been the introduction of XML (extensible mark-up language) to complement HTML and to improve the usefulness of the Web. Whereas HTML has provided a predominantly formatting function for data on a page, XML provides valuable information on what the data means. For example, in HTML, we may only know whether a numerical integer has a certain textual attribute such as bold, body or title in the text. In contrast, XML will tell us what the integer means, whether it's a speed, a date or a sales figure. This extra information on a Web page allows new computer software to automatically interpret, manipulate and perform operations without direct human intervention. This additional information is often termed 'metadata' or data about data.

Metadata is directly linked to the resource and provides direct access to it. In bibliographic circles, a metadata standard or schema named 'Dublin Core' was developed in 1995 to allow greater bibliographic control over networked resources. The data elements include title, author, subject and keywords, description, publisher, other contributor, date, resource type, format, resource identifier, source, language, relation, coverage and rights management. Other standards are emerging across different industries and the standards are contained within an XML document type definition (DTD), often simply called a 'dictionary'. To allow internationalisation of the Web, XML has been firmly rooted in unicode which provides all kinds of text characters from different languages around the world. XML incorporates the direction in which text moves across a page (e.g. right to left in Arabic), hyphenation conventions and cultural assumptions on ways of addressing one another.

The beauty of XML is that it enables companies to provide access to their own data to customers and suppliers at relatively low developmental costs by addressing the schemas in the DTD for each party concerned. Another advantage of XML is that it provides output in many forms and on different platforms such as PCs and PDAs from one source document. As the information in XML documents is described so precisely, it also means that quality of information retrieval from search engines is likely to increase substantially. One casualty and potential danger may be the built-in bias on XML-driven search engines towards specific information, opinions, products and services based on future industry standards.

Critical thinking and reflection

Reflect on how the internet and your company's intranet have increased your knowledge base. What are the strengths and limitations of this new medium? How can the internet or extranet help your organisation share knowledge across your value chain? Do you foresee any dangers in using the internet as a knowledge-sharing medium? Are there any concerns over sharing ideas and intellectual property rights? Given the widespread nature of the internet, what are the implications for you and your future work using this medium?

The future direction of the Web as described by Tim Berners-Lee, its inventor, is one moving more towards a semantic Web. This would allow the user to access precise information for decision making immediately rather than having to browse through lots of documents to find the information. The goal is to make the Web more intelligent. The language and schemas chosen for the semantic Web are RDF rather than XML as information found in RDF (Resource Description Framework) maps links directly and unambiguously to a decentralised model and there are instruments known as parsers that can decipher this information more easily.

With the expanding bandwidths and processing power, multimedia technology is no longer an aspiration but a reality on the Web. Image technology has advanced to an extent whereby images can be sent as scalable vector graphics in small abstract packets and reassembled on computers or small personal digital assistants in a style and resolution appropriate to the device. The quality of the image is much better than the traditional pixel graphics found in GIF or JPEG files. The independence of device and software has provided major advances in this area. Another standard called the synchronised multimedia integration language (SMIL) has offered a direction for integrating the different components of a multimedia experience into one. Increasingly, the disabled user is being brought to the forefront of Web developments with an emphasis on supplying alternative mediums such as soundtracks with subtitles, images with descriptions and mouse movements with keyboard alternatives.

An intranet is a network that exists exclusively within an organisation and is based on internet technology. It can provide an e-mail system, remote access, group collaboration tools, an application sharing system and a company communications network (Laudon and Laudon 2010). It protects information from unauthorised use through a software mechanism called a 'firewall' that blocks unwanted access from the outside but allows internal users to gain access to the internet. Some traditional applications of intranets are:

- access to databases;
- forum for discussion;
- distribution of electronic documentation;
- administering payroll and benefits packages;
- providing online training;
- frequently asked questions (FAQs) to provide answers to commonly raised questions.

When building intranets, organisations need to be mindful of the dangers of developing large and sophisticated solutions that nobody visits. The technology needs to be user led to meet explicit needs. Another danger is the use of intranets to develop 'electronic fences' in organisations contrary to the espoused principle of knowledge sharing (Swan *et al.* 1999).

❱ Security of intranets

Most organisations have adopted 'firewall' technologies to prevent intruders from gaining access to their sensitive organisational information. The most important goals of firewall systems are (Loew *et al.* 1999):

- access control at different levels;
- control at the application layer;
- user rights administration;
- isolation of certain services;
- proof back-up and analysis of the log;
- alarm facilities;
- concealment of internal network structure;
- confidentiality;
- resistance of firewall against attacks.

Firewalls examine every packet of information between networks (using packet filters) and analyse their characteristics to decide whether to deny any unauthorised messages or access attempts. A high-level security firewall can be constructed using two packet filters. The weakness of one packet filter is supported by the other. Attacks on these servers will not endanger the internal network. However, there can never be any guarantee of total security. In the future, it is likely that encryption technologies will be used to strengthen the security of firewalls.

❱ Text-based conferencing

There are a number of text-based conferencing channels through which individuals can share knowledge and information. Usenet newsgroups are worldwide discussion forums on a multitude of topics where discussions take place on an electronic bulletin board, with individuals posting messages for others to read. Another public forum for sharing knowledge within predefined groups is discussion lists that individuals can subscribe to. These lists are generally moderated, in comparison with newsgroups which are not. An individual subscribes and joins a discussion group and receives e-mail messages sent by others concerning the topic. The individual can reply to the group and their offerings are distributed to all subscribers to the group.

Various chat tools have been developed to allow two or more individuals on the internet to hold live interactive conversations. If the number of contributors increases substantially, chat groups can be divided into different themes and topic areas. Some enhancements are providing voice chat capabilities. Individuals can arrange to meet at predefined times to share their knowledge and ideas, particularly in cases where the phone may not be the appropriate medium. Discussion groups can also be set up on a variety of topics on an organisation's intranet to enable knowledge sharing. Sensitivities relating to the membership of these groups need to be considered so that full, frank and open discussions and dialogues can be promoted. For example, in a work context, people may be guarded in their contributions if they are aware that their boss or senior management may be party to the conference.

▶ Web 2.0 platform

Web 2.0 is now seen as a driver of the knowledge and network economy. There are numerous definitions of Web 2.0. Some emphasise the technological dimension. This includes the small shift to XML script where content is separated from its form. Others argue that it is Ajax – a form of JavaScript on the Web used by programs such as Google Maps. This makes pages look like dynamic applications and allows pages to work with one another in so-called 'mashups'. Another technology associated with Web 2.0 is RSS (Really Simple Syndication), a technology standard, where information can be broadcast over the internet as feeds. The general technologist view is that Web 2.0 is a shift from the rather static web pages of Web 1.0 technologies to a more dynamic social Web applications and services.

The other end of the spectrum is the social dimension of Web 2.0. Here people are proactively shaping the Web through their clickstreams, uploads and downloads each day. Rather than passive users of Web 1.0 technology, nowadays people are much more dynamic and interactive and uploading their own content daily. This is the social web of podcasts, wikis, blogs and mashups. The difference in Web 2.0 technologies is that individuals and businesses can make money by providing customer services for free. Take Google, for example, which provides a free search engine and yet has annual sales of $10 billion and a market valuation of $200 billion. Similarly, YouTube, a free video-sharing website is worth $1.6 billion; or Facebook, a free social networking site, worth $15 billion.

The term Web 2.0 was coined at a conference organised by O'Reilly Media, John Battelle and CMP in 2004. Tim O'Reilly (2006) has summarised the Web 2.0 phenomena as:

> *'Web 2.0 is the business revolution in the computer industry caused by the move to the internet as platform, and an attempt to understand the rules for success on that new platform. Chief among those rules is this: Build applications that harness network effects to get better the more people use them.'*

The range of Web 2.0 tools are shown in Figure 7.11. Network effects are critical to the success of Web 2.0. Take Flickr, a Web 2.0 free photo-sharing site, for example. Users can upload their photographs and add comments and captions (metadata) for immediate public access. This creates a sense of community with positive network effects and collective user value. The more people interact with the photos adding their own captions and comments, the more valuable is the photographic database. The site has resulted in over 100 million photos uploaded by some 2 million users. Users were able to integrate their photos on Flickr with blogs, social networking and syndication via RSS. Users could subscribe to photos as RSS feeds and the website soon became the choice for the active blogging community. The financial success of Flickr comes from three sources of revenue: annual subscription fees for unlimited storage of photos with no advertising, revenue from advertising per click of its free services and transaction fees from its photo development revenue. The main free photo-sharing part of its business can be seen as a loss leader.

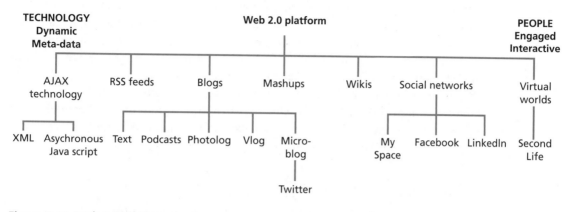

Figure 7.11 Web 2.0 platform tools

Positive network effects can explain the success of Google. There are direct network effects where the value of goods and services increases as more people use it. As new people join the network, its value increases and more people are willing to pay for network services. Indirect network effects result from greater use of a product or service that has an influence on related goods and services, adding value to the original entity. Social network effects such as instant messaging can also affect the decisions of some consumers. In the case of Google, each new query to its search engine dynamically updates the user relevance, providing an instant feedback loop. To increase user traffic, Google has made deals with AskJeeves and AOL. This has resulted in increased advertising revenue based on a pay-per-click model. They have also employed 'AdRanking' to create dynamic pricing for keywords to advertisers. Advertisers were willing to pay premiums for demand-side networks effects related to these keywords as they were targeted to the businesses concerned.

Facebook is a good example of a Web 2.0 online social network. It has attracted more than 47 million customers in less than three years. These customers are highly interactive, engaged and use the site to communicate and work together. There is the potential for people with highly specialised interests to find each other and create groups. In *The Tipping Point* (2000), Malcolm Gladwell suggests that there are three kinds of people that make a difference, 'a tipping point', in word-of-mouth epidemics:

- **Connectors**: the 'social glue' who want to connect you with everyone you should know;

- **Mavens**: the 'information brokers' who want to tell you about the best deals and what to buy;

- **Salesmen**: the 'evangelists' who are good at convincing you and getting you to act.

People play many different roles in social networks and each are important in convincing people whether or not to buy a good or use a service. Social networking is vital for Flickr's success even though it is conventionally thought of as a photo-sharing website. Similarly, Amazon is reliant on the ranking of its reviewers to develop the necessary trust with its customers.

'Six degrees of separation' is the notion that there are predominantly six links between you and anyone else in the world (Milgram 1967). Recent research on Facebook has found that there are, on average, 5.73 degrees of separation between its 4.5 million users. In social network analysis the degrees of separation can be shortened if there are 'hubs' and 'brokers' between you and the target person. These are strong connectors in the network which increase the speed of digital connectivity. Professional networks such as LinkedIn are based on trying to reduce these degrees of separation. They allow you to connect and expand your network to meet the appropriate person for your business (Shuen 2008).

▶ Conversational media: Blogs

A blog, short for 'web log', is a website for adding an individual's thoughts, commentary or a diary of events. These can be text based, pictures or be expressed in video form. An audio blog is called a podcast, an image blog is called a photoblog and a video blog, a vlog. Essentially, blogs are online journals and individuals who write blogs are called bloggers. Blog entries or posts are normally maintained in reverse chronological order. Blogs can contain links to other blogs and stimulate further discussion.

Each blog has a title rather like a newspaper headline to entice the reader. The blogger can supply a tag with the post, rather like metadata, to help index the blog. Bloggers can see who is linking into their blogs through applications such as 'Trackbacks'. These applications also allow readers to see what different bloggers are saying about a posting and to assess its popularity.

The 'blogosphere' is the collective term given to blogs on the internet as the blogs can be searched through search engines such as Technorati. In March 2008 there were 184 million people who had started a blog and 346 million who had read a blog. Each day there are almost a million posts placed on the Web by bloggers.

Blogs can exist internally within an organisation to prevent posts slipping outside corporate boundaries. They can act as an alternative to face-to-face meetings and allow employees to engage with organisational problems and decision-making processes. Individual can follow 'threads', postings on the same topic, easily and see how ideas have progressed. Blogs can be archived and retrieved easily using a search engine.

Organisations can use external blogs to engage with customers and other stakeholders outside organisational boundaries. They are useful for gathering knowledge and information from external parties that would be impossible to gain in any other way. In addition, an external blog can act as the public face for the organisation influencing perceptions within the market place. An external blog allows the voice of the customer to come centrally within the organisation and allows greater trust to be generated. Blogs reach consumers who are intensely engaged with a particular subject area.

Micro-blogging is a form of multimedia blogging where users can publish brief texts, micro-audio and video clips using instant messaging, email or the Web. The main difference between traditional blogs is the micro nature of the file size. They tend to provide information on what someone is doing at a particular time. Twitter is one of the most famous free social networking and micro-blogging sites. Users send out tweets (up to 140 characters text-based posts) to their subscribers (called followers).

For example, celebrities such as Stephen Fry can send out tweets to inform followers of their daily logs and activities as SMS texts.

❱ Syndication and RSS feeds

Syndication is commonly used in the entertainment industry where information in the form of TV programmes, photos and articles are remixed and repackaged for different customers. The same approach is applied to digital content on the Web where information is broadcast as feeds by online publishers using RSS as the technology standard. RSS (Really Simple Syndication) feed is a standardised format to publish frequently updated content on websites. Normally an RSS feed contains a headline, author's name, date and either the fully updated article or a summary. The feed is created using XML language and can contain images. Organisations can place feeds showing latest offers of their products and services or provide consumer information such as traffic news and weather forecasts.

Gmail provides a news aggregator which alerts users to new content from their favourite sites on the internet. RSS has become the viral distribution engine for bloggers. Syndication uses RSS and feedreader applications to convert XML blogs to third-party websites in real time. Most popular Web browsers have RSS readers built into their applications. Users can initiate the RSS button to receive new material from their favourite bloggers as soon as it is posted on the internet. Most blogging software generates these feeds and provides them free to their readers. However, sites have arisen which gather and filter these feeds in terms of user interest. This is not dissimilar to that used in the entertainment industry.

❱ Mashups

In the music world, mashups combine two or more songs to create a new song or dance track. In the technology world, mashups are a way of combining data and applications in diverse ways to make them more valuable to the user than the sum of their parts. Often the mashup arises from different service providers. Developers can now mix, match, reuse Web content, data and services. A mashup allows content from different data sources to be combined with applications from different business processes, thus avoiding the need for a diverse set of applications.

An example of a mashup is getting an insurance quote from a website. Here the mashup may combine Google Maps with aggregate information from a multitude of insurers, all interfaced to the site via XML. Tourist offices have used mashups to combine Google Earth with tourist information. The user enters their postcode and receives a local map showing locations of hotels, restaurants and other information. Starbucks have used a similar mashup to help customers locate their nearest café on a map once they've entered their postcode. Digg, a website where people discover and share content from the Web is powered by a mashup. Data from different internet sources are brought together with site reviews and rankings from the Digg online community.

Mashups are not without their fair share of risks. Information used from external sources may be inaccurate and outside your control if the site closes down or alters significantly in the future. Also, external mashups are prone to greater levels of threat from malware.

◗ Wikis

Wikis are Web pages that can be viewed and modified by anyone with access to a Web browser and the internet or intranet. The term was coined by Ward Cunningham from the Hawaiian word for quick. He didn't want this application to be called the 'quick web'. Wikis allow anyone to create or change the content of Web pages. Wikis are collaborative tools and can be used in a number of ways. They can be repositories of knowledge such as 'Wikipedia' (an online encyclopaedia), composition systems, media for discussions or mailing systems. Centrally they allow users to create and edit any page on a website. Collections of pages are usually well interconnected using hyperlinks. Wikis engender a certain democracy and level playing field. The simplicity of wikis firmly places power and freedom in the hands of users rather than some external 'expert' source. Anyone with a non-technical or technical background can contribute to wikis. This is known as 'open editing' and the level of technical expertise required to contribute to wikis is minimal. There is no HTML to learn or specialist software to master. Users can include text, images and video material in their wikis. Wikis are built from a combination of CGI scripts and a collection of plain text files.

Wikis started around the mid-1990s and were initially used in the domain of technical users. Nowadays, they are more widespread with a diverse range of users. They have been successfully employed as collaborative tools in organisations: as replacements to static Web pages on corporate intranets. Any new user can look at a wiki and read what that particular community has written. They can edit any page and update it instantaneously. They are about community building where multiple users can create or edit a collection of articles online. Openness is a key characteristic of wikis, where users can contribute their thoughts and experiences 'on the fly' and are happy for others to amend and develop their contributions. Their flexibility allows involvement and engagement by community members and greater adoption of the material generated. In essence, wikis are databases comprising continual works in progress on virtual 'white boards'.

In organisations, wikis can prevent e-mail overload by allowing relevant material for any project to be placed on a wiki. Agenda and minutes of meetings can be placed on wikis. Additional information such as hotel and restaurant information in different cities can be added. Corporate wikis are more dynamic than traditional content management systems, as they allow users to create and edit the content. Users can also create 'structured wikis' that are specific to their needs. These combine the power of plain wikis with corporate databases. From basic to-do lists, they can include inventory systems to employee handbooks. Wikis encourage collaborative writing where different ideas can be expressed, discussed and debated on each page. Participation of wikis can be limited to certain groups, internal communities or departments.

Wikis do carry some risks. They can be open to manipulation and vandalism. Users can use inappropriate language or place incorrect or inappropriate material on the wiki. In the extreme, a user could erase all the content from pages. As such, maintenance of wikis can be labour intensive and time-consuming. A number of interventions can help counteract these risks. An administrator can block or ban any user or IP address that is continually destructive. Users can alert community members to vandalism. Administrators can delete inappropriate pages or restore pages to their pre-vandalism state. Edit wars can occur on controversial topics where two sides of a community become polarised in almost opposite views. Here it is about gaining consensus about the wording on the Web page to the satisfaction of both parties. This may lead to an emphasis on factual agreement by both camps or on interpretations by two or more schools of thought. A small shortcoming of wikis is their collective bias. Over time, wikis can become embedded in certain assumptions, values and perspectives shared by the community and become resistant to new ideas and approaches.

The current English language version of Wikipedia has over 2,892,068 entries from 151,937 contributors (as of May 2009). This compares with 55,000 entries in Columbia Encyclopedia, the best one-volume encyclopedia in the world. Anyone can initiate an entry on Wikipedia, though there is a voluntary army of editors who oversee the whole process. The editors can place an issue up for vote by other users if there is ever any doubt over an entry. There is considerable policing in Wikipedia by a 'Recent Changes Patrol' who pick up any obscenities or absurdities. Wikipedia tries to balance surveillance and the anonymity of new entries by focusing on the needs of user communities. One of the consequences of this process is that many entries can be preoccupied with the immediate past rather than with providing a more rounded entry such as may be found in an encyclopedia (Lih 2009).

▶ Online social networks

Online social networks are internet communities where individuals can interact with others in the community through their profiles, which represent their public persona and networks of connections. Social network sites (SNS) have proliferated over the past ten years as a means of maintaining friends and colleagues. The most popular social networking sites include MySpace, Friendster, Facebook and LinkedIn. Each site has tailored its content and user experience to a particular audience. MySpace was oriented towards teenagers, Friendster towards meeting new friends or dates, Facebook towards college students and LinkedIn towards professionals. However, the boundaries of each social networking site have expanded as they have developed and gained broader appeal. Traditionally each social site has been composed of community members who share a common interest. Social networks have moved from a niche to a mass adoption phenomena.

Current research on social networking sites has focused on the benefits to social capital, self-presentation, privacy issues and network analysis. Most SNS tend to support pre-existing social relationships rather than the development of new ones through browsing new profiles (Ellison *et al* 2007). SNS are closed systems that tend to support three principal activities:

- construction of a public or semi-public profile;
- creation of a list of other users with whom people have a connection;
- viewing and interacting with different connections in the network.

SNS are unique in that they allow users to meet complete strangers and to make their social networks public. Individuals start by articulating their public persona as a profile in a number of Web pages. This can be done through completing a form with questions such as age, location and interests. A profile is generated from the responses and users are encouraged to upload a photograph. Users can modify their profiles and add multimedia content. Some sites allow users to choose whether their profiles are accessible publicly or not, whereas other sites such as LinkedIn control what viewers can see whether they are members or not.

The second stage for users is the development of a public display of people with whom they have a connection within the network. The nature of the connection can be differentiated by terms such as 'Contacts', 'Friends' and 'Fans'. These delineations vary on each SNS. Though terms such as 'Friends' can be misleading when compared to their everyday usage.

Users can interact with one another by leaving messages as comments on each other's profiles. These comments are made public and some SNS do provide private messaging as well. Other facilities on SNS include photo-sharing and video-sharing capabilities, blogging and instant messaging technologies (Boyd and Ellison 2007).

The major risk of SNS concerns privacy. The threats to privacy come from third parties securing personal information such as location and date of birth. Researchers have shown that personal details of Facebook users and their friends can be stolen by submitting malicious applications. There are a number of ways to protect one's privacy and militate against embarrassing material getting into the public domain. These include:

- using private Friends lists in the SNS;
- removing your profile from SNS and Google search results;
- manually configuring your photo and video privacy pages to specific Friends;
- configuring your News feed page to prevent your stories appearing on friends news feeds;
- ensuring your contact information remains private;
- keeping your friendships private.

▶ 3-D virtual worlds

Millions of people interact with one another through virtual worlds each day. These are computer-simulated worlds online where users interact in real time through 'avatars'. Avatars are computer-generated, three-dimensional depictions of the user; a form of alter ego. These user representations are similar in form to 3-D electronic cartoons. Users can experiment with identity, express themselves and explore their alter egos in three dimensions – a factor that is lacking in social network sites such as MySpace and Facebook. Second Life started in 2003 and is the most popular 3-D virtual world used by businesses and the education sector, with over 15 million user accounts. Users, called 'Residents', can traverse the virtual world known as the 'grid'. This is a 3-D world of land, buildings and shopping districts. There are reconstructed townscapes made to look like Elizabethan England. Avatars can walk, fly or use vehicles to traverse the grid.

Each Resident has a single avatar which can be animal, mineral or vegetable and can resemble themselves in real life. They can change their avatars over time. They choose how their avatar looks and the mode of dress they adopt. When avatars meet other avatars they can communicate via text in a chat channel or through voice communication in two ways:

- Initiate a public 'chat' with two or more avatars. As in real life, this chat can be heard by others with a local area.
- Initiate a private conversation through global instant messaging known as IM. These private communications can be between two avatars or members of a group.

There is an internal currency in Second Life known as Linden dollars (L$) which can be exchanged for US$ dollars. The currency can be used to purchase a variety of goods and services including land and property. In education, Second Life is used as a medium to reach students, particularly distance-learning ones. A class can begin with the tutor and students sitting in some idyllic location. Discussions can continue about different aspects of the teaching programme. Field trips can be arranged to a virtual nuclear power plant such as the one established by University of Colorado, or construction testing facilities. The virtual space can also be used for online conferences. Some institutions such as Strathclyde and Coventry University have bought islands on Second Life and invested in related staff and building costs. In terms of learning, Second Life allows students to role-play, explore and experiment in virtually risk-free environments. Simulations can be conducted without any fear of health and safety hazards. Students have the added benefit of interacting with others from around the world. Second Life can provide the opportunities for business executives to provide business insights for students without stepping outside their offices. One shortcoming of Second Life is that avatars can create a barrier to teachers getting to know their students better and their unique learning needs. Eye contact is currently limited.

In business Second Life can be used as a way of conducting meetings, workshops or hospitality parties with different people around the world. Mazda launched a new car model inside Second Life which wasn't available in the real world. More than 50 multinational companies such as Ericsson, IBM and Dell have a presence on Second Life. Charities have used the 3-D virtual environment to raise money for themselves. Bain & Co. and IBM have used Second Life for recruitment of MBA students and for interacting with senior Bain staff. Prospective students attend virtual recruitment centres, meet company employees, listen to video and slide presentations and download any necessary information.

Groupware tools

The raison d'être behind groupware is to encourage collaboration between people to enhance knowledge sharing. In commercial terms the assumption is that greater collaboration will lead to increased productivity, lower costs and higher quality through better decision making. Groupware, as a concept, tends to be applied to information communication technologies (ICTs) that support collaboration, communication and coordination of activities over space and time as well as shared information spaces

(Robertson *et al.* 2001). Two common technologies used in groupware are e-mail and Lotus Notes discussion databases. Lotus Notes is generally considered as the first groupware product to provide discussion databases, e-mail with attachments, shared databases, workflow automation and applications development. Other systems have included (Williams 1996):

- group decision support systems (GDSS) with brainstorming, ideas generation and voting systems;
- collaborative writing and whiteboards;
- computer-based conferencing;
- schedule meetings and diary organisers;
- e-mail systems used proactively.

▶ Videoconferencing

Desktop videoconferencing (DTVC) provides a means for two or more people to see and hear each other from their desktop computer, enabling them to collaborate and share knowledge without leaving their desk. A small camera and microphone are attached to the top of a PC and these relay the video information to a distant user. Using this technology, organisations can improve their workflows and save on travel time and costs. Most products provide a simple shared workspace or 'whiteboard' so that users can explain their ideas through drawings. More sophisticated applications allow users to work together on the same documents or spreadsheets. Poor picture quality issues of videoconferencing are normally associated with a lack of internet bandwidth.

▶ Skills directories: expertise yellow pages

To enable knowledge sharing in organisations, there is often a need to find the individual or groups with the necessary skills and expertise that may be required in another part of the organisation. Many firms now produce 'expert yellow pages' and directories of communities. Expert yellow pages comprise a listing of all the employees in an organisation, with a summary of their knowledge, skills and expertise. This is accessible to all employees who can access the 'expert' through keywords on an intranet-based search engine. A similar searchable listing may be developed for communities, groups and discussion lists within organisations.

▶ E-learning

E-learning is the generic term used to describe online learning, computer-based training and Web-based training. It is the application of internet technologies to support the delivery and management of learning, skills and knowledge. E-learning does not have to occur exclusively on the internet. More reputable offerings tend to provide an integration of various learning technologies such as:

- mentoring;
- chat forums;
- expert-led discussions;
- Web seminars;
- online meetings;
- virtual classroom sessions.

E-learning initiatives need to be considered as part of an organisation's portfolio of HRD interventions to meet training and development needs rather than being adopted as a panacea for cutting costs.

Storing and presenting knowledge

▶ Data warehouses

A data warehouse is a large physical database that holds a vast amount of information from a wide variety of sources. The data warehouse needs to serve as a neutral data storage area that can be used for a variety of analytical tools. The characteristics of a data warehouse are (Inmon 1992):

- subject orientation – data may be organised around business subjects;
- uniformity – common data elements related to multiple applications are treated consistently;
- time variant – data is updated as conditions change;
- non-volatile – data is loaded into the warehouse and retrieved easily from it.

Data warehouses can be structured to contain data at various levels (as shown in Figure 7.12) including current detail data, older detail data, lightly summarised data (often for middle management), highly summarised data (for top management) and meta-data. The 'older level of detail' is often placed at the bottom of the data warehouse structure as it may be two or three years old and infrequently accessed (Ma *et al*. 2000). Meta-data is used to describe the meaning and structure of the data as well as how it was created, accessed and used (Devlin 1997). The meta-data can help the user locate the contents of the warehouse and map their elements. In addition, it may provide a guide to the algorithms used to summarise the data in different ways.

Relational database management systems (RDBMS) are widely used today as data warehouses to store, manipulate and query large data sets in a variety of applications. They are used in virtually every major organisation to manage tasks such as payroll, sales and marketing.

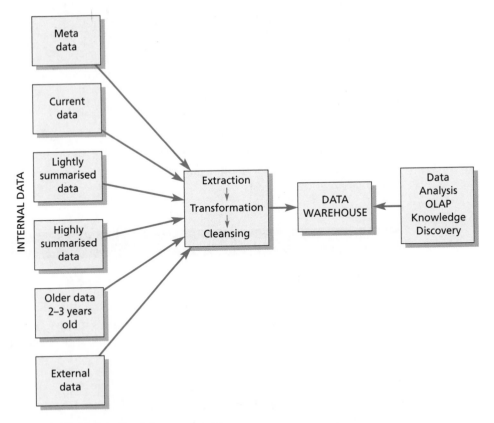

Figure 7.12 **Model of a data warehouse**

Critical thinking and reflection

Relational databases are very popular in organisations nowadays. What are your experiences of using these databases? How useful do you find them, particularly databases of customer records? Are there inherent limitations in using them for particularly large databases? How would you rate your statistical skills and ability to understand complex statistical analyses? Do you see any problems arising from managers misinterpreting complex analyses from OLAP or data mining tools? How could you overcome this potential problem?

▶ Visualisation

Visualisation is an emerging technology which allows users to understand the complexity of information through the use of rich computer graphics. This can be an invaluable tool, particularly for visualising analysis from data mining and information-retrieval techniques, as shown in Figure 7.13. For example, data in an information retrieval system can be represented and modelled in the following manner (Song 2000):

- 2-dimensional (2D) or 3-dimensional (3D) scatterplots;
- 2D or 3D vector field topology plots with geometric data points;

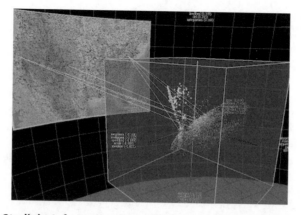

Figure 7.13 **The Starlight Information Visualisation System developed at the Pacific Northwest National Laboratory** (reproduced courtesy of Pacific Northwest National Laboratory)

- tree or hierarchical visualisation techniques to simplify complex data by branching data into levels;
- network techniques to represent information structures as spatial networks;
- maps related to a domain's geography;
- bibliometric mapping techniques to represent authors and their writings on a landscape and clustering authors based on various commonalities.

More advanced visualisation techniques have adopted colour as well as a combination of rendering and photo-realism techniques (Cawkell 2001). Rendering is a technique to make computer-generated images appear as realistic as photographs. The emphasis is on modelling the way light creates shadows on surfaces, textures and objects and removing the transparency of obscuring objects. In the film industry photo-realism techniques have been employed to create animation and special effects so that computer-generated graphics can blend seamlessly into the action in movies. These techniques have been used in films such as *Star Wars*, *Jurassic Park* and *Titanic*. It is notable that one of the greatest challenges in photo-realism is the ability to render human skin on animated objects. Many of these techniques are likely to enter knowledge management domains as the complexity of information and related analyses increases in the long term.

Royal Dutch Shell (Netherlands/UK)

Peter Kemper arrived for a long awaited meeting with Jeroen van der Veer, CEO at Royal Dutch Shell. There were three things on Jeroen van der Veer's mind. The first was Second Life and how virtual worlds could be effectively utilised at Shell. The second was the recent implementation of wikis at Shell and how effective they had been. Lastly, he was interested in any further initiatives that could mobilise knowledge more effectively across Shell, such as their earlier investment in SiteScape and development of virtual communities. They had 20 minutes to discuss these matters before Jeroen van der Veer was expected at another meeting.

Peter Kemper, Knowledge Management Portfolio Manager (IT Department), was a keen believer in user-generated content and the simplicity of Web 2.0 solutions. He started by suggesting that wikis had reduced the problem of information overload with much fewer documents. He estimated that there were probably between 300 and 500m documents within Shell archives. This was too great for even the most determined search engines in the world. 'To overcome this problem', he added

> 'We followed the Google/Wikipedia approach as much as possible: no traditional big bang implementation but entirely bottom up supported by "smart marketing". We concentrated on keeping it as simple as possible (e.g. transparent login/NO access control). On the content management side we linked to our existing discipline structures (e.g. geology, production chemistry, wells technology etc.).'

The wikis were also connected to Global Networks or discussion threads within Shell. These had been established in 1997 to assist with community collaboration and community self-regulation. He continued that they had added 'information similarity checking' to the wiki environment. This allowed the system to provide a list of existing documents that were 'similar' in content to the wiki. The emphasis was on reducing the number of documents in Shell's knowledge base and eliminating duplicate documents.[1]

Prior to the wikis, Shell's main media for maintaining and sharing knowledge had been e-mails and Powerpoint presentations. He gave the example of the geological structures of the Atlantic Margins held as a series of images and added: 'It would be a nightmare to maintain this kind of information in Powerpoint! No offence meant: Powerpoint is good for presentations but not for creating and maintaining a knowledge base.' Peter maintained that the wikis achieved six times more productivity than their former Powerpoint presentations and allowed content to be linked directly together. He showed that wikis had been used successfully in translating 400-page contracts into crystal-clear prose that could be acted upon by ordinary employees. There was a groundswell in dialogue and activity across Shell where staff were communicating with creators of wikis especially when they wanted to go beyond the knowledge found directly in the wiki. They did this directly via e-mail or using the discussion pages with each wiki. Authors were also alerted via a 'watch list' function if anyone amended their entry.

Peter Kemper offered a picture of progress with wikis at Shell. He confirmed that there were roughly 40,000 registered users compared to the overall employee population of 150,000. He noted that the numbers of active users remained relatively constant even though user numbers had increased. He observed that there were three types of users: content owners who created the content, content editors who improved syntax and the overall presentation of wikis and information consumers. He reminded Jeroen van der Veer that 60 per cent of all staff would go into retirement over the next eight years and that wikis provided a useful medium for capturing and sharing this vital organisational knowledge.[2] All Shell Open University courses had their content successfully converted into a wiki. This allowed course members as well as the wider Shell community to access this knowledge. However, Peter insisted that the most valuable knowledge was that found in the heads of co-workers. Wikis had provided the fastest and most effective medium for employees to tap into their co-worker knowledge.[3] This knowledge included aspects of production engineering, technical handbooks and the non-technical aspects of their roles. He tried to illustrate the level of activity with wikis each day. There were around 100 registered new users each day, around 300 edits of wikis each day and over 5,000 views of wikis each day. This represented substantial activity in both knowledge creation and knowledge sharing. There were also over 1,300 users who had created new content in wikis since its inception at Shell. Peter Kemper added: 'We have definitely met the needs of many users in the company, who were looking for efficient and flexible ways of sharing their knowledge, and who wanted to co-write and co-publish information'.[3]

Peter Kemper viewed the emergence of wikis as an extension of Shell's communities of practice (CoPs). In both, insights were shared and they brought people together with common interests. This was important as many Shell employees shared their expertise by moving between different projects around the world. As many as 80 per cent of Shell's technical professionals were away from home at any given time. Hence communities of practice originally developed more through electronic means rather than regular face-to-face contact. At first, there were 107 different CoPs around the world but the difficulty was that there was little communication within them. In 1999 Shell rationalised the 107 CoPs into three global networks: Surface, Wells and Subsurface. In addition, eight CoPs were formed that were cross-cutting across functional areas. These included benchmarking, competitor intelligence, procurement, knowledge management and IT. There were around 20 subject experts in each CoP and one full-time global coordinator (facilitator). Sitescape Forum was the social software adopted underpinning Shell's CoPs thanks to its ease of use and administra-

tion. Most messages and requests for information were responded within a few hours.

Peter Kemper tried to demonstrate the costs and benefits of the Sitescape system. In any one CoP, there were around 80 new postings each day and around 350 logins and files viewed by users. Each posting had at least 60 views and most new entries were responded within 24 hours. There were likely to be multiple responses to each new entry as each community had at least 1,000 members. Given the global nature of Shell's operations, users were encouraged to place entries in their own language and to use the language tool to translate information from one language to another. However, users were warned about the pitfalls of vital knowledge being lost in translation and encouraged to check source languages with colleagues. Peter Kemper estimated the overall cost of Sitescape Forum was around €600 per person per year. Much of this cost was human costs rather than IT costs with some 20 staff coordinating the system. He evaluated the cost savings from effective advice around the organisation at around €200m each year.[4]

On the question of Second Life, Peter Kemper was clear that a paradigm shift had occurred at Shell with a desire among users to explore new ways of creating and sharing knowledge. In terms of user needs, he continued:

'However, these needs are changing quickly. For example, these days, more and more users are familiar with Web 2.0 sites such as Facebook or SecondLife, and so we are also exploring the use of virtual worlds to add a new dimension to learning at Shell – for example, with interactive 3D simulations and training modules. Shell Wiki has shown us that our users are ready to share their knowledge in new ways.'

Jeroen van der Veer's PA interrupted their discussions and informed them that the next meeting had been cancelled. Jeroen van der Veer suggested that they continue their discussions of virtual worlds and Second Life over lunch.

References

1 Kemper, P. 2008 'Interview with Peter Kemper', [cited 22 June 2009]; available from http://i-know.tugraz.at/blog/?p=59.

2 Hervig, J. (2008) 'Wikis for knowledge engineering, and in global businesses', [cited 22 June 2009]; available from http//blog.semantic-web.at/tag/peter-kemper+mediawiki/.

3 Hendrix, D. and G. Johannsen (2008) 'A knowledge sharing and collaboration platform', *Inside Knowledge*, 11(8).

4 Boyd, A. *Shell's communities of practice –12 years of experiences*, 2004. London: EBK – Knowledge Sharing Across Boundaries.

Questions

1 What benefits have wikis brought to Shell?

2 How would you promote greater user engagement with wikis in Shell?

3 What are the benefits of virtual worlds such as Second Life for Shell?

Summary

This chapter has elaborated five main technologies in the development of new knowledge in organisations:

1 Tools for organising knowledge emphasised the importance of ontology and taxonomy generation tools to categorise knowledge at an individual, organisational or knowledge-domain level.

2 Tools for capturing knowledge examined cognitive mapping tools to help make tacit knowledge more explicit, information retrieval tools and the technology behind Web-based search engines. Automation of knowledge capturing tasks was explored in relation to personalisation tools and agent technology.

3 Tools for evaluating knowledge considered the potential of case-based reasoning, OLAP, data mining and machine-based learning tools.

4 Tools for sharing knowledge focused on the power of the internet and Web 2.0 tools and how sharing could be facilitated through involvement and engagement of users in active communities.

5 Tools for storing and presenting knowledge highlighted data warehouses and the latest visualisation techniques.

Questions for further thought

1 Assuming high developmental costs, what can organisations do if they find their intranets and data warehouses are rarely visited by their employees?

2 How could second-generation semantic webs co-exist with first-generation, HTML-based webs? Are there potential opportunities and challenges for knowledge sharing?

3 In group processes, how do you manage conflicting 'collective maps' of tacit routines?

4 A 2002 thesis proposed by Stephen Wolfram, chief executive of Mathematica, was that all knowledge could be described as an algorithm. How far do you agree with such a proposition and is the end goal of KM tools to discover these underlying algorithms?

5 What are the barriers facing human–computer interaction and the ability of humans to place greater trust in personalisation and agent technologies to meet their needs?

6 If knowledge-discovery techniques can analyse only 5–10 per cent of data in large databases, what are the dangers of making decisions and building strategies on partial information?

7 What parameters are likely to encourage the adoption of certain tools and technologies over others in organisations?

8 Apart from saving travel costs, what are the likely advantages of using video-conferencing tools in an organisation?

9 What is the best way of managing two large data warehouses in a merger or acquisition situation?

10 When are traditional tools of knowledge creation and sharing such as a blank piece of paper or telephone more useful than more sophisticated tools outlined in this chapter?

Further reading

1 Laudon and Laudon (2010) is an easily accessible text on some of the tools outlined in this chapter. It also provides a good introduction to management information systems.

2 Amy Shuen (2008) provides a good oversight on Web 2.0 technologies from a strategic perspective.

References

Ambrosini, V. and Bowman, C. (2002) 'Mapping successful organizational routines', *Mapping Strategic Knowledge*, A. S. Huff and M. Jenkins, eds, Sage, London.

Baeza-Yates, R. and Ribeiro-Neto, B. (1999) *Modern Information Retrieval*, Addison-Wesley Longman Limited, Harlow, Essex.

Barney, J. B. (1991) 'Firm resources and sustained competitive advantage', *Journal of Management*, 17(1), 99–120.

Boyd, A. (2004) *Shell's Communities of Practice –12 Years of Experiences*: EBK – Knowledge Sharing Across Boundaries, London.

Boyd, D.M. and Ellison, N. B. (2007) 'Social network sites: Definition, history and scholarship', *Journal of Computer Mediated Communication*, 13, 210–30

Cawkell, T. (2001) 'Progress in visualisation', *Journal of Information Science*, 27(6), 427–438.

Devlin, B. (1997) *Data Warehouse: From Architecture to Implementation*, Addison-Wesley, Reading, MA.

Ding, Y. and Foo, S. (2002) 'Ontology research and development. Part 1 – a review of ontology generation', *Journal of Information Science*, 28(2), 123–36.

Domingos, P. (2002) 'Machine learning', *Handbook of Data Mining and Knowledge Discovery*, W. Klösgen and J. M. Zytkow, eds, Oxford University Press, Oxford.

Eden, C. and Ackermann, F. (1998) *Making Strategy: The Journey of Strategic Management*, Sage, London.

Eden, C. and Ackermann, F. (2002) 'A mapping framework for strategy making', *Mapping Strategic Knowledge*, A. S. Huff and M. Jenkins, eds, Sage, London.

Ellison, N. B., Steinfield, C. and Lampe, C. (2007) 'The benefits of Facebook "Friends": Social capital and college students' use of online social network sites', *Journal of CMC*, 12, 1143–68.

Fayyad, U., Piatetsky-Shapiro, G., Smyth, P. and Uthurusamy, R. (1996) *Advances in Knowledge Discovery and Data Mining*, MIT Press, Cambridge, MA.

Friedman, J. H. (1997) 'Data mining and statistics: What's the connection?', Keynote Speech of the Proceeding of the 29th Symposium on the Interface Between Computer Science and Statistics, Houston TX.

Gargano, M. L. and Raggad, B. G. (1999) 'Data mining – a powerful information creating tool', *OCLC Systems & Services*, 15(2), 81–90.

Gharajedaghi, J. and Ackoff, R. L. (1994) 'Mechanisms, organisms and social systems', *New Thinking in Organizational Behaviour*, H. Tsoukas, ed., Butterworth & Heinemann, Oxford, 25–39.

Gladwell, M. (2000) *The Tipping Point: How little things can make a big difference*, Back Bay Books, New York.

Grant, R. M. (1991) 'The resource-based theory of competitive advantage: Implications for strategy formulation', *California Management Review*, 33(3), 114–35.

Grant, R. M. (1996) 'Toward a knowledge-based theory of the firm', *Strategic Management Journal*, 17, 109–22.

Gruber, T. R. (1993) 'A translation approach to portable ontology specifications', *Knowledge Acquisitions*, 5, 199–220.

Hendrix, D. and Johannsen, G. (2008) 'A knowledge sharing and collaboration platform', *Inside Knowledge*, 11.

Huff, A. S. and Jenkins, M. (2002) '*Mapping Strategic Knowledge*', Sage, London.

Inmon, W. H. (1992) 'Data warehouse – a perspective of data over time', *Database Management*, February, 370–90.

Jennings, N. R., Faratin, P., Johnson, M. J., Norman, T. J., O'Brien, P. and Wiegand, M. E. (1996) 'Agent-based business process management', *International Journal of Cooperative Information Systems*, 5(2), 105–30.

Jennings, N. R. and Wooldridge, M. J. (1998) *Agent Technology: Foundations, Applications and Markets*, Springer-Verlag, Berlin.

Kelly, G. A. (1955) *The Psychology of Personal Constructs*, Norton, New York.

Klösgen, W. and Zytkow, J. M. (2002) *Handbook of Data Mining and Knowledge Discovery*, Oxford University Press, Oxford.

Lih, A. (2009) *The Wikipedia Revolution*, Aurum Press Ltd, London.

Laudon, K. C. and Laudon, J. P. (2010) *Management Information Systems: Organization and Technology in the Networked Enterprise*, 11th edition, Prentice-Hall, Upper Saddle River, NJ.

Littlestone, N. (1997) 'Learning quickly when irrelevant attributes abound: A new linear threshold algorithm', *Machine Learning*, 2, 285–318.

Loew, R., Stengel, I., Bleimann, U. and McDonald, A. (1999) 'Security aspects of an enterprise-wide network architecture', *Internet Research: Electronic Networking Applications and Policy*, 9(1), 8–15.

Ma, C., Chou, D. C. and Yen, D. C. (2000) 'Data warehousing, technology assessment and management', *Industrial Management & Data Systems*, 100(3), 125–34.

Mack, R., Ravin, Y. and Byrd, R. J. (2001) 'Knowledge portals and the emerging digital knowledge workplace', *IBM Systems Journal*, 40(4), 925–55.

Maes, P. (1994) 'Agents that reduce work and information overload', *Communications of the ACM*, 37(7), 31–40.

Marwick, A. D. (2001) 'Knowledge management technology', *IBM Systems Journal*, 40(4), 814–30.

Mertins, K., Heisig, P. and Vorbeck, J. (2000) *Knowledge Management: Best Practices in Europe*, Springer-Verlag, New York.

Milgram, S. (1967) 'The small world problem', *Psychology Today*, 2, 60–67.

Nelson, R. and Winter, S. (1982) *An Evolutionary Theory of Economic Change*, Harvard University Press, Cambridge, MA.

O'Dell, C., Hasanali, F., Hunbert, C., Lopez, K. and Raybourn, C. (2000) *Stages of Implementation: A Guide for Your Journey to Knowledge Management*, American Productivity and Quality Center, Houston, Tex.

Ribeiro, F. L. (2001) 'Project delivery system selection: A case-based reasoning framework', *Logistics Information Management*, 14(5/6), 367–375.

Robertson, M., Sørensen, C. and Swan, J. (2001) 'Survival of the leanest: Intensive knowledge work and groupware adaption', *Information Technology & People*, 14(4), 334–52.

Ruggles, R. (1998) 'The state of the notion: Knowledge management in practice', *California Management Review*, 40(3), 80–9.

Scholkopf, B., Burges, C. and Smola, A. (1998) *Advances in Kernel Methods: Support Vector Machines*, MIT Press, Cambridge, MA.

Shaw, M. J., Subramaniam, C., Tan, G. W. and Welge, M. E. (2001) 'Knowledge management and data mining for marketing', *Decision Support Systems*, 31, 127–37.

Shuen, A. (2008) *Web 2.0: A Strategy Guide*, O'Reilly Media, Inc., Sebastopol, CA.

Smith, R. G. and Farquhar, A. (2000) 'The road ahead for knowledge management: An AI perspective', *American Association for Artificial Intelligence*, Winter, 17–40.

Sofia Pinto, H., Gomez-Perez, A. and Martins, J. P. (1999) 'Some issues on ontology integration', Proceedings of IJCAI-99 Workshop on Ontologies and Problem-Solving Methods: Lessons Learned and Future Trends, in conjunction with the Sixteenth International Joint Conference on Articial Intelligence, Stockholm, Sweden.

Song, M. (2000) 'Visualization in information retrieval: A three-level analysis', *Journal of Information Science*, 26(1), 3–19.

Spender, J. C. (1996) 'Making knowledge the basis of a dynamic theory of the firm', *Strategic Management Journal*, 17, 45–62.

Swan, J., Newell, S., Scarbrough, H. and Hislop, D. (1999) 'Knowledge management and innovation: Networks and networking', *Journal of Knowledge Management*, 3(4), 262–75.

Uschold, M. and Gruninger, M. (1996) 'Ontologies: Principles, methods and applications', *Knowledge Engineering Review*, 11(2), 93–155.

Weick, K. E. and Bougon, M. G. (1986) 'Organisations as cognitive maps', *The Thinking Organization*, H. P. J. Sims, ed., Jossey-Bass, San Francisco, 125–35.

Williams, A. (1996) 'Groupware: The next ware of office automation', *Industrial Management & Data Systems*, 96(6), 11–13.

Wolfram, S. (2002) *A New Kind of Science*, Wolfram Media Inc., Champaign, IL.

Chapter 8

Knowledge management systems

Learning outcomes

After completing this chapter the reader should be able to:

- explain the component technologies involved in different KM systems;
- describe the different quality management processes driving KM systems;
- outline a plan for the selection and effective implementation of KM systems for any given business problem;
- construct a breakdown of overall costs for a KM system.

Management issues

The use and application of knowledge management systems implies these questions for managers:

- How do you select an appropriate KM system to meet current and future business needs given the multitude of offerings in the marketplace?
- What are the key factors that lead to effective implementation and adoption of KM systems?
- Can higher-quality information from new KM systems lead to poorer-quality decisions?
- Do KM systems achieve the necessary return on investment and expectations for the end customer?

Links to other chapters

Chapter 4   explores the role of KM systems in knowledge strategies.

Chapter 7   describes the component tools and technologies found in KM systems.

Chapter 10   concerns change management and the effective implementation of KM systems in organisations.

Decision-making software in the fast lane   **FT**

In the heat of Formula One motor racing, success and failure are separated by hundredths of a second and a poor decision on the part of either driver or pit crew is punished immediately and irrevocably.

A good decision, on the other hand, can lead to victory. In the 2005 F1 Grand Prix at Monte Carlo, Kimi Raikkonen was leading the race when an accident brought the safety car into play. Conventional wisdom at Monte Carlo, where the narrow streets make overtaking almost impossible, dictates that cars should head for the pits for refuelling and new tyres whenever the safety car is deployed.

But the McLaren software said otherwise and Raikkonen continued to circulate, posting some super fast laps and eventually winning the race by a comfortable margin. The McLaren strategists, based not at the trackside but in the company's technology centre just outside London, had just 10 seconds after the safety car was deployed to act on the various scenarios presented by the software.

Business strategists have, hopefully, a little longer to make the right decision. But the repercussions of their decisions can be just as devastating.

Large pharmaceutical companies, for example, regularly spend almost a billion dollars developing a new drug and the success rate can be as low as one in 20. With such vast sums, finely judged and timely decisions can be worth small fortunes.

Here, too, technology can help: 'If the company can make the right decision a day earlier, it saves it $1m,' says Simon Williams, chief executive of SmithBayes, a UK company that has developed software to make business decision-making easier, faster and more accurate. What distinguishes SmithBayes Playmaker software from other decision support systems is its heritage. It was conceived and nurtured in the high-speed world of Formula One racing. It combines a number of mathematical techniques, including Monte Carlo (the casino, not the Grand Prix) simulations, with advanced visualisation.

MacLaren's engineers have been developing the software for eight years and using it to help with race strategy for six. The system is capable of analysing 8m scenarios for each race based on 3,000 variables. It recalibrates the race strategy every two seconds based on what is happening on the track and other information including, for example, informed guesses about competitors' intentions: 'The whole platform embraces uncertainty rather than being based on hard data,' Mr Williams says, which is why he believes it is well suited to analysing the business world. Monte Carlo methods, for example, are used when a solution depends on a large number of variables.

All the big F1 teams use systems of this kind. But McLaren has gone further than the others in seeking to open its technology to business use.

'McLaren is set up to take its assets, its technologies and its innovations and do other things with them,' Mr Williams says.

Like other SmithBayes founders, he is a former Reuters senior executive. A small group of them had been seeking new business possibilities when they serendipitously came across the MacLaren technology: 'Our ambition was to be the equivalent of a Bloomberg or Reuters terminal for the corporate decision maker,' Mr Williams says. 'We had worked in financial markets and we saw that, over time, the pace of change meant that people that made faster, more precise decisions, held an advantage. We felt that held true across many business sectors.'

Furthermore, in terms of business analysis, Mr Williams explains:

'We believed it was pointless focusing on decimal places on what were essentially guesses and better to focus on flexibility and agility. As in sport, the organisations that can respond to change with better insight, faster and with more precision have an advantage. We believe that agility will be a key element of competitive advantage for the next 10 years.'

MacLaren gave SmithBayes access to its technology in exchange for a 40 per cent equity stake in the newly formed company.

The motor racing group is no longer involved, however, following a management buy-out late last year, the financial details of which are not being disclosed. MacLaren will continue to use the core technology to support its racing programme but SmithBayes is entirely responsible for developing the business logic and marketing outside the motorsport arena. The underlying architecture has beeen re-engineered and rebuilt on .net3 to run on the Microsoft's Vista operating system.

So who could make use of the software? Customers are unwilling to be named because of the competitive advantage they hope the system will yield but any big company facing difficult business decisions based on inadequate data could benefit, Mr Williams says, giving as an example an aerospace manufacturer planning a new engine with four technical options to choose between.

'This is a big decision. The company is betting on a technological horse today that will have an impact on its engine development cycle for 10 years; the engines themselves will be on aeroplanes for a further 30 years, so it's a 40-year business decision.' Mr Williams says that, for a 5 per cent price premium, the SmithBayes software provides a way to keep a final decision on three of the four technologies open for three years.

SmithBayes says it has four large customers and two smaller ones after six months or so of marketing. The system costs £50,000 a year for the core application plus £1,000 a month per seat.

Customers are typically opting for five to six seats to begin with, representing an expenditure of about £100,000–£120,000 a year – small beer if the software brings the claimed advantages. McLaren, meanwhile, is fine-tuning the core technology to continue to support its race strategies. But computers don't win races on their own. After a poor 2006, it must be hoping that its drivers, current world champion Fernando Alonso and rookie Lewis Hamilton, will be equal to the challenge.

Source: from Decision-making software in the fast lane, *The Financial Times*, 28/02/2007 (Cane, A.), copyright © The Financial Times Ltd.

Questions

1 What do risk managers look for in decision making systems?

2 What are the advantages of the SmithBayes platform?

3 What are the shortcomings of the SmithBayes platform?

Introduction

The knowledge-based view of the firm emphasises the strategic importance of knowledge within firms. Many organsations have developed information systems to facilitate sharing and mobilisation of knowledge. Such systems that manage organisational knowledge processes are referred to as Knowledge Management Systems (KMS). The organisational processes supported by KMS may include knowledge creation, storage/retrieval, transfer and application. Even though considerable knowledge management theory emerges from strategy and organisational research, the majority of knowledge management initiatives employ a significant level of information technology. Alavi and Leidner (2001) have compared a number of perspectives on organisational knowledge and suggested a number of implications for knowledge management and knowledge management systems. Their approach highlights the changing role of IT and knowledge management focus and is summarised in Table 8.1. They argue that information technology plays a substantial role in knowledge sharing within organisations by increasing 'weak ties' between individuals and creating informal links. Knowledge is transferred from individual to group to organisation through an interplay of tacit and explicit knowledge assisted by knowledge management systems (KMS).

Table 8.1 Knowledge perspectives and their implications for Knowledge Management Systems

Perspectives		Implications for Knowledge Management (KM)	Implications for Knowledge Management Systems (KMS)
Knowledge vis-à-vis data and information	Data is facts, raw numbers. Information is processed/interpreted data. Knowledge is personalised information	KM focuses on exposing individuals to potentially useful information and facilitating assimilation of information	KMS will not appear radically different from existing IS, but will be extended towards helping in user assimilation of information
State of mind	Knowledge is the state of knowing and understanding	KM involves enhancing individual's learning and understanding through provision of information	Role of IT is to provide access to sources of knowledge rather than knowledge itself
Object	Knowledge is an object to be stored and manipulated	Key KM issue is building and managing knowledge stocks	Role of IT involves gathering, storing and transferring knowledge
Process	Knowledge is a process of applying expertise	KM focus is on knowledge flows and the process of creation, sharing and distributing knowledge	Role of IT is to provide link among sources of knowledge to create wider breadth and depth of knowledge flows
Access to information	Knowledge is a condition of access to information	KM focus is organised access to and retrieval of content	Role of IT is to provide effective search and retrieval mechanisms for locating relevant information
Capability	Knowledge is the potential to influence action	KM is about building core competences and understanding strategic know-how	Role of IT is to enhance intellectual capital by supporting development of individual and organisational competences

A multitude of knowledge management systems have been developed by configuring different component technologies shown in Chapter 7 and integrating them in different ways. For certain business applications, generic and standard software has been developed for mass-market appeal. A frequent dilemma for firms is whether to acquire off-the-shelf solutions or develop customised KM systems. A major issue concerning off-the-shelf solutions is whether organisations want to follow practices and ontologies embedded within the software. The underlying premise of KM systems is that they will meet expectations of senior management for return on investment or increased effectiveness. The current reality is that many KM systems have failed to deliver on these expectations owing to their strong IT orientation and scant regard to links with business strategy and the end customer.

In determining the appropriateness of KM solutions, one needs to be mindful of the five major concerns of senior executives related to IT investments in organisations (PriceWaterhouse 1995):

● integrating IT with corporate objectives;

● transforming through IT;

- infrastructure;
- uncertainty;
- cost control.

This chapter opens by exploring the notion of a system and examines the key contributors to systems thinking and methodologies. It argues that the dominant driver behind the development of KM systems is the improvement of quality management processes in organisations. In this regard, the chapter deliberates on the dominant contributors of the quality management movement starting with Deming and Juran and moving on to principles such as TQM (total quality management), BPR (business process re-engineering) and lean production. To reach these continuous improvement goals, a variety of KM systems are examined, including document management systems, decision support systems, group support systems, executive information systems, workflow management systems and customer relationship management systems. The emphasis throughout is to elaborate on the nature of these systems, their component technologies and shared good practice on their effective implementation. The economic and hidden costs of KM systems are also explored given the scaling back of IT spend in many organisations globally. In a study of 431 US and European firms conducted in 1997 exploring what firms are doing to manage knowledge, the following project priorities (in descending order) were discovered related to KM systems (Ruggles 1998):

- creating an intranet (47 per cent);
- creating data warehouses and knowledge repositories (33 per cent);
- implementing decision support tools (33 per cent);
- implementing groupware to support collaboration (33 per cent);
- creating networks of knowledge workers (24 per cent);
- mapping sources of internal expertise (18 per cent).

These figures are likely to have changed dramatically in the interim in response to changing organisational needs and market developments. The key question remains: can KM systems deliver individual and management expectations around knowledge creation and sharing? If not, what are the additional ingredients needed in the collective 'knowledge management' pot?

Systems thinking

Early management thinking tended to adopt a mechanistic view of reality and treat organisations and people more like machines. This mechanistic view is typified by Frederick Taylor's theory of scientific management (Taylor 1911) and Weber's notion of bureaucracies (Weber 1947). Scientific management stresses repetitive work cycles, detailed planning of work sequences and motivation based on economic rewards. Bureaucracies are characterised by top-down authority hierarchies, breakdown of jobs into routine and well-defined tasks, and a formal set of rules to ensure predictable behaviour. Despite numerous criticisms of this mechanistic conception of organisation, many commentators have argued that developments in information technology and virtual organisations have tended to refine this perspective.

Systems thinking emerged in the 1940s in the biological sciences as the traditional mechanistic view failed to explain the complexity of organisational phenomena. Soon this new perspective found its way into organisational thinking with an adoption of biological analogies such as survival, development and stability.

So what is a system? A system can be characterised as a series of elements connected by relationships or links surrounded by a clearly defined boundary to the external environment and with a role of transforming its inputs into desired outputs, as shown in Figure 8.1. Each element and relationship has an attribute depending on how they are measured, such as size, intensity and strength. The system is termed an 'open' one if the boundary allows inputs from and outputs to the environment. A state of homeostasis is achieved when the system is able to control its internal environment and maintain a dynamic steady state with its changing external environment.

One early conception of organisations by Eric Trist was to view them as 'sociotechnical' systems (Trist 1959). The goal of such systems was to find a 'best fit' between the social (capabilities, needs, relationships) and the technical (material, apparatus, operational stages) aspects of the system. Such a conception still has some relevance in knowledge management with its preoccupations with technical or human resource aspects of knowledge creation and distribution. In the field of systems science, a wide range of other system methodologies has been forwarded, as shown in Table 8.2. There is currently no consensus on the best systems methodology for a given knowledge management situation, but rather an understanding of the strengths and limitations of different systems methodologies as well as the advantages of combining methods to offer creative solutions to complex and ill-defined situations (Gao *et al.* 2002).

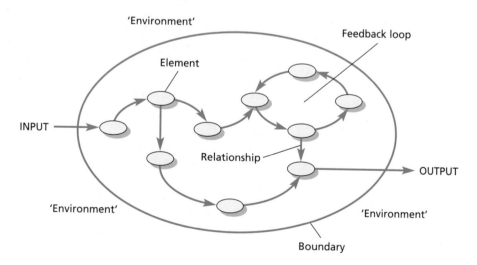

Figure 8.1 **General characteristics of a system**

Table 8.2 **Summary systems methodologies** (adapted from Gao *et al.* 2002)

Author	*Systems methodology and key points*
Churchman (1970)	Social systems design (SSD) Uses dialectic process of thesis, antithesis and synthesis to better understand a situation.
Beer (1972)	Viable systems diagnosis (VSD) Belief that system is viable if capable of responding to environmental changes by achieving variety. Important role played by information flows and organisational structure. Subsystems labelled as implementation, coordination, control, development and policy.
Ackoff (1979)	Interactive planning (IP) Facilitates participation of all stakeholders in planning to generate consensus, commitment; mobilises creativity and eases implementation.
Checkland (1981)	Soft systems methodology (SSM) Emphasises systems as cyclical learning processes. 1 Enter unstructured problematic situation 2 Express problem situation 3 Formulate root definitions: CATWOE – Customers, Actors, Transformation process, *Weltanschauung* (view of the world), Owners, Environmental constraints 4 Build conceptual models 5 Compare models with real-world actions 6 Define feasible and desirable changes 7 Take action to improve problem situation.
Mason & Mitroff (1981)	Strategy assumption surfacing and testing (SAST) Useful for ill-structured problems with differences of opinion. Can be adversarial, participative, integrative and managerial mind supporting. Allows group formation, assumption surfacing, dialectic debate and synthesis of perspectives.
Ulrich (1983)	Critical systems heuristics (CSH) Attempts to link systems with practical reasons of a problem. Encourages debate in terms of practical relevance rather than theoretical justification. Contains twelve critical heuristic categories.
Flood and Jackson (1991)	Total systems intervention (TSI) Finds strengths and weaknesses of available systems and uses a range of systems to promote creativity. Supported by five pillars: 1 Critical awareness 2 Social awareness 3 Dedication to human emancipation 4 Complementarism at theoretical level 5 Complementarism at methodological level.
Linstone (1994)	Technical, organisational and personal perspectives (TOP) Views reality from multiple perspectives: scientific and technological, group or institutional, individual and self.

Drivers of KM systems: quality management processes

The raison d'être of most organisations is to provide products and services that meet the changing needs of their customers. For commercial organisations in highly competitive markets, this means developing systems and processes continually that produce higher-quality services or products at a lower cost than competitors. The key driver of knowledge management systems in organisations is argued to centre around improving quality management processes linked to an organisation's ability to capture, share and apply new knowledge.

▶ Deming and Juran

The pioneers of quality management were Dr William Deming and Dr Joseph Juran. Both quality 'gurus' were influenced by the principles of statistical quality control (SQC) developed by Dr Walter Shewhart. Shewhart (1931) believed that every task had controlled and uncontrolled variations that could be understood through simple statistics, with the possibility of reducing or even eliminating the variations. In most cases, Deming believed that the uncontrolled (his term was 'special' – under operator control) variations accounted for around 15 per cent of the variations and the rest of the controlled ('common causes') variations were to do with the systems and processes and the responsibility of management. This emphasised the importance of leadership and the responsibility of senior management for initiating change.

It is noteworthy that the ideas of these two pioneers were almost ignored in their home country of America until the 1980s but found tremendous recognition in Japan. After defeat in the war, Japan was a country in ruins. In 1950 Deming met a group called the Union of Japanese Scientists and Engineers (JUSE), formed to promote revival of Japanese industry, and spoke to packed audiences across Japan. He became acquainted with the *Kei-dan-ren*, the association of Japan's chief executives, and proposed the importance of statistical process control (an adaption of Shewhart's ideas) to meet consumer demands for high-quality products. Having lost all in the war, the Japanese followed Deming's advice and his conviction that it would make them supremely competitive in global markets within five years. Japanese manufacturers went from strength to strength and by the 1980s had become a major economic threat to the US. Deming was a hero, with the national quality prize in Japan named after him, and was awarded the Second Order of the Sacred Treasure by Emperor Hirohito in 1960.

Deming's method of ensuring quality of every task was based on a form of learning cycle, the PDCA (plan, do, check, act) cycle that could be applied repetitively and continuously to every task (Deming 1986). His beliefs can be summarised into the following stages that lead from one to another:

● improve quality;
● costs decrease because of less rework, fewer mistakes, fewer delays, snags, better use of machine time and materials;
● productivity improves;

- capture the market with better quality and lower price;
- stay in business;
- provide jobs and more jobs.

After publication of his book (Juran 1950), Dr Joseph Juran was invited by JUSE to lecture in Japan. He developed the concept of company-wide quality management (CWQM) as a way of disseminating quality throughout an organisation. This was based on a trilogy linking together planning, control and improvement:

- *planning* – identify and ensure customer needs are easily understood by every person. Ensure that the process will produce something to meet customer needs. Produce a product for the customer;
- *control* – continuously monitor processes for variations. Management take responsibility for the majority (80 per cent) of controlled variations in processes;
- *improvement* – take all necessary steps to improve system including attitude and cultural change.

Juran's lectures were translated and sold in kiosks across Japan as well as being broadcast on radio. They were also used in 'reading circles' in organisations to help improve literacy. These reading circles were a precursor to 'quality circles' and were used to improve quality through joint problem solving in teams.

Critical thinking and reflection

Reflect on your own organisation. How important is Deming and Juran's message to your organisation? Describe how quality is managed in your organisation. To ensure high and consistent levels of quality, what other factors do you think need to be taken into account apart from statistical quality controls? How important are customer perceptions of quality? One of the goals of modern-day marketing is to achieve one-to-one marketing rather than mass marketing. How do your organisational systems measure up to this goal in providing up-to-date knowledge of each customer?

▶ Total quality management (TQM)

Following the discovery in the west of Deming's work and in response to threats of Japanese imports, the concept of total quality management (TQM) was developed. TQM built on earlier concepts of quality control and quality assurance. Quality control was an extension of inspection to collect data and understand variations using statistical techniques. In contrast, quality assurance was about developing organisational structures, procedures, processes and resources to ensure that tasks were performed in a consistent manner. Some firms have opted to follow a quality standard such as ISO 9000, which defines different aspects of their quality system and the nature of third-party assessment. Verification in quality assurance is a major departure from quality control and allows an independent assessment of quality systems and procedures to be made.

TQM moves beyond the mechanistic orientation of quality assurance and emphasises the need to facilitate cultural change. It is linked with a commitment to total customer satisfaction achieved through continuous improvement and encourages the contribution and involvement of people in the process. It offers a multidisciplinary approach to empower employees at all levels and moves beyond the conformance needs to customer-driven needs. For example, in the automobile industry, TQM may focus more on what delights the customer, such as electric windows, rather than purely on the basic conformance needs such as the power of the engine. The key elements of TQM are:

- a total process involving all units in the organisation and led from the top;
- customer is king, with every strategy, action and process directed at satisfaction of customer needs;
- information is gathered and analysed rationally using ICT;
- all organisational processes that add to costs of poor quality are examined;
- greater involvement of people as an untapped resource;
- the use of multidiscipline and multilevel teams to solve problems related to meeting customer needs;
- the promotion of creative thinking to develop innovative solutions.

▶ Business process re-engineering (BPR)

In the mid-1990s, a controversial approach to quality and cost improvements was forwarded called business process re-engineering (BPR). The pioneers of BPR (Davenport 1993; Hammer and Champy 1993) defined BPR as:

The fundamental re-thinking and radical redesign of business processes to achieve dramatic improvements in critical, contemporary measures of performance, such as cost, quality, service and speed.

BPR offered a fresh start to organisational redesign, with a blank sheet of paper ignoring past history or present structures and practices. It focused on the horizontal analysis of work along an activity chain and challenged the very foundations of traditional operations. As most organisations are structured vertically around functions, BPR represented a total shake-up of organisations into horizontal cross-functional processes. One result of the BPR approach was to flatten hierarchies and remove many middle managers with the necessary skills, knowledge and expertise. For some organisations, this lack of regard to 'context-specific' issues has had untoward consequences. Many senior executives have had to manage day-to-day operational issues for which their expertise has been clearly lacking.

A typical BPR project has four stages (Huczynski and Buchanan 2001):

- *process mapping* – drawing flowcharts of work activity sequences;
- *identifying 'moments of truth'* – deciding which steps are critical, add value and introduce errors;
- *generating redesign proposals* – streamlining processes and avoiding duplication and overlap;
- *implementation* – putting the redesign into effect.

Table 8.3 **Differences and similarities between TQM and BPR**

TQM	BPR
Based on process flow to accomplish work	Same
Starts with the customer of the process	Same
Works within existing framework	Seeks to break from existing practices
Based on continuous incremental improvement	Seeks breakthrough
Focus on enhancing continually, facts, data, participation, teamwork, job design, based on technology application	Focus on entirely new information systems, a 'different approach to change management'

Some commentators argue that TQM has been overtaken by BPR whereas others view each approach as complementary to another. Could TQM be seen as a form of single-loop learning (Argyris and Schon 1978) and the radical redesign of BPR as double-loop learning? The distinctions between the two methodologies are shown in Table 8.3 (Hammer and Champy 1993).

▶ Lean production

In 1990 a new concept of 'lean production' was forwarded to explain the increased performance and competitiveness of certain automobile manufacturers around the world (Womack *et al.* 1990). The goal of lean production was to achieve increased productivity, reduced lead times and costs, and improved quality across the organisation. The principles and techniques in lean production have focused on manufacturing firms and contain the following features (Sánchez and Pérez 2001):

- elimination of zero-value activities – anything that doesn't add value to the product or service (Womack and Jones 1996);
- search for continuous improvement in products and processes – involve production teams and management to develop creative solutions to the identification and adjustment of defective parts;
- multifunctional teams – to facilitate task rotation and flexibility to accommodate changes in production levels. Increased training effort on quality control and remuneration to compensate for new flexibility in workforce;
- just-in-time (JIT) production and delivery – integration of automation equipment with production information system to enable delivery of any part in the necessary quantity at the right time. This contributes to the reduction of inventories and lead times;
- integration of suppliers – with key departments to enhance buyer–supplier relationships such as R&D for new component prototypes;
- flexible information systems – to provide timely and useful strategic and operational information to all levels. Strategic information may contain organisation's production plans and sales forecasts whereas operational information may contain the factory's current productivity or quality performance.

Document management systems

Organisations tend to publish a variety of documents for internal consumption or for external sources such as suppliers, customers and shareholders. There is a growing tendency for the volume of these documents to increase substantially each year and an urgent need to manage them adequately for efficient storage and retrieval. Paper files can take up a lot of space in filing cabinets, with the likelihood that they are rarely retrieved for many years. Document management systems have developed to address these problems and have typically employed the intranet as an electronic medium rather than conventional document printing and circulation methods. The primary driving force has been the cost savings compared with conventional publication and distribution methods, together with the dynamic nature of intranets. Documents can be published and updated on the intranet when needed and become available instantly to all interested users (Frazee 1996). The types of documents may include policy and procedure manuals, corporate phone directories, online help, human resource guidelines, sales and marketing literature, customer data, price lists and press releases.

Implementing a document management system constitutes an important stage in a quality management strategy but may result in considerable resistance and even opposition within organisations. To overcome this resistance, many organisations have begun with a pilot study using documents that were originally being delivered on paper and where costs and results could be monitored and measured. Apart from emphasising the reduced costs of intranet-based document management systems, the pilots have focused on the value of enhanced access to information for users. Anecdotal statements focused on value derived from the document management systems can help erode some of the resistance to change. For example, value statements such as (Wen *et al.* 1998):

> *'I was able to win three new accounts over the telephone because I had the information at my fingertips, and I knew it was current. With the old system, I was always putting the customer on hold and asking the other reps for information.'*

Document management systems can be 'cheap and cheerful', operating on a limited number of functions, or can be full-blown, expensive systems with a multitude of functions and potentially frightening in terms of their impact on organisational processes and administrative practices. The 'value-adding' facilities of document management systems may include (Raynes 2002):

- control to ensure only one user modifies a document at a time;
- audit trail to monitor changes in a document over time;
- security processes to control user access to documents;
- organisation of documents into related groups and folders;
- identification and retrieval of documents according to text they contain (free-text searching);
- recording information associated with the document as meta data such as author, creation date and title;
- ability to route documents from one user to another in a controlled fashion based on the workflow;

- converting paper documents into electronic format by scanning;
- organising documents into groups to enable them to be distributed to target audiences.

The choice of document management system is likely to influence the culture of the organisation or, depending on its scale, may simply reflect the dominant culture. It is important to consider clearly the current or future problems the system is likely to solve and the advantages over traditional paper-based methods. The process of implementing a document management system can be divided into a number of phases, as shown in Table 8.4 (Rowley 1999).

Some of the typical remaining organisational challenges presented by document management systems have included (Wen *et al.* 1998):

- *privacy* – the need to balance the desire to track visitors through site logs and the need for privacy. Also, the need to deliver sensitive information in a largely anonymous manner;
- *currency of information* – whether documents are updated regularly. This can be overcome by simply adding 'date of last change' to each page;
- *performance* – becomes an issue in high-volume, transaction-oriented applications. This can be overcome by increasing the bandwidth of the network but results in increased costs;
- *security* – to bar access to unauthorised personnel from sensitive financial, company or personnel records.

Table 8.4 **Phases of implementing a document management system**

Phase	*Description*	*Initiated by*
Identify content	Identify a subset of documents to be indexed and made available on the intranet	System administrator
Database set-up	Define a database template or framework for the text database, which will store the indices of the processed documents	System administrator
Populate database	Perform indexing and populate database with the indices of the processed documents	System administrator
Intranet enable/publish	Once the documents are processed and appropriate intranet/internet connections are made, an interface is created through which users can enter their search requests	User/client
Process search requests	Using the search criteria, the text-retrieval engine performs a search on the document repository	User/client
Present results	Displays search results in the form of a hit list. Users can make selections from hit list to view particular documents	User/client
View/download original	User can be presented document in a viewable format (such as PDF) or can download the required file	User/client

Decision support systems

Decision support systems (DSS) combine data analysis and sophisticated models to support non-routine decision making. They are particularly useful in helping managers make decisions on ill-defined problems in rapidly changing environments. They provide the user with an interactive interface and bring together analyses and models to make sense of existing internal and external data. The major capabilities of DSS are that they (Turban and Aronson 2001):

- provide support in semi-structured and unstructured situations;
- support several sequential and interdependent decisions;
- support intelligence, design, choice and implementation phases of decision making;
- support a variety of styles and processes;
- are adaptive and flexible over time;
- are user-friendly with strong graphical capabilities;
- improve accuracy, timeliness and quality of decision making;
- have substantial modelling capability to allow experimentation with different strategies under different scenarios.

There is a multitude of DSS on offer in the marketplace. A simplistic distinction would be to separate them into model-driven DSS and data-driven DSS, as shown in Figure 8.2. Model-driven DSS provide a range of statistical, financial, forecasting and management science models that may be applied at strategic, tactical or operational levels. They allow the user to conduct 'what if' analyses under a range of scenarios. Typically, they are end user-led such as the Bloomberg portal designed by a former financial trader

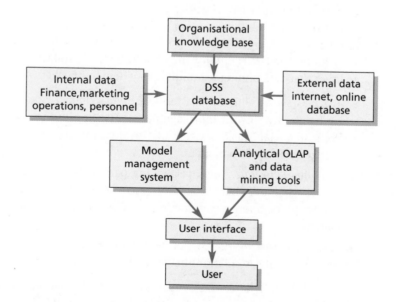

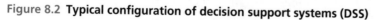

Figure 8.2 **Typical configuration of decision support systems (DSS)**

to meet the information needs of other traders in the financial markets. The DSS may contain between a few and several hundred models encompassing strategic models, tactical models, operational models and analytical models. Strategic models tend to help high-level strategic planning processes within organisations. Tactical models assist in allocating and controlling organisational resources such as capital budgeting and human resource planning. Operational models help support day-to-day decision making, such as loans approval and quality control processes. Analytical models may cover methods of analysis such as statistical models or specific financial models.

Critical thinking and reflection

Imagine your ideal decision support system. What would you consider to be the optimal characteristics of a DSS that would allow you to solve organisational problems effectively? Given that the reality for most managers is incomplete information in decision making, how could a DSS be best employed? The quality of outputs in any system is based primarily on the quality of inputs. What measures could you take to ensure high quality of information was fed into a DSS in your organisation?

In contrast, data-driven DSS are more focused on examining patterns and relationships in large amounts of data. As described in Chapter 7, they use knowledge evaluation tools such as online analytical processing (OLAP) to provide multidimensional analyses and data mining techniques looking at associations, sequences, classifications, clustering and forecasting with the data (Laudon and Laudon 2010). Associations are occurrences linked to a single event. Sequences are events linked over time. Classification recognises patterns in certain groups such as loyal or fraudulent customers. Clustering techniques can help determine different groupings of certain customers where classifications don't necessarily exist. Forecasting techniques can help predict values for certain variables. Data mining techniques vary considerably in the variety of approaches adopted, from fuzzy logic to neural networks (see Chapter 7 for more details). The following uses in different industrial sectors illustrate typical analyses that data mining techniques may help to uncover:

- *Banking industry* – identify patterns of fraud, conduct risk analysis of customers who are habitually slow in mortgage payments, find hidden correlations between different financial indicators, identify loyal customers and predict customers likely to change credit card companies.
- *Retail and marketing* – discover buying patterns such as certain customers regularly buying wine and cheese together, uncover associations in buying habits linked to demographics, forecast customer responses to advertising and perform a market-basket analysis.
- *Insurance* – discover patterns of behaviour of risky customers, perform claims analyses and identify associations between claims.

In order to purchase a DSS, organisations need to decide between custom-made or off-the-shelf solutions. The advantage of off-the-shelf solutions are the lower costs, flexibility and applicability of many business problems in the same sectors. In contrast, custom-made solutions allow organisations to differentiate themselves from competitors and use a more sophisticated approach based on different configurations of the following seven classifications (Holsapple and Whinston 1996):

- *Text-oriented DSS* – using technologies such as Web-based documents, hyperlinks and intelligent agents.

- *Database-oriented DSS* – featuring strong report generation and query-searching capabilities.

- *Spreadsheet-oriented DSS* – such as Excel which uses statistical and financial models and techniques.

- *Solver-oriented DSS* – functions or procedures used for optimising certain variables such as the optimal ordering quantities of certain resources based on historical data.

- *Rule-oriented DSS* – often expert systems linked to procedural and inferential (reasoning) rules such as evacuation of a tall building in case of fire in certain parts of it.

- *Compound DSS* – containing two or more aspects of the above five classifications.

- *Intelligent DSS* – similar to rule-oriented DSS that can learn using agent technology and machine learning techniques.

Group support systems

Teamwork is part of most organisations in one form or another. It is relatively rare to find even freelance individuals purely working by themselves. In response to global and competitive pressures, organisations are increasingly having their activities geographically dispersed and using internet technologies to communicate over long distances. The growth of teleworking since its inception in the 1960s has given rise to virtual teams and virtual organisations. Distance and time differences globally are less of a barrier nowadays with a variety of technologies employed such as e-mail, video conferencing, mobile phones and co-authoring systems. The important feature is the development of appropriate technologies to facilitate collaboration and cooperation in groups and teams. The five basic team processes supported by group support systems (GSS) and found in many commercial products such as Lotus Notes and Microsoft NetMeeting are (Andriessen 2003):

- *communication* – these include easy, fast and cheap technologies such as e-mail, voice-mail and video systems;

- *knowledge sharing and learning* – these include quick, reliable and inexpensive tools for knowledge storage and retrieval;

- *cooperation* – these include document sharing and co-authoring facilities as well as group decision support systems to support brainstorming, evaluating ideas and decision making;

- *coordination* – provided using synchronisers to synchronise work processes of a team using group calendars and workflow tools;

- *social interaction* – using cameras and monitors near coffee machines or other locations where people can meet each other unintentionally. An example of such a system is Media Space.

The term 'group decision support systems' can be misleading as teams may often convene in virtual environments for short periods of time without the opportunity for traditional face-to-face cohesion. They are designed to support simultaneous and anonymous idea generation with group displays, the evaluation and structuring of information, and the facilitation of agenda setting and group priorities. To meet social needs, advanced video systems have been developed to give group members the sense that they are sitting at the same table as colleagues. Further developments have moved to virtual spaces where symbols of group members are depicted in virtual reality. A typology of group support systems is shown in Table 8.5 (Andriessen 2003).

Table 8.5 **Typology of group support systems** (Andriessen 2003)

Group process systems	Support between encounters: asynchronous communication	Support for synchronous electronic encounters	Support for synchronous face-to-face meetings
	Different place/different time	Different place/same time	Same place/same time
Communication	• Fax • E-mail • Voice-mail • Video-mail	• Telephone/ Mobile • Audio systems • Video systems • Chat system	
Knowledge sharing and learning·	• Document sharing systems • Message boards	• Tele-consultation systems • Co-browser	• Presentation systems
Cooperation·	• Document co-authoring	• Shared CAD, whiteboard, word processor, spreadsheet·	• Group decision support systems
Coordination	• Group calender • Shared planning • Shared workflow management system • Event manager • Subgroup spaces	• Notification systems, e.g. active batch	• Command and control centre support systems
Social encounters		• Media spaces • Virtual reality	

Critical thinking and reflection

Think about the ways you communicate with people in your organisation. What would you say is your optimal approach? What role do face-to-face encounters play in your relationships with colleagues? What technological or collaborative tools do you use for communication and team working? If you use group support systems, how effective are they? For true collaborative working, how can you enhance trust in your dealings with colleagues using group support systems? Given the power of the internet to cover geographical boundaries, how important are face-to-face meetings?

Experience has shown that the success of group support systems relies on more than technology. Hence the development of future systems is likely to place the end user more centrally in the design process through a better understanding of socio-technical processes. Such group support systems are not a quick fix and may require a champion, a pilot and an effective communications process for their success. A few noteworthy guidelines to improve the effectiveness of group support systems include (Andriessen 2003):

- if possible, start group with face-to-face meetings;
- learn about each other's backgrounds through 'yellow pages' (expertise directory);
- prepare and structure synchronous meeting well, with minutes;
- use video links where possible to develop trust and cohesion;
- provide regular information on progress and milestones;
- pay attention to training and intercultural differences.

Even though group support systems provide a forum for knowledge sharing, learning and enhanced problem solving, they can pose certain challenges for groups. For example, there may be 'free-riders' relying on others to do all the work, a tendency to make riskier decisions, compromised solutions of low quality and information overload. However, improvements can be made through effective facilitation and by making these dangers explicit to group members. The results can lead to decreased costs, saved travel time and greater creativity through the anonymity of the systems. Group support systems have also been successfully used for distance learning programmes in universities to increase a student's learning experience through greater dialogue with peers and the faculty tutors.

Executive information systems

Executive information systems (EIS) were developed in the mid-1980s with a primary goal of enhancing the strategic planning and control processes of executives through the provision of quality, timely, accurate and accessible information (O'Brien 1991). In addition, to compensate for the computer illiteracy of many senior executives, they were designed intuitively so that even a ten-year-old child could use such systems. They provided a broad understanding of company information by summarising large quantities of data and allowed the user to drill down to different levels of data to gain insight into the detail of information. The challenges in EIS have been in understanding the rich and complex nature of executive decision making and especially the dynamic and fast-changing information needs of executives. As with many other systems, there has often been resistance to EIS from data owners in organisations who fear loss of control over data and the potential implications for changes in power structures. In addition, the high costs of EIS have been difficult to justify in comparison with opportunity costs of using the same resources for other activities.

One dilemma facing the high-quality information requirements of EIS is the fact that data is often input using unskilled and untrained operatives, which may lead to gross errors and misleading analyses. Careful consideration must be taken to avoid the dangers of 'garbage in, garbage out' syndrome and the potential risk of making the wrong decisions. Research on the effective implementation of EIS has found a number of factors linked with continuous improvement that increase the success of initiatives (Zairi *et al.* 1998):

- need for a committed executive sponsor to drive project and provide feedback on product quality and expectations for improvement;
- need for a pro-active operating sponsor (often in an IT/IS department) to act as market researcher with the executives, confidence builder, product designer and operational line manager;
- the bringing together of business knowledge and IT skills through teamwork;
- coordinating systems and processes lower in the organisation with EIS to ensure alignment of effort;
- visually attractive graphics.

The traditional alternative to EIS is having managers providing analyses of complex data at board meetings. The arguments in favour of EIS are that it provides a tool as a supplement to managerial knowledge and experience and allows decisions to be made in dynamically changing environments where the privileged recourse to managers may not always be available. The leading question is whether there is an alignment between a manager's decision-making patterns and the analyses generated from an EIS. The answer may lie more closely in the distinction between EIS providing rational modes of analyses and managers relying more on irrational information and political factors. A comparison of TQM and effective EIS practices is shown in Table 8.6 (Zairi *et al.* 1998).

Table 8.6 **Impact of TQM factors on effective EIS practices**

TQM	EIS practices
Goal	
Customer satisfaction	Meeting executives' information requirements
Quality product/service	Quality information
Cost effectiveness	Reducing cost of decision making and communication
Concept	
Customer–supplier chains	Operational level – managers – executives
Customer requirements	Identifying executives' information requirements
Performance measurement	Using key performance indicators (KPIs)
Failure prevention	Preventing wrong decision making and error in data input
Implementation	
Top management commitment	Strong support from an executive sponsor
Involvement of every employee	Everyone's information system
Cross-function teamwork	Teamwork including IT and business knowledge
Learning process	Executives' receptivity by learning
Benchmarking	Internal and external (competitor) information

▶ Workflow management systems

One of the ideal tools in business process re-engineering has been the use of workflow management systems (WMS). WMS are a part of enterprise resource planning (ERP) and may be considered as the back-office integration processes in organisations. An important function of WMS is the modelling of workflows. WMS can be seen as repositories of an organisation's procedures and processes. They are predominantly suited to the efficient processing of a large number of 'cases' within a small number of predefined processes. Ad hoc workflows with a separate workflow defined for each case is more likely to occur in future developments of WMS. Examples of cases include customer orders, insurance claims, university applications and tax returns. Each case (let's say a university application from Fred Bloggs) has a *unique identity* and a *limited finite lifetime*. The lifetime begins from the moment the university receives Fred Bloggs' application and ends when the university notifies Fred Bloggs of the outcome of his application. In the case of Fred Bloggs' application, the procedure may be broken down into a number of phases, each with a number of *conditions* that need to be fulfilled before certain other tasks are carried out. The conditions allow the user to see how far a case has progressed. The contents of the case may be held manually in a filing cabinet or electronically in a database.

Tasks in a WMS are logical units of work such as writing reports and assessing candidates, and can be manual, semi-automatic or automatic. The combination of a task and a case is termed a work item and the application of a task on a case is seen as an activity. There are a number of ways that a case can go through a process and this determines the nature and order of tasks to be performed. This *routing* of a case may be sequential (one task after another), parallel (tasks performed simultaneously) or selective (choice made between two or more tasks depending on the case attributes). The spark or trigger that initiates the work item may come from a resource such as an employee or an external event or a time signal (van der Aalst and van Hee 2002).

The traditional and formal analysis of processes is the use of '*Petri Nets*' (see Figure 8.3) to ensure precise definitions of processes and prevent ambiguities. A Petri Net enables processes to be described graphically and is composed of places and transitions. Places indicate states within a process and are indicated with a circle whereas transitions may denote different activities between states and are shown by a rectangle. Places and transitions are often linked together using arcs shown by the arrows in the diagram.

Critical thinking and reflection

Imagine you were asked to manage workflows in a virtual organisation. How would you go about conducting this role? What KM systems would you employ to manage the changing knowledge base of your supply chain from customers to suppliers? On a practical level, what measures would you adopt to ensure that there weren't any blockages in your workflow particularly from staff illnesses or poorly performing sub-contract workers? How influential do you consider time differences when working in a global virtual environment?

In a quest to develop standards with the multitude of WMS offerings, the Workflow Management Coalition (WFMC) was set up to define terminology and provide standards for exchange of data between different systems. The WFMC has produced a workflow reference model as a general description of architecture in WMS, as shown in Figure 8.4.

The different aspects of WMS are as follows:

- *Workflow enactment service* – is at the heart of any WMS and creates new cases and work items and ensures that activities are conducted in the right order at the right time. It may be composed of several workflow engines that handle a certain number of cases and processes.

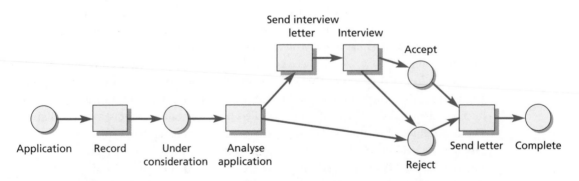

Figure 8.3 **Example of a Petri Net for a university application**

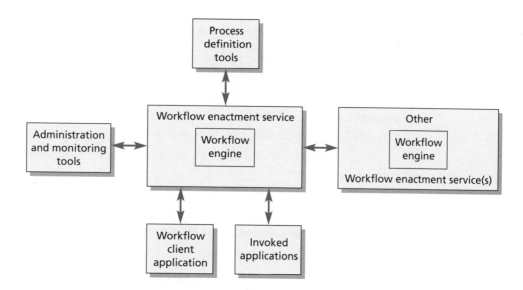

Figure 8.4 **Typical workflow systems architecture (WFMC)**

- *Process definition tools* – comprise tools for modelling process definitions (using Petri Nets), resource classifications (such as qualifications and expertise of individuals, groups and departments) and analysis (such as semantic correctness of process definitions).

- *Workflow client application* – is the main contact employees often have with a WMS. Each employee has a worklist (in-tray) showing which work items need action. Work items can be locked to a user or passed on to another employee. Figures can be generated on individual or group performance.

- *Invoked applications* – the performance of certain activities may require the starting and use of various applications such as different spreadsheets and databases. Applications are started by the workflow engine so that the activities may be completed satisfactorily. These applications may perform the tasks automatically, such as a mathematical analysis, or may be interactive and require human intervention.

- *Administration and monitoring tools* – contain day-to-day operational management tools as well as recording and reporting tools. Operational tools allow the user to examine bottlenecks and faults in the systems from a case perspective, such as reconfiguring the workflow system, or from a resource perspective, such as addition or removal of employees due to illness or holidays. Recording and reporting tools allow managers to analyse the performance of the WMS using indicators such as average completion rates for cases, average waiting times and average resource capacity utilisation. As the magnitude of recording increases substantially, OLAP and data mining techniques can be employed to analyse the data, as shown in Chapter 7.

There are traditionally two methods of developing WMS using business process re-engineering (BPR) or rapid application development (RAD). As shown earlier in this chapter, BPR aims to discover the most efficient and effective business processes without recourse to existing processes. The BPR lifecycle is traditionally initiated by senior management and contains the four phases:

- *diagnosis* – an analysis of existing working processes and their problems;
- *redesign* – starting with a clean slate, new processes are designed looking at the most efficient ways of converting inputs to desired outputs;
- *reconstruction* – the infrastructure to support the new processes are considered, such as IT systems and organisational structures;
- *operations* – performance of processes is measured, analysed and modified accordingly.

In contrast, RAD uses a more evolutionary method for developing WMS and has a strong emphasis on user participation. The RAD approach comprises four phases and there is less of a distinction between separate and consecutive design and construction phases:

- *requirements planning phase* – intended results and functionality of system defined;
- *user design phase* – user consultation results in designers making clear specifications in a CASE tool. Users can test specifications against prototypes of WMS;
- *construction phase* – WMS software is perfected and validated through testing by users;
- *delivery phase* – comprises acceptance testing by users and minor modifications as well as user training.

The future trends in WMS are towards modelling ad hoc workflows with separate processes defined for each case (van der Aalst and van Hee 2002). More attention is likely to be paid to the scheduling of people using sophisticated timetabling systems and labour flexibility arrangements. The internet and corporate intranets provide future challenges for developing effective WMS to cater for the burgeoning e-business markets as well as providing easy access and protection to confidential information.

Customer relationship management systems

In contrast to the back-office aspects of WMS, customer relationship management systems are firmly rooted in front-office integration and revolve principally around marketing. The motivation is to integrate technology and business processes to meet customer requirements at any given moment. Customer relationship strategy is about cementing long-term, collaborative relationships with customers based on trust (Crosby 2002). Such strategies are not about short-term revenue gains from customers but more about enhancing the customers' lifetime value to the firm. In this sense, CRM technology needs to be aligned with business goals of maintaining and enhancing customer relationships.

In the 1980s firms were preoccupied with a marketing orientation based around *customer segmentation*. This meant that firms tried to establish groups of customers with similar needs and wants around characteristics such as demographics and behavioural traits. This was a cost-effective method of satisfying many customer needs but by no means all of them. As competition increased in the 1990s, market segmentation was seen as a starting point for many firms and the focus turned towards *customer-centric orientations*. This perspective was about relationships with customers and treating each customer individually and uniquely. It was one-to-one marketing. During this time advancements in technology meant that fast, low-cost storage and retrieval of individual customer preferences and needs became a reality. CRM emerged so that firms could concentrate on a share of each customer in the long term rather than a share of the overall market in the short term. The underlying premise was the difficulty and huge resources involved in gaining new customers rather than retaining existing ones. This resulted in a marked shift from mass marketing and communications towards focusing on successful interactions with existing customers at every turn.

Critical thinking and reflection

The ultimate goal in marketing is to achieve one-to-one marketing where each customer is treated individually in terms of their preferences and needs. How could you use CRM systems rather than purely segmentation marketing to achieve this goal? What incentives could you provide customers to gather regular, up-to-date knowledge on their changing needs? What ethical issues could such data collection present, particularly in connection with the internet?

Effective CRM systems are not confined to partnerships between marketing and IT departments but are likely to span divisional boundaries such as finance, operations and human resources. The component technologies involved with CRM systems are likely to include data warehousing, data mining techniques and World Wide Web integration through a website, intranet and phone support systems. The development and integration of a CRM system within an organisation can be painful and fraught with difficulties. There may be little user support and the user interfaces may not fit with users' working styles. There may be a tendency to focus on technology rather than process improvements. The scope of the project may change frequently and political infighting may result in lack of senior management commitment. Cost overruns and substantial time delays may result in firm and user disillusionment. Also, the CRM system may fail to integrate and support mobile communications (Corner and Hinton 2002). To overcome some of these problems, a CRM development plan based on a project lifecycle is outlined below (Bose 2002):

- *Planning* – identifying how managers will use customer information at various levels in the organisation and gaining senior management support. Identifying how, when and where employees will interact with customers such as help desks, website, sales person, mail or phone. Also, identifying decision interaction points on how managers and executives will use the knowledge to improve the quality of their decision making.

- *Research* – assessment of the firm's organisational structure, culture, hardware, software, vendors and suppliers.

- *Systems analysis* – identifying employee information needs to interact successfully with a customer. Exploring the need for automated interaction using Web or automated phone systems. Implementing system in a number of stages. Integrating customer data across a firm, expanding customer data profile to include non-transactional information such as inquiries, management comments and complaints, integrating with legacy systems where data may be functionally based. Conducting a feasibility study.

- *Design* – to include a detailed specification of needs and core technologies. Any modifications required to link to existing KM systems.

- *Construction* – developing software to meet design plan.

- *Implementation* – including a solid training programme at all levels, including managers and executives, particularly in areas such as data mining and statistics. Erroneous conclusions may arise from managers confusing correlations with causation and using unreliable data.

- *Maintenance and documentation* – evaluation and modification of the system dependent on data quantity and quality.

- *Adaptation* – continuous improvement of CRM system from learning more about the customer.

There is a paradox with CRM systems. Even though CRM collects vast amounts of data to allow managers to make better quality decisions, the contrary may be true. Higher quality information may result in poorer decisions, especially where a decision maker fails to interpret and understand the true relationships between different variables (Raghunathan 1999). Future developments in CRM systems are likely to result in greater integration with decision support systems and executive information systems. In addition, as partnerships and alliances develop due to competitive pressures, CRM systems are likely to cross organisational boundaries and facilitate information sharing between different partners in the supply chain. Data mining techniques will also need to improve to cope with the needs of large data warehouses over and above the current performance limitations concerned with analysing only 5–10 per cent of data in these huge knowledge repositories.

Economics of KM systems

Early development considerations of KM systems by senior management need to take into account the overall costs of implementing and maintaining these systems. These can be divided into costs related to implementing a KM system including overheads, and the salary costs of employees with designated KM functions. The implementation costs of KM systems include (Maier 2001) the following:

- *Hardware* – networked PCs, high storage capacity databases, Web servers running client–server applications, internet broadband connections and mobile technology such as mobile phones, palmtops, laptops and bluetooth (wireless) technology.

- *Software* – for KM systems to meet specific organisational needs. May use off-the-shelf solutions with significant customisation or develop own solutions.

- *Training and education* – continual communication about benefits of new system as well as structured training programme for all levels on use of KM system.

- *Literature, conferences, consulting and proactive participation in KM activities* – KM budget to spend on literature, funding (university) KM research programmes, attending conferences and employing consultants.

- *Organisation of KM events* – announcing and communicating KM initiative and facilitating 'communities of practice'.

- *KM overhead* – to coordinate KM initiative.

- *KM systems administration* – especially to protect system against hackers.

- *KM staff* – salaries, overheads and expenses of staff taking different KM roles.

In contrast, the benefits of KM systems can be determined using a variety of intellectual capital approaches outlined in Chapter 3.

CASE STUDY

Tata Consultancy Services (India)

Mr N. Chandrasekaran, Chief Operating Officer at Tata Consultancy Services (TCS), stood up and walked over to the display terminal. His plane had been delayed by 50 minutes. This gave him time to reflect on his meeting today with John Chambers, Chairman and Chief Executive of Cisco. Cisco had grand plans for market growth and development in the global internet networking market and saw Tata Consulting Services as an important strategic partner in this quest. Mr Chandrasekaran pondered on the strategic implications of such an alliance so that he could report back his own thoughts to Mr Subramanian Ramadorai, Chief Executive Officer of Tata Consulting Services. Mr Chandrasekaran's main concern was over the alignment of short- and long-term goals of both organisations and the value of a strategic alliance in the current downturn in global markets.

Cisco is a US-based world leader of networking services and has ambitions to increase its market share in internet networking solutions for the banking, financial services, telecom and state sectors in the US, UK and India. Cisco has recognised the low-cost advantage of operating in India as well as the high pool of technology talent and expertise.[1] John Chambers was confident about India's future growth in the technology sector adding, 'If I had to bet on one country at this moment, it would be India.' Cisco had operated in India for the past ten years and recognised major opportunities for developing next generation virtualised data centres using a strategic alliance with TCS.[2]

Tata Consultancy Services provides IT consultancy services to businesses around the world. It has over 130,000 consultants based in 47 countries. The company offers some of the most complex applications and next-generation IT infrastructures in the world. The consultancy is highly competitive in global markets as it optimises onsite consultancy with offshore back office functions based in more economical India. TCS's in-depth knowledge of different business domains combined with its technological prowess makes it a significant player in global markets. The organisation is driven by a thirst for knowledge.

TCS was founded in 1968 as an arm of Tata Sons Limited, the largest industrial conglomerate in India which now owns Jaguar cars and Land Rover. The break for TCS came in the 1970s when Mr Ramadorai convinced US clients to send work to India while maintaining high levels of service quality and capabilities.[3] As the organisation expanded, there was a need for greater agility and shift from a centralised structure to a more decentralised one. Mr Ramadorai recalls: 'The fundamentals of TCS are the same. But now we have more of a team approach. I try and make the core team as visible as possible. The age profile has come down, the hierarchical structure is much broader and decision making is spread all over the organisation.'[4] TCS has started developing cross-cultural capabilities with its workforce comprising 9.1 per cent foreign nationals and 30 per cent women.

The three pillars of knowledge management at TCS are People, Processes and Technology. In terms of people, one of TCS's key values is 'learning and sharing'. The company has introduced two initiatives to promote a greater learning culture: PEEP and PROPEL. PEEP stands for 'Proactive Employee Engagement Program'. Here senior managers have arranged face-to-face meetings with employees across various functions and grades. These forums have allowed employees to express problems and share their suggestions and opinions. The other HR initititiative PROPEL has promoted a 'share-care-grow' culture and encouraged individuals to advance their own ideas and resolve issues at a local level. PROPEL stands for Professional excellence, Role enhancement, Ownership culture, Personal growth, Employee involvement and Learning. PROPEL is composed of confluences and camps. Confluences are cross-functional and cross-grade forums of around 40 members based around a particular theme and can last for 3–4 hours. In contrast, a camp is a forum for improvement initiatives on some aspect of the business.[5]

TCS has a global training hub at Technopark in Thiruvananthapuram, Kerala, where it trains new recruits in different aspects of software engineering, quality systems and different technologies. Included within this training is soft-skills development such as leadership and teamwork. The trainers are drawn from different parts of the business with significant subject expertise and experience.

TCS has developed six additional training centres overseas in line with its global expansion. The company invests around 4 per cent of its annual turnover in training and development. Each employee spends around 20 days each year developing their domain knowledge, technical capabilities and managerial skills.

As a technological champion, TCS has developed a number of ICT interventions to encourage knowledge sharing. The initial knowledge repository was called KBases and contained information on organisational processes, technologies, best practice, customer feedback, tips, project and management-related information. This was superseded by an enterprise resource planning platform named Ultimatix that has integrated 50 core applications and streamlined internal collaboration of 700 business processes. This was important for supporting workflow, HR, finance and project management processes for TCS's 130,000 staff based at 150 offices worldwide. As part of this system, there were Process Asset Libraries (PAL) that provided information on technology, processes and case studies from previous learning on projects as part of their quality management system. The Integrated Project Management System (IPMS) provided key project guidelines and procedures from project planning, work allocation, project execution to delivery of projects.

Mr Chandrasekaran's deliberations recognised that there were opportunities in a strategic alliance with Cisco with clear benefits for both sides. In his mind he thought:

'Customers are demanding greater dynamism from their IT infrastructure and application environment to address current challenges. This strategic alliance will take advantage of Cisco's industry-leading data centre networking solutions and TCS's global network delivery model to help our customers increase the efficiency and agility of their IT operations.'[6]

Knowledge, learning, and skills development would be central in this strategic alliance. However, he recalled Mr Ramadorai's words of the current business environment:

'It is impossible to predict what is really happening. We are living in times where everything is unpredictable. Such an event (global meltdown) has not happened in anyone's living memory. So it is such unpredictable times we are living in.'[7]

Mr Chandrasekaran decided that he would suggest to Mr Ramadorai that TCS start a small venture with the formation of a Cisco Technology Lab at their campus in Chennai. The Cisco Technology Lab could allow TCS to develop network-based solutions, test frameworks, develop skills and certify employees in Cisco data centre technologies.[8] Before he could formulate any further thoughts, an announcement was made that Mr Chandrasekaran's flight was ready to board. He picked up his coat and proceeded to board his plane.

References

1 Bonasia, J. (2008) 'TCS wary of rivals, wage hikes: Falling U.S. dollar, too; India's Tata Consultancy offers high-end services, cultivates Europe, Asia, *Investor's Business Daily*, National edn.

2 *Agence France Presse* (2009) 'India's TCS and Cisco form strategic alliance', *Agence France Presse*, Mumbai.

3 Choudhury, A. R. (2005) 'The quiet software czar; Amit Roy Choudhury meets a driving force behind India's thriving IT services industry', *The Business Times Singapore*, Singapore.

4 De, A. (2003) 'Chip off a new block', *Tata Consultancy Services Media Reports*, India.

5 *The Financial Express* (2004) 'TCS gets a peep into employee minds', *The Financial Express*.

6 *Associated Press Financial Wire* (2009) 'Cisco and Tata Consultancy Services announce strategic alliance', *Associated Press Financial Wire*.

7 Balaji, F. (2008) 'India IT industry caught in unpredictable times: Ramadorai', *Indo-Asian News Service*, Bangalore.

8 *Associated Press Financial Wire* (2009) 'Cisco and Tata Consultancy Services announce strategic alliance', *Associated Press Financial Wire*.

Questions

1 What advice would you give Mr N. Chandrasekaran about the potential strategic alliance with Cisco?

2 What are the current weaknesses in Tata Consultancy Services' approach to knowledge management?

3 How could these weaknesses be improved?

Summary

This chapter has argued that KM systems are primarily driven by an organisation's desire to improve quality management processes. Current trends in quality management are explored covering practices such as TQM, BPR and lean production. The intrinsic nature of systems and the development of systems thinking and methodologies are also explored. Key KM systems are detailed, with an emphasis on their component technologies and their effective implementation. The financial implementation costs of KM systems are considered in greater depth. The KM systems elaborated in this chapter are:

1 *Document management systems* – getting the right information or knowledge to the right person at the right time.

2 *Decision support systems* – creating and evaluating knowledge through data analysis or using sophisticated models to support decision making.

3 *Group support systems* – systems designed to enhance communication, knowledge sharing, cooperation, coordination and social encounters within groups.

4 *Executive information systems* – providing high-quality information and knowledge to executives to aid strategic planning and control processes.

5 *Workflow management systems* – knowledge associated with workflows and aligning 'cases' with resources such as employees.

6 *Customer relationship management systems* – developing knowledge about customers' individual preferences and needs using knowledge repositories and knowledge discovery techniques.

Questions for further thought

1 Are there differences between information management systems and KM systems? Or is it a case of 'old wine in new bottles'?

2 The complexity of a system increases with the addition of different perspectives and subprocesses. How does one find a balance between simplicity and complexity of systems models in problem solving?

3 If conformance quality is a given starting point in today's competitive environment, how do organisations develop KM systems in order to delight their customers?

4 How would you advise a firm about the strengths and pitfalls of a business process re-engineering approach?

5 Decision-support systems use a variety of models and analytical tools ranging from fuzzy logic to neural networks. How would you interpret the range of findings from different DSS using the same data warehouse? Are there lessons for designing the optimal DSS for structured and unstructured data?

6 If group support systems predominantly act to facilitate team meetings and coordination of tasks, how can the systems be developed to generate greater cohesion and build longer-term relationships?

7 Should a course in statistics be a pre-requisite for all managers and executives using KM systems for decision making?

8 How effective are workflow management systems for managing processes requiring high levels of skills and expertise? Do WMS encourage Frederick Taylor's view of scientific management with a disregard for the psychological and social needs and capabilities of workers?

9 The customer-centric orientation of CRM systems nowadays can lead to firm's holding sensitive information about customers. In the quest for understanding each customer uniquely, how can organisations prevent such information seen as private by some customers backfiring on them and destroying the very trust they were hoping to build?

10 How can firms develop faith in their KM systems investments when the speed of change in hardware and software may alter dramatically every 18 months?

Further reading

1 Flood and Jackson (1991) provides a good historical background on systems thinking and methodologies.

2 Laudon and Laudon (2010) is particularly good as an introduction and general overview of information and knowledge management systems.

3 Turban and Aronson (2001) is a more in-depth text on KM systems and focuses more on decision support systems including groupware.

4 van der Aalst and van Hee (2002) provides an accessible and detailed text on workflow management systems.

5 Alavi and Leider (2001) provide an overarching theoretical framework for analysis of knowledge management systems.

References

Ackoff, R. L. (1979) 'Resurrecting the future of operations research', *Journal of the Operational Research Society*, 30(3), 189–99.

Agence France Presse (2009) 'India's TCS and Cisco form strategic alliance', *Agence France Presse*, Mumbai.

Alavi, M. and Leidner, D. E. (2001) 'Knowledge management and knowledge management systems: conceptual foundations and research issues', *MIS Quarterly*, 25, 107–36.

Andriessen, J. H. E. (2003) *Working with Groupware: Understanding and Evaluating Collaboration Technology*, Springer-Verlag, London.

Argyris, C. and Schon, D. A. (1978) *Organizational Learning: A Theory of Action Perspective*, Addison-Wesley, Reading, MA.

Associated Press Financial Wire (2009) 'Cisco and Tata Consultancy Services announce strategic alliance', *Associated Press Financial Wire*.

Balaji, F. (2008) 'India IT industry caught in unpredictable times: Ramadorai', *Indo-Asian News Service*, Bangalore.

Beer, S. (1972) *Brain of the Firm*, Allen Lane, London.

Bonasia, J. (2008) 'TCS wary of rivals, wage hikes: falling U.S. dollar, too; India's Tata Consultancy offers high-end services, cultivates Europe, Asia', *Investor's Business Daily*, National edn.

Bose, R. (2002) 'Customer relationship management: Key components for IT success', *Industrial Management & Data Systems*, 102(2), 89–97.

Checkland, P. B. (1981) *Systems Thinking, Systems Practice*, Wiley, Chichester.

Churchman, C. W. (1970) 'Operations research as a profession', *Management Science*, 17(2), 37–53.

Choudhury, A. R. (2005) 'The quiet software czar; Amit Roy Choudhury meets a driving force behind India's thiving IT services industry', *The Business Times Singapore*, Singapore.

Corner, I. and Hinton, M. (2002) 'Customer relationship management systems: Implementation risks and relationship dynamics', *Qualitative Market Research*, 5(4), 239–51.

Crosby, L. A. (2002) 'Exploding some myths about customer relationship management', *Managing Service Quality*, 12(5), 271–77.

Davenport, T. H. (1993) *Process Innovation: Re-engineering Work Through Information Technology*, Harvard Business School Press, Boston, MA.

De, A. (2003) 'Chip off a new block', *Tata Consultancy Services Media Reports*, India.

Deming, W. E. (1986) *Out of the Crisis*, MIT Press, Boston, MA.

Flood, R. L. and Jackson, M. C. (1991) *Creative Problem Solving: Total Systems Intervention*, John Wiley & Sons, Chichester.

Frazee, V. (1996) 'Six reasons for going paperless', *Personnel Journal*, 75(11), 70–1.

Gao, F., Li, M. and Nakamori, Y. (2002) 'Systems thinking on knowledge and its management: systems methodology for knowledge management', *Journal of Knowledge Management*, 6(1), 7–17.

Hammer, M. and Champy, J. (1993) *Re-engineering the Corporation: A Manifesto for Business Revolution*, Nicholas Brealey, London.

Holsapple, C. W. and Whinston, A. B. (1996) *Decision Support Systems: A Knowledge-Based Approach*, West Publishing, St. Paul, MN.

Huczynski, A. and Buchanan, D. (2001) *Organisational Behaviour*, Pearson Education Limited, Harlow, Essex.

Juran, J. M. (1950) *Quality Control Handbook*, McGraw-Hill, New York.

Laudon, K. C. and Laudon, J. P. (2010) *Management Information Systems: Organization and Technology in the Networked Enterprise,* 11th edition, Prentice-Hall, Upper Saddle River, NJ.

Linstone, H. A. (1994) *The Challenge of the 21st Century*, State University of New York, Albany, NY.

Maier, R. (2001) *Knowledge Management Systems: Information and Communication Technologies for Knowledge Management,* Springer-Verlag, Berlin.

Mason, R. O. and Mitroff, I. I. (1981) *Challenging Strategic Planning Assumptions*, Wiley, New York.

O'Brien, R. (1991) 'Brief case: EIS and strategic control', *Long Range Planning*, 24(5), 125–7.

PriceWaterhouse (1995) *Information Technology Review 1995/6*, PriceWaterhouse, London.

Raghunathan, S. (1999) 'Impact of information quality and decision-maker quality on decision quality: A theoretical model and simulation analysis', *Decision Support Systems*, 26(4), 275–86.

Raynes, M. (2002) 'Document management: Is the time right now?', *Work Study*, 51(6), 303–08.

Rowley, J. (1999) 'Document publishing systems: A review of current issues', *Online & CD-ROM Review*, 23(1), 3–9.

Ruggles, R. (1998) 'The state of the notion: Knowledge management in practice', *California Management Review*, 40(3), 80–89.

Sánchez, A. M. and Pérez, M. P. (2001) 'Lean indicators and manufacturing strategies', *International Journal of Operations & Production Management*, 21(11), 1433–51.

Shewhart, W. (1931) *Economic Control of Quality of Manufactured Product,* Van Norstrand, New York.

Taylor, F. W. (1911) *Principles of Scientific Management*, Harper, New York.

The Financial Express (2004) 'TCS gets a peep into employee minds', *The Financial Express*.

Trist, E. L. (1959) *Socio-technical Systems*, University of Cambridge: Department of Engineering & Psychology, Cambridge.

Turban, E. and Aronson, J. E. (2001) *Decision Support Systems and Intelligent Systems*, Prentice Hall, Upper Saddle River, NJ.

Ulrich, W. (1983) *Critical Heuristics of Social Planning*, Haupt, Berne.

van der Aalst, W. and van Hee, K. (2002) *Workflow Management: Models, Methods, and Systems*, MIT Press, Cambridge, MA.

Weber, M. (1947) *The Theory of Social and Economic Organization*, A. M. Henderson and T. Parsons, translators, Oxford University Press, Oxford.

Wen, H. J., Yen, D. C. and Lin, B. (1998) 'Intranet document management systems', *Internet Research: Electronic Networking Applications and Policy*, 8(4), 338–46.

Womack, J. P., and Jones, D. T. (1996) *Lean Thinking: Banish Waste and Create Wealth in Your Corporation*, Simon and Schuster, New York.

Womack, J. P., Jones, D. T. and Ros, D. (1990) *The Machine That Changed the World*, Rawson Associates, New York.

Zairi, M., Oakland, J. and Chang, S. (1998) 'Achieving a successful EIS: Linking TQM and best practice', *Integrated Manufacturing Systems*, 9(1), 50–61.

Part 5

MOBILISING KNOWLEDGE

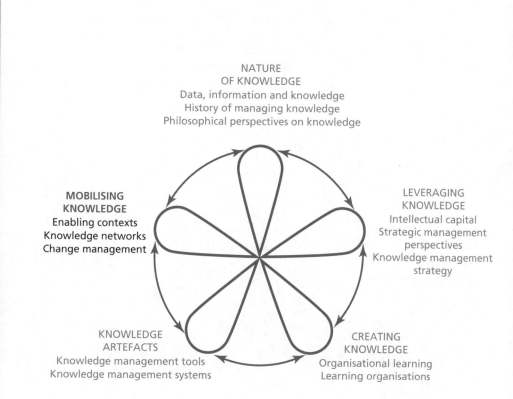

NATURE
OF KNOWLEDGE
Data, information and knowledge
History of managing knowledge
Philosophical perspectives on knowledge

MOBILISING
KNOWLEDGE
Enabling contexts
Knowledge networks
Change management

LEVERAGING
KNOWLEDGE
Intellectual capital
Strategic management
perspectives
Knowledge management
strategy

KNOWLEDGE
ARTEFACTS
Knowledge management tools
Knowledge management systems

CREATING
KNOWLEDGE
Organisational learning
Learning organisations

Chapter 9

Enabling knowledge contexts and networks

Learning outcomes

After completing this chapter the reader should be able to:

- explain the distinctions between organisational culture and organisational climate;
- understand the surface manifestations and deeper aspects of organisational culture;
- discuss different approaches to developing knowledge-sharing cultures;
- apply the notion of 'communities of practice' to organisations.

Management issues

An understanding of cultural issues and the development of knowledge-sharing cultures and communities of practice implies these questions for managers:

- How do you embed knowledge management technologies to a given culture?
- What types of cultures are likely to facilitate knowledge sharing and how do you achieve them?
- What is the role of the manager in cultivating communities of practice?

Links to other chapters

Chapter 3   concerns intellectual capital which is clearly an intended outcome of knowledge-sharing cultures and communities of practice.

Chapter 4   examines knowledge management strategies where cultural factors and communities of practice may play a central role.

Chapter 10   explores implementation of knowledge management initiatives and the role of cultural management of the change process.

Building bridges for success

The conventional view that business is all about competition is being challenged by the idea of collaboration, as companies look to find ways of exploiting the power of partnership.

It was not so long ago that business leaders viewed competition as the most appropriate way to achieve their goals. The basic premise was that in any industrial environment there was a finite amount of potential value and the savvy executive tried to beat other companies by gaining as much of the cake as possible.

This focus on competition was played out in many ways. Executive boardrooms were filled with the language of competition, with words such as 'winners', 'losers' and 'battlefields' the norm. People-management practices extolled the virtues of competition through the high value placed on individualised bonuses and rewards.

Over the past five years, however, it has been striking how this fundamental premise has begun to falter. Instead of competition, the discussion in the executive offices is increasingly of collaboration. While the former idea focuses on bosses and hierarchies, and is about withholding knowledge and the exercise of personal power, this new way of management thinking is about working with peers, colleagues and other businesses.

Why collaboration is crucial

The emergence of collaboration is the result of a number of intersecting trends.

The rise of partnership strategies

The first trend is a fundamental change in what constitutes good business strategy and strategic positioning. Over the past decade, it has become clear that executives and their businesses are not, in fact, competing for a piece of finite cake. Instead, they are more interested in making the cake bigger. In the jargon of business strategy, the emphasis is less on 'value appropriation' and more on 'value creation', often in the context of co-creation. According to this logic, new markets can be created – but to do so often requires erstwhile competitors, customers and clients to work together.

This first became apparent in the pharmaceutical industry, which had created and marketed its products through alliances and joint ventures for decades. These relationships allowed individual companies to pull together the breadth of talent and experience required to bring major drugs to the market. The focus on working with partners has forced the companies in this sector to hone their partnership skills and build their collaborative capabilities.

These patterns of collaborative working are now apparent in the telecommunications sectors and IT where it is becoming increasingly untenable to 'go it alone'. Alliances and partnerships require the capacity to work collaboratively with others whom you consider to be more like peers than suppliers.

The knowledge economy

The second trend is a rapid move into the knowledge economy and the focus on innovation of products or services. Research into the history of innovation shows clearly that in the majority of cases, innovations arise as the result of the collective experience and conversations of groups of people. Yet – and here is the real issue – people do not willingly work with each other and share knowledge unless they respect and trust each other. Simply put, innovation is unlikely to occur without some degree of a collaborative culture.

The working styles of Generation Y

While the first two trends are about the business environment, the third trend involves the subtle but profound generational changes that are becoming apparent. To understand these developments, step back for a moment and think about the basic attitudes and values of many of today's CEOs and senior executives. These postwar baby boomers entered a world of competition and individual endeavour.

Typically they had to battle to get a university education, to get a job and to succeed in their career. Competition was the name of the game and they honed their competitive skills and practices as they rose through the corporate hierarchy. These generational cohorts are now in their late 40s and 50s. They may still have their hands on the corporate steering wheel – but coming up after them are two generations with very different attitudes: Generation X and Generation Y.

Generation Y, now up to age 27, is particularly adept at collaborating with others. This is a community-based generation that places enormous value on working with their peers and shies away from the individual competitive nature of the baby boomers. So, as the baby boomers are succeeded in the business world by a generation for whom collaboration is a basic attitude and competency – and for whom collaborative technology is second nature – it is entirely plausible that a more finely tuned collaborative style will emerge.

Advances in collaborative technology

The final trend is technological. As I will show, many of the collaborative experiences in companies take place in highly complex forms that rely on advanced technology to support them. For example, it is not easy to collaborate with someone in another country without asynchronous communication technology such as voicemail and e-mail. It is also difficult to share information without a shared repository of knowledge.

Technology has made possible what demography has made plausible: a wired-up generation for whom communities is central. You may not be on Facebook or Second Life – but your teenage children certainly are.

The complex nature of collaboration

How is collaboration actually taking place? At its most simple, collaboration involves two or more people actively engaging with each other. They could be working on a joint project and sharing an office, or even meeting each other over a coffee to discuss a mutual issue. However, in most cases, collaboration takes an altogether more complicated form.

The magnitude of this complexity was illustrated in a recent study at London Business School supported by the Advanced Institute of Management. Over a period of three years, we studied 52 teams in 15 companies located in both the US and Europe. It became rapidly apparent that collaboration is inevitably occurring in highly complex situations.

Types of collaboration

Complexity of collaboration typically takes a number of forms. It can be created by the sheer number of people involved. At companies such as Nokia, PwC and Reuters, we found collaborative teams of over 100 people to be the norm. Not only is this an incredible scale of collaboration, but these situations are also complex because often the people who are collaborating are scattered across the globe. What is more, given the virtual and international scale of collaboration, the groups are diverse and their members are often strangers. Collaboration is simple when people are interacting with a relatively low number of people, when they are of a similar age, gender, nationality or education level, and when they are located in the same place and already know each other. It is a whole lot more difficult when teams are large, diverse, virtual and unfamiliar with each other.

Supporting complex collaboration

If collaboration is so crucial, what can be done to create a culture of collaboration? Our research shows that collaboration emerges when the culture and expectation are in place, and when the task itself encourages it.

A culture of collaboration

We examined almost 100 factors that could potentially support the emergence of a culture of collaboration. Four were most important:

1 Leadership role modelling: employees are unlikely to behave collaboratively and to value collaboration if they see senior executives competing with each other.

2 There are a number of people practices that appear to support a culture of collaboration: in particular, selecting for collaborative attitudes and induction are particularly important.

3 Individual reward structures act as a barrier to collaboration and should be removed if collaboration is to be encouraged.

4 Collaboration is more likely to take place when people also collaborate in more informal ways, for example, through shared social activities, communities of practice or social enterprise activities.

Together, these four enablers create a culture where the probability of collaboration is increased. However, for collaboration to be productive there needs to be a focus on the competencies of people and the task itself. The general skills of appreciating diversity, managing conflict and commitments are crucial to productive collaboration. Tasks that encourage collaboration are complex, ambiguous and meaningful, and require people to collaborate if the goal is to be achieved.

The ongoing challenges of collaboration

As collaboration becomes one of the defining competencies and strategies for this decade, there are two major issues that will require greater insight. First, technology plays a central role in complex collaboration, particularly when many of the players are virtual. Our research shows that, while most teams currently use asynchronous technology in the form of voicemails and e-mails, surprisingly few make use of video conferencing. Yet in a virtual world, visual identification can be enormously useful as visitors to Second Life can see. The challenge is to understand how technology can support complex collaboration.

At IBM, for example, there are a number of ongoing experiments into using Second Life and personal avatars as a platform for the interactions of virtual teams. These early experiments have been very successful – and so we can expect to see more collaboration mediated by the virtual world of technology. Over the past couple of years, I have worked with a number of people to create a simulation of collaboration in which individuals work in a virtual environment to create an innovative product. As they go through the challenges of attracting people to work with them, assigning tasks, giving feedback and sharing knowledge, they experiment with the styles that work best for them. I believe that these simulated environments will become ever more central to the development of collaborative competencies. Expect some exciting developments over the next couple of years as more and more collaboration is played out in the virtual world with avatars – with possibly multiple identities – standing in for you.

A second challenge over the next decade will be to build a more sophisticated and finessed understanding of the leadership techniques that enable and encourage collaboration. While some of the competencies that we have already will be useful, others need to be realigned and adjusted. In our work, for example, in one paper colleagues and I tried to establish exactly when team leaders should bring the group together. While many leaders had presumed to do so at an early stage, we found this was more likely to create the fault lines that can break collaboration and teams. Working in complex collaborative forms and supporting a cooperative culture are some of the most pressing leadership challenge executives face. They are also some of the most challenging and exciting.

Lynda Gratton is professor of management practice at London Business School. Her latest book, *Hot Spots: Why Some Teams Buzz with Energy and Others Don't*, explores how complex collaboration takes place. For more information, visit Prof Gratton's website at www.lyndagratton.com

For more information on 'Hot Spots', go to www.hotspotmovement.com.

'Bridging faultlines: Overcoming fractures in diverse teams', by Lynda Gratton, Andreas Voigt and Tamara Erickson is published in the Summer 2007 edition of the *Sloan MIT Management Review*.

Source: Article by Lynda Grattan, *Financial Times*, 29 June 2007, copyright © Linda Gratten.

Questions

1 What are the drawbacks of collaborative working?

2 How can technology support complex collaborations?

3 What are the challenges of collaborating in virtual environments?

Introduction

The failure of many information or knowledge management systems is often as a result of cultural factors rather than technological oversights. Culture, by its nature, is a nebulous subject with a variety of perspectives and interpretations. In practice, we may be left with expressions such as 'We don't do it that way around here!'. To the puzzled inquirer, this chapter is about gaining some clarity about the notion of culture and its historic roots in the organisational climate literature. We explore the variety of surface manifestations of culture in organisations as well as its deeper expressions in values, beliefs, attitudes and assumptions. We follow this path so as to better understand the emerging literature in knowledge-sharing cultures. The current literature suggests that such cultures can be cultivated through the deployment of certain artefacts, the promotion of certain values such as 'care' and a healthy dialectic between cooperative and competitive cultures. We proceed to understand the nature of informal groupings called 'communities of practice' in organisations and how they differ from more formal groupings such as project teams. The importance of storytelling and narratives for embedding tacit knowledge cognitively and socially is investigated in detail. The organisational benefits of communities of practice are explored and a blueprint for their development is provided.

Understanding organisational culture and climate

In an attempt to understand social environments and their effects or interactions with individuals, there have been two distinct concepts that have developed in the literature: organisational climate and organisational culture. Organisational climate has much older roots in psychology and was strongly influenced by field theory (Lewin 1948; Lewin 1951). In the Lewinian understanding of social environments, the individual is assumed to be separate from the environment, acting either as a subject or an agent, and the underlying framework for field theory can be expressed simply as:

$$B = f(P,E)$$

where the social processes equate to B = behaviour, P = person and E = environment. In its early conception, climate could be created through leadership styles which produced dependable social situations in three categories, namely autocratic, democratic and laissez-faire (Lewin *et al.* 1939). The climate literature comes from a positivist, functionalist paradigm and measurement of this concept has been strongly influenced by the quantitative measurement of attitudes using the Likert scale (Likert 1967). The use of surveys has been predominant in this approach. One early example is a study of the impact of organisational climate on individual motivation (Litwin and Stringer 1961) which classifies organisational climate along nine dimensions: structure, responsibility, reward, risk, warmth, support, standards, conflict and identity. Most research in this area has focused on measuring either the individual's perception of individual attributes (the 'psychological climate') or the perceptions of organisational attributes (the 'organisational climate'). Hence, debate has continued on whether climate is a 'shared perception' or a 'shared set of conditions' (Denison 1996).

The weakness in the organisational climate literature has been the lack of agreement on metrics, the poor contingent relationships and the lack of clear categorisations of climate that could be used by managers. In response to these weaknesses and a critique of the dominant positivist paradigm of the climate literature, the study of organisational culture developed from strong anthropological and sociological roots. The literature on organisational climate has been relatively neglected recently. Cultural researchers have taken a more qualitative approach and become more interested in inductive accounts to understand the complexity of social phenomena.

One of the most influential anthropologists in cultural studies has been Geertz's (1973) interpretative theory of culture. Geertz's approach is 'semiotic' and focuses on language and symbols to discern what ordinary people consider to be significant in the 'organisational glue' or social contexts that develop through interaction. Other anthropological roots of cultural studies come from symbolic interaction (Mead 1934) and questioning values and practices in western societies. The other main intellectual tradition of cultural research is sociology, looking at social reality from a variety of social construction perspectives (Berger and Luckmann 1966; Durkheim 1984; Weber 1947) such as myths, rituals, symbols, norms and ambiguity. An interesting development of cultural scholarship has been the promotion of culture from a postmodern and critical theory perspective (Alvesson 2002). Culture is not inside people's heads but exists in the interactions and material objects where symbols and meanings are publicly expressed.

Critical thinking and reflection

Culture is often described as the way we do things around here. How would you describe the culture of your organisation? How homogeneous would you describe this culture? Are you aware of subcultures that exist within your organisation? How prevalent are they? Have you observed any changes in your organisational culture over the past few years? What were the driving forces for these changes and how effective were these changes in your opinion?

As ontological and epistemological assumptions of climate and culture begin to merge, it is clear that these two concepts become less differentiated (Ashkanasy *et al*. 2000b). Quantitative survey-based research is seen in climate research (O'Reilly *et al*. 1991) and interpretivist dimensions can be found in cultural studies. A realist perspective that tries to integrate these two concepts and builds on the popular three-level model of culture (Schein 1985b) is shown in Figure 9.1. Organisational climate is the static or temporary phenomenon found in norms and organisational artefacts that can be determined through traditional survey-based approaches. In contrast, organisational culture is the result of processes that arise from dynamic interactions between individuals or members of a social system. The 'cultural soup' or structures that underlie organisational cultures are the deeply held values, beliefs, attitudes and assumptions in the organisation.

There are a multivariate number of definitions on organisational culture and climate which are based on the ontological and epistemological positions of the researchers. One definition that tends to contrast the widely accepted distinctions between the two phenomena is (Denison 1996):

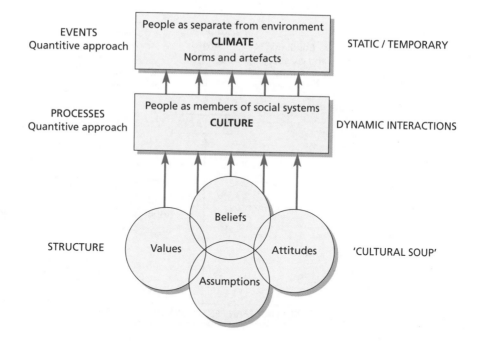

Figure 9.1 Distinction between culture and climate in organisational environments

'Culture refers to the deep structure of organizations, which is rooted in the values, beliefs and assumptions held by organizational members. Meaning is established through socialization to a variety of identity groups that converge in the workplace. Interaction reproduces a symbolic world that gives culture both a great stability and a certain precarious and fragile nature rooted in the dependence of the system on individual cognition and action.

Climate, in contrast, portrays organisational environments as being rooted in the organisation's value system, but tends to present these social environments in relatively static terms, describing them in terms of a fixed (and broadly applicable) set of dimensions. Thus, climate is often considered as temporary, subject to direct control, and largely limited to those aspects of the social environment that are consciously perceived by organisational members.'

Norms, artefacts and symbols

At a more surface or superficial level, we have the manifestation of culture as norms, artefacts and symbols, as shown in Figure 9.2. Norms are expectations of appropriate and inappropriate behaviour. This may be norms about dress code or issues such as expectations surrounding performance and handling conflict (bottling it up or confronting it). Norms attach approval or disapproval to holding certain beliefs and attitudes and acting in particular ways. They can vary along two dimensions (O'Reilly 1989):

- intensity of approval or disapproval attached to an expectation;
- degree of consistency with which a norm is shared.

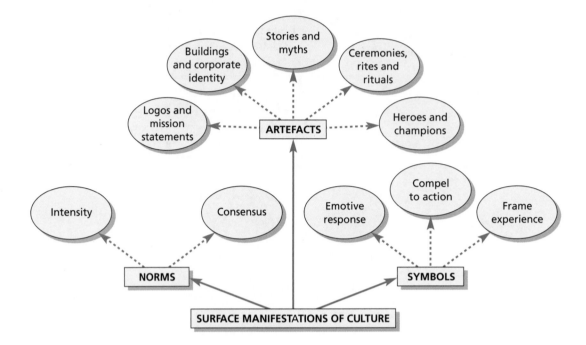

Figure 9.2 **Surface manifestations of organisational culture**

For example, there may be consensus over senior management values such as respect and integrity but little intensity one way or the other. Or there may be strong approval and disapproval for the same value such as excellence in the organisation leading to great intensity but little consensus. When great intensity and consensus exists in an organisation, this leads to a strong culture where organisational members share a common set of expectations. If there is a weak culture in the organisation (low intensity and consensus), there is a greater likelihood of sub-cultures forming. An example of norms for promoting innovation in organisations is provided in Table 9.1. These collective norms are based on a study of over 500 managers from diverse industries sharing very similar expectations on what they saw as necessary for innovation in organisations. A useful tool in a change management programme would be to conduct a survey of existing and desired norms and base organisational interventions on assisting a convergence between these two norms.

Table 9.1 **Examples of norms that promote innovation** (O'Reilly 1989)

Norms to promote creativity	Norms to promote implementation
Risk taking	**Common goals**
• Acceptance of mistakes	• Eliminate mixed messages
• No punishment for failure	• Build consensus
Rewards for change	**Autonomy**
• Ideas are valued	• Freedom to act
• Top management support and attention	• Minimise bureaucracy
Openness	**Belief in action**
• Listen better	• Anxiety about timeliness
• Encourage lateral thinking	• Eagerness to get things done

Artefacts also provide us with shared systems of meaning that construct organisational life. They can exist as material objects, physical layouts, technology, language and behaviour patterns as well as procedures and practices in organisations (Brown 1998).

Material artefacts can exist as company logos and mission statements. Company logos give us clear signals of the meaning and values behind them. Mission statements inform the reader about company aspirations in terms of its principal aims, beliefs and values. However, there may be a serious gap between the senior management rhetoric glossed over in these mission statements and the reality at ground level.

The corporate architecture and identity in terms of appearance and uniform also provide clues about an organisation's culture. The nature of the building, its external appearance, its internal layout and furniture can provide signals to organisational members about how the company values them and their interactions with others. For example, the organisation may provide open-plan offices, water fountains and subsidised restaurant facilities to encourage interaction and dialogue with different levels of the organisation. Or the corporate building may be compartmentalised to prevent dialogue and reinforce divisional or operational boundaries. In each case, we learn a bit more about the organisational culture. Many large organisations commission buildings by renowned architects to reinforce their identity and show clear signs of opulence.

Stories are powerful artefacts that tell us about problems and solutions, disasters and triumphs. They also tell us about informal rules and procedures; how things are done around here. War stories encourage an understanding of what happened and why in a particular circumstance. They also convey indicators of status and the norms of compliance and deviation from rules. Stories enable organisations to develop their own unique identity. A common deviant of stories are myths. They are based on unjustified beliefs and recounted as stories. They serve the purpose of influencing action in particular contexts. For example, there may be myths about superhuman characteristics of certain individuals or groups and derogatory characteristics of some others. These may be perpetuated as part of the organisational culture even though they bear little resemblance to reality.

Recurrent patterns of behaviour such as ceremonies, rites and rituals remind and reinforce organisational members of cultural values (Brown 1998). Ceremonies may include presentations and prizes for high achievers. Corporate heroes or champions may be celebrated in order to share their success stories and the values communicated through them. Rites may be planned activities such as rites of passage from one role or status to another. Rituals may include company retreats and away days. In each case, these cultural artefacts help individuals develop a deeper sense of company values.

Organisational culture can be construed as a network of meanings or shared experiences that provide members with a shared and accepted reality (Pettigrew 1979). This shared reality can derive from certain symbols that may stand for a multiplicity of meanings that serve to link emotions and interpretations and compel people to action. For example, working late at night above one's contracted hours may symbolise loyalty to an organisation. Accordingly, symbols can act to reflect aspects of organisational culture, frame experiences that may be vague or controversial, and mobilise members to action through their emotional response to a symbol (Ashkanasy *et al.* 2000b). Symbols are rich in meaning and can occur as a word, a statement, an action or a material phenomenon. There are private symbols and collective symbols which stand ambiguously for something else or more than the object itself (Alvesson 2002).

Values, beliefs, attitudes and assumptions

All too often, senior managers and chief executives place considerable effort in formulating their corporate values statement. However, why is it that many of these values statements can be bland, hollow and meaningless? They may lack credibility and have the undesired effect of generating cynicism, alienation and insincerity. The corporate values may stand for nothing with organisational members and a gulf emerges between organisational rhetoric and reality.

Instead of differentiating a company by clarifying its identity and motivating employees, they may actually have the opposite effect of being destructive to the organisation. For example, the relatively meaningless corporate values of Enron are: Communication, Respect, Integrity and Excellence.

Critical thinking and reflection

What do you see as potential problems in a values-led organisation or a values-led society? How would you describe your own values? From your experience, have you had encounters where your values have differed dramatically from your organisation's values? If so, please describe the nature of disparity in values and how you managed the situation? Given that many organisations work in multicultural environments, what would you consider to be some pitfalls in organisational values?

In contrast, real values are far from being bland and can be painful for organisations as they constrain strategic and operational freedom as well as individual behaviour. They demand constant monitoring and may leave executives open to criticism for minor breaches. Organisational values fall into four categories and it is important to avoid confusion between them (Lencioni 2002):

- Core values are deeply ingrained principles that guide a company's actions. They are never compromised for convenience or economic gain and often reflect the values of the company founders.

- Aspirational values are values to support a new strategy. They are values that the company needs to compete in the future but currently lacks.

- Permission-to-play values are the minimum behavioural and social standards required of employees in the organisation.

- Accidental values are values that arise spontaneously over time. They reflect the common interests or personalities of employees. They may be positive, such as inclusivity of employees, or negative, such as an ingrained mistrust of management.

But what is the best way of developing a corporate values statement? The traditional method of the HR departments conducting numerous surveys and focus groups to build consensus is to be avoided because such consensus may integrate values that do not belong to the organisation and give an equal weighting to all employee contributions. For example, senior managers may feel that certain values espoused by certain employees might better belong to other organisations than their own. Hence, a more appropriate response to values statement development is to form a small team of executives including the chief executive to discuss values over a long time frame and provide enough time for reflection of the consequences of these values in the workplace (Lencioni 2002). Core values guide every action and decision that a company makes. They form the fabric underlying every recruitment, selection, appraisal and rewards policy. If the core values are poorly implemented, they can lead to mistrust and cynicism of senior management motives. Core values require constant vigilance to make explicit what a firm stands for and to act as a rallying call to employees to guide their actions. They can reinforce individual commitment and willingness to give energy and loyalty to an organisation. Individuals may make sacrifices and investments based on corporate values.

Values have considerable potency as they tend to link the social, cognitive and behavioural dimensions of an organisation. The social aspects characterise the history of experiences and understandings of groups within the organisation. The cognitive aspects draw on the history and experiences of individuals within these groups and the behavioural aspects show how these values affect individual actions and interactions (Ashkanasy *et al.* 2000b).

Beliefs are another core manifestation of culture and concern what people think is true. For example, some executives may believe that focusing organisational efforts on efficiency is more likely to lead to greater organisational performance whereas others may believe it is an innovation strategy. Sometimes values and beliefs may be hard to distinguish, especially where the belief and value such as innovation are closely related. Values could be considered as enduring beliefs where certain actions are considered socially more appropriate than others (Rokeach 1973).

Our attitudes connect our beliefs and values with feelings (Brown 1998). They are a learnt predisposition to act in a favourable or unfavourable manner to a given circumstance and involve evaluations based on our feelings. Attitudes are more enduring than opinions and have an impact on an individual's motivation. They can result in prejudices and stereotypes, such as the negative attitudes towards quality circles in the United States as workers did not feel that sitting down in groups and talking about quality was beneficial.

Basic assumptions are the taken-for-granted solutions to particular problems (Brown 1998). They are the 'theories-in-use' (Argyris and Schon 1978) that perpetuate organisational routines and single-loop learning. Assumptions are unconsciously held, making them difficult to confront or make explicit. They are highly complex interpretations based on our beliefs, values and emotions. One typology of basic assumptions considers five dimensions (Schein 1985a):

- whether an organisation dominates the external environment or is dominated by it;
- whether truth and reality are received dogma, rules and procedures, a consequence of debate or what works;
- whether people are inherently lazy or self-motivated;
- whether 'doing' and work are more primary than 'being' and valuing employees' private lives;
- whether human interaction is based on individualism or collectivism.

Typologies of organisational culture

In the language of organisational culture, it may be useful to provide classifications for different configurations of culture found in organisations. It is not expected that organisations will necessarily fall into these idealised types, but their characteristics may help organisations understand their social environments. Two popular typologies of organisational culture are provided below (Brown 1998; Deal and Kennedy 1982; Handy 1985; Scholz 1987). The Handy typology has been very influential among cultural scholars and suggests four types of culture (Handy 1985), as shown in Figure 9.3:

- *Power cultures* are characterised as a web with a person or small group of people at the centre. There are few rules and people tend to act politically and are more concerned about ends rather than means. Such organisations can react quickly to environmental changes but may suffer from high turnover rates if suitable people are not recruited.
- *Role cultures* are characterised by bureaucracies where rules, procedures and job descriptions tend to predominate. They are successful in stable environments but may have difficulties adapting to more turbulent environments.
- *Task cultures* are characterised by project or matrix organisations that bring together the appropriate resources and competence required for effective team functioning. Mutual respect is based on ability rather than status or age. These cultures can be highly effective for innovative projects but are less successful where there is an emphasis on cost rationalisation and economies of scale.

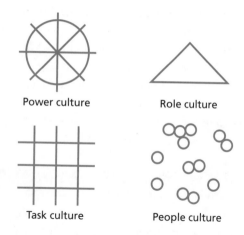

Figure 9.3 **Handy's typology of culture** (Handy 1985)

- *Person cultures* are characterised by individual autonomy and collective action based on fulfilling individual self-interests. Individuals decide on their work allocations rather than it being a function of a central body. Examples of person cultures may be found in academia, among architects or barristers.

Another popular cultural typology is based on the degree of risk in company activities and the speed of feedback on actions and decisions, as shown in Figure 9.4 (Brown 1998; Deal and Kennedy 1982). In this framework, the four idealised cultural typologies are:

- tough-guy, macho culture characterised by high risks and fast feedback on actions. This culture focuses on speed and can lead to internal competition and tensions as individuals take high risks. These cultures are predominantly uncooperative and can lead to high staff turnover. Similarities with the power culture?

- work-hard, play-hard culture characterised by low-risk but quick-feedback environments. These cultures can be fun and action oriented but may suffer from 'quick-fix' solutions and lack of reflection in crisis situations. Similar to a task culture?

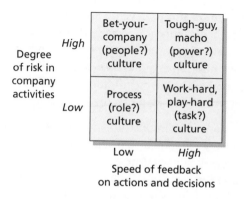

Figure 9.4 **Deal and Kennedy's typology of culture**

- bet-your-company culture characterised by high-risk but low-feedback environ-ments. There is a greater tendency towards cooperative endeavours and producing innovations in such cultures. Similarities with a people culture?

- process cultures exist in low-risk and slow-feedback environments. Due to the low levels of feedback, the organisations are characterised by procedures, rules and hier-archies. They can be threatening in highly changeable environments as they are unable to respond quickly. Similarities with a role culture?

Measuring organisational culture

Despite the strong anthropological and sociological roots of cultural research, there have been numerous attempts to conceptualise and quantify the construct of 'organis-ational culture'. In this sense, the quantification of culture as an instrument has adopted the traditional methodologies found in climate research. This relates to the more observable and accessible levels of culture, the surface manifestations. If one accepts the realist notion of organisational culture as a process (see Figure 9.5), is it fea-sible or meaningful to quantify this process?

Currently, there is little consensus about the nature of the 'organisational culture' construct and its various subconstructs. Hence, a number of instruments have been developed with a varying level of homage to existing theory. The types of surveys can be classified into two categories (Ashkanasy *et al.* 2000a):

- *Typing surveys* classify organisations into particular typologies such as the Handy or Deal and Kennedy ones shown above. Such instruments attempt to generate a number of organisational culture 'types' that have certain behaviours and values linked with them. These surveys can provide senior managers with snapshots on their current positions and their desired outcomes from a cultural change manage-ment programme. The drawbacks with these typing surveys is that they assume that organisations fit neatly into strictly defined categories rather than conforming to a number of different types that demonstrate their uniqueness. The different types do not assume a continuity between the different typologies.

- *Profiling surveys* aim to develop a profile of the organisation on multiple categories of norms, behaviours and values. There are three types of profiling surveys, namely effectiveness surveys, descriptive surveys and fit profiles. *Effectiveness surveys* tend to assess organisational values associated with high levels of performance. *Descriptive surveys* purely measure organisational values. *Fit profiles* tend to assess the level of fit between an individual and an organisation.

Organisational culture instruments can be used in a variety of contexts: to monitor and evaluate organisational change, to identify cultures of high-performing teams and to facilitate mergers and acquisitions. There are numerous culture instruments available but few that meet the acid test of high levels of reliability and show clear evidence of validity (convergent, discriminant, nomological and known groups). One such instrument that meets these rigours of instrument development and is widely used is the 'Organizational Culture Inventory®' (OCI®) (Cooke and Lafferty 1987). The instrument is based on two

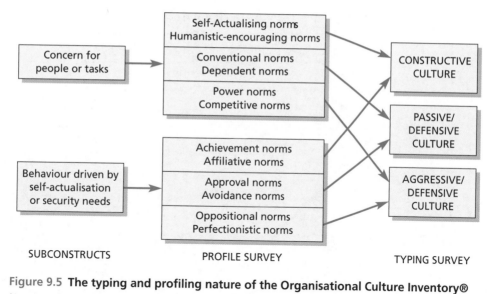

Figure 9.5 **The typing and profiling nature of the Organisational Culture Inventory®**
(OCI cluster and style names from R. A. Cooke and J. C. Lafferty, *Organizational Culture Inventory*, Human Synergistics International. Copyright © 1987–2010. All rights reserved. Organizational Culture Inventory® and OCI® are registered trademarks of Human Synergistics International)

subconstructs of 'concern for people or tasks' and 'behaviour driven by security or self-actualisation needs', as shown in Figure 9.5. The instrument provides a typing survey in terms of three categories of culture as well as a profile survey of the organisation against a variety of norms. The twelve norms for any organisation can be plotted on an OCI circumplex, as shown in Figure 9.6, and the description of each norm is given below.

▶ Description of the twelve OCI styles

The following style descriptions and sample items are from *Organizational Culture Inventory* by R. A. Cooke and J. C. Lafferty, 1983, 1986, 1987, 1989, Plymouth, Michigan, USA: Human Synergistics. Copyright © 1989 by Human Synergistics International. Reproduced by permission.

Constructive norms (styles promoting satisfaction behaviours)

Achievement: an Achievement culture characterises organisations that do things well and value members who set and accomplish their own goals. Members are expected to set challenging but realistic goals, establish plans to reach those goals, and pursue them with enthusiasm. (Pursue a standard of excellence)

Self-Actualising: a Self-Actualising culture characterises organisations that value creativity, quality over quantity, and both task accomplishment and individual growth. Members are encouraged to gain enjoyment from their work, develop themselves, and take on new and interesting activities. (Think in unique and independent ways)

Humanistic-Encouraging: a Humanistic-Encouraging culture characterises organisations that are managed in a participative and person-centred way. Members are expected to be supportive, constructive and open to influence in their dealings with one another. (Help others to grow and develop)

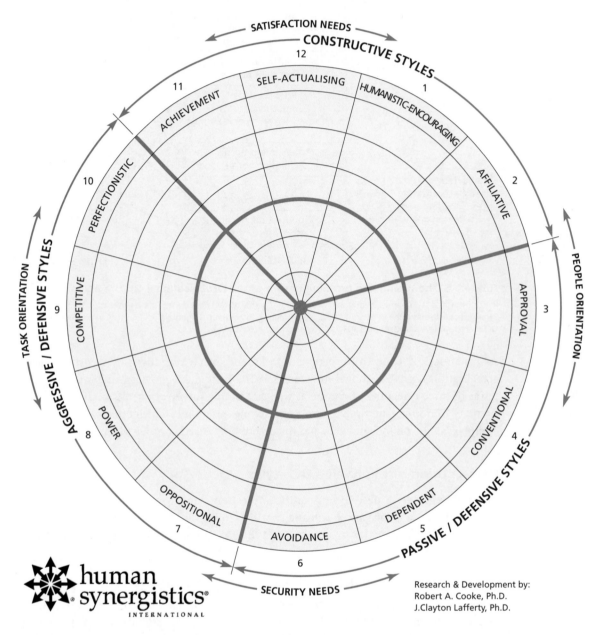

Figure 9.6 **Organizational Culture Inventory circumplex** (© 1987–2010 by Human Synergistics International. All Rights Reserved. Reproduced by permission)

Affiliative: an Affiliative culture characterises organisations that place a high priority on constructive interpersonal relationships. Members are expected to be friendly, open and sensitive to the satisfaction of their work group. (Deal with others in a friendly way)

Passive/Defensive norms (styles promoting people-security behaviours)

Approval: an Approval culture describes organisations in which conflicts are avoided and interpersonal relationships are pleasant – at least superficially. Members feel that they should agree with, gain approval of, and be liked by others. ('Go along' with others)

Conventional: a Conventional culture is descriptive of organisations that are conservative, traditional and bureaucratically controlled. Members are expected to conform, follow the rules and make a good impression. (Always follow policies and practices)

Dependent: a Dependent culture is descriptive of organisations that are hierarchically controlled and non-participative. Centralised decision making in such organisations leads members to do only what they are told and to clear all decisions with superiors. (Please those in positions of authority)

Avoidance: an Avoidance culture characterises organisations that fail to reward success but nevertheless punish mistakes. This negative reward system leads members to shift responsibilities to others and avoid any possibility of being blamed for a mistake. (Wait for others to act first)

Aggressive/Defensive norms (styles promoting task-security behaviours)

Oppositional: an Oppositional culture describes organisations in which confrontation and negativism are rewarded. Members gain status and influence by being critical and thus are reinforced to oppose the ideas of others. (Point out flaws)

Power: a Power culture is descriptive of non-participative organisations structured on the basis of authority inherent in members' positions. Members believe they will be rewarded for taking charge, controlling subordinates and, at the same time, being responsive to the demands of superiors. (Build up one's power base)

Competitive: a Competitive culture is one in which winning is valued and members are rewarded for outperforming one another. Members operate in a 'win–lose' framework and believe they must work against (rather than with) their peers to be noticed. (Turn the job into a contest)

Perfectionistic: a Perfectionistic culture characterises organisations in which perfectionism, persistence and hard work are valued. Members feel they must avoid any mistake, keep track of everything and work long hours to attain narrowly defined objectives. (Do things perfectly)

In international contexts and particularly among multinational corporations, there has been considerable interest in the role of national cultures on organisational cultures. For example, do 'American organisational cultures' or 'Japanese organisational cultures' lead to greater effectiveness? One seminal study in this area conducted a descriptive survey of national culture across 40 nations and derived distinctions between national cultures along four value dimensions (Hofstede 1980). The theoretical basis for this study arises from a psychological, anthropological and sociological review of national character (Inkeles and Levinson 1969). The four value dimensions that differentiate national character are (Hofstede 1980):

- *power distance* – the extent to which the less powerful members of organisations and institutions accept and expect that power is distributed unequally. (Example: high power distance – Malaysia and Venezuela; low power distance – Sweden, New Zealand);

- *individualism versus collectivism* – the extent to which individuals are integrated into groups. (Example: individualist – USA and Netherlands; collectivist – Ecuador and Indonesia);

- *masculinity versus femininity* – assertiveness and competitiveness versus modesty and caring. (Example: Masculine – Japan and Mexico; feminine – Norway and Costa Rica);
- *uncertainty avoidance* – intolerance for uncertainty and ambiguity. (Example: high uncertainty avoidance – Greece and Guatemala; low uncertainty avoidance – Singapore and Denmark).

Critical thinking and reflection

Reflect on situations where you have had cultural misunderstandings among friends or colleagues at work. How did you manage those situations and what lessons did you learn? How could some of those misunderstandings have been avoided and better cultural understanding be promoted in your organisation?

Creating knowledge-sharing cultures

Many executives aspire to develop knowledge-sharing cultures where knowledge is shared easily among organisational members through social and electronic networks. This aspiration is also a primary assumption behind the knowledge management literature that knowledge-sharing cultures are more conducive to knowledge creation and enhanced performance. But how do we turn this aspirational value of knowledge sharing into a core value? Let's assume that the culture in many organisations may be hostile to knowledge sharing and more conducive to knowledge hoarding. For example, 'power' or 'tough-guy' cultures may be highly political and uncooperative environments. What interventions are likely to help senior managers in these circumstances steer a clear path in managing cultural change? (See next chapter.) If the interventions are successful, have we unintentionally changed strong effective cultures with little consideration of their strategic impact?

Are there dangers in assuming that knowledge-sharing cultures are effective in all situations? If we follow this line of reasoning, one could argue that ultimately organisations need to move towards idealised forms of cultures such as task or person cultures that promote knowledge sharing. However, we know that there is a diversity of cultures that are equally effective in different industries. The reality is that cultural research in this area is limited and has not begun to address the complexity of managing aspirational values of knowledge sharing and their likely impact on the organisation. If such values are managed wrongly, they may appear hollow, lack credibility and generate widespread cynicism. Organisational members will pay lip-service to these perceived management fads and the interventions will fail to win over 'hearts and minds'.

Our current understanding of developing cultures for knowledge creation is based on the deployment of artefacts (Nonaka and Konno 1998), the promotion of certain values (von Krough 1999), a healthy cultural dialectic (Jashapara 2003) and certain prescriptions based on a few case studies (McDermott and O'Dell 2001; Newell *et al.* 2002). The deployment of artefacts, 'Ba' or spaces builds on an earlier 'SECI' model of knowledge conversion between different forms of tacit and explicit knowledge (Nonaka 1991), as shown in Figure 9.7.

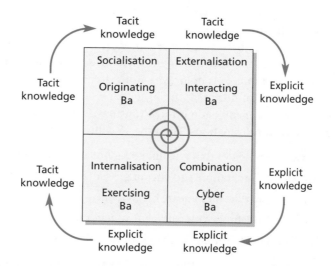

Figure 9.7 Knowledge conversion and characteristics of 'Ba' (Nonaka and Konno 1998)

The concept of 'Ba' is new to many western palettes and translates to a place or space in Japanese. This artefact of space or 'Ba' can be physical, virtual or mental. On first impressions, this model is examining the surface manifestations of culture in terms of artefacts. The model does not suggest whether the 'mental spaces' of 'Ba' go more deeply and manifest as attitudes, beliefs and values. There are four types of 'Ba' which tend to facilitate the different aspects of the knowledge conversion process (Nonaka and Konno 1998):

- Socialisation involves sharing tacit knowledge between individuals. Tacit knowledge is considered as more than 'know how' and can include intuitions, hunches and insights. It is deeply embedded in a person's values and beliefs. The space that contributes to socialisation is 'Originating Ba' where individuals share feelings, emotions, experiences and mental models. The values that support the transfer of this tacit knowledge are care, love, trust and commitment.

- Externalisation involves the articulation of tacit into explicit knowledge. This conversion normally occurs through dialogue and the use of figurative language, metaphors, narratives, images and creative inference. The space required to facilitate this knowledge conversion is 'Interacting Ba'. The main characteristic of this artefact is dialogue where individuals share their mental models and reflect and analyse their own understandings.

- Combination involves conversion of explicit knowledge into more complex explicit forms. This may arise from capturing, collecting, sorting, editing and integrating new explicit knowledge. Such conversions are promoted through 'Cyber Ba'. These cyber spaces encourage the documentation of knowledge and the use of databases and groupware tools.

- Internalisation relies on converting explicit into tacit knowledge. This usually occurs through experience (learning-by-doing) and training. The spaces that encourage such conversions are 'Exercising Ba', characterised by reflection through learning, training and mentoring.

A development of the 'Originating Ba' artefact promoting socialisation is the suggestion that the primary value in knowledge creation is 'care' (von Krough 1998). Care is characterised by considerable mutual trust, active empathy, access to help, lenience in judgement and courage. Sounds like love but without the organisational embarrassment! The emphasis is on organisations to cherish the value of care/love at all costs. If this value is not nurtured, the likely consequences are the emergence of greater levels of fear where members reinforce routines and scare stories, abandon good ideas and stunt any transformations. The ways to cultivate care are:

- incentive schemes that encourage care-related behaviour;
- mentoring programmes to encourage senior members to transfer their knowledge;
- training programmes in care behaviour;
- project debriefings with sufficient time for reflection;
- social events to improve organisational relationships.

The assumption from the 'care' perspective is that supportive or cooperative cultures are more likely to result in knowledge creation. This view is challenged as highly cooperative or supportive environments (such as a kibbutz) can discourage change and, if organisational members perceive a need for change, they may be forced to challenge the dominant ideology which breeds politics and fear. Instead, research shows that effective organisations tend to operate in a 'zone of knowledge creation' in a dialectic between the internal forces of cooperation and competition (Jashapara 2003), as shown in Figure 9.8. Extreme forms of these idealised cultures are likely to suppress the very knowledge they are trying to create. In this conception, the dialectic of knowledge-sharing cultures can be viewed as a continual struggle by groups of organisational members to impose their values and identities on the role of others (Carroll 1995).

Critical thinking and reflection

Reflect on your experiences of knowledge sharing. What social environments have made you feel more comfortable about sharing your knowledge? Do you think that incentives would help you share knowledge more easily in your organisation? If so, what form do you think these incentives should take? Are there aspects of your knowledge base that you would be unwilling to share under any circumstance? If so, can you elaborate on the unique quality of this prized knowledge asset?

Efforts in cultural engineering are often doomed to fail if they do not support the more deeply held organisational values and assumptions. An alternative approach adopted by many effective companies is to build knowledge management interventions that fit the embedded culture. In some organisations, such as PricewaterhouseCoopers (PwC) and American Management Systems (AMS), knowledge sharing was explicit and directly informed corporate strategy. Clear knowledge-sharing programmes were developed including reward and recognition initiatives, and distinct roles and responsibilities related to knowledge sharing, such as the appointment of a chief knowledge

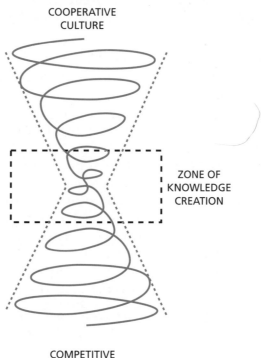

COOPERATIVE
CULTURE

ZONE OF
KNOWLEDGE
CREATION

COMPETITIVE
CULTURE

Figure 9.8 The zone of knowledge creation and the dialectic between cooperation and competitive cultures

officer. In other organisations like Ford and Lotus Development, knowledge sharing was more implicitly embedded into everyday routines and projects. There were different degrees of formal, informal and electronic networks to promote knowledge sharing. A number of lessons arise from different attempts to create a knowledge-sharing culture (McDermott and O'Dell 2001; Newell *et al.* 2002):

- make a visible connection between sharing knowledge and practical business goals;
- match the style of the organisation to the intervention (e.g. developing artefacts such as social events, language and websites);
- promote appropriate reward and recognition interventions;
- provide adequate resources to encourage human networks of knowledge sharing such as time to share ideas and information in communities of practice;
- try to link knowledge sharing with widely and deeply held core values rather than aspirational values;
- encourage 'boundary-spanning' individuals who can translate knowledge and experiences from one group to another;
- support a committed project champion who can enthuse and motivate others with the knowledge-sharing initiative. Bring together people in the organisation who already share ideas and knowledge.

Cultural stickiness: developing communities of practice

Explicit knowledge is relatively easy to codify, store and retrieve as knowledge objects using traditional technologies. However, how do we tackle the externalisation, sharing and integration of tacit knowledge that may be embedded within the minds of organisational members? The holy grail of competitive advantage may be closely related to exploiting the cognitive and social aspects of tacit knowledge. It is often through dialogue and interaction with others that we are able to contact the inner depths of our tacit knowledge and generate new ideas and insights. Many organisations have recognised the intrinsic value of water coolers, coffee machines, subsidised canteens and common rooms as being instrumental in facilitating this creative process.

Another approach to cultivating tacit knowledge that moves beyond organisational artefacts is the notion of 'communities of practice' (Brown and Duguid 1991; Lave and Wenger 1991). Communities of practice are informal, self-selecting groups that are open ended, without any deadlines or deliverables. They exist to serve a number of cognitive and social interests, set their own agendas and elect their own leadership. Communities of practice can be defined as follows (Wenger *et al.* 2002):

'Communities of practice are groups of people who share a concern, a set of problems, or a passion about a topic, and who deepen their knowledge and expertise in this area by interacting on an ongoing basis.'

The World Bank sees communities of practice as the main component of its knowledge management strategy in its attempts to become a 'knowledge bank'. In this context, tacit knowledge is acknowledged as embedded in organisational practice and interactions rather than simply in the domain of an individual's head. Communities of practice can also exist online as communities of transaction (buying and selling), communities of interest (related to a topic), role-playing communities and communities of relationships (around a shared life experience) (Newell *et al.* 2002). But what are the characteristics of communities of practice that distinguish them from other organisational groupings? A comparison of different groupings in organisations is shown in Table 9.2.

In formal groupings, the common approach to team learning is to adopt tools such as brainstorming or cognitive mapping to encourage dialogue and discussion. However, the success of such approaches may often depend on the motivations (or lack of) of team members, their composition and power relations underlying the team and organisational culture. For example, the use of 'quality circles' was highly successful in Japan where team members got together regularly to share problems and discuss ways of improving work practices. However, the same concept failed to gain acceptance in the US or the UK due to major cultural reservations about discussing problems.

Table 9.2 Characteristics of formal and informal groupings in organisations (Wenger and Snyder 2000)

	Formal groupings 'canonical practice'		Informal groupings 'non-canonical practice'	
	Work group	Project team	Informal network	Community of practice
What is their purpose?	To deliver a product or service	To accomplish a specific task	To collect and pass on business information	To develop members' capabilities; to build and exchange knowledge
Who belongs?	Everyone who reports to group's manager	Employees assigned by senior management	Friends and business acquaintances	Members who select themselves
What holds it together?	Job requirements and common goals	Project's milestones and goals	Mutual needs	Passion, commitment and identification with the group's expertise
How long does it last?	Until the next reorganisation	Until the project is completed	As long as people have a reason to connect	As long as there is interest in maintaining the group

The major interest in communities of practice is that they provide significant benefits to organisations than do more formalised forms of activity. On the social side, they provide individuals with a sense of identity, confidence and trust through meeting like-minded individuals who share similar problems and outlooks. In terms of tacit knowledge, they provide a forum to facilitate knowledge creation through externalisation of tacit knowledge, the sharing of knowledge and increasing knowledge flows, enhanced creativity and integration of collective knowledge. Some direct benefits of communities of practice in organisations are (Wenger and Snyder 2000):

- they help drive strategy;
- they start new lines of business;
- they solve problems quickly;
- they transfer best practices;
- they develop professional skills;
- they help companies recruit and retain talent.

The informal interactions of organisational members in communities of practice are considered to encourage reflection of practice rather than simply reworking everyday processes. People come together from similar backgrounds from around the organisation with a passion and interest in improving practice. Communities of practice can allow organisational members to think outside the box and to question organisational routines where appropriate. This does not necessarily mean that such questioning will always lead to radical innovation, dynamic capabilities or double-loop learning (Swan et al. 2002; Zollo and Winter 2002).

The commonly cited example of communities of practice is a network of technical reps at Xerox who got together regularly over breakfast, lunch and coffee breaks to share their 'war stories' about problems in servicing photocopiers (Orr 1996). Stories were central to sharing such tacit knowledge and making sense of the collective knowledge. A repertoire of stories formed the collective knowledge over time which was greater than anything one could find in organisational repair manuals. In fact, repair manuals on their own would be incapable of solving many of the problems encountered by these reps. There was banter in their dialogue, laughing at mistakes and frequent questioning of the storyteller to test their own understanding. One story recounted two highly competent reps addressing a near impossible situation that defied all standard procedures. A dialogue pursued between these two reps all afternoon where they went through their reasoning associated with the collective knowledge and stories until they were able to narrow down the potential causes and solve the problem through trial and error. This story of course went back into the collective knowledge and psyche of the reps.

Critical thinking and reflection

Reflect on different stories you may have heard in your organisation over the past few months. Describe some of the stories that are foremost in your mind. What role do these stories play in your working life? For example, do they help you to work much better? If so, what aspects of stories have you found useful? How important is the storyteller and can you describe their role in your organisation? How far do these stories make you feel like a communal part of the organisation?

The role of storytelling and narratives for embedding tacit knowledge socially in a community of practice is shown in Figure 9.9. Each story has a connection with certain ideas, lessons and best practice. These ideas relate to different actors in the community of practice who are joined together by strong and weak ties. It is these linkages that provide the embedding of collective tacit knowledge and make it 'sticky' (von Hippel 1994) as it is difficult for other organisations to imitate the complexity of the social and cognitive linkages. This can become a potential source of competitive advantage as it is difficult to commodify the 'sticky' knowledge. Stories are self-perpetuating, creating knowledge that reinforces and renews itself through these connections embedded in work practice. Stories are a powerful way of understanding what happened in a sequence of events and the causes of why they happened (Brown and Duguid 2000). They allow preservation of knowledge and its subsequent diagnosis (Brown and Duguid 1991).

The use of stories and narratives for embedding knowledge in work practice may be considered as a 'perspective making' (Boland and Tenkasi 1995). This is the process by which a community of practice develops and strengthens its knowledge domain and practices. But how do communities of practice facilitate radical innovation or double-loop learning? Many commentators suggest a need for some interaction between different communities of practice as isolated communities can become self-reinforcing and self-deluding, turning core competences into core rigidities (Blacker 1995; Swan et al. 2002). Communication that improves a community's ability to take the knowledge of another community into account is known as 'perspective taking' (Boland and

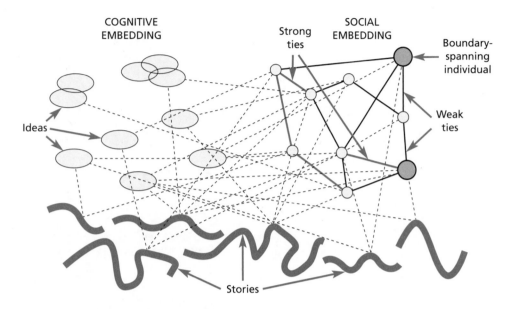

Figure 9.9 **The ontology of storytelling**

Tenkasi 1995). Radical innovation may require embedding new knowledge and work practices and, at the same time, discarding obsolete practices and routines. The sharing of this new knowledge between communities can be promoted in a number of ways (Brown and Duguid 1998):

- Organisational translators can frame the interests of one community in terms of another's perspective. They may be external mediators or consultants.

- Knowledge brokers or boundary-spanning individuals can participate in several communities. The strength of their 'weak ties' may help facilitate knowledge flows between communities.

- Boundary objects such as documents, contracts and architectural plans may coordinate links between communities who may view the boundary objects from many different perspectives. These boundary objects may also include the use of powerful metaphors.

In many organisations, some members may be engaged in professional or occupational networks outside the organisation. Such communities or 'networks of practice' are different from traditional communities of practice as they are not self-selecting but rely on formal institutional arrangements such as examinations to control membership. They engender shared identity between professionals or occupational groups and could be characterised as an intermediate form between canonical and non-canonical practice (see Table 9.2). When communities of practice are composed more of professional networks or networks of practice as shown in Figure 9.10, the issue of power relations between network members and managers becomes more prominent. Communities of practice cease to fulfil many of the emancipatory needs of members as they pursue a greater managerial or professional agenda (Swan *et al.* 2002). This breeds organisational politics due to competing interests and power struggles requiring more conventional interventions such as negotiation and persuasion of community members.

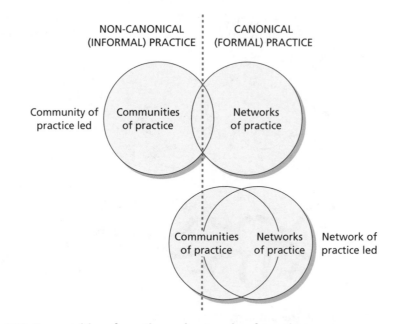

Figure 9.10 Communities of practice and networks of practice

There are a number of measures that organisations can actively take to cultivate rather than constrain communities of practice. Too much control and intervention may have adverse consequences on their development. The following design features are recommended as enhancing communities of practice (Wenger 2000):

- *events* – to bring the community together and tuned to its sense of purpose;
- *leadership* – use of multiple leaders such as 'community coordinator', thought leaders and pioneers;
- *connectivity* – brokering relationships between people to enhance trust and generate dialogue;
- *membership* – critical mass of members but not too large to dilute participation or interest;
- *learning projects* – taking responsibility for learning agenda;
- *artefacts* – producing documents, tools, stories, symbols and websites.

Knowledge across organisational boundaries

Organisational boundaries can be construed as the demarcations between an organisation and its environment. There are currently four distinct conceptions of boundaries: efficiency, power, competence and identity (Santos and Eisenhardt 2005). Each is important for our understanding of how knowledge may flow across boundaries within and outside the firm. Current research is shaped by transaction economics and assumes that knowledge transfer across boundaries is related to exchange-efficiency perspectives. The efficiency conception of a boundary explores whether a transaction is governed by a market or on organisation. The organisation is seen as a set of governing mechanisms and boundaries are set at a point that minimises the cost of these mechanisms. Organisational boundaries are managed in atomistic ways through a number of make-or-buy decisions, and knowledge is conceived as a possession. This notion of efficiency boundaries is most applicable in stable industries characterised by price competition. The limitation of this view is empirical support over causality.

The power conception of boundaries focuses on the sphere of organisational influence. This conception draws on the industrial organisation tradition, and the assumption is that organisational members exert powers of influence outside the firm in the external environment and markets. The organisational focus from this perspective is to maximise strategic control over external forces through exerting organisational influence. This may be to use boundaries that allow firms to protect their knowledge and positions in markets. The sphere of organisational influence on external strategic relationships can affect overall performance. This conception introduces the notion of a permeable boundary and is suitable in cases of imperfect competition.

The competence conception of a boundary focuses on the choice of organisational resources needed with different dynamic environments. This view is informed by contingency theory (Chandler 1962) and the resource-based view of the firm (Penrose 1959). Boundaries develop dynamically through the co-evolution of resource deployment (including knowledge) and the changing nature of environments. Organisational processes such as dynamic capabilities are prevalent in moderately dynamic and high-velocity environments and shape the nature of these boundaries. This perspective draws attention to internal organisational boundaries as well as external ones.

The identity conception of a boundary seeks to explore who the organisation is and whether coherence exists between an organisation's identity and its activities. Organisations are viewed as social contexts for sense-making (Weick 1995). Identity may emerge from the founding fathers of the firm or through social interactions among members, industry and other institutions over time. This conception of boundary reflects all organisational activities consistent with organisational identity. An identity boundary is particularly useful for enabling action in ambiguous environments. This perspective takes into account how unconscious, cognitive and emotional factors related to identity help co-create boundaries (Santos and Eisenhardt 2005).

Carlile (2002, 2004) recognises that the nature of knowledge in organisations is problematic, particularly as knowledge has the capacity to drive innovative problem solving across functions but also to hinder the same processes. From his ethnographic study, he describes knowledge as localised, embedded and invested in practice, and proposes a three-level framework for managing knowledge across boundaries as shown in Figure 9.11. Each level is differentiated by an increasing level of novelty. As the complexity increases, the exact delineation of each boundary becomes less clear, though the higher boundaries do need the capacities of those beneath them.

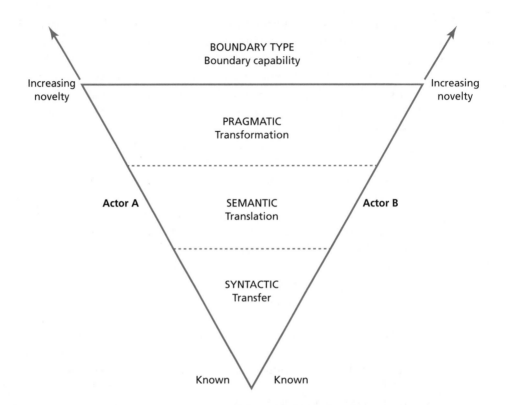

Figure 9.11 Integrated framework for managing knowledge across boundaries
(Carlile 2004, p. 558)

The syntactic approach assumes a mechanical notion of communication with a sender and receiver (Shannon and Weaver 1949) where there is a shared and stable syntax (language) between them. This allows a high quality of information exchange and relies on the information-processing capacity of the sender and the receiver. The key insight of this approach is that knowledge transfer is optimised through greater amounts of information, communication and strategies. Where this perspective becomes unstuck is the introduction of new knowledge and new conditions which lie outside the boundaries of the current syntax (language).

As novelty increases in the environment, some meanings can become ambiguous and interpretive differences become wider especially across different epistemic communities with different world views. Communication between these different 'thought worlds' can become difficult. The need is to develop a common meaning to address interpretive differences across semantic boundaries. The key role here is one of knowledge translation. The communities of practice literature shows how individuals develop shared meanings after participating in informal networks.

As novelty increases even further, there is a recognition that knowledge is embedded, localised and invested in practice. This is the pragmatic knowledge boundary which recognises the need to transform existing knowledge in order to resolve the different interests among actors. This perspective recognises knowledge processes as 'creative abrasion' and focuses on the negotiation of practice. Boundary objects (Star 1989) such as drawings and protypes have proved effective in representing different interests and facilitating negotiations between parties to help transform knowledge. This is about negotiating and transforming common knowledge and domain-specific knowledge from the past (Carlile 2002; Carlile 2004).

CASE STUDY

Fluor (United States)

Alan Boeckmann, CEO of Fluor, met John McQuary, Vice President of Knowledge Management, at his offices. 'We have a major challenge, John, and I need your help. Until the end of 2008 most of our activities in South America were focused in Puerto Rico through Fluor Daniel Caribbean. At Board level, we have now made a decision to expand across South America and we have opened offices in Buenos Aires in Brazil, Santiago in Chile, Lima in Peru, Caracas in Venezuela and Mexico City in Mexico. Our corporate knowledge and expertise is critical to our success in these countries. Please tell me where we are with our global knowledge management activities and what we need to do to ensure success across new markets in South America.'

Mr McQuary began by confirming that Fluor had been winners of the 2008 Most Admired Knowledge Enterprise (MAKE) awards. 'At Fluor, we take a true enterprise-wide approach to knowledge management. This requires an expanded mindset for deploying and maintaining communities beyond what is required when the KM approach is targeted to a segment of the company, is regional, or is not open to all employees. We have also adopted a broad definition of knowledge communities that includes the global network of people and a technology platform providing integrated content, expertise, and discussions. Every employee has access to every community, a rigorous community deployment process is followed, community performance measurement and auditing programs align communities with strategic business direction, and knowledge-sharing behaviors are integrated into all aspects of company operations.[1]

Mr Boeckmann interrupted and said: 'Take me slowly through what this means and how we can apply it to South America.'

Fluor is one of the world's leading engineering, procurement, construction and maintenance (EPCM) firms in a range of heavy industrial sectors: oil and gas, industrial and infrastructure, government, global services and power. Fluor employs more than 40,000 employees in 25 countries and had an annual turnover in excess of $22 billion in 2008 with profits of $721m. Fluor's knowledge management journey started in 1997 when they became aware that much valuable knowledge was being lost at the end of projects. The nature of their work meant that teams disbanded at the end of projects and reformed into new project teams. Lessons learnt on projects weren't necessarily passed on, with new project teams making the same costly mistakes and dissemination of new approaches having limited success.

This problem is inherent in any large project-based organisation whether it be IT, shipping or construction. Fluor was clear from the start that a community-based solution was required and that technology would be needed in some form to allow its large employee base to be connected. They were interested in allowing employees to access and share their collective knowledge, which would result ultimately in benefits for the customer. They built a Web-based knowledge management platform called 'Knowledge OnLine' as part of their solution. In essence, this technology platform combined aspects of social networking with a document-management system that was constructed, owned and managed by the company. The focus was on open knowledge-sharing across organisational, regional and project boundaries. In 1999 Fluor started with two communities as a pilot. In 2000 the success of the pilot communities led to 32 communities with 4,000 members. Now there are 43 communities with 26,000 members including almost all of Fluor's professional staff (21,000).

Each community has its own homepage with news stories, featured content and knowledge objects such as best practice guidelines, specifications and tips and tricks. The emphasis is on material that other employees will find useful. The other aspect of the homepage is the community dimension. Users are provided with contact details for Community Leaders and Subject Matter Experts (SMEs). There is a section on community mission and charter, community help and links to community discussion forums, a calendar of activities and a search function. Apart from traditional search functions sorting results for relevance, Knowledge OnLine provides the user with contributor profiles for each knowledge object or discussion list searched. The user can see the contributor's past experience and projects and determine whether to contact them directly. Another approach is for the user to start a discussion in the community forum by posting to 'Asking a Question'. Apart from the content and context of the question, the user also provides the date by which the response is needed.[2]

An example of the responsiveness of the Knowledge OnLine discussion forums can be shown by a process study conducted for a Kuwaiti client wanting a dehazing solution for diesel and gas oil to meet the Haze-2 specification at 77°C. The client's initial judgement was to use an electrostatic coalescer and salt-bed drier with a water-cooled chiller. The project team found the salt-bed drier manual as a knowledge object on Knowledge OnLine and placed a request for any design and operational experience of electrostatic coalescers and salt-bed driers. They received three responses in three days from their Netherlands and Canadian offices with different design options and project references to each. The underlying advice was to pre-cool the diesel and oil to 60°C which would avoid the need for a salt-bed drier. The project team packaged this solution as the Dehazing Facility Design and offered it to the client. The client was extremely pleased as the new solution saved them €1m in equipment costs and future operating costs. This process study using Knowledge OnLine led to new work for Fluor with the same client.[3]

Employee participation was difficult in the early days of Knowledge OnLine. Fluor decided against the 'points'-based incentive scheme used in other organisations. Instead, they engaged new employees to use the new platform from day one and tried to show existing employees through Global Communications that most of the resources used in their everyday work could be found either as knowledge objects or within one of the communities. The main incentives came from recognition awards annually from their KM success-story contest and 'KM Pacesetter' award where employees were nominated by peers for epitomising exceptional knowledge-sharing behaviours. Over the past ten years there has been a distinct shift from a management-driven KM directive towards a more employee-focused one. The emphasis is on performing communities that can add corporate value to the organisation.

To coordinate the KM system, John McQuary adds: 'At Fluor there is a central KM team of seven, but only two are assigned full-time to KM. Those two maintain the technology platform for Knowledge OnLine. The rest are part-time. Other team members focus on improving community performance and communication. I myself split my time between the KM programme and technology strategies. Each community also has a knowledge-manager responsible for maintaining the content and people connections through the online community. Like the community leaders and central staff, KM responsibilities are either part of the job description or fulfilled by volunteers. In total, there are 200+ people globally providing explicit support for what looks like a corporately managed system'.[3]

Alan Boeckmann interjected and asked about the nature of the 43 communities and how they would operate with their recent South American expansion. Mr McQuary explained that all their communities fall into functional or business categories. The functional communities represent different aspects of the project such as procurement and project management. Business communities are linked to certain sectors of their work such as mining, oil and gas and life sciences. Mr Boeckmann laboured the point and asked how their new employees would cope in these large online communities with over 1,000 members when Spanish or Portuguese was their first language. He asked Mr McQuary to reflect on whether there was any need for changes to Knowledge OnLine given their South American expansion and to arrange another meeting with him with some concrete plans. He confirmed that he was impressed with the way knowledge management had engaged staff at all levels over the past ten years and provided lasting value to the organisation.

References

1 McQuary, J. (2009) 'Lessons from a decade of knowledge management', *KM Edge*.
2 Will, A. J. (2008) 'The institutionalization of knowledge management in an engineering organization', *Collaboratory for Research on Global Projects – Stanford University*, Working Paper no. 40, 1–24.
3 Ash, J. (2007) 'Connecting people', *Inside Knowledge*, 10(9), 20–23.

Questions

1 What changes to Knowledge OnLine should John McQuary recommend to Alan Boeckmann in light of Fluor's rapid expansion in South America?

2 What are the shortcomings of Fluor's online communities and how could they be improved?

3 How can Fluor get employees to share project mistakes on Knowledge OnLine for the benefit of other employees and the organisation?

Summary

This chapter has elaborated five areas that need to be considered when developing a knowledge-sharing culture and communities of practice:

1 The importance of norms, artefacts and symbols in providing explicit clues to a given culture and how knowledge management interventions can be aligned to the prevailing culture.

2 The development of core values that guide every action and decision in a company to prevent them from becoming meaningless and generating cynicism with senior management.

3 The different approaches to measuring culture fall into typing surveys or profiling surveys such as effectiveness surveys, descriptive surveys and fit profiles.

4 The debates related to knowledge-sharing cultures arising from the promotion of different forms of 'Ba' (space) in the knowledge-conversion process or the development of cooperative cultures through the values of 'care' or the result of an interplay or dialectic between cooperative and competitive cultures.

5 Communities of practice as informal, self-selecting groups that are open-ended, without any deliverables. They play an important role in embedding tacit knowledge cognitively and socially through storytelling and narratives shared regularly between actors.

Questions for further thought

1 If culture is so difficult to change let alone understand, why should managers concern themselves with such a construct?

2 Communities of practice place considerable emphasis on stories and narratives for embedding tacit knowledge. What are the dangers in the current literature for not considering other surface manifestations of culture in communities of practice?

3 What issues need to be considered when the culture of different communities of practice may differ significantly from the dominant organisational culture?

4 Is radical innovation or double-loop learning asking for cultural change when its tenets are to question the underlying assumptions and values in an organisation?

5 What is the relevance of measuring organisational or group cultures?

6 How does the concept of 'Ba' add to the SECI model of knowledge conversion?

7 In what ways could the development of values of 'care' be detrimental to an organisation?

8 If communities of practice are the main component of a firm's knowledge management strategy, how do you evaluate them?

9 What are the advantages and disadvantages of online communities of practice or threaded discussion groups?

10 How do you discard obsolete practices and routines that are embedded in a community of practice?

Further reading

1 Brown (1998) is an excellent book providing a grounding and elaboration of the organisational culture literature. It has a clear and easily accessible style.

2 Ashkanasy, Wilderom and Peterson (2000b) provides a more heavyweight elicitation of the current debates in the organisational culture and climate literature. This may be useful if you wish to conduct a more in-depth study of this area.

3 Wenger, McDermott and Snyder (2002) provides an erudite background to the different approaches related to communities of practice.

References

Alvesson, M. (2002) *Understanding Organizational Culture*, Sage Publications, London.

Argyris, C. and Schon, D. A. (1978) *Organizational Learning: A Theory of Action Perspective*, Addison-Wesley, Reading, MA.

Ashkanasy, N. M., Broadfoot, L. E. and Falkus, S. (2000a) 'Questionnaire measures of organizational culture', *Handbook of Organizational Culture and Climate*, N. M. Ashkanasy, C. P. M. Wilderom and M. F. Peterson, eds, Sage Publications, Thousand Oaks, CA.

Ashkanasy, N. M., Wilderom, C. P. M. and Peterson, M. F. (2000b) *Handbook of Organizational Culture and Climate*, Sage, Thousand Oaks, CA.

Berger, P. L. and Luckmann, T. (1966) *The Social Construction of Reality: A Treatise in the Sociology of Knowledge*, Penguin, New York.

Blacker, F. (1995) 'Knowledge, knowledge work and organizations: An overview and interpretation', *Organization Studies*, 16, 1021–46.

Boland, R. J. and Tenkasi, R. V. (1995) 'Perspective making and perspective taking: In communities', *Organization Science*, 6, 350–72.

Brown, A. D. (1998) *Organisational Culture*, Pearson Education Ltd, London.

Brown, J. S. and Duguid, P. (1991) 'Organizational learning and communities-of-practice: Towards a unified view of working, learning and innovation', *Organization Science*, 2, 40–57.

Brown, J. S. and Duguid, P. (1998) 'Organizing knowledge', *California Management Review*, 40(3), 90–111.

Brown, J. S. and Duguid, P. (2000) 'Balancing act: How to capture knowledge without killing it', *Harvard Business Review*, May–June, 73–80.

Carlile, P. R. (2002) 'A pragmatic view of knowledge and boundaries: Boundary objects in new product development', *Organization Science*, 13, 442–55.

Carlile, P. R. (2004) 'Transferring, translating, and transforming: An integrative framework for managing knowledge across boundaries', *Organization Science*, 15, 555–68.

Carroll, C. (1995) 'Rearticulating organizational identity: Exploring corporate images and employee identification', *Management Learning*, 26(4), 463–82.

Chandler, A. D. (1962) *Strategy and Structure: Chapters in the History of the Industrial Enterprise*, Cambridge, MA, The MIT Press.

Cooke, R. A. and Lafferty, J. C. (1987) *Organizational Culture Inventory*, Human Synergistics, Plymouth, MI.

Deal, T. E. and Kennedy, A. A. (1982) *Corporate Cultures: The Rites and Rituals of Corporate Life*, Addison-Wesley, Reading, MA.

Denison, D. R. (1996) 'What is the difference between organizational culture and organizational climate? A native's point of view on a decade of paradigm wars', *Academy of Management Review*, 21(3), 619–54.

Durkheim, E. (1984) *The Division of Labour in Society*, W. D. Halls, translator, Free Press, New York.

Geertz, C. (1973) *The Interpretation of Cultures*, Basic Books, New York.

Handy, C. B. (1985) *Understanding Organizations*, Penguin, Harmondsworth.

Hofstede, G. (1980) *Culture's Consequences: International Differences in Work-related Values*, Sage Publications, Beverly Hills, CA.

Inkeles, A. and Levinson, D. J. (1969) 'National character: The study of modal personality and sociocultural systems', *The Handbook of Social Psychology*, G. Lindzey and E. Aronson, eds, Addison-Wesley, Reading, MA, 418–506.

Jashapara, A. (2003) 'Cognition, culture and competition: An empirical test of the learning organization', *The Learning Organization*, 10(1), 31–50.

Lave, J. and Wenger, E. (1991) *Situated Learning: Legitimate Peripheral Participation*, Cambridge University Press, Cambridge.

Lencioni, P. M. (2002) 'Make your values mean something', *Harvard Business Review*, July, 113–17.

Lewin, K. (1948) *Resolving Social Conflicts*, Harper & Row, New York.

Lewin, K. (1951) *Field Theory in Social Science*, Harper & Row, New York.

Lewin, K., Lippitt, R. and White, R. K. (1939) 'Patterns of aggressive behavior in experimentally created "social climates"', *Journal of Social Psychology*, 10, 271–99.

Likert, R. (1967) *The Human Organization*, McGraw-Hill, New York.

Litwin, G. H. and Stringer, R. A. (1961) *Motivation and Organizational Climate*, Harvard Business School Press, Boston, MA.

McDermott, R. and O'Dell, C. (2001) 'Overcoming cultural barriers to sharing knowledge', *Journal of Knowledge Management*, 5(1), 76–85.

Mead, G. (1934) *Mind, Self, and Society*, University of Chicago Press, Chicago.

Newell, S., Robertson, M., Scarbrough, H. and Swan, J. (2002) *Managing Knowledge Work*, Palgrave, Basingstoke, Hampshire.

Nonaka, I. (1991) 'The knowledge-creating company', *Harvard Business Review*, 69 (November–December), 96–104.

Nonaka, I. and Konno, N. (1998) 'The concept of "Ba": Building a foundation for knowledge creation', *California Management Review*, 40(3), 40–54.

O'Reilly, C. A. (1989) 'Corporations, culture and commitment: Motivation and social control in organizations', *California Management Review*, Summer, 9–25.

O'Reilly, C. A., Chatman, J. and Caldwell, D. F. (1991) 'People and organizational culture: A profile comparison approach to assessing person–organization fit', *Academy of Management Journal*, 34(3), 487–516.

Orr, J. (1996) *Talking About Machines: An Ethnography of a Modern Job*, IRL Press, Ithaca, NY.

Penrose, E. T. (1959) *The Theory of Growth of the Firm*, Oxford, Blackwell.

Pettigrew, A. M. (1979) 'On studying organizational cultures', *Administrative Science Quarterly*, 24, 570–81.

Rokeach, M. (1973) *The Nature of Human Values*, Free Press, New York.

Santos, F. M. and Eisenhardt, K. M. (2005) 'Organizational boundaries and theories of organization', *Organization Science*, 16, 491–508.

Schein, E. H. (1985a) 'How culture forms, develops and changes', *Gaining Control of the Corporate Culture*, R. H. Kilmann, M. J. Saxton and R. Serpa, eds, Jossey Bass, San Francisco, CA.

Schein, E. H. (1985b) *Organizational Culture and Leadership: A Dynamic View*, Jossey-Bass, San Francisco, CA.

Scholz, C. (1987) 'Corporate culture and strategy – the problem of strategic fit', *Long Range Planning*, 20(4), 78–87.

Shannon, C. and Weaver, W. (1949) *The Mathematical Theory of Communications*, Urbana, IL, University of Illinois Press.

Star, S. L. (1989) 'The structure of ill-structured solutions: Boundary objects and heterogeneous distributed problem-solving', *Distributed Artifical Intelligence*, 2, 37–54.

Swan, J., Scarbrough, H. and Robertson, M. (2002) 'The construction of "communities of practice" in the management of innovation', *Management Learning*, 33(4), 477–96.

von Hippel, E. (1994), '"Sticky information" and the locus of problem solving: Implications for innovation', *Management Science*, 40, 429–39.

von Krough, G. (1998) 'Care in knowledge creation', *California Management Review*, 40(3), 136–7.

Weber, M. (1947) *The Theory of Social and Economic Organization*, A. M. Henderson and T. Parsons, translators, Oxford University Press, Oxford.

Weick, K. E. (1995) *Sensemaking in Organizations*, Thousand Oaks, CA, Sage Publications.

Wenger, E. C. (2000) 'Communities of practice and social learning systems', *Organization*, 7(2), 225–46.

Wenger, E. C., McDermott, R. and Snyder, W. M. (2002) *Cultivating Communities of Practice: A Guide to Managing Knowledge*, Harvard Business School Press, Boston, MA.

Wenger, E. C. and Snyder, W. M. (2000) 'Communities of practice: The organizational frontier', *Harvard Business Review*, January–February, 139–45.

Zollo, M. and Winter, S. G. (2002) 'Deliberate learning and the evolution of dynamic capabilities', *Organization Science*, 13(3), 339–51.

Chapter 10

Implementing knowledge management

Learning outcomes

After completing this chapter the reader should be able to:

- understand the different dimensions and interventions that contribute to successful change management;
- successfully apply the different leadership and human resource interventions to a knowledge management initiative;
- analyse the training and development needs at individual and job level in a change management process;
- explain the critical factors that will lead to the successful implementation of knowledge management practices.

Management issues

The use and application of knowledge management systems implies these questions for managers:

- What are the most effective ways of implementing a knowledge management initiative?
- How can knowledge management programmes be managed with moderate levels of support from senior managers?
- How can resistance to change be minimised?

Links to other chapters

Chapter 4   concerns strategic management of knowledge management and institutional practices linked with change and everyday learning.

Chapter 5   examines the different forms of learning linked with the change process resulting in organisational routines and dynamic capabilities.

Chapter 9   explores the nature of culture and climate rather than the effective management of cultural change programmes.

Box clever and keep your star performers happy   **FT**

Something else to worry about. When business is bad, your best people get twitchy. They struggle. They start looking around for something better to do. 'Clever, creative people want to go to work and have fun,' says Gareth Jones, a fellow of the centre for management development at London Business School (LBS). 'They don't like gloomy workplaces.'

We have heard enough for one lifetime about the 'war for talent'. But this doesn't mean that leaders can ignore who is on their team. Last week I went to a seminar hosted by the Corporate Research Forum which, thankfully, injected new life into that increasingly tired debate over talent, knowledge workers and the rest of it. It is time to reframe this debate. What we should be thinking about, you see, are clever people.

Clever is a slippery word. It is never a good idea to be thought 'too clever by half'. Many people are told at some stage in their lives that 'you are not as clever as you think you are'. But clever people are important. They create 'disproportionate value', in the words of the aforementioned Prof Jones and his colleague, Rob Goffee, who is a professor of organisational behaviour, also at LBS.

The Jones/Goffee double act might be familiar to readers of these pages. Their first big hit came more than 10 years ago with *The character of a corporation*, an insightful analysis of corporate culture. They followed up a few years later with the provocatively titled *Why should anyone be led by you?*, an original (and subversive) book on leadership.

This year they will publish *Clever – leading your smartest, most creative people*, and last week's seminar, run by the authors, offered a chance to sample some of the ideas that are explored at greater length in the new book.

Who are these clever people? They work in research and development for pharmaceutical businesses, they develop new computer games for software companies, they are partners (or rising stars) in professional service firms, they are mechanics and designers in Formula One racing

teams. But clever people are not all earning huge sums of money in the private sector. Some are also working in intensive care in children's hospitals, or curating special exhibitions in museums.

What are they like, and why are clever people difficult to lead and manage? Having researched the subject, Profs Jones and Goffee have come up with a 10-point checklist for managers.

1 Cleverness is central to their identity. They take negative feedback badly.
2 Their skills are not easily replicated. Not many people can do what they do.
3 They know their worth.
4 They ask difficult questions.
5 They are organisationally savvy. Their projects will get funded.
6 They are not impressed by corporate hierarchy. Job titles don't mean much to them, but status does.
7 They expect instant access to the chief executive. If they don't get it they may lose interest, slipping rapidly from obsession in their work to indifference.
8 They are well connected both inside and outside the organisation.
9 They have a low boredom threshold.
10 They won't thank you. They do not feel they need to be led.

But there is also good (and slightly less daunting) news for business leaders. Clever people need organisations. Their work usually involves complex tasks that are performed in a team setting. They want 'a high degree of organisational protection,' Goffee and Jones say. And they are more effective when they are well led.

Who is good at leading clever people? Sir Martin Sorrell, chief executive of the global marketing services group WPP, gets the professorial thumbs up. He has to deal with a lot of powerful creatives. In conversation with the authors he plays down the big impact he makes on his colleagues: 'I'm a boring little micro-managing, number-crunching accountant.'

Too modest. In reality, Sir Martin constantly reminds his people that he is running a creative business. WPP's boss enforces commercial discipline, offering the tough love of a benevolent guardian. He also uses reverse psychology: 'If you want them to turn left, tell them to turn right.' Do we risk overestimating the importance of cleverness at work? Famously, the clever people at Enron were 'the smartest guys in the room'.

Fred Hilmer, now vice-chancellor of the University of New South Wales in Australia but previously a McKinsey partner, business school dean and CEO of the Fairfax media group, says that, while you need some clever people, organisations with lots of them can go wrong fast. The global banking crisis would seem to bear this out.

Still, you need to hold on to your cleverest people, especially at a time like this. Try to cre-

ate the right amount (neither too much nor too little) of sociability and solidarity within your organisation. Where do clever people flourish? 'In complicated value chains, where there is plenty of "unarticulated reciprocity",' Prof Goffee explains. Build a culture that is hard to copy, and which will give you a significant competitive advantage.

Source: from Box clever and keep your star performers happy, *The Financial Times*, 26/05/2009, p.14 (Stern, S.), copyright © The Financial Times Ltd.

Questions

1 How do you best lead clever 'knowledge workers'?

2 Why do smart people find it difficult to learn?

3 How would you test the assumption that 'clever people' create 'disproportionate value' in an organisation?

Introduction

Change is an ephemeral word and its nature is increasingly uncertain and unpredictable. It affects people in different ways and the traditional emotional response can provide considerable resistance to change. All knowledge management initiatives such as implementing new technical solutions or promoting knowledge-sharing cultures can provide considerable challenges to their effective implementation. The reasoning adopted in this chapter is that a contingency approach using different interventions depending on context is more likely to be successful than a single solution. A KM framework showing the different dimensions and interventions likely to lead to successful implementation of KM initiatives is shown in Figure 10.1.

This chapter begins by examining the nature of change and the personal response to it. Leadership is considered vital in any change programme and the nature of situational skills is explored for developing a vision and goal commitment towards the new initiative. The change management strategy adopted follows a cycle of three phases of unfreezing, moving and refreezing (Lewin 1951) and using a variety of interventions to reduce the resistance to change (Kotter and Schlesinger 1979). The chapter then proceeds to explore in detail the variety of human resource interventions that can be used in the change process. Of particular interest are the variety of employee involvement practices, the diversity of training and development interventions, and the role reward and recognition schemes can play to smooth the implementation of KM initiatives. Finally, the chapter explores the politics of change and how they can undermine and cause failure in a rationally determined change programme.

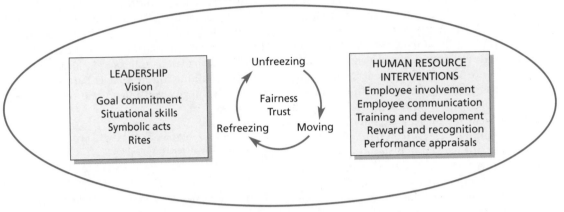

Figure 10.1 **KM initiatives and change management**

The nature of change

Change in organisations can occur at almost any time internally or externally. There may be periods of 'incremental change' followed by periods of increased turbulence or complexity as well as periods of major disequilibrium or 'discontinuous change'. Such patterns are often referred to as 'punctuated equilibrium,' as shown in Figure 10.2. Prior to the 1970s the dominant form of change experienced by many organisations was 'incremental change', characterised by stable markets, the past repeating itself in the future and predictable organisational challenges (Ansoff and McDonnell 1990). The common tool adopted to meet these challenges was forecasting by extrapolating from past experiences and figures and forecasting into the future. This worked well for annual budgeting purposes but soon many organisations started to experience strategic drift where they found their incremental change strategies were no longer moving at the same pace as forces in the environment.

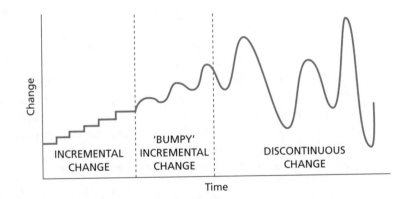

Figure 10.2 **The nature of change**

Change was no longer slow and predictable but showed much greater flux due to increased internal complexity and turbulence in the external environment. Such 'bumpy incremental change' (Grundy 1993) or flux can often result in periodic reorganisations to increase the organisation's ability to respond to the quickening pace of daily problems and perceptions of work overload (Senior 1997). The organisational focus in periods of incremental change tends more towards 'doing things better' or single-loop learning (Argyris and Schon 1978).

The logic of organisations responding incrementally to changes can also lead to serious consequences. For example, using the 'boiled-frog' analogy (Handy 1993) shows that if a frog is placed in cold water and slowly heated, the frog will let itself be boiled to death. Like the organisation, the frog attempts to respond slowly to the changing environment until it is too late. In contrast, if a frog is placed in boiling water it will jump straight out in order to survive.

In the 1970s the consequence of the oil price shock forced many companies such as Shell to reappraise how they conducted business. Such unpredictable surprises or discontinuous changes led to major periods of disequilibrium where unexpected events occurred at a faster rate than the ability of organisations to respond to them. The old ways of prediction and forecasting were no longer valid and new tools and techniques were needed to manage such transformational change. One such tool developed by Shell during this period was 'scenario planning' to obtain a number of plausible futures against which to test organisational responses. The organisational focus in periods of discontinuous change tends more towards 'doing things differently' or double-loop learning (Argyris and Schon 1978).

Personal response to change

Organisations are about people. In order to manage change effectively, we need to understand how change affects people at an emotional and cognitive level. There are a number of relatively predictable transition phases that people encounter linked with their ability to exercise control over a new situation, as shown in Figure 10.3. These transition phases in the cycle of change include (Hayes 2002):

- *shock* from an individual feeling overwhelmed and paralysed by the new situation or event. This can lead to rejection of the change process and an assertion that the change won't happen;

- *denial* as the individual clings to the past and their everyday routines. Resistance to change is at its highest level at this stage, leading to a defensive reaction. If the individual panics, this may also lead to sabotage of the change process. This is characterised by the individual response of 'I'm not going to let this happen';

- *depression* as the individual feels that the situation is beyond their control, resulting in sadness, anger, confusion and withdrawal from the change process;

- *letting go* by the individual. The individual acknowledges and accepts the change but does not necessarily like it. This represents a turning point in the change process;

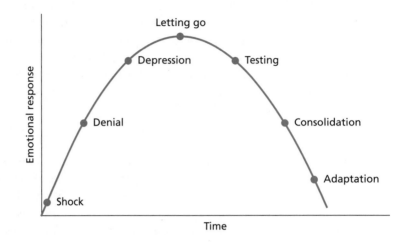

Figure 10.3 **Emotional response to change**

- *testing* as the individual tries out new behaviours and ways of working;
- *consolidation* of new experiences and ways of behaving to develop new norms and routines;
- *internalisation*, reflection and learning leading to effective adaptation of change process. The individual response tends to be 'things are changing, let's work with it'.

> ### Critical thinking and reflection
>
> Reflect on a time of major change in your life. Describe the nature of your feelings at this time. What did you find helped or hindered you through this change process? What lessons have you learnt from this personal introspection? How do you feel that your experiences could help you in future change processes or if you were tasked with leading a major change initiative?

This emotional response to change can lead to considerable resistance to change for four primary reasons (Kotter and Schlesinger 1979):

- *parochial self-interest* as people feel that they will lose something of value through the change such as resource allocation, career prospects and power imbalances;
- *misunderstanding* and lack of trust arising from poor communication of the change process and how it will affect individuals. Trust also depends on the background of employee relations between senior management and staff;
- *different assessments* as conflicting views and interpretations arise about the nature and benefits of the change process;
- *low tolerance* for change, especially when it means job losses, reskilling or relocation.

Leadership and change

It is clear that outstanding leaders can play a vital role in the change process and particularly in enabling effective transformations to occur. But what are the leadership skills and abilities that are required? First, leaders offer a vision of what is possible that mobilises, energises and empowers people to reach that vision. Second, they play a role in goal setting connected with building and articulating clearly accepted goals and expectations. Last, they play a role in gaining commitment to the goals in the change process. This is not purely an awareness of the goals ('I know') or a knowledge of the goals ('I understand') or a belief in the goals ('I can') but a commitment to the goals ('I will'). This requires an active involvement of people in the development of goals. It is noteworthy that there are no conclusive studies showing that certain leadership styles, such as a participative style or an autocratic style, are more effective than others.

There is much debate about the difference between a leader and a manager. One distinction is that managers 'do things right' whereas leaders 'do the right thing' (Bennis and Nanus 1985). Managers are more concerned with the activities related to the formal structure and goals of the organisation whereas leaders are more concerned with establishing a direction, aligning, motivating and inspiring people (Senior 1997). The two main skills for managing people in the change process are:

- creating energy through motivation by getting the right people in the right places in the change programme. Selecting the right person is about more than simply their skills and abilities. It is about their motivation and attitudes towards the role. Does the person enjoy their role and do they feel proud of their work? Choosing the right person frees up energy for leadership as the leader isn't sidetracked into purely managing resistance to change;
- channelling energy through leadership and goal commitment.

One common practice in the leadership of change is to adopt a three-phase approach over roughly a three-month period. The first consultative phase is where the leader asks questions and actively listens to managers, employees, customers, suppliers and other stakeholders. This phase serves as a business analysis to understand problems and opportunities. The leader also builds relationships and conducts a human resource analysis to find out what managers are good at, what makes them tick, what they would fight for or against and what turns them on. The second phase is testing out reactions to a goal or a plan. The aim of this phase is to test for commitment to the change process by simulating the benefits and challenges of the change. The third phase is the announcement of the change process through conferences, meetings, newsletters and other media. The aim of this phase is to encourage concrete action and commitment to the change rather than further discussion and argument.

As we do not live in a perfect world, the leader may not be able to gain the perfect commitment to a vision or goal as desired. In this case, leaders often rely on situational skills. In order to influence people, the leader needs to understand the readiness of people along two dimensions: job readiness (their knowledge, skills and experience) and psychological readiness (their confidence, commitment and motivation). Once the person or group's readiness is understood as well as their level of supportive behaviour, the leader can choose the appropriate situational skill as shown in Figure 10.4. In cases of low levels

Leadership style	Level of leadership behaviour with staff	Maturity level of staff	Characteristics of leadership style
Telling	High task/Low relationship	Low maturity	*Give instruction*: one-way communication on what, how, why, when and where to do task
Selling	High task/High relationship	Medium maturity but limited skills	*Explain decisions*: two-way communication where leader influences staff to proceed in a certain direction
Participating	Low task/High relationship	Medium maturity but lacking confidence	*Share ideas*: shared decision making on how task is accomplished while maintaining high relationships
Delegating	Low task/Low relationship	High maturity	Hand over decisions: decision making process and responsibility passed to staff while leader monitors progress

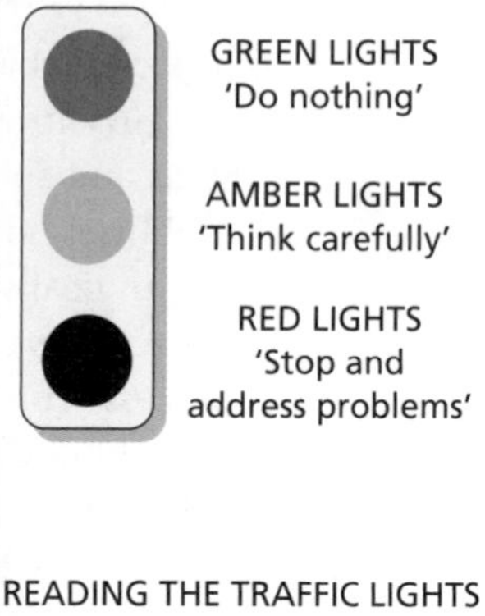

GREEN LIGHTS
'Do nothing'

AMBER LIGHTS
'Think carefully'

RED LIGHTS
'Stop and address problems'

READING THE TRAFFIC LIGHTS

Figure 10.4 **Leadership situational skills in change management** (Source: left based on Hersey *et al.* 2000)

of job and psychological readiness, the leader may use 'telling' or 'selling' styles depending on the level of support required. In contrast, with high levels of job and psychological readiness, the leader is more likely to use follower directed styles of 'participating' and 'delegating'. In high trust styles of delegation, the person or group are given full responsibility for their work and the leader is kept informed if they run into any problems.

The second situational skill used by many leaders is 'reading the traffic lights' to provide appropriate direction and control, as shown in Figure 10.4. If the lights are 'green' where things are running smoothly towards agreed goals, the leader recognises that it would be best not to intervene in these circumstances. If the lights are 'red', where major problems are gathering, the leader is best informed to stop, change their agenda and pay close attention to the problems. If not, the problems could mushroom out of all proportion. The real challenge for leaders is reading the amber/orange lights to see whether or not to intervene: are the amber lights in a given situation on their way to green or on their way to red? This is part of the armoury of an outstanding leader.

Change management strategies

The underlying assumption of the change management process among many managers is that it follows a three-phase process. The three phases assume that there is a need for some permanency or stability within organisations, even if this happens to be temporary. The three phases advocated for helping individuals, groups and organisations manage change are (Lewin 1951):

- unfreezing and loosening current sets of behaviours, mental models and ways of looking at a problem;

- moving by making changes in the way people do things, new structures, new strategies and different types of behaviours and attitudes;

- refreezing by stabilising and establishing new patterns and organisational routines.

Even though this model is predominant in many organisations, it has been criticised for its emphasis on stability, particularly when organisations are faced with turbulent environments and discontinuous change. Such cycles may perpetuate single-loop learning in the refreezing process rather than double-loop learning through continual adaptation to the external environment.

An important tool used by managers to understand the dynamics of change in any given situation is a force-field analysis (Lewin 1951), as shown in Figure 10.5. This uses a military metaphor of examining the driving forces and restraining forces that create a 'quasi-stationary equilibrium' at any given moment. The intention of any manager is to strengthen the driving forces while reducing the influence of restraining forces. Such an analysis will provide the manager with a number of problems to be tackled to help drive the change process in the desired direction.

Once a manager has understood the restraining forces and the change management problems, there are a number of approaches and options for managing resistance to change (Kotter and Schlesinger 1979):

- *Education and persuasion*. This involves explaining the problems and issues concerned with current working practices and how the change management programme can benefit individuals, groups and the organisation as a whole. Persuasion is about convincing people about the benefits of changing practices and the costs of continuing with current practices. Managers need to guard against defensive reactions from overcritical analysis of current practices and the problems of misinformation or, at worst, no information at all.

- *Participation and involvement*. This is an important approach to engage people and get 'buy-in' for the change process. It involves relinquishing some control and involving organisational members in diagnosing the problems, addressing options, finding

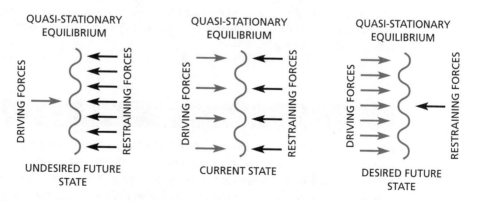

Figure 10.5 **Forcefield analysis**

solutions and implementing the change process. The result is that champions are created with much greater motivation and shared understanding for the change programme. It empowers individuals and reduces the victim mentality often associated with change. The drawback is that the consultative process can be very time consuming and the people may not have the necessary technical expertise to conduct an effective analysis of the current situation. The threat is that a suboptimal solution may result from the consultation process (Hayes 2002).

- *Facilitation and support.* Resistance to change often results from the loss of something that is valued by organisational members. Some of this can be overcome by offering individual opportunities for training and development in new skills. However, loss also implies grief and staff may need emotional support and a listening ear in the change process.

- *Negotiation and agreement.* If an individual or a group such as the unions has significant power to resist change, one approach is to engage in negotiations to secure an agreement. In this case, the negotiations are about reaching a compromise so that both parties can gain some benefits from the new situation. However, negotiations can be time consuming and add costs to the change management programme.

- *Manipulation and cooption.* The common term used for this approach nowadays is 'spin'. This involves a covert operation to bias information and communications in an organisation in order to gain support. However, this can result in coopted members feeling deceived in the long term and can act as a restraining agent.

- *Coercion.* This approach is used in more extreme cases where a manager has the ability to exercise power over granting or withholding a valued outcome, such as promotion or pay, from an organisational member (Hayes 2002). Such threats tend to be used when commitment to the change process is very low within a workforce. The dangers of this approach are that it can lead to resentment and loss of goodwill from organisational members.

Critical thinking and reflection

Some managers adopt bullying tactics in order to manage change. As a manager, what do you think could be some of the benefits or limitations of this approach? What do you envisage could be some of the short-term and long-term consequences of bullying behaviour? If one of your colleagues was being bullied, what would you advise them as their best course of action?

Gaining commitment for change

For successful implementation of knowledge management practices and encouraging knowledge-sharing behaviour, organisational commitment is a major asset to be nurtured. But what is the nature of commitment and its root causes? Commitment affects how employees behave and their attitudes towards their workplace. Commitment can be seen as an attitudinal consequence of the psychological contract (Guest and Conway

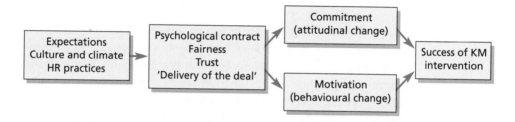

Figure 10.6 **Psychological contract and commitment** (Guest and Conway 1997; Hislop 2002)

1997; Hislop 2002), as shown in Figure 10.6. The psychological contract is the perceptions that the individual and organisation bring to the employment relationship. The core components of a psychological contract are fairness, trust and 'delivering the deal' by meeting expectations of key obligations and promises on both sides. Fairness in daily practices relates to the level of equity in the way people are valued and rewarded for their contributions. Trust concerns the level of confidence in an organisation to meet expectations of future outcomes. Much depends on the mutual expectations within a psychological contract.

There are criticisms of this model of commitment as it doesn't take into account the complexity of this construct. There may be different types of commitment and individuals may be committed to certain parts of the organisation rather than the organisation as a whole. Similarly, employees may develop psychological contracts with key individuals or groups rather than with the organisation (Hayes 2002).

As knowledge-based organisations are dependent on the commitment and ideas of their employees, the role of a fair process becomes crucial as it affects attitudes and behaviours of individuals to achieve superior performance. Employees will commit to a manager's decision even though they may disagree with it as long as they feel that the process has been fair (Kim and Mauborgne 2003). They will cooperate freely with a situation even though they may not benefit from its consequences. However, if employees feel that there is something deceitful in a manager's actions and a general lack of respect, the level of trust and commitment is likely to deteriorate. This will probably result in employees hoarding their knowledge rather than sharing it. Being valued is a basic human need in all employees; people like to contribute their ideas and have them taken seriously. There are three basic principles underlying a fair process (Kim and Mauborgne 2003):

- *Engagement* is about involving and consulting people in the decision-making processes. Such engagement makes people feel valued and conflicting views help sharpen understanding and gain commitment. There is ownership of the process.

- *Explanation* allows employees to understand the rationale behind certain decisions and gain trust in a manager's intention even though their own ideas may be ignored.

- *Expectation* clarity is about managers defining the new behaviours expected of employees and the rewards and penalties for achieving certain standards. This allows new rules and policies to be understood and minimises allegations of favouritism.

Average performance often occurs in organisations due to 'distributive justice'. This arises when employees receive outcomes they deserve (such as compensation) and feel drawn towards a compulsory form of cooperation. However, superior performance and strong knowledge-sharing behaviours are more likely to occur through 'procedural justice'. This involves a fair process, building trust and commitment and leading to voluntary cooperation and behaviours where individuals go beyond the call of duty. It affects people's everyday attitudes and behaviours. There are often three stages in achieving employee commitment (O'Reilly 1989):

● *compliance*, where an individual accepts the rules of the game in expectation of some reward such as pay;

● *identification*, when an employee accepts influence to maintain a satisfying relationship with individuals and groups;

● *internalisation*, when an employee finds the organisational values intrinsically rewarding and aligned with their personal values.

Cults and religious groups exhibit high levels of commitment marked by the internalisation of group values with personal values.

Critical thinking and reflection

As a manager, what strategies could you use to make your staff feel valued at work? Think of your own experiences of being valued at work. What were effective interventions that made you feel valued? One of the pitfalls of valuing some staff over others is described as favouritism. How could you avoid this pitfall? What are the likely consequences if you are unable to do so?

Employee involvement

In many organisations there is an increasing shift away from control towards commitment. As we have seen, an important factor in gaining this commitment is engagement or employee involvement. But what is the nature of employee involvement and what impact does it have on the power relations between a manager and their teams? Employee involvement implies a certain loss of management prerogative in decision-making processes. However, the spectrum of employee involvement practices can span from one-way communication of management decisions to full-blown democratic systems in decision making. Employee involvement is time consuming and many senior managers may feel that it detracts from their focus on tight cost control or other strategic directions and leave themselves open to criticisms about lack of investment in human resources such as training and development.

The history of involving the workforce in the decision-making process can be traced back to the Second World War. In response to the strong demand for products and services during the war, works committees or joint consultative committees were set up across many organisations. These committees lost favour with unions and employers alike soon after the war. Instead, direct collective bargaining between unions and employers was preferred. In the 1960s and 1970s there was a greater focus on 'industrial democracy', with union members fulfilling consultative roles in organisations. The extent of power delegated to them was unclear. In the 1980s industrial democracy interventions became tarnished by left-wing ideologies and 'employee involvement' schemes became much more popular. Power relations between management and the workforce still play an important role in the nature of employee involvement. It has been argued that there may be waves of participation, especially linked to the perceived threat or loss of control of labour in some manner (Beardwell and Holden 2001).

A spectrum of different employee involvement practices linked to the level of management or worker control is shown in Figure 10.7. In reality, the nature of employee involvement practices in organisations is likely to have significant overlaps and behave more dynamically than that shown, due to environmental pressures. The nature of employee involvement schemes can be divided into four groupings (Beardwell and Holden 2001; Marchington *et al.* 1992):

- *downward communication* or one-way communication from management using company newsletters, the intranet and regular team briefings. Newsletters are a popular form of communication but can be seen as a medium to convey management rather than worker views. Team briefings are an effective face-to-face medium to allow management goals to be addressed and any misunderstandings to be clarified. They involve small numbers of people in short meetings with a question and answer session at the end;

- *upwards, problem-solving forms* which aim to capture employee knowledge and expertise. These may include attitude surveys, quality circles, TQM and suggestion schemes. Quality circles are about teams getting together focusing on problems, using statistical techniques and presenting managers with potential solutions. They have declined in popularity in many countries for cultural reasons (they originated in Japan) and the fact that they may undermine union authority;

- *financial participation* which aims to link employee effort with performance of the organisation. This may include organisation-wide rewards such as profit-sharing schemes, share ownership or bonus schemes. The aim is to achieve greater identification with the organisation among employees with the assumption that this will lead to greater levels of commitment;

- *representative participation* of employees through their representatives such as union members. These may include joint consultative committees (JCC), works councils, co-determination and collective bargaining.

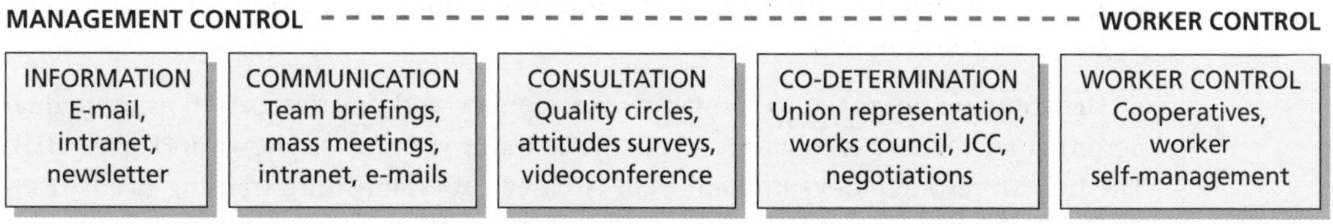

MANAGEMENT CONTROL – WORKER CONTROL

| INFORMATION E-mail, intranet, newsletter | COMMUNICATION Team briefings, mass meetings, intranet, e-mails | CONSULTATION Quality circles, attitudes surveys, videoconference | CO-DETERMINATION Union representation, works council, JCC, negotiations | WORKER CONTROL Cooperatives, worker self-management |

Figure 10.7 **Spectrum of employee involvement**

Even though there has been a decline in union membership in many countries, there are still examples of industrial democracy such as co-determination practices, particularly in countries with a strong union presence. In Sweden, there is the Co-determination at Work Act (MBL) which places an obligation on organisations to extend their collective bargaining to areas of strategic management and operational changes. Hence, the emergence of any new practices or organisational direction has to be negotiated with the workforce, often through the unions.

In Germany the co-determination law places similar obligations on employers to consult and consider the views of their workforce through works councils, supervisory boards and management boards. Employees and their representatives have a right to participate in any personnel matters and planned changes in a company likely to affect employees. The different committees can make suggestions to employers but they are not obliged to accept them. The impact of co-determination schemes often varies with economic cycles and the change in power relations between the government, employers and the workforce. For instance, the power of unions during times of recession may be reduced and the role of works councils correspondingly weakened.

Training and development

For change management strategies to be successful, one core element is the use of training and development to provide the necessary education, facilitation and support in the change process. Training is a planned process to help modify the attitudes, knowledge or skill behaviour of an individual through a learning experience. Development is more long term and can be associated with an individual's maturity. Development can be described as a journey starting with some level of confusion and leading through highs and lows towards a new understanding. Nothing is changed at the end of the journey but the individual is transformed internally (Daloz 1986).

Many organisations have a propensity to send their employees on courses as the mainstay of their training programmes. However, this can result in the common problem of 'Del the Delegate'. He returns from a course full of new ideas only to be faced with scepticism and cynicism from colleagues and bosses. His enthusiasm is undermined and he reverts to old patterns of behaviour and routines. If this is to be avoided, organisations need to adopt formalised or focused approaches to training and development (Barham *et al.* 1987):

- formalised approach is linking the planned training and development programme to performance appraisal and career-planning processes;
- focused approach is linking training and development activities to organisational goals and continuous learning.

The common approach to human resource policy and practice as well as individual performance reviews is to adopt a systematic training cycle, as shown in Figure 10.8. The human resource development plan is based on establishing training needs from business objectives as well as training needs of employees and determining the gap between these two entities. Appropriate training methods are decided and the human

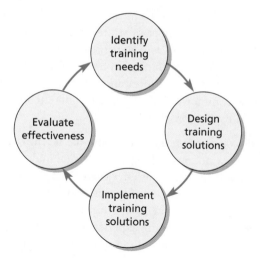

Figure 10.8 **Systematic training cycle** (Stewart 1999)

resource development plan contains material on responsibilities and how the plan will be implemented, monitored and evaluated.

Training needs need to be linked closely to organisational objectives and exist at organisation, job and individual levels. At the job level, it is the body of knowledge, the range of skills and the necessary attitudes required to perform a certain job. At the individual level, it is the gap between the knowledge, skills and attitudes (KSA) held by the individual and those required for a job. At the organisational level, the training needs are the summation of all the individual training needs or gaps in order to deliver performance objectives. There are a number of analytical techniques that can be adopted in a change-management programme to identify training needs at individual or job level (Reid and Barrington 2000):

- *comprehensive analysis* of all job tasks. This is useful for repetitive tasks that are difficult to learn and in which the potential cost of error is unacceptable;

- *key task analysis focusing on core tasks*. This form of analysis is useful when a job is changing and the focus is on the tasks critical for performance;

- *problem-centred analysis*. Here the need for training is urgent and resources are unavailable to conduct an extensive analysis;

- *stage and key points analysis*. This provides a breakdown of training needs at stages and key points;

- *manual skills analysis*. Isolates the knowledge and skills required by experienced workers performing tasks requiring high levels of manual dexterity;

- *faults analysis*. Where certain faults are costly and keep recurring. A fault specification is produced to help the trainee understand the nature of faults, what causes them, who is responsible for them and how to best act when a fault occurs;

- *critical incident analysis*. Examines the training needs related to critical incidents in problem situations;

- *job-learning analysis*. Looks at the processes in performing a job and the generic learning skills required.

Once the training needs have been identified, the training solution can be designed by considering a number of strategies and interventions. The appropriateness of the training interventions will depend on how they meet organisational objectives, the likelihood of learning transfer in terms of the organisational climate ('Del the Delegate' syndrome), the available resources and learner-related factors such as their learning style. The common training and development strategies found in organisations include (Reid and Barrington 2000):

- *on-the-job training.* This may involve learning by doing or 'sitting next to Nellie'. There is a potential danger that *Nellie* may not have the necessary skills to transfer knowledge and skills effectively. Work shadowing can be another useful training intervention. However, if this is poorly planned, trainees can feel unwelcome and be seen by other workers as a hindrance to their everyday routines. Job rotation can provide a good learning experience for workers, equipping them with new skills and providing greater flexibility for managers in times of crisis or change;

- *planned organisation experience.* This can involve mentoring or coaching. In mentoring, a senior or experienced employee acts as an adviser to a trainee in terms of professional and emotional support. The roles are similar to a master–apprentice. Coaching has parallels to mentoring as they are both learning processes that support and encourage learning. The distinction is one of contextual roles. A mentor seeks to develop a special relationship with an employee and is rarely a learner's line manager. In contrast, a coach is more concerned with immediate performance results and is more likely to be a person's line manager (Parsloe and Wray 2000);

- *in-house programmes.* These may include part-time courses leading to externally validated qualifications. There is also a rise in the use of the intranet as a medium for e-learning, particularly for developing technical knowledge and skills. Interactive computer learning packages are also used for developing IT skills;

- *planned experiences outside the organisation.* These may include secondments to other divisions or other companies. In addition, study tours and visits to competitors and suppliers can provide fruitful learning experiences;

- *external courses.* These may comprise short full-time courses or more longer (usually part-time) courses, often leading to a qualification. In both cases, it is important to examine how well the courses meet the person's training needs and link to the organisational objectives;

- *self-managed learning.* This is an ultimate goal of employees rather than human resource departments taking full responsibility for their learning. Logbooks and records of progress are often used and provide a stimulus for further learning.

Critical thinking and reflection

A common situation in many organisations is that training and development budgets are insufficient to cover all training needs. How would you decide on the most effective ways to prioritise these limited budgets? Can you suggest any internal low-cost training alternatives that could be adopted? What could be some of the dangers of relying too heavily on internally driven training solutions?

The staff appraisal process has become an important method for evaluating training interventions. The trainee and line manager can discuss the effectiveness of certain interventions and how they affected the individual's performance. There are a variety of other approaches used to evaluate training and often a combination of these is used (Beardwell and Holden 2001; Harrison 2000):

● questionnaires or feedback sheets often known as 'happy sheets' on training courses;

● tests leading to qualifications help identify a trainee's progress;

● interviews with trainees and tutors to gain feedback on training;

● observation of training provision can provide additional valuable feedback;

● participation and discussion with participants at the end of a training intervention.

The change process may also need to address the management development needs in the organisation. Without engaging in the debates about the precise nature of management, there are numerous interventions to meet a manager's development needs. Even though each manager has unique needs, some organisations have adopted a portfolio approach to management development (Odiorne 1984), as shown in Figure 10.9. The portfolio approach allows resources to be targeted cost effectively to particular groups of managers where there is a higher likelihood of immediate or long-term benefit to the organisation. At the same time, resources may be withheld from poorly performing managers described as 'deadwood' in this model. The danger with this approach is that certain managers may become stigmatised and their efforts to change perceptions through their performance may go unheeded. Such an approach also has implications for the individual manager's career progression.

A management development needs analysis can be conducted using the same tools described above for training and development of employees. The traditional forms of management development interventions are (Beardwell and Holden 2001):

● management education and training interventions such as MBA programmes;

● action learning through tackling problems that have defied solutions in the organisation;

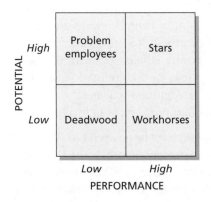

Figure 10.9 **Portfolio approach to management development** (Odiorne 1984)

- mentoring using a personal development plan. Checking that goals are 'SMART' (specific, measurable, achievable, relevant and timescaled). Mentor encourages learner to solve problems and acts as a sounding board (Parsloe and Wray 2000);

- coaching, which can be hands-on for inexperienced learners or hands-off for more experienced learners relying on questioning and feedback skills (Parsloe and Wray 2000);

- secondments;

- outdoor management development to develop team and leadership skills by giving managers physical, mental and emotional challenges in an unfamiliar outdoor environment;

- management team development involving workshop and game playing at informal residential venues;

- self-development through self-learning groups, psychometrics, books, distance-learning materials and e-learning.

Reward and recognition

Reward and recognition schemes are an important tool in the change-management process to increase employee motivation and gain commitment. For example, some organisations have adopted 'Miles for Knowledge Sharing' schemes similar to Airmiles used by travel companies and retail outlets. Each employee is given a notional number of miles, say 500, and is able to give away different numbers of miles to others in the organisation for their helpful knowledge-sharing behaviours. Individual totals are added up at the end of the year and prizes are awarded annually at an awards ceremony to those exhibiting exceptional knowledge-sharing behaviours. Other companies, such as Buckman Laboratories, have held one-off events at a fashionable resort with 150 employees attending who had exhibited the greatest knowledge-sharing behaviours. Each employee was given a new laptop and participated in a workshop on how to improve knowledge management practices in the organisation. Such initiatives found that participation in knowledge management practices rose dramatically (Newell *et al.* 2002).

The assumption behind reward and recognition schemes is that employee engagement and effort will lead to greater performance. This performance will be rewarded, leading to greater employee satisfaction and commitment, as shown in Figure 10.10. The rewards may be a combination of employee salary incentive schemes, employee benefits and recognition schemes.

There are four broad types of incentive-based schemes (Casey *et al.* 1992):

- *Individual payment by results (PBR).* This depends on the relationship with incremental pay and incremental output, the threshold output for receiving PBR over and above an employee's salary and the capping level of PBR. Such schemes can give employees greater freedom and opportunities to achieve high earnings. However, they can ignore the fact that many effective change processes are a result of team effort.

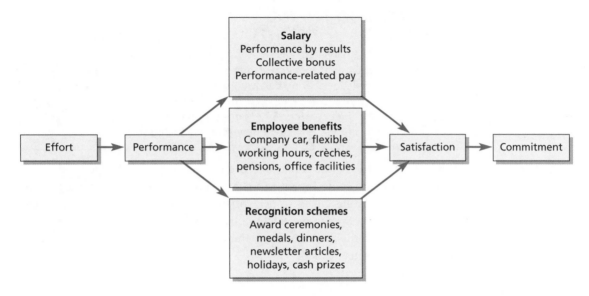

Figure 10.10 **Commitment through reward and recognition schemes** (Beardwell and Holden 2001; Porter and Lawler 1968)

- *Collective payment by results.* This is similar to individual PBR but more focused on a group, division and department. It acknowledges that individual PBR can be divisive for group working and long-term knowledge sharing. Instead, it rewards cooperative behaviours.

- *Collective bonus schemes.* The aim of these schemes is to foster greater cooperation between departments to achieve corporate objectives and to attract and retain the right staff. They may include profit-sharing schemes in the form of company shares or allow staff to buy company shares at a discount. A critical factor is the proportion of bonuses to an employee's total compensation. If it is small, it is unlikely to persuade individuals to change their behaviours.

- *Performance-related pay (PRP).* This is an incentive scheme based on an assessment of performance, often conducted through a staff appraisal process. This can allow managers to identify high-achieving employees as well as the 'deadwood'. The aim of PRP is to increase employee motivation and encourage certain behaviours and attitudes in the change process through performance norms. Institutionalising knowledge-sharing behaviours as part of these performance norms brings knowledge management practices clearly on to the everyday agenda. However, PRP can undermine the cooperation and cohesiveness of a work group. Employee performance cannot be judged in isolation but is often a result of group effort. Also, there is a danger that the psychological contract is changed from relational to transactional. Employees are more concerned with their performance (transactional) rather than all the altruistic or helpful behaviours (relational) that allow an organisation to meet its objectives (Beardwell and Holden 2001).

Critical thinking and reflection

Reflect on your role as a knowledge worker. What reward and recognition schemes do you feel are most appropriate for knowledge workers? Do you believe that PRP schemes related to knowledge-sharing behaviours could work in your organisation? What are the likely problems with this approach? How would you devise a scheme to measure knowledge-sharing behaviours? As 'game playing' behaviours could distort the results, how would you attempt to prevent game playing among staff?

Another aspect of the rewards package is the employee benefits for increasing employee motivation and commitment to a change process. These are benefits that the employee values and can be linked to performance and achievement of targets. The benefits may be flexible, known as 'cafeteria benefits', where the employee chooses from a selection of rewards and constructs their own benefits package. The types of potential employee benefits include:

- company cars;
- flexible working practices;
- pensions;
- upgraded office accommodation and facilities;
- private healthcare;
- sports facilities;
- assistance with educational fees;
- assistance with crèches.

Lastly, organisations use recognition schemes to acknowledge and recognise the efforts of high-performing individuals in the direction of the change process. This is more than an everyday 'pat on the back' and may include:

- article or story in company newsletter;
- annual awards ceremony;
- medals, plaques and certificates for exceptional performance;
- paid luxury holidays;
- business accessories such as laptops;
- cash prizes.

Cultural change management

Organisational culture concerns the underlying values and assumptions that define prevailing norms and behaviours. But what if the norms are not compatible with organisational goals and objectives? What if the prevailing norms are knowledge-hoarding behaviours rather than the desired knowledge-sharing behaviours? How do organisations effect and manage a cultural change process? A widely accepted frame-work for managing the cultural change process involves five stages (Kilmann 1984):

● surfacing actual cultural norms;
● articulating new directions;
● establishing new cultural norms;
● identifying gaps in cultural norms;
● closing gaps in cultural norms.

As shown earlier in this chapter, there are predominantly two drivers for cultural change management: leadership and human resource interventions. Leadership and commitment from senior managers is vital to the success of cultural change pro-grammes. Leaders have tremendous power to influence employees through personal enactment. They can resort to symbolic actions frequently and consistently to reinforce certain beliefs values and assumptions. Symbolic acts can include the way they use their time, such as visiting operational sites and customers to show what they consider to be important. The way a chief executive announces new directions or ways of work-ing with stories and anecdotes can shape individual understandings. Placing certain topics continually at the top of the agenda in meetings informs employees about what is important to a leader (Brown 1998).

Leaders can also employ rites to facilitate cultural change. Rites are organised and planned activities. Existing rites can be modified to include new values and assump-tions in an organisation. Certain rites can be eliminated if they are no longer desirable and maintain the status quo. A more risky approach is to develop new rites which express the desirable beliefs and values in an organisation. For example, rites of passage involving recruitment, selection and induction procedures may shift from a legislation-led, equal-opportunities emphasis more towards valuing diversity in the organisation. Rites of enhancement may reward employees for exhibiting behaviours associated with new values and beliefs through various reward and recognition schemes as described above. Leaders can use rites of degradation for demoting or removing employees resist-ant to the change process. Other rites include rituals of conflict reduction through committees between warring factions and, more informally, using sporting contest or humour. Last, the leader can use rites of integration to develop greater social cohesion through recreational activities such as drinking, dancing and picnics.

Apart from clear leadership in the cultural change process, there are a number of human resource interventions that can be employed to reinforce the desired norms, beliefs and values. The ultimate goal is to have all aspects of the human resource programme using a 'consistent cues' approach (Brown 1998) to ensure that consist-ent signals are sent to achieve the desired cultural end state. The spectrum of human resource interventions to manage culture includes:

● changes in recruitment and selection norms;
● changes in induction, socialisation and training norms;
● changes in performance appraisal norms;
● changes in reward and recognition norms.

Politics of change

Many organisational change programmes fail because of resistance to the change process. People use organisational politics to resist and influence the change process, particularly if it is not going in their preferred direction. The majority of managers find that politics becomes more intense when change is radical, complex and wide ranging (Buchanan *et al.* 1997). In fact, many managers feel that change programmes are likely to fail unless managers and leaders are adept in political skills. A common approach in the politics of organisational change is to focus on the 'dominant coalition'. Such coalitions of senior executives have considerable influence over decisions and resources. They decide organisational direction and what is important. Coalitions are dynamic and can become unstable depending on the nature of external market changes, social ties and internal politics.

Major changes, such as delayering in organisations, use of teamwork and business process re-engineering practices, recently have meant that the prevalence of political behaviour is a norm rather than an exception (Browning 2003). People are responding less to rational argument and more to egotistical motives such as personal security and career advancement (Stone 1997). Research in this area can be a minefield, since managers are reluctant to discuss the subject in case it lowers their image, and often fail to legitimise the power and influence of organisational politics (Paton and McCalman 2001). The political tactics often employed in organisations include (Carnall 1990):

- selective use of performance criteria to manage credibility;
- use of external consultants to support their views;
- control of agenda in formal meetings;
- building internal alliances and coalitions;
- use of promotions;
- control of access to information and key decision-makers;
- group pressure for employee conformity.

CASE STUDY

Woods Bagot (Australia)

Group Managing Director, Ross Donaldson, was visiting Dubai and wanted to gain some strategic insights from Mark Mitcheson-Low, their Middle-East Managing Director. He explained: 'So far we haven't felt the pinch with the global downturn in construction. However, I'm mindful that some $166 billion worth of projects have been shelved in Dubai. We need a new way of working to differentiate ourselves from other architectural firms and I believe that the way we utilise knowledge will be crucial for our future endeavours. Our 'PUBLIC' initiative was a start in the right direction but we need to do much more to remain competitive. What are your thoughts, Mark?' Mark Mitcheson-Low pondered the question and replied: 'It appears to me that the next steps are really around developing cohesive and responsive communities globally. We need to be able to tap into our collective intelligence quickly and share knowledge wherever it is needed in the organisation. This is easier said than done, given architects are highly individualistic creatures with strongly held views. That is the real challenge we face or a significant opportunity if we can crack it.'

Woods Bagot is a 139-year-old Adelaide building design practice with 14 offices and over 1,000 staff globally. It has sales of around $140m accounting for some $4 billion worth of building projects. There is no single headquarter at Woods Bagot. Instead there are 49 principals with the responsibility to make decisions and manage projects. The organisational structure is relatively flat and each principal has a shareholding in the firm. Each year, the firm invests 2 per cent of its revenue in research.[1] In 2006 the outputs of this research were published in a corporate journal named 'PUBLIC'. This journal is more than a series of papers and information source. Instead, it conveys Wood Bagot's culture and unique approach to architecture. Research underpins their modus operandi in their three key market sectors: education, lifestyle and workplace. PUBLIC provides a forum to challenge conventional thinking and generate new ideas and fresh approaches. It is about thought leadership derived from continuous learning, knowledge transfer and research.

Ross Donaldson elucidates the Woods Bagot approach: 'Woods Bagot has dared to be different; developing a global network of studios in five regions that sets us apart. This innovative structure has resulted in the creation of a super-niche global service, unique to the firm. Woods Bagot's continued investment in research, fundamentally underpinning all of the practice's "Design Intelligence", has allowed our studios across the globe to gain a competitive advantage. Our knowledge-based approach, coupled with a vast amount of global experience, assists in producing a consistently high standard of design across all sectors and regions. Our global network further feeds this ethos, creating a very different value proposition for our clients, which is evident in the number of our repeat global clients.'[2]

Ross Donaldson spent 17 years of his early career teaching architecture and is a proponent of a new approach to learning spaces. He wonders whether the same ideas could be applied

virtually or physically to foster learning and knowledge exchange between staff at their offices. He is aware that organisations spend millions on setting up IT networks to facilitate knowledge creation and sharing. However, little thought is often given to knowledge transfer that occurs through casual interactions and how spaces can be designed to facilitate these informal processes. He recognises that in higher education designers used a model of circulation pathways which allowed 'serendipitous encounters' to occur between academics. He adds: 'The stories that are always told are of the critical conversations held at the coffee machine or when two people met in the corridor and started chatting. How do you plan for that? You plan away from circulation pathways that separate people and you plan for ones that will lead people together. One option the designers considered was a prominent lounge in the open centre of the building. In order for academics to move around the building, they would have to pass through the lounge, increasing their opportunities to interact.'[3]

An example of Woods Bagot's use of its intellectual capital can be shown by its innovative design solution for the Nakheel Harbour and Tower development in Dubai. The masterplan for the harbour covers 270 hectares and the tower will be over 1 kilometre in height. The design has been inspired by Islamic principles and geometric patterns common in Middle Eastern architecture. Mark Mitcheson-Low explains: 'The Nakheel Harbour & Tower is a feat of design excellence on all levels and across all disciplines – it is truly a mark of the epoch. The project demonstrates Nakheel's drive to provide a reflection of the future Arabia – a modern, global city of significance rightly assuming its place in the world. The design is an example of the human ability to overcome the forces of nature and harness them to create a monument dedicated to past, present and future generations of the Gulf. Nakheel and Woods Bagot have pushed the design envelope with a project that will be central to the development of one of the world's most exciting cities.'[4] The tower is an advancement of traditional skyscraper design and is composed of four towers. Each tower is linked to one another at intervals using 'sky bridges'. Apart from binding the towers together, the sky bridges demarcate different uses of the building. They provide a space for people to engage and interact with one another and can be considered as 'living' bridges. In emergencies, the sky bridges also provide safe crossing points between towers.

The design solution reduces the effect of wind loadings as air can pass easily through the building – normally a significant problem in many skyscrapers. Wind tunnel testing has shown that the wind loading can be reduced by three-fold with this design especially with the use of vertical gills. This has the result of increasing floor areas at higher levels rather than the tapering effect of floor areas normally found in other skyscrapers. The building has been designed for multiple community uses from commercial offices to residential and hotel accommodation and a two-storey observation deck at the top of the tower. The precinct has a substantial transportation hub to minimise car use and to maximise train, bus and water transport use.

Mark Mitcheson-Low suggested to Ross Donaldson that virtual communities could be their answer to knowledge sharing where architects in their Dubai offices could connect instantaneously with architects in their London or Adelaide offices. He adds that there are two key knowledge bases within the organisation; one technical and the other architectural. The technical knowledge is around latest thinking in structural, mechanical and electrical engineering whereas the architectural knowledge is more around changes in aesthetics, fashions and design. Ross Donaldson interjected: 'Mark, can you and your Principals put a plan together to start a pilot virtual community with our Dubai studio and Adelaide one? If successful, we could then roll it out to our other studios! If you have any difficulties, let me know! In the meantime, I think it's time for lunch! Where shall we go?'

References

1 Ross, E. 'Empire building', 7 November 2008 [cited 7 July 2009]; Available from: http://www.smartcompany.com.au/Premium-Articles/Hot-Innovator/20081106-Empire-building.html.
2 Inglis, G. 'Woods Bagot wins international gong', 1 July 2009 [cited 7 July 2009]; Available from: http://www.propertyoz.com.au/Article/NewsDetail.aspx?p=16&id=1558.
3 Clem, W. 'Learning environment: Changing times spur new-look classroom', *South China Morning Post*, 2008, p. 6.
4 Williams, J. 'The Nakheel Harbour and Tower offers the ultimate symbol of Dubai's evolution', *Middle East Company News Wire*, 2008.

Questions

1 What advice would you give Mark Mitcheson-Low to set up a virtual community between their Dubai and Adelaide studios?

2 What changes can Woods Bagot make to their offices to encourage greater engagement and interaction between staff?

3 What knowledge management strategy is most appropriate for Woods Bagot?

Summary

This chapter has elaborated five key areas that need to be considered when developing a change management plan or the successful implementation of a knowledge management initiative:

1 The importance of leadership to develop a vision and goal commitment towards the change process. This is done through getting the right people in the right place and using situational skills. Additional leadership skills are the use of symbolic acts and rites, especially in cultural change programmes.

2 Change is most effectively managed in a three-phase process of unfreezing, moving and refreezing. A number of options can be used to overcome resistance to change including education and persuasion, participation and involvement, facilitation and support, negotiation and agreement, manipulation and cooption and coercion.

3 Fairness, trust and 'delivering the deal' are important components for generating high levels of commitment towards a change programme.

4 Successful human resource interventions in a change process include the use of different levels of employee involvement, the use of training and development and management development practices and a mixture of reward and recognition schemes.

5 The importance of politics in the change process cannot be underestimated.

Questions for further thought

1 As many of the interventions suggested in this chapter are time consuming, how can organisations manage effectively in times of discontinuous change?

2 How would you manage redundancies as part of a KM initiative?

3 What are the dangers of the three-phase change management strategy of unfreezing, moving and refreezing (Lewin 1951)?

4 What determines the nature and level of consultation given that a manager could lose control in the change process?

5 What is the most effective approach to training and development if the organisation has limited resources?

6 What are the ethical issues associated with a portfolio approach to management development?

7 Discuss the advantages and disadvantages of individual and collective incentive schemes.

8 What type of recognition schemes are likely to be most effective in knowledge management initiatives?

9 Some commentators believe that cultural change programmes do not deliver their goals. How feasible is it for human resource interventions to influence the deeper values, beliefs and attitudes rather than purely affect surface level norms?

10 What is the best way of developing political skills in the change process?

Further reading

1 Senior (1997) is an excellent book covering the different approaches and challenges in the change management process and explores the hard systems and soft systems approach to change.

2 Brown (1998) is strong on cultural change management.

3 Beardwell and Holden (2001) provides a contemporary text on different human resource interventions in the change process.

References

Ansoff, I. H. and McDonnell, E. J. (1990) *Implementing Strategic Management*, Prentice-Hall, Englewood Cliffs: NJ.

Argyris, C. and Schon, D. A. (1978) *Organizational Learning: A Theory of Action Perspective*, Addison-Wesley, Reading, MA.

Barham, K., Fraser, J. and Heath, I. (1987) *Management for the Future*, Ashridge Management College, Ashridge.

Beardwell, I. and Holden, L. (2001) *Human Resource Management: A Contemporary Approach*, Pearson Education, Harlow, Essex.

Bennis, W. and Nanus, B. (1985) *Leadership: The Strategies for Taking Charge*, Harper and Row, New York.

Brown, A. D. (1998) *Organisational Culture*, Pearson Education Ltd, London.

Browning, G. (2003) 'Office politics: the new game', *Management Today*, May, 54–9.

Buchanan, D. A., Claydon, T. and Doyle, M. (1997) 'Organization development and change: the legacy of the nineties', Leicester Business School Occasional Paper, De Montford University, 43.

Carnall, C. A. (1990) *Managing Change in Organizations*, Prentice Hall, Hemel Hempstead, Hertfordshire.

Casey, B., Lakey, J. and White, M. (1992) *Payment Systems: A Look at Current Practice*, Policy Studies Institute, Department of Employment, London.

Daloz, L. A. (1986) *Effective Mentoring and Teaching*, Jossey-Bass, San Francisco.

Grundy, T. (1993) *Managing Strategic Change*, Kogan Page, London.

Guest, D. and Conway, N. (1997) *Employee Motivation and the Psychological Contract*, IPD, London.

Handy, C. B. (1993) *The Age of Unreason*, Century Business, Chatham, Kent.

Harrison, R. (2000) *Employee Development*, Chartered Institute of Personnel and Development, London.

Hayes, J. (2002) *The Theory and Practice of Change Management*, Palgrave, Basingstoke.

Hersey, P., Blanchard, K. H. and Johnson, D. E. (2000) *Management of Organizational Behaviour: Leading Human Resources*, Prentice-Hall, Upper Saddle River, NJ.

Hislop, D. (2002) 'Linking human resource management and knowledge management via commitment: A review and research agenda', *Employee Relations*, 25(2), 182–202.

Kilmann, R. H. (1984) *Beyond the Quick Fix: Managing Five Tracks to Organizational Success*, Jossey-Bass, San Francisco, CA.

Kim, W. C., and Mauborgne, R. (2003) 'Fair process: Managing in the knowledge economy', *Harvard Business Review*, January, 127–36.

Kotter, J. P. and Schlesinger, L. A. (1979) 'Choosing strategies for change', *Harvard Business Review*, March/April (2), 106–14.

Lewin, K. (1951) *Field Theory in Social Science*, Harper & Row, New York.

Marchington, M., Goodman, J. P., Wilkinson, A. and Ackers, P. (1992) *New Developments in Employee Involvement*, Manchester School of Management, Manchester.

Newell, S., Robertson, M., Scarbrough, H. and Swan, J. (2002) *Managing Knowledge Work*, Palgrave, Basingstoke, Hampshire.

Odiorne, G. S. (1984) *Strategic Management of Human Resources: A Portfolio Approach*, Jossey-Bass, San Francisco.

O'Reilly, C. A. (1989) 'Corporations, culture and commitment: Motivation and social control in organizations', *California Management Review*, Summer, 9–25.

Parsloe, E. and Wray, M. (2000) *Coaching and Mentoring: Practical Methods to Improve Learning,* Kogan Page, London.

Paton, R. A. and McCalman, J. (2001) *Change Management: A Guide to Effective Implementation,* Sage, London.

Pfeffer, J. (2001) 'Fighting the war for talent is hazardous to your organization's health', *Organizational Dynamics,* 29(4), 248–59.

Porter, L. W. and Lawler, E. E. (1968) *Management Attitudes and Performance,* Irwin, Homewood, Ill.

Reid, M. A. and Barrington, H. (2000) *Training Interventions: Promoting Learning Opportunities,* Chartered Institute of Personnel and Development, London.

Senior, B. (1997) *Organisational Change,* Pearson Education Ltd, Harlow, Essex.

Stewart, J. (1999) *Employee Development Practice,* Pitman Publishing, London.

Stone, B. (1997) *Confronting Company Politics,* Macmillan, Basingstoke.

KNOWLEDGE MANAGEMENT

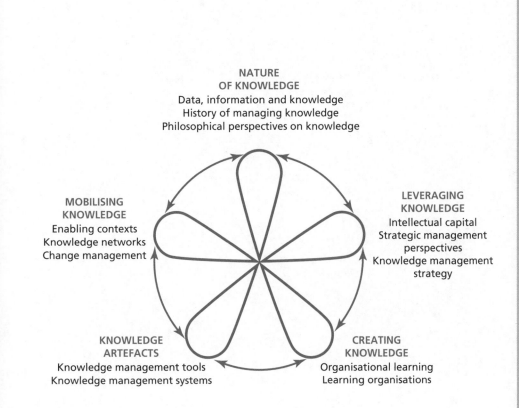

**NATURE
OF KNOWLEDGE**
Data, information and knowledge
History of managing knowledge
Philosophical perspectives on knowledge

**LEVERAGING
KNOWLEDGE**
Intellectual capital
Strategic management
perspectives
Knowledge management
strategy

**MOBILISING
KNOWLEDGE**
Enabling contexts
Knowledge networks
Change management

**KNOWLEDGE
ARTEFACTS**
Knowledge management tools
Knowledge management systems

**CREATING
KNOWLEDGE**
Organisational learning
Learning organisations

Epilogue

Introduction

The depth and breadth of material in this book has tried to demonstrate that knowledge management is more than a management fad or buzzword and has established itself as an important area of inquiry for practitioners, consultants, researchers and academics. The fact that this emerging discipline is highly fashionable need not detract from the fact that it aims to contribute to real-life problems and issues which organisations face today.

Knowledge is not new and has been part of human experience from the beginning of time. The current challenge is developing our theoretical and practical understanding of this concept. One approach is to engage practitioners, researchers and consultants with fellow philosophers on this journey to help move beyond our simplistic notions of this prized entity. In general, philosophy tends to be neglected in many business schools and for years the relevance of ontological and epistemological issues on academic curricula has been widely debated. This is not surprising as business studies as a major academic discipline has a pedigree from around the 1960s. In its attempt to gain legitimacy as a serious discipline, it has adopted the rigours of the scientific approach in the main. However, there have been healthy signs questioning this orthodoxy and its shortcomings. The emergence of knowledge management may help shape those debates as it is critical that we understand the nature of knowledge beyond a scientific paradigm before we attempt to manage it.

The importance of knowledge management derives from an assumption that we are moving into a post-industrial society or a knowledge-based economy (Bell 1973). Former factors of production in the economy such as technical and craft skills of mass production are less important than the more intangible and intellectual skills concerning 'knowledge'. These intangible resources are considered valuable as they constitute the difference between an 'excellent' and a mediocre organisation. Such assumptions imply significant changes in our society, particularly as new classes emerge on the basis of their control over knowledge (Kalling and Styhre 2003).

Even though the notion of knowledge management may have a recent lineage, the idea of managing knowledge has existed among practitioners and scholars for much longer than is commonly assumed (Etzioni 1964). The literature concerning knowledge management derives from the more mature field of organisational learning and the more recent applications of information technology to capture, organise, evaluate, share and store knowledge in organisations. Without this technology, knowledge management would have laid dormant within the organisational learning and strategy literatures. Technology, and in particular Web-based technologies, have provided major advances in this field but have been found wanting with their preoccupation with historic and explicit knowledge. The newer Web 2.0 technologies such as Facebook show that social interaction is vital for the negotiation and co-production of knowledge. The Holy Grail of knowledge management is the ability for organisations to inform their actions through 'knowledge' in original and creative ways that differentiate them from their competitors. In the financial sector, the life of many newly developed financial instruments has been shown to be limited to a maximum of three months. Firms make their profits during this brief period before competitors copy the instruments and profit margins disappear. Such knowledge-intensive industries are indicative of competitive environments pervading more traditional industries such as construction where knowledge and creativity have become key drivers.

The rest of this chapter shall attempt to draw on key lessons learnt on our journey of knowledge management throughout this book and summarise the current status of this discipline, its shortcomings and potential ways forward.

Wrestling with knowledge: some reflections

How do we develop a consensus on the nature of knowledge in organisations when philosophers have been unable to derive a consensus on this valuable asset from their studies over 2,000 years? A useful starting point might be that an absolute consensus on the nature of knowledge may remain elusive indefinitely and that any conclusion about its nature can be only temporary as we wrestle with the shortcomings of our own arguments in relation to it. A Socratic approach to questioning is suggested as the optimal way forward.

From a scholarly perspective, another approach is the recognition that each scholar views knowledge from a particular ontological and epistemological perspective (Burrell and Morgan 1979), as shown in Figure 11.1. A useful analogy is to imagine practitioners, researchers and consultants wearing 'invisible coloured glasses'. Each of these glasses bears different assumptions written all over them whether the wearer is aware of them or not. In the final analysis, these 'coloured glasses' or our 'theory-laden' perceptions are 'value neutral', implying that no particular ontological or epistemological understanding of reality has a monopoly over truth. Each has its contribution to knowledge which adds to the richness and diversity of our understanding of organisations. Such a liberal or possibly a radical perspective to some will undoubtedly be challenged by the dominant orthodoxy in any discipline but it acts to question the established norms and values within a field. For example, the dominant positivist, functionalist paradigm pervasive in management research and literature can suffocate scholarship and threaten the development of new possibilities in this field. A frequent response to the failure of aspiring doctoral students to explore different paradigms or 'coloured glasses' found at the Academy of Management was (Morgan 1990):

'Those who do so will fail to "get published", and fail to "get tenure".'

In a similar manner, the current dominant notions of knowledge are the distinctions between 'tacit' and 'explicit' knowledge (Polanyi 1967; Ryle 1949). This book has argued that many of the current typologies of knowledge are little more than abstractions to denote the continuum between 'know how' and 'know that'. However, there

Figure 11.1 Burrell and Morgan's four paradigms and different epistemologies (adapted from Burrell and Morgan 1979)

are green shoots developing in the literature that are providing a more sophisticated and critical postmodernist perspective (Hassard and Kelemen 2002; Kalling and Styhre 2003; Styhre 2003). This increasing diversity within the literature and continued questioning of the dominant tacit–explicit distinction is likely to lead to a deepening and greater maturity of our understanding of knowledge management.

At practitioner level, knowledge tends to be characterised in its relation to data and information. Simplistically, data is perceived as a signal acquired through our senses. It is important to recognise that our senses and our minds are not 'theory neutral', meaning that we project our stored mental images on to any data we may observe. We are not neutral observers and are informed by our experiences and cultural backgrounds. Information can be considered as organised data where we endow meaning, relevance and purpose to it (Meadows 2001). In this conception, many scholars consider knowledge as information that allows us to act in any given situation or context. Action becomes the distinguishing feature of knowledge. However, action may come at the price of reflection. In many organisations, there may be dangers of neglecting the 'reflection' phase of knowledge development, particularly if organisations are engaged in 'action-fixated' learning cycles. In pressurised business environments focused on results, it is not difficult to see the negative consequences of a lack of reflection or foresight on impending problems, particularly when there are continual competitive demands on people's time.

The practical implication of these debates is to ascertain the most effective way to conceptualise knowledge in organisations. Is it using the distinction between tacit and explicit knowledge? Or is it considering knowledge as 'actionable information'? The predominant difficulty arises in articulating the subtle differences in common language between notions such as tacit knowledge, knowing and intelligence in organisations.

Knowledge management – is there an optimal approach?

Numerous knowledge management models and frameworks have been forwarded in the literature. There is little consensus among practitioners or academics on the optimal approach but these are early days on a burgeoning literature. However, there are some strands and commonalities that link them together. Some models come from a human resource perspective, focusing more on learning processes, whereas others come from a technological perspective, focusing more on information systems to transform an organisation. The approach adopted in this book has been to integrate these two dominant dimensions of knowledge management under a coherent model, as shown in Figure 11.2.

An alternative and popular framework in knowledge management literature is one that develops a hypothesis of the four modes of knowledge (tacit and explicit) conversion (Nonaka 1991; Nonaka 1994). Processes are forwarded such as 'externalisation' where an organisation may use metaphors and figurative language to help convert its tacit base to explicit knowledge. The conceptual gap in this framework is that it considers tacit and explicit knowledge as distinct entities rather than existing along a continuum as commonly understood (Polanyi 1967). The assumption is that organisational knowledge can somehow be 'ground, lost or reconstituted' (Tsoukas 1996). Tacit knowledge as an entity is much more sophisticated and may come in different forms. The fashionable knowledge conversion framework does not acknowledge that

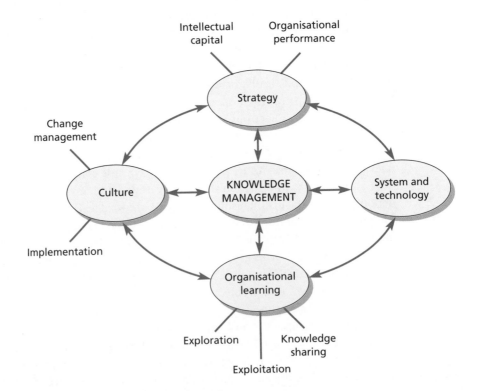

Figure 11.2 **Integrated model of knowledge management**

things may remain unspoken in a workplace (tacit knowledge) based on a wide variety of reasons such as (Boisot 1998):

- things that everyone understands and takes for granted;
- things that nobody understands;
- things that may have a personal cost to the individual if spoken.

Organisational gymnastics: balancing learning with routines and dynamic capabilities

Moderate levels of failure may be good for organisations, as shown in Figure 11.3. This is our conclusion from studying the organisational learning literature. Success can result in maintaining the status quo, complacency and risk aversion as managers follow tried and tested patterns of behaviour. This 'exploitation' of past behaviours may lead to greater efficiency in organisations but may not save them in dynamic environments where greater innovation rather than efficiency is required. In contrast, moderate levels of failure and making mistakes can lead to 'exploration' behaviours where people are more inclined to reflect and experiment with new strategies, procedures and processes.

One of the enduring organisational learning frameworks that has attempted to integrate different dimensions of the literature comes from an information-processing perspective and focuses on four constructs (Huber 1991): knowledge acquisition, information distribution, information interpretation and organisational memory. A common criticism of this approach is that it tends to focus more on the outputs of learning rather than its processes. To overcome this criticism, one can explore the different

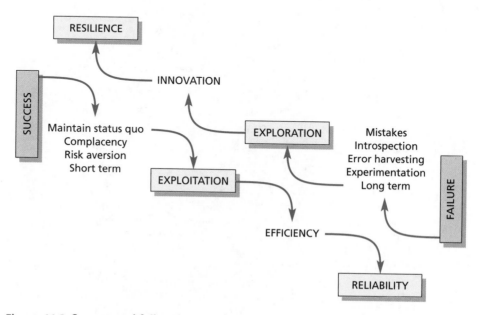

Figure 11.3 **Success and failure in organisation**

facets of organisational learning in relation to processes characterised as single-loop and double-loop learning. Single-loop learning is considered as behavioural learning where organisations follow their traditional ways and patterns in response to a problem. In contrast, double-loop learning is considered as cognitive learning where organisations question their underlying assumptions and values and explore new ways of responding to a problem (Argyris and Schon 1978).

There are similarities between single- and double-loop learning and the more recent notions of organisational routines and dynamic capabilities. Organisational routines are regular and predictable patterns of behaviour whereas dynamic routines are a firm's ability to integrate, build and reconfigure its competences to address dynamic environments. One could argue that the former concept appears to be a reworking of single-loop learning whereas the latter one is of double-loop learning. Is this an example of old wine in new bottles or are there real and major distinctions with earlier concepts?

Knowledge management between nations

A useful typology for grouping different knowledge technologies is one that acknowledges the knowledge development cycle, as shown in Figure 11.4. Even though many technologies tend to focus on explicit knowledge, a number of tools exist to mobilise tacit knowledge:

● tools for capturing knowledge, particularly using cognitive mapping and mind mapping tools;

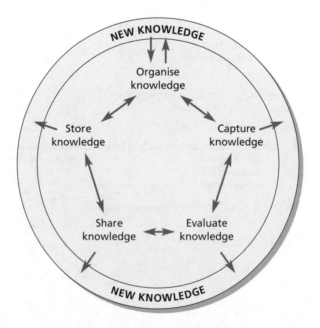

Figure 11.4 **A typology of knowledge tools and component technologies**

- tools for sharing knowledge, particularly utilising the power of the internet, intranet, extranets and e-mail to share tacit knowledge over a firm's value chain. The technologies can be used to develop virtual communities of practice online to help share ideas and tacit knowledge. Another tool is 'expertise yellow pages' to assist in finding the right people with the relevant tacit knowledge to solve pressing organisational problems. This cannot be underestimated in large organisations. The use of videoconferencing allows organisations to share tacit knowledge over geographic boundaries and maintain the richness of communication which derives from a combination of our body language, spoken words and tone of voice.

More traditional tools for codifying, storing and evaluating explicit knowledge include:

- tools for organising knowledge, which include ontology and taxonomy generation tools. The challenge is maintaining taxonomies with high levels of flexibility so that they can respond dynamically to our changing perceptions of concepts and schemas over time;

- tools for storing knowledge, which include sophisticated data warehouses that have the ability to store and summarise internal and external data over different time horizons;

- tools for evaluating knowledge, which include data mining, OLAP, case-based reasoning and machine-based learning tools. Interpretation of knowledge using these tools needs to be carefully handled as patterns and relationships may be suggested that are misleading to the untrained eye. Most tools tend to adopt statistical and probabilistic analyses rather than more qualitative insights into a particular problem.

The types of KM systems employed in many organisations include:

- document management systems – involve getting the right information or knowledge to the right person at the right time;

- decision support systems – entail creating and evaluating knowledge through data analysis or using sophisticated models to support decision making;

- group support systems – designed to enhance communication, knowledge sharing, cooperation, coordination and social encounters within groups;

- executive information systems – provide high-quality information and knowledge to executives to aid strategic planning and control processes;

- workflow management systems – integrate knowledge associated with workflows and alignment of 'cases' with resources such as employees;

- customer relationship management systems – develop knowledge about customers' individual preferences and needs using knowledge repositories and knowledge-discovery techniques.

Institutionalist perspective and the knowledge-based view of the firm

Much strategic management theory and practice today is based on assumptions of the industrial organisation tradition (Ansoff 1965; Chandler 1962; Porter 1980). Here the relationship between the firm and the market structures of any given industry is deemed critical. Rational microeconomic theory is the mode of analysis concerned more with the price elasticity or inelasticity of demand. Firms can reduce competition by collusion, creating higher barriers to entry, differentiating their products and services or lowering their costs. This industrial organisation tradition has influenced the dominant planning approaches to strategy prevalent on MBA programmes across the world. The assumption is that executives can use their prized strategy tools to plan ahead effectively each year. The fact that these strategic plans have often been found wanting on implementation strategies is often telling. It is not surprising that only a small proportion of formulated strategies ever gets implemented in organisations (Mintzberg *et al.* 1998).

An alternative approach that has been argued in this book is the institutionalist perspective (Barney 2001; Penrose 1959; Selznick 1957). Institutional theory tries to explore the homogeneity between organisations in an industry and places greater emphasis on the individual in an organisation and their day-to-day learning. Strategy is considered synonymous with strategic change and is informed by a manager's learning and understanding of a situation over time. From this perspective, competition and strategic change are intimately linked. Core competences of a firm (Prahalad and Hamel 1990) become much more important in defining superior performance as the collective learning of a firm depends on these capabilities.

Such core competences or firm's resources that lead to competitive advantage are premised on the 'resource-based theory' of the firm (Barney 2001). This assumes that it is the firm's internal resources, tangible and intangible, that lead to competitive advantage. These internal resources are seen as rare, valuable and not easily replicated or transferable. One subset of the resource-based view of the firm has been the emergence of a knowledge-based view (Grant 1996; Spender 1996). Here the most important internal resource of an organisation is argued to be its tacit and explicit knowledge. Knowledge sharing and knowledge integration become key factors in achieving competitive advantage from this perspective.

From a knowledge-based view of the firm, the most common form of knowledge management strategies found among US management consultancy firms were 'codification' and 'personalisation' strategies (Hansen *et al.* 1999). A dialectic of knowledge management strategies that develops these findings is shown in Figure 11.5.

Codification strategies are heavily based on technology and use large databases to codify and store explicit knowledge. In contrast, personalisation strategies are less about technology and more about getting people together to share their tacit knowledge over any given problem. As suggested in Figure 11.5, codification strategies are likely to be more prevalent in organisations where competitive forces based on efficiency are dominant. Similarly, personalisation strategies are likely to be found in firms where creative insight and innovation are prevailing forces. Knowledge management strategies have

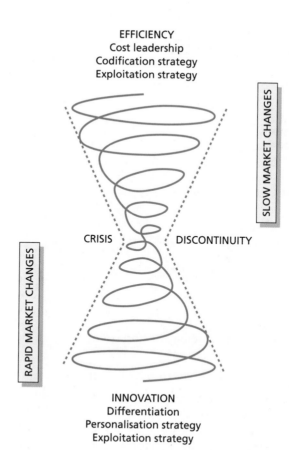

EFFICIENCY
Cost leadership
Codification strategy
Exploitation strategy

SLOW MARKET CHANGES

RAPID MARKET CHANGES

CRISIS   DISCONTINUITY

INNOVATION
Differentiation
Personalisation strategy
Exploitation strategy

Figure 11.5 **The dialectic of knowledge management strategies**

been conceptualised as a dialectic as firms exist in dynamic market environments where the strength of external competitive forces may vary considerably over time.

Communities of practice

One of the key channels for enhancing tacit knowledge sharing in organisations is the promotion of 'communities of practice'. The World Bank sees communities of practice as the main component of its knowledge management strategy to fulfil its aims of becoming a 'knowledge bank'. Communities of practice are informal, self-selecting groups that are open ended without any deadlines or deliverables (Wenger *et al.* 2002). They can be informal groups that meet regularly around physical environments such as water coolers or canteens or they may be virtual communities that meet in discussion forums over the internet. They are not formalised work groups or project teams but are like-minded individuals who share similar problems and outlooks.

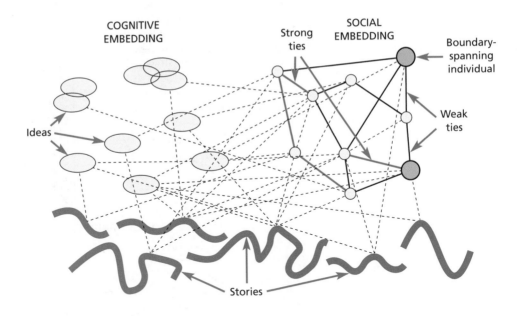

Figure 11.6 **The ontology of storytelling**

The informal interactions found in communities of practice tend to encourage reflection of practice rather than simply reworking everyday processes. Storytelling and narratives play an important role in embedding tacit knowledge socially and making it 'sticky', namely, making it difficult for competitors to replicate such socially embedded knowledge. One of the potential dangers of communities of practice is that they may become self-reinforcing and self-deluding, turning core competences of an organisation into core rigidities. An ontology of storytelling showing how stories embed tacit knowledge cognitively in the form of ideas or socially in the relationships between community members is shown in Figure 11.6.

Personal knowledge management

If knowledge is likely to be the core commodity of future 'knowledge' markets, there is relatively little literature on its implications for the individual. Each individual's worth on the market could be described as their personal capital. Like other forms of capital on the stock market, personal capital has a value dependent on the demand for certain capabilities and a cost related to acquiring certain levels of knowledge and skills. In a knowledge era, it is argued that each of us needs to take our personal capital seriously and take ownership for the development and maintenance of our knowledge. Like many commodities, it may soon become outdated and valueless.

One model forwarded for exploring ways we acquire and distribute our personal capital is the 'K-profile' (Cope 2000), as shown in Figure 11.7. This model is based on different facets of an individual knowledge cycle from discovering new knowledge to delivering it to market. The model makes a distinction between our tacit and explicit

Personal K-profile		Discover New knowledge	Delay Stored knowledge	Discard Redundant knowledge	Diffuse Shared knowledge	Deliver Market knowledge
EXPLICIT	**HEAD** (our thoughts) **HAND** (our actions) **HEART** (our emotions)	Acquire new codified knowledge	Store codified knowledge for later retrieval	Discard codified knowledge	Share codified knowledge	Sell codified knowledge in the market
TACIT	**HEAD** (our thoughts) **HAND** (our actions) **HEART** (our emotions)	Acquire new intuitive knowledge	Store intuitive knowledge for later retrieval	Discard intuitive knowledge	Share intuitive knowledge	Sell intuitive knowledge in the market

Figure 11.7 **The personal knowledge map or K-profile** (Cope 2000)

knowledge base (termed 'knowledge stock') and our knowledge currency. The knowledge currency is the different ways we use to acquire new knowledge and exchange it with the world. It is suggested that this knowledge currency has three principal components:

● head – representing our thinking and cognitive abilities;

● hand – representing how we act or behave in a situation;

● heart – representing our emotions and ways we manage our relationships with ourselves and others.

The three components of knowledge currency are easily identified in relation to explicit knowledge. However, these distinctions can break down in relation to tacit knowledge. Do intuitive insights or knowledge arise as a consequence of a person's cognitive or emotional abilities or both? Also, the model does not acknowledge that tacit and explicit knowledge may exist along a continuum rather than behave as distinct entities. However, the strength of the model is its ability to allow individuals the ability to reflect on different dimensions of their personal capital along a knowledge cycle, from discovering new knowledge to delivering it to market. Like the use of psychometrics in the field of personality measurement, the K-profile allows individuals to assess their strengths and weaknesses in relation to their personal capital and take restorative measures as necessary.

Knowledge management between nations

As with personal knowledge management, the current literature has paid scant attention to knowledge flows and exchanges between nations, assuming that we are moving towards a global knowledge-based economy. The unit of analysis in knowledge management has remained at the level of the organisation. Many bodies such as the World Bank and the United Nations have become increasingly concerned at the relative lack of knowledge transfer to local communities on major funded projects. There are difficulties in sustaining knowledge generated on these projects or embedding knowledge deeply in everyday roles and practices of local communities. Such development projects can provide an insight into knowledge management between nations, particularly when there is a diverse number of countries involved and collaborating over a common concern. Civil servants in each country act as guardians of governmental knowledge and can play an important role in promoting knowledge sharing or inhibiting its progress. Political sensitivities come to the fore as well as cultural and historic differences between countries. Tensions may also exist between different government ministries that may contribute towards a lack of cooperation and knowledge sharing resulting in suboptimal practices.

For example, a United Nations Development Programme project named 'PEMSEA' involving twelve nations in the Far East (Ganapin *et al.* 2003) showed that there were differences in organisational learning within local communities in each of these countries. One major distinction was between 'centralised learning' and 'decentralised learning', as shown in Figure 11.8. Project sites based in command economies such as China and Vietnam favoured centralised learning aimed more at mobilising committees rather than communities. Progress in these countries appeared much faster due to the strong committee decision-making structures in local government. In contrast, decentralised learning was much more evident at project sites such as Bali based more on community-oriented decision making. Progress appeared to be much slower as greater efforts were made to mobilise community leaders and local stakeholders.

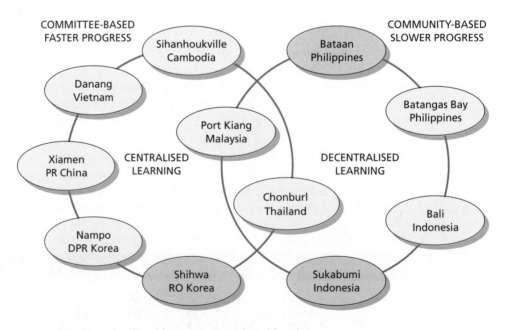

Figure 11.8 **Organisational learning at national levels**

Concluding remarks

Conclusions have no major status in Socratic dialogue. They are purely temporary and tell us which point we have reached in our understanding at any moment in time. They are dynamic and likely to change dependent on our continuous questioning of the status quo. The starting point behind the current knowledge management literature is that it is no longer resources such as land, technology or manual labour that are primary factors of production in society but rather intellectual resources such as knowledge that are the dominant concern. This assumption has led to the emergence of notions such as knowledge economies and knowledge societies.

In the knowledge management arena, there still exist two dominant camps, championed on one side by human resource professionals and on the other by technologically oriented information systems ones. Similar in fate to modern-day architects and engineers, the language and discourse of each side can be incomprehensible to the other. This book has been an attempt to break down these barriers and integrate these two perspectives by providing a language for mutual dialogue (Styhre 2003). Each has valuable lessons to challenge and enhance the other. One cannot remain blind to the incredible technological advances such as the internet that allows us to almost instantaneously share knowledge across the world. Nor can firms remain blind to the fact that their intellectual capital is primarily driven by people. Out of organisational necessity, firms need to foster and develop their human and social capital as a matter of competitive survival.

Beyond these two common approaches, the book has examined knowledge management strategy in organisations from an institutionalist perspective and has challenged the common orthodoxy of the industrial organisation tradition. The individual and the spoils of their learning are placed more centrally in an organisation as the source for competitive success. Such assumptions have led to the emerging knowledge-based view of the firm.

The most pressing challenge in knowledge management today is around fostering and cultivating knowledge sharing in organisations. Explicit knowledge is relatively easy to codify and transfer around an organisation using tools such as data warehouses. However, the ability to share tacit knowledge is much more elusive. Much of the knowledge-sharing literature is concerned with how the more intangible tacit knowledge can be transferred, diffused and disseminated in an organisation. This may occur through formal teams, formal and informal networks and across organisational boundaries (Kalling and Styhre 2003).

One of the principal aspects of knowledge sharing appears to be the ability of organisations to create environments that foster dialogue between related groups. The importance of dialogue is that it allows us to tap into the rich tacit base in organisations and to play with ideas. It is unclear whether formal groupings can suffice in generating this tacit knowledge through tools such as brainstorming or whether there is a need for more informal groupings termed as 'communities of practice'.

Finally, as a caution, the reader needs to guard against the 'old wine in new bottles' syndrome that may exist in some writings in this field. Like Alice in Wonderland, different terms can become confused as they mean the same thing. Despite this shortcoming, this book has demonstrated the breadth and depth of the corpus of knowledge underlying a serious and emerging discipline. Knowledge management and its practices have significant contributions to make in the reality of a knowledge-based economy. Like the development of English as a discipline in the early twentieth century, the study of knowledge management is here to stay and likely to pervade every facet of organisational life.

Further reading

1 Newell *et al.* (2009) is a good all-round book on knowledge management predominantly from a human resource perspective and contains some good case-study material. I have used it successfully with postgraduate students.

2 Davenport and Prusak (1998) helped popularise the field of knowledge management and comes from a consultancy and practitioner background.

3 Styhre (2003) is an excellent book providing a much-needed critique of our current understanding of knowledge management from a postmodern perspective.

4 Cope (2000) is the only book that explores the notion of personal knowledge management. This may be useful for readers wishing to reflect on their personal capital profiles and explore ways of overcoming blocks or shortcomings such as marketing their knowledge more appropriately.

References

Ansoff, H. I. (1965) *Corporate Strategy*, McGraw Hill, New York.

Argyris, C. and Schon, D. A. (1978) *Organizational Learning: A Theory of Action Perspective*, Addison-Wesley, Reading, MA.

Barney, J. B. (2001) 'Resource-based theories of competitive advantage: Ten-year retrospective of the resource-based view', *Journal of Management*, 27, 643–50.

Bell, D. (1973) *The Coming Post-industrial Society*, Basic Books, New York.

Boisot, M. H. (1998) *Knowledge Assets: Securing Competitive Advantage in the Information Economy*, Oxford University Press, New York.

Burrell, G. and Morgan, M. (1979) *Sociological Paradigms and Organizational Analysis*, Heinemann, London.

Chandler, A. D. (1962) *Strategy and Structure. Chapters in the History of the Industrial Enterprise*, The MIT Press, Cambridge, MA.

Cope, M. (2000) *Know Your Value? Value What You Know*, Prentice Hall, Harlow, Essex.

Davenport, T. H. and Prusak, L. (1998) *Working Knowledge: How Organizations Manage What They Know*, Harvard Business School Press, Boston, MA.

Etzioni, A. (1964) *Modern Organizations*, Prentice-Hall, Englewood Cliffs, NJ.

Ganapin, D., Burbridge, P. and Jashapara, A. (2003) *Building Partnerships in Environmental Management for the Seas of East Asia (PEMSEA): Mid-Term Evaluation*, United Nations, New York.

Grant, R. M. (1996) 'Toward a knowledge-based theory of the firm', *Strategic Management Journal*, 17, 109–22.

Hansen, M., Nohria, N. and Tierney, T. (1999) 'What's your strategy for managing knowledge?', *Harvard Business Review*, March–April, 106–16.

Hassard, J. and Kelemen, M. (2002) 'Production and consumption in organizational knowledge: The case of the "paradigms debate"', *Organization*, 9(2), 331–55.

Huber, G. P. (1991) 'Organizational learning: The contributing processes and the literatures', *Organization Science*, 2, 88–115.

Kalling, T. and Styhre, A. (2003) *Knowledge Sharing in Organizations*, Copenhagen Business School Press, Copenhagen.

Meadows, J. (2001) *Understanding Information*, K.G. Saur, München.

Mintzberg, H., Ahlstrand, B. and Lampel, J. (1998) *Strategy Safari*, Pearson Education Limited, Harlow, Essex.

Morgan, G. (1990) 'Paradigm diversity in organizational research', *The Theory and Philosophy of Organizations*, J. Hassard and D. Pym, eds, Routledge, London.

Newell, S., Robertson, M., Scarbrough, H. and Swan, J. (2009) *Managing Knowledge Work and Innovation*, Palgrave Macmillan, Basingstoke, Hampshire.

Nonaka, I. (1991) 'The knowledge-creating company', *Harvard Business Review*, 69 (November–December), 96–104.

Nonaka, I. (1994) 'A dynamic theory of organizational knowledge creation', *Organization Science*, 5(1), 14–37.

Penrose, E. T. (1959) *The Theory of Growth of the Firm*, Blackwell, Oxford.

Polanyi, M. (1967) *The Tacit Dimension*, Doubleday, New York.

Porter, M. (1980) *Competitive Strategy*, Free Press, New York.

Prahalad, C. K. and Hamel, G. (1990) 'The core competence of the corporation', *Harvard Business Review*, 68(3), 79–91.

Ryle, G. (1949) *The Concept of Mind*, Hutcheson, London.

Selznick, P. (1957) *Leadership in Administration: A Sociological Interpretation*, Row, Peterson and Co., Evanston, IL.

Spender, J. C. (1996) 'Making knowledge the basis of a dynamic theory of the firm', *Strategic Management Journal*, 17, 45–62.

Styhre, A. (2003) *Understanding Knowledge Management – Critical and Postmodern Perspectives*, Copenhagen Business School Press, Copenhagen.

Tsoukas, H. (1996) 'The firm as a distributed knowledge system: A constructionist approach', *Strategic Management Journal*, 17, 11–25.

Wenger, E. C., McDermott, R. and Snyder, W. M. (2002). *Cultivating Communities of Practice: A Guide to Managing Knowledge*, Harvard Business School Press, Boston, MA.

A posteriori presupposes our sensory experience and reasons information derived through our sense perceptions.

A priori is taken to be independent of sensory experience and reasons from abstract general premises.

Abductive inquiry presenting theories for consideration.

Adaptability the ability of an organisation to adapt to internal or external changes in its environment.

Agent technology computer systems that are capable of autonomous action in certain environments to fulfil their design objectives.

Artefacts can be material objects, physical layouts, technology, language and behavioural patterns.

Associative memories where pairs of associated data are memorised using a long-term memory network model.

Ba physical, virtual or mental space for helping convert tacit into explicit knowledge and vice versa.

Balanced scorecard a balanced approach to organisational performance which takes into account the customer, innovation and learning and internal business processes as well as traditional financial measures.

Behaviourism body of psychological theory concerned with identifying conditions that stimulate patterns of human behaviour.

Boolean operators locate records containing matching terms (AND, NOT, OR) in specified fields.

Business process re-engineering (BPR) rethinking and radical redesign of business processes.

Case-based reasoning information retrieval systems that allow the storage of past problems, their solutions and their reasoning for future retrieval.

Cleavage paralysis arising from two or more forces confronting each other in an organisation.

Clustering techniques the grouping together of closely related data.

Coaching where instructor observes student completing tasks and provides helpful hints, suggestions and feedback as needed.

Codification strategy heavily based on technology and uses large databases to codify and store knowledge.

Cognitive mapping visual representation of a domain through concepts and their interrelationships.

Cognitive perspective the study of mental processes associated with perception, learning, reasoning and memory.

Communities of practice groups of people who share a common concern or passion and interact informally on an ongoing basis.

Configuration competitive state when one external force dominates.

Congenital learning learning influenced by the founding fathers of an organisation.

Contamination problem when the dominant external force undermines equally valid forces.

Conversion move from one competitive force and form in an organisation to another.

Core competence proposition that competition between firms is as much a race for competence mastery as it is for market position and power.

Crawlers software programs that send requests to remote Web servers looking for new or updated pages.

Customer capital the value of organisational relationships with customers including their intangible loyalty.

Customer relationship management (CRM) systems systems that integrate technology and business processes to meet customer requirements at any given moment.

Data known facts or things used as a basis of inference or reckoning.

Data processing (DP) use of technology to automate tasks.

Data warehouses large physical databases that hold vast amounts of information.

Decision support systems (DSS) systems that combine data analysis and sophisticated models to support non-routine decision-making.

Decision tree a graphical representation of a decision process drawn as branches of a tree stemming from the initial decision point to the final outcomes.

Deductive inquiry preparing theories for test.

Dialectic fundamental process of development in thought and reality from thesis to antithesis to synthesis.

Dialogue involves active listening and the suspension of one's assumptions to explore complex issues and divergent thinking.

Discussion involves presentation and defence of different views to find the best view to support a decision or convergent thinking.

Document management systems the systematic management of documents in an organisation.

Double-loop learning doing things differently or doing different things.

Dynamic capabilities the learning abilities of organisations to adapt their daily routines to meet the challenges of volatile environments.

Economic rent profits to any asset whose sale exceeds its competitive price.

Effectiveness the ability to meet customer requirements on product or service features at a given cost.

Efficiency developing cost advantages of operations.

E-learning education delivered via the internet.

Empiricism reliance on experience as the source of ideas and knowledge.

Employee involvement engagement of employees in order to gain commitment.

Encryption security measure to prevent non-authorised party from reading or changing data.

Epistemology relates to our grounds of knowledge and what we can know.

Excellence and turnaround perspective centred around managerial remedies and recipes of successful companies.

Executive information systems (EIS) systems to enhance strategic planning and control by summarising large quantities of data and allowing the user to drill down to different levels of detail.

Existentialism emphasises the primacy of individual existence and its unqualified freedom.

Experiential learning learning acquired from direct experience.

Expert systems systems designed to mimic the reasoning skills of experts.

Expertise 'yellow pages' list of employees in an organisation with a summary of their knowledge, skills and expertise.

Explicit knowledge 'know that'.

Exploitation learning to perform the same processes better or faster.

Exploration experimenting with new strategies, procedures and processes to work differently.

Figurative language not literal form of speech.

Forcefield analysis examines the driving and restraining forces in any change process.

Fuzzy expressions use a thesaurus to expand a query into related terms.

Genetic algorithms involve complex data structures and are based on biological mechanisms.

Grafting employing new members with the knowledge or skills required rather than developing them in-house.

Group support systems systems to aid communication, knowledge sharing, cooperation and coordination in groups.

Groupware tools software that allows groups of people to collaborate on a project using the internet or intranet.

Human capital the value on the knowledge, skills and abilities that allow individuals to produce goods and services.

Human resource management a managerial perspective which argues for integrated personnel policies in alignment with organisational strategy.

Idealism belief that only mental entities are real, so that physical things exist only in the sense that they are perceived.

Inductive inquiry assessing results of test.

Industrial organisation tradition design and planning model of strategy where the relationships between the firm, industry and market structures are central to competitive advantage.

Information systematically organised data.

Information overload the saturation of information by an individual leading to impaired reasoning and judgement.

Information systems interrelated components working together to collect, process, store and disseminate information to aid organisational activities.

Information systems (IS) capability relates to an organisation's information system's capability as a source of competitive advantage.

Institutionalist perspective belief that experience and learning of individuals is central to competitive advantage.

Intellectual capital the economic value of two categories of intangible assets of a company: organisational capital and human capital.

Intellectual property the collective intellectual assets such as documents, drawings, software programs, data, inventions and processes.

Intelligence know how or tacit knowledge.

Internet an international collection of computer networks.

Intranet a collection of private computer networks within an organisation.

Inverted file a list of words in a set of documents and their occurrences in terms of their precise storage locations.

Just-in-time production (JIT) integration of automation with production information system to deliver any part in the necessary quantity at the right time.

Knowledge philosophically there is no consensus on term. Practically may be regarded as actionable information or tacit or explicit knowledge.

Knowledge economy an economy based fundamentally around knowledge rather than other factors of production such as labour or technology.

Knowledge management the effective learning processes associated with exploration, exploitation and sharing of human knowledge (tacit and explicit) that use appropriate technology and cultural environments to enhance an organisation's intellectual capital and performance.

Knowledge workers individuals who need to use a high level of knowledge in their everyday activities.

Leadership situational skills learning the appropriate use of 'telling', 'selling', 'participating' and 'delegating' interventions.

Lean production form of manufacturing that uses less human effort, manufacturing space, tools, hours and inventory compared with mass production.

Learning organisation organisation that sustains competitive advantage through learning faster than its competitors.

Lexical analysis identifies the words in the text and their interrelationships.

Machine-based learning the ability of a machine to improve its performance based on previous results.

Management information system (MIS) system to provide managers with information for monitoring and controlling their business processes.

Mentoring learning process where a mentor can serve as a role model, counsellor or teacher.

Metaphor imaginative use of a name or description for an object or action to which it is not literally applicable.

Method-of-doing business (MDB) patent patent to provide protection of a firm's business methods.

Networks of practice more formalised networks such as professional networks where power relations may become more prominent.

Neural networks tools to mimic the physical thought processes of the brain.

Norms expectations of appropriate or inappropriate behaviour.

Noun groups clustering nouns found near each other into a single indexing component.

Online analytical processing (OLAP) allows organisations to analyse large sets of data along more than three dimensions.

Ontology (philosophy) relates to our assumptions of reality such as whether it is external or a construct of our minds.

Ontology (systems) overall conceptualisation of a field of knowledge that may not be represented in a hierarchical manner.

Organisational alignment the ability of an organisation to align its processes with changes in the external environment.

Organisational capital the value of the knowledge assets remaining in the organisation when people have left their workplace.

Organisational climate an understanding of social environments where individuals are considered separate from their environments.

Organisational culture a study of social environments predominantly from an anthropological or sociological perspective.

Organisational learning the processes of improving organisational actions through better knowledge and understanding.

Organisational routines repeated patterns of behaviour and processes in organisations.

Personal knowledge management ways of developing and managing an individual's personal capital.

Personalisation strategy focused on gaining deeper insights into problems through people rather than technology.

Perspective making process by which a community of practice develops its knowledge domain.

Petri nets allow processes to be described graphically in terms of places and transitions.

Phenomenology the description of experience through careful analysis of intellectual processes.

Positivism belief that the natural sciences comprise the whole of human knowledge.

Postmodernism expresses grave doubts about universal truth, rejects artificially sharp dichotomies and delights in the ironies of language and life.

Pragmatism explains meaning and truth in terms of the application of ideas or beliefs to observable actions.

Probabilistic expressions assign probabilities to documents that the query assumes users will find relevant.

Rationalism reliance on reason as the only reliable source of human knowledge.

RDF Resource Description Framework is a metadata standard.

Realism belief that universals exist independently of the particulars that instantiate them.

Resource-based view belief in the firm's resources as the principal determinant of (RBV) competitive advantage.

Rule induction statistical techniques to discover rules related to frequency of correlation and accuracy of predictions.

Semantic web an extension of the current web in which information is given well-defined meaning, better enabling computers and people to work in cooperation.

Signature files index structures that divide text into blocks for analysis, primarily to aid retrieval.

Single-loop learning doings things better.

Slogan a short catchy phrase.

Smart patents a method of extending the life of a patent through using continuation patents.

Social capital the value on the strength of linkages, connections, interactions and shared understandings among social networks in organisations.

Stemming removal of affixes of a word to improve retrieval.

Stopwords words that occur too frequently in the text that do not provide good discriminators for the purposes of retrieval.

Strategic information systems (SIS) systems that integrate customers more fully in business process, develop new products based on information and provide support for strategy development and implementation.

Strategic intent a firm's obsession with winning in the short or long term.

Strategic management includes an understanding of a firm's strategic position, its strategic choices and ways of turning its strategy into action.

Strategic positioning is concerned with impact of strategy on the external environment, a firm's internal resources and expectations of its stakeholders.

Strategy plan of actions to achieve one's goals.

Suffix file forms a tree data structure of words in the text.

Symbols can occur as words, statements, actions or a material phenomenon.

Systems thinking focuses on the way that a system's constituent parts interrelate and how systems work over time and within the context of larger systems.

Tacit knowledge 'know how' or intelligence.

Taxonomy the hierarchical structuring of knowledge in subcategories related to its essential qualities.

Team learning ability to balance dialogue and discussion in groups as necessary.

Text-based conferencing internet-based discussion forums or chat groups.

Tobin's q ratio compares the market value of an asset with its replacement cost (book value).

Total quality management (TQM) structured system of integrating the business environment and continuous improvement with development, improvement and cultural change.

Unlearning process by which individuals discard obsolete or misleading information.

Vector expressions assign weights to index terms linked to their frequency in a document.

Vicarious learning imitating strategies, practices or technologies of competitors.

Videoconferencing conferencing with people through the use of video and computer technology.

Visualisation technology that allows users to understand complex information through use of rich computer graphics.

Wisdom ability to act critically or practically in a given situation.

Workflow management systems effectively model organisational processes into workflows and allow the efficient processing of large numbers of cases through predefined cases.

XML eXtensible Markup Language. A subset of SGML constituting a particular text markup language for interchange of structured data.

Index